Freedom's Horizon

AMERICA IN THE NINETEENTH CENTURY

Series editors: Brian DeLay, Steven Hahn, Amy Dru Stanley

America in the Nineteenth Century proposes a rigorous rethinking of this most formative period in U.S. history. Books in the series will be wide-ranging and eclectic, with an interest in politics at all levels, culture and capitalism, race and slavery, law, gender, and the environment, and regional and transnational history. The series aims to expand the scope of nineteenth-century historiography by bringing classic questions into dialogue with innovative perspectives, approaches, and methodologies.

A complete list of books in the series is available from the publisher.

Freedom's Horizon

Black Abolitionism in Nineteenth-Century Brazil

Isadora Moura Mota

PENN

UNIVERSITY OF PENNSYLVANIA PRESS

PHILADELPHIA

Published by
University of Pennsylvania Press
Philadelphia, Pennsylvania 19104-4112
www.pennpress.org

Printed in the United States of America on acid-free paper
10 9 8 7 6 5 4 3 2 1

A Cataloging-in-Publication record is
available from the Library of Congress

Hardcover ISBN 978-1-5128-2761-3
eBook ISBN 978-1-5128-2762-0

For Dudi (in memoriam) and Chloe

CONTENTS

Map 1. The Empire of Brazil in South America. Based on the *Atlas do Império do Brazil* (Rio de Janeiro: Lithographia do Instituto Philomathico, 1868). Erin Greb Cartography.

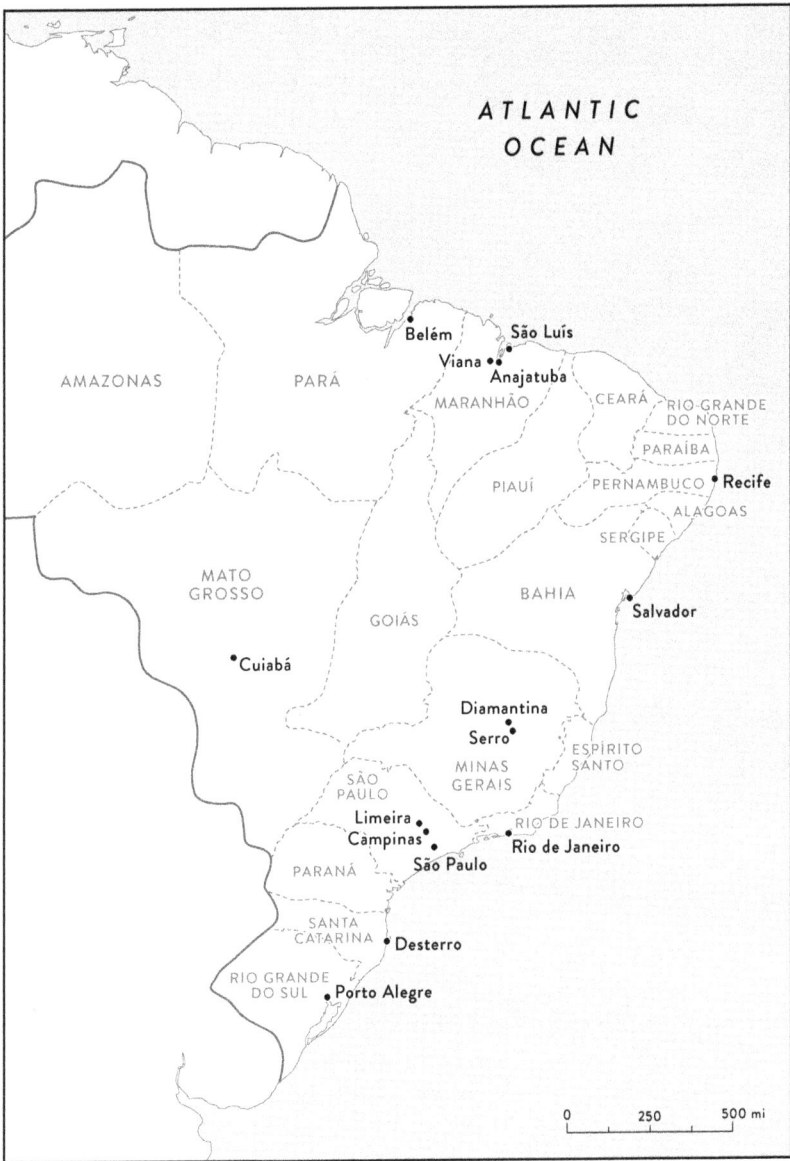

Map 2. Brazilian provinces in the 1860s. Based on the *Atlas do Império do Brazil* (Rio de Janeiro: Lithographia do Instituto Philomathico, 1868). Erin Greb Cartography.

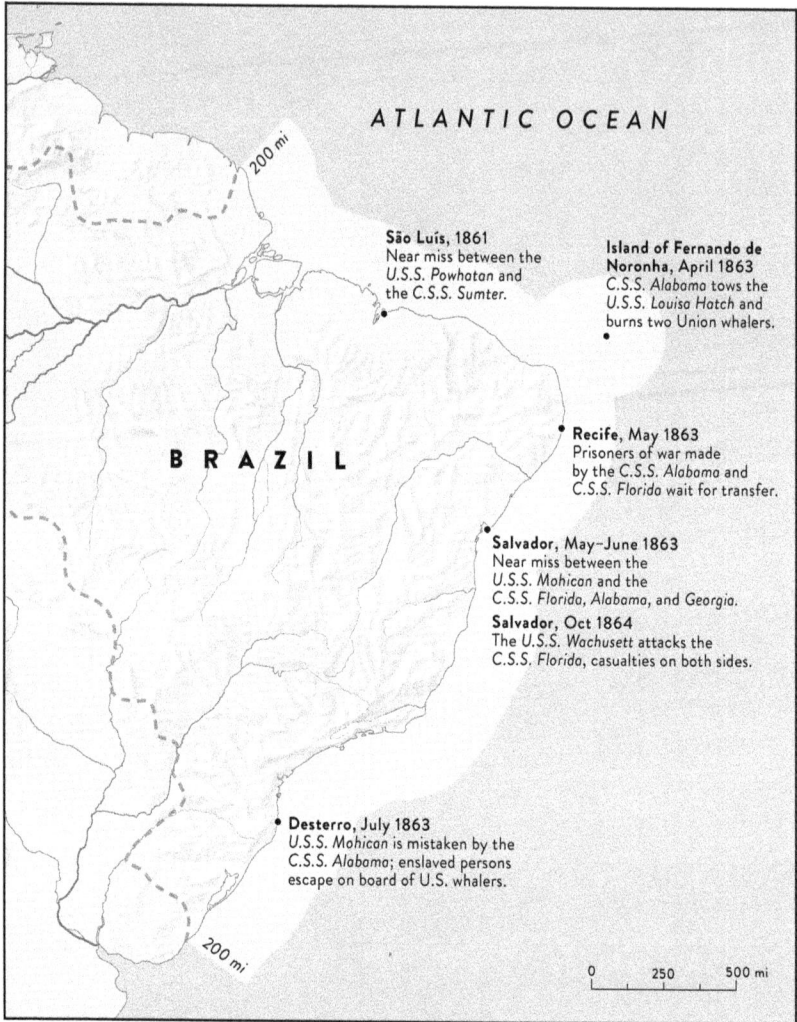

ATLANTIC OCEAN

200 mi

São Luís, 1861
Near miss between the
U.S.S. Powhatan and
the *C.S.S. Sumter*.

**Island of Fernando de
Noronha, April 1863**
C.S.S. Alabama tows the
U.S.S. Louisa Hatch and
burns two Union whalers.

B R A Z I L

Recife, May 1863
Prisoners of war made
by the *C.S.S. Alabama* and
C.S.S. Florida wait for transfer.

Salvador, May–June 1863
Near miss between the
U.S.S. Mohican and the
C.S.S. Florida, Alabama, and *Georgia.*
Salvador, Oct 1864
The *U.S.S. Wachusett* attacks the
C.S.S. Florida, casualties on both sides.

Desterro, July 1863
U.S.S. Mohican is mistaken by the
C.S.S. Alabama; enslaved persons
escape on board of U.S. whalers.

200 mi

0   250   500 mi

Map 3. The US Civil War in Brazil. Based on the Map of Brazil's Hydrographic Divisions (including its territorial waters), 2021, IBGE. Erin Greb Cartography.

Introduction

In October 1864, the African-born Faustino spoke to José, both men enslaved by Thereza Joaquina de Jesus, about the imminence of an uprising in Serro, a town in the Brazilian province of Minas Gerais. "The chicken was dead and ready, just waiting to be roasted,"[1] he uttered, using the metaphoric language that had energized black networks of communication stretching within a five-mile radius of Serro. Abolitionist talk flowed from its source in the Serra do Espinhaço (Espinhaço Mountain Range) down the steep side of the Jequitinhonha River valley into the mines and *quilombos* (maroon communities) of neighboring Diamantina. This slavery-based mining region, the economic heart of Portuguese America in the eighteenth century, continued to rely on enslaved workers to secure Brazil's place as the world's largest producer of raw diamonds in the 1800s.[2] Faustino, José, and nearly five hundred men and women prepared to "wage a war against the whites" in the region "for they had been reading the papers and, through them, realized that all slaves were free but that the whites were hiding the fact."[3] The insurgents followed press coverage of a "war over the freedom of the slaves but not of this country," and noted that the US Civil War coincided with the first debates on gradual emancipation in Brazil. Their story was one of survival in the throes of a regime that lasted until 1888, long enough to face the currents of hemispheric abolition in the 1860s, when every other part of the Americas except Cuba, Puerto Rico, and the United States had abolished slavery. Times were changing, they reckoned, and the newspapers placed emancipation on the horizon, making the US Civil War part of the history of Brazilian abolition.[4]

The 1864 uprising in Serro and Diamantina was one of several others to take place in that war-torn decade, bookmarked on one end by the threat of an Anglo-Brazilian war in 1863 and, on the other, by the Triple Alliance War, which pitted Brazil, Argentina, and Uruguay against Paraguay from 1865 to

1870. In the first half of the 1860s alone, enslaved people throughout Brazil organized more than sixty uprisings demanding immediate emancipation.[5] As actors at the center of the major geopolitical disputes of the nineteenth century in the Americas, black insurgents produced a specific narrative of emancipation that immersed Brazil in the global politics of abolition by reinforcing the idea that meaningful freedom was to be born out of conflict. News of sectional warfare in the United States traveled in the holds of Union merchant ships and Confederate raiders engaged in naval operations in the South Atlantic, spreading both orally and through the literacy practices of Afrodescendants. If in the landlocked province of Minas Gerais enslaved rebels learned about the Civil War via print, on the Brazilian coast others gauged the odds of abolition by watching ships like the CSS *Sumter*, the USS *Powhatan*, and the CSS *Alabama* land prisoners, capture and tow war prizes at will, and recruit crew members in waterfront communities. Insurgency flourished in Brazil when the enslaved generated their own stories about liberation.

Once read or listened to, freedom news traveled far and wide, both in distance and in the antislavery imagination of bonded people. In 1864, the collective reading of newspapers fostered solidarity among insurgents with varying levels of literacy and provided them with opportunities to discuss Brazil's position in the larger context of slavery's undoing. Led by the literate stonemason José Cabrinha, enslaved rebels planned to gather on the last Sunday of October in front of the black Church of Our Lady the Rosary in Serro. From there they would descend on the town, setting fire to the homes of diamond merchants and seizing weapons from the National Guard headquarters. In preparation, they also exchanged letters, which were read aloud in the fields and mines to educate illiterate rebels. Ultimately, a betrayal compromised the initial outbreak in Serro, and the village of São João da Chapada, a mining outpost on the outskirts of Diamantina heavily populated by workers from Central West Africa, became the center of the rebellion. From trenches dug deep into the diamond mines of Duro and Barro, enslaved miners and *quilombolas* (maroons) fought a two-month guerrilla war against private and public forces, eventually losing to provincial troops.[6]

The uprising in Minas Gerais drew the horizon of freedom inland, connecting the oceanic interface of slavery with urban and mining areas usually overlooked by the scholarly focus on plantation slavery in nineteenth-century Brazil. Bound in a country that participated extensively in the transatlantic slave trade until the 1850s, Africans and their descendants struggled for emancipation while slavery remained a viable institution of national proportions.

Although political life in Brazil was centered in Rio de Janeiro, the seat of the national government, and coffee production made the southeast the economic engine of the country, black struggles for freedom demand that we decenter the writing of Brazilian history. The enslaved contested the proslavery nationalism of an agrarian elite that constituted the political class all over the country, as well as the reluctance of liberals in urban areas who, even when sympathetic to gradual emancipation, defended the need to maintain bondage to avoid economic collapse.[7] In doing so, they often drew on knowledge of the nineteenth-century world of reform and acted on an internationalist vision of emancipation based on diasporic experiences.[8]

Abolitionism in the Americas owes much to anonymous rebels like José Cabrinha and Faustino. Their sustained struggle against the longest-lasting slave regime in the Western Hemisphere produced a version of antislavery thought that deserves a prominent place in narratives of Atlantic emancipation alongside more famous figures like Simón Bolívar or William Lloyd Garrison. Insurgent logic located black freedom at the nexus of multiple histories, forging connections invented by Africans and Afro-descendants throughout the hemisphere that have remained largely invisible to conceptual frameworks centered on the nation-state.[9] Through flight, marronage, and rebellion, they thought broadly about political geographies, reading the imminence of abolition into Brazil's entanglements with the world. This explains events as diverse as rebels divining freedom in São Paulo as Brazil and Britain clashed over the end of the African slave trade in 1848, quilombolas in Maranhão swearing allegiance to Britain in 1863, or fugitive enslaved people claiming the prerogatives of wartime emancipation as news of Paraguayan victories over the Brazilian army spread through newspapers in 1865. Be it through Afro-Atlantic oral cultures, relationships to print, or the religious vernaculars of Islam, Catholicism, and Candomblé, insurgents recast abolition as a process also rooted in black interpretations of nineteenth-century history, which inspired them to claim historical change as the product of both prophecy and war.[10]

Freedom's Horizon examines how Africans and their descendants fashioned abolitionism in Brazil. It traces the development of a black geopolitical imagination in the context of transnational events they envisioned as turning points in the process of emancipation in the Americas. The book is first and foremost a social history of abolition written from Brazil outward that documents the kind of black politics on which struggles for radical emancipation rested in the nineteenth century. I see abolitionism as both a lived experience and a political movement built by self-liberating activists who thought of freedom as a phenomenon that connected black people everywhere slavery existed. Their visions of emancipation, I argue, offered to an era of antislavery pluralism a diasporic way of envisioning a political community based on the collective experience of enslavement.

In this study, a mode of historical storytelling that emerges organically out of black freedom struggles takes precedence over interstate affairs so that Brazil's insertion into a global context can also unfold as an act of black world-making.[11] Embracing the analytical possibilities of thinking with the enslaved, not merely about them, the book emphasizes the decades between the 1840s and the 1860s to account for the emancipation politics that drew from the impact of British abolitionism, the US Civil War, and the Triple Alliance War in Brazil.[12] Although enslaved people's readings of the geopolitics of abolition found precedents in Latin America's independence era, deeply steeped in narratives of revolution and nation-building, the wars and diplomatic tensions of midcentury spurred grassroots activism in a new way. They resonated among enslaved persons for whom independence had meant the entrenchment of forced labor alongside the expansion of an Atlantic public sphere awash in discourses of freedom.

Coming to terms with black abolitionism from below requires taking the literacy of Africans and Afro-descendants seriously, thus pushing the boundaries of how historians have understood the intellectual life of ordinary people in a country where literacy rates in general hovered around 15 percent in the 1870s.[13] Brazil's past is covered in layered stories, some written, others oral, and most combining both. Some of the enslaved could read well enough to make out the headlines on newspapers and pamphlets, effectively transforming periodicals into a genre of antislavery literature.[14] Crediting newspapers with truth-telling, they claimed the authority of print to recruit allies against slavery. Others were reader-listeners or writer-dictators who talked the terms of their own emancipation into written form.[15] This book leans into the dynamic tension between orality and literacy to explore abolitionism as a movement deeply rooted in the ways the enslaved storied the world, that is, as the product of oral thinking, collective textual interpretation, and grassroots organizing through writing. Literacy is here more than a figurative tool to describe black perspectives of the geopolitical context; it is a window into social practices and interpretive activities that sustained the struggle for abolition over time.

In the nineteenth century, regardless of one's literacy in the strict definition of the term, reading (in the sense of interpreting) the world involved, at some level, appraising something in print, including the enslaved.[16] Ordinary people who were semiliterate, partially educated, or even illiterate could also be skilled practitioners of antislavery. *Africanos livres*—Africans seized after the prohibition of the transatlantic slave trade—for instance, produced hundreds of petitions to Brazilian authorities to contest their lack of access to emancipation after the expiration of their terms of forced apprenticeship. Those who were literate in Portuguese often sent the imperial government handwritten documents, while others enlisted the assistance of curators, lawyers, and British consuls to challenge the slave order in writing. In either case, africanos livres created emancipationist jurisprudence and shaped abolitionist thought within the realm of foreign affairs by advancing their own definitions of freedom in Brazil.[17]

Viewed mostly as an illiterate population, the enslaved have often been excluded from the histories of education, the book, and print culture in the Americas. Nevertheless, they were both interpreters of text and political actors engaged in the pursuit of alliances and support through the written word.[18] The texts that speak of a black abolitionist imagination hardly fit standard definitions of "written culture"; insurgent strategies circulated through communal reading, handwritten notes, and symbols drawn on skin and paper.[19] However, literacy wedded itself to individual and collective demands for social justice all over Latin America.[20] In the "unpracticed acts of writing" and collective literacy of black insurgents, one can find vestiges of a worldview from which to rethink the Atlantic currents that produced the era of slave emancipation in the Americas.[21]

Abolitionism and the Enslaved

To speak of slave activism as a constitutive element of abolitionism in Brazil is not a foregone conclusion. The effort requires touching on the very optics of history: What is it that we call abolitionism? Where, when, and how does it take place? Who are its protagonists and antagonists? The quest for a visibly articulated abolitionist campaign has led scholars to focus largely on the 1870s and 1880s, the moment when abolitionism emerged as Brazil's first national mass political movement leading up to the passage of the Golden Law in 1888, which officially ended slavery.[22] This was the country's antislavery moment, one might say, a time when an interracial coalition similar to those in the North Atlantic took to the streets, colleges, theaters, and the press to demand the liberation of the enslaved. Brazilian abolition took place amid a profound social and political crisis that also brought down the constitutional monarchy in 1889.

The historical process that gave rise to such a robust social movement had deep roots in the mid-nineteenth century. The suppression of the slave trade, the wars of the 1860s, and the process of gradual emancipation in Cuba combined to accelerate deliberations about the future of slavery in Brazil. A wave of associationism followed the Triple Alliance War while Parliament revived emancipationist debates that culminated in the Free Womb Law of 1871.[23] That year, the imperial government created an emancipation fund to free a certain number of enslaved persons annually, preferably family members and women, and mandated that masters matriculate their captives in a national registry under penalty of losing their human property. The measure liberated the newborn yet established that minors remain in the custody of their mothers' owners until the age of eight, at which point slaveholders could either receive indemnification from the state or keep minors in their service until the age of twenty-one years.[24] The Free Womb Law also endorsed the accumulation of savings by the enslaved, established their right to use it in manumission bids, and prohibited the separation of husband and wife or children under twelve years of age from father or mother in cases of property alienation or transfer.[25] State recognition of slaves' rights paved the way for judicial activism in Brazilian courtrooms, and enslaved people who arrived in Brazil over the preceding decades filed civil suits that claimed their bondage violated the 1831 prohibition on the slave trade.

The growing public presence of abolitionism in the 1880s responded to and accentuated political polarization in Brazil, with massive slave desertions from plantations giving the movement a radical edge. As dissident members of the imperial elite advocated for legal reform, a proslavery countermovement coalesced around landowners' fears of social upheaval. Plantation conferences and clubs formed in opposition to the institutionalization of abolitionism, then organized nationally by the Abolitionist Confederation (1883) and active through liberal electoral coalitions. However, when the Conservative Party took over the executive branch in late 1884, conflict intensified.[26] In 1887 the armed forces came out in support of emancipation. Ultimately, a combination of free-soil campaigns (the provinces of Ceará and Amazonas freed their slaves in 1884), the formation of abolitionist quilombos, urban rallies, slave rebellions, and widespread civil disobedience made the crisis untenable for the Brazilian monarchy and Parliament in 1888.

Abolitionism as a struggle for black freedom, however, hardly follows this timeline to the letter.[27] A movement of multiple genealogies, it also sprang from an earlier black radical tradition that called for immediate emancipation at least since midcentury.[28] This movement emerged from cultures nurtured underground along the roads, around water fountains, in taverns, among quilombos, and within *senzalas* (slave quarters) and streets where the enslaved exchanged and elaborated on conceptions of radically different futures for themselves throughout the 1800s. Black abolitionist thought, I argue, was a diffuse form of political discourse belonging to the context of daily life. It survived, and at times thrived, despite elite attempts to undermine anything that fell outside the acceptable modes of political participation in Brazil. Some of these repressive efforts extended to the control of the written word itself. Locating black abolitionism thus depends on a methodological approach that positions the enslaved as agents of social and political change despite their exclusion as historical subjects in the archives of slavery.

As elsewhere in the Americas, black presence in Brazilian sources is predicated on the curtailment of self-representation: historical records portray Africans and Afro-descendants as backward rebels who stay clear from the domain of abolitionism.[29] Take quilombos as an example. The Brazilian government referred to fugitive slave settlements with the language of racial condemnation: they were sites of otherness, unclaimed lands inhabited by dissolute outlaws who had to be eradicated. From the perspective of the enslaved, however, quilombos questioned the spatial practices of traditional plantations and the modern state, functioning as central nodes in black networks of communication. Quilombos rendered freedom stories geographic as they marked insurgent ground and structured routes of survival for those living on the margins of Brazilian society.[30]

Depending on the ebbs and flows of Atlantic history, Brazilian authorities preferred to charge the Haitians, French, Paraguayans, North Americans, and, above all, the British with prodding the enslaved awake.[31] In their telling, seemingly everyone waged a war against slavery except the enslaved themselves. In *Freedom's Horizon*, I seek to summon the archives of black abolitionism by going against this kind of counterinsurgent discourse that denied oppressed people the ability to conceive of a different political order.[32] The chapters ahead analyze exactly what slaveholders derided as improbable or fantastic: multilayered literacy practices, black evocations of international freedom struggles, syncretic religious beliefs, nonlinear understandings of time, and dreams of a reversal of racial hierarchies.

The enslaved understood the symbolism of their personal and collective acts of allegiance to foreign powers as Brazilian slavery became increasingly isolated in the international sphere. They often engaged in what I call "grassroots diplomacy," a kind of popular activism that grew out of subversive representations of the abolition era.[33] Enslaved people wielded power, for instance, by exploiting the perennial enmity between Brazilian authorities and British diplomats to win manumission or by staging rebellions on the home front while the Brazilian army fought a war in Paraguay.[34] The politics of black emancipation mapped opportunities onto the shifting geographies of freedom that increasingly crept into Brazilian territory over the nineteenth century.[35]

Rethinking Hemispheric Ties

Recognizing that the nation was not the only context for the black experience, *Freedom's Horizon* approaches Brazilian history from a transnational perspective that illuminates both its internal workings and its place in Latin America and the Afro-Atlantic. Brazil has earned well-deserved mentions in the English-language historiography as the staunchest bastion of slavery in the age of abolition, yet much remains to be said about it as a cradle of black freedom movements.[36] Abolitionism, in particular, continues to be studied mostly as an Anglo-American phenomenon, with hemispheric connections muddled by an Atlantic paradigm that does not sufficiently take intra-American exchanges as part of its canon.[37] This book situates the enslaved as essential producers of a subaltern current of antislavery thought and activism based on comparative thinking about the unfolding of abolition.[38] It presents hemispheric history not only as a field of inquiry into the processes that held the Americas together but also as a product of the intellectual experiences of Africans and Afro-descendants whose transnational journeys laid the groundwork for such connected histories.[39]

The following chapters offer insights into black narratives of freedom without attempting to tell a story of origins. They are grounded in the understanding that abolition has a long and protracted history that connects Brazil to broader processes of Atlantic decolonization, social revolutions, and the formation of modern nation-states in the Americas. For example, the Haitian Revolution and the wars of independence in mainland Spanish America (1810–25) filtered through the everyday politics of information exchange between the enslaved, the freed, and maroons, broadening the scope of opposition to slavery. Haiti, in particular, embodied for the first time the promise of immediate emancipation for black people worldwide, helping Africans and Afro-descendants in Brazil to imagine themselves as part of a larger community based not only on literal connections but also on common experiences, assumptions, and cultural practices.[40]

Brazil, like most of South America, gained independence during the age of revolution but took a different path after decolonization. Unlike nations that established themselves as republics, Brazil became a constitutional monarchy led by Pedro I, the authoritarian son of the late Portuguese king, who used his power to crush alternative political projects emanating from the provinces and the disenfranchised. In the 1820s, rather than embarking on a process of gradual abolition like its republican neighbors, the Brazilian Empire evolved into an entrenched slave society of continental proportions, entirely dependent on the human trade with Africa. As a result, Brazil remained largely Atlantic-facing due to its economic dependence on Britain and its commercial relations with Africa. Nevertheless, the abolition of slavery in Spanish America reverberated far and wide. The continent's shifting geopolitics kept Brazil's borders porous to insurrectionary ideas and made the South American republics important interlocutors in the field of antislavery.[41]

In Bahia, independence unfolded through a prolonged armed struggle between Brazilian and Portuguese troops not unlike what was taking place in Spanish America.[42] On July 2, 1823, after besieging the Portuguese in Salvador for eighteen months, the Brazilian Pacifying Army took Brazil's second-largest city and first colonial capital. Recruitment cast a wide net over the population of Bahia, involving black and *pardo* (mixed-race) militias as well as enslaved people (usually recruited against the will of their masters) in battles that occurred especially in the sugar plantation belt around the Bay of All Saints. In fact, the most concerted effort to arm the enslaved in Brazil at that time took place precisely during Bahian independence under the French mercenary Pierre Labatut, appointed by Pedro I as commander of the patriot forces in 1822. Having served briefly in Simón Bolívar's insurgent armies in Gran Colombia, Labatut enlisted enslaved people who either escaped from Brazilian masters or were abandoned by the Portuguese, causing quite a controversy among local planters fearful of slave uprisings and the specter of Haiti.[43]

At its peak, the Pacifying Army in Bahia gathered fifteen thousand soldiers, including a few hundred enslaved men who were eventually emancipated by imperial decree between 1823 and 1824. The measure was not a precedent to state abolitionism; the government of Pedro I ordered the

manumission of slave soldiers with compensation to masters reluctant to free
them spontaneously as a means of enforcing obedience after the upheavals of
independence. Some of these freedmen were eventually deported to Rio de
Janeiro and other parts of Brazil with free black soldiers, spreading popular
notions of sovereignty and antislavery beyond Bahia.

Despite the emperor's rhetoric of national unity, many parts of Brazil only
accepted the monarchical pact on the condition that local autonomy and constitutional rights be respected. Pedro I's closing of the Constituent Assembly
in October 1823 and imposition of his own Constitution in 1824 destabilized
the country. Republican and regional conspiracies largely inspired by the
same ideals debated in Spanish-American often involved pardo militiamen
in Brazil, of whom Emiliano Felipe Benício Mundrucu (1791–1863) is probably the most famous. Mundrucu is said to have used the example of the
Haitian Revolution to inspire the separatist rebels of Pernambuco in 1824,
and he later went to Gran Colombia to fight in the Bolivarian army of General Antonio José Paez in 1826.[44] He eventually settled in the United States,
where he filed the first known lawsuit on segregated transportation in 1832,
linking the upheavals of Brazilian independence to the American abolitionist
movement.[45]

During Mundrucu's brief stay in Spanish America, Brazil's territorial
boundaries were still being reinvented after the collapse of the Iberian empires.
The country's western border with the Viceroyalty of Upper Peru, now Bolivia,
was one such contested frontier.[46] Those loyal to or opposed to Spain often
sought refuge in Brazil, leading to periodic rumors of a possible invasion
of the western province of Mato Grosso. In 1824, the Brazilian government
even feared that Portugal might launch an expedition to reconquer Brazil via
Upper Peru, just as Bolívar imagined that the Holy Alliance might wage war
against Spanish American forces from Brazil. By early 1825 only the governments of Buenos Aires, the United States, and the African kingdom of Benin
recognized Brazil's independence.[47]

In 1826 black struggles for freedom intersected with Mato Grosso's short-
lived annexation of the royalist province of Chiquitos, in the department of
Santa Cruz de la Sierra. Although the creation of the "United Province of
Mato Grosso" without the prior approval of Pedro I was rescinded after two
months, continuous talk of liberation among the Spanish American insurgents led by General José Antônio Sucre kept tensions alive in Mato Grosso.[48]
In April 1826 rumors of an imminent invasion of Brazil by Bolívar inspired
the enslaved to rise in support of revolutionary freedom. The prospect of

an attack was so real that Mato Grosso's army commander summoned his troops to Vila Maria, on the border with Bolivia, to prevent the outbreak of a black rebellion.

Manoel Joaquim, a fugitive slave who had just been returned to his master in Mato Grosso after escaping to Santa Cruz de la Sierra, was at the center of the conspiracy.[49] He spread word that "Bolivar had freed the slaves in that Province [Santa Cruz] and that he had a large army to enter here and that the same Spanish soldiers wanted to come to this province, and that it was natural that if they came here they would Free the slaves as well."[50] In the village of Diamantino, Manoel Joaquim would even have mentioned that "General Bolivar, in the Provinces of Spain, had already established himself as the Universal Liberator."[51] The projected rebellion combined with the information that the so-called Periquitos (Parakeets), soldiers of color enlisted in the Brazilian army during the independence wars in Bahia, planned a mutiny and the proclamation of a republic.[52] In May 1826, the government of Mato Grosso rendered investigations inconclusive, leaving underlying tensions unresolved.

From the era of independence, then, Africans and Afro-descendants in Brazil would carry forward an elastic sense of abolitionist possibility that facilitated the rallying of rebellious collectivities over time. Black struggles for freedom shared characteristics across the Spanish republics and the Brazilian Empire, as Afro-descendants perceived emancipation as an interconnected process that spanned slave and emancipated societies. Although the abolition of the slave trade and the enactment of free womb laws in most of Spanish America date from the 1810s and 1820s, abolition itself was a long process that dragged on throughout the region until the 1860s.[53] By midcentury, black people in Brazil were able to draw on a tradition of grassroots diplomacy (or shaping interstate relations from below) to "imagine otherwise," giving radical meaning to foreign wars, government actions, religious beliefs, and possibilities for black self-determination.[54] Cumulatively, they crafted a version of abolitionism that would lay the groundwork for the emergence of the mass movement against Brazilian slavery in the 1870s and especially the 1880s.

Abolition as Afro-Atlantic History

Freedom's Horizon takes an Afro-Atlantic perspective on black insurgency. More than simply identifying black strategies for radicalizing international antislavery, this approach involves using the lived experiences of diasporic people as sources for interpreting how black communities' abolitionist practices were intertwined. The book considers their activism as formative of political discourses on race, labor, and freedom or, paraphrasing the historian Laurent Dubois, as zones of engagement and debate with broader issues in the Atlantic world.[55]

Brazil holds a unique position in the history of the African diaspora: as the largest landing point of the transatlantic slave trade, it is still home to the biggest black population outside Africa itself.[56] From 1501 to 1875, 45.5 percent of the total 12.5 million Africans sent to the Americas were disembarked on Brazilian shores. Of these, almost 700,000 died during the forced trip westward, approximately 37 percent of all Africans who perished during the Middle Passage.[57] Thus Brazilian history can hardly be contained within national borders and must be extended beyond mainland South America to include Africa.[58]

Slavery and freedom coexisted in Brazil for most of the nineteenth century, fueling various forms of contestation of the world of forced labor created in the era of abolition. From 1800 to 1850 alone, about two million and a half enslaved Africans arrived in the country on Luso-Brazilian vessels, a number that corresponds to roughly 40 percent of all the Portuguese and Brazilian slave trade over the course of 350 years.[59] Black abolitionism in Brazil was therefore also distinctly African. The surge in human trafficking in the nineteenth century dovetailed with a coffee boom that undergirded the development of the Brazilian nation-state despite British pressure to outlaw the trade. The expansion of slavery, however, occurred in the presence of the largest freed African and free Afro-descendant population in the Americas, emboldening many to articulate seemingly scattered Afro-Atlantic influences into an abolitionist practice in Brazil.[60] Freedom was never absolute, though, as high rates of manumission were often conditional, and reinforced the physical and social vulnerability of black people.[61]

Slave-trade suppression started in earnest in 1822, when Britain established the end of the trade as a condition to recognize Brazilian nationhood. But since the Congress of Vienna in 1815, Portugal had pledged to suppress the slave trade above the equator, which included the Bight of Benin ports that supplied enslaved Africans to Bahia. In 1817, the British claimed the right to search ships suspected of involvement in the illegal trade to Brazil and created mixed commission courts in Rio de Janeiro, the Cape of Good Hope, and Sierra Leone to adjudicate confiscated vessels.[62] Authority over the emancipation of illegal captives—the africanos livres—consistently put Britain and

Brazil at odds, as first the Portuguese and later the Brazilian government protested against coastal patrolling as well as seizures of slave ships by the British squadron. Britain's global policy of diplomatic pressure assumed coercive overtones in both Brazil and the African coast, feeding anti-British sentiment among Brazilian government officials and enslavers. Africans in diaspora, though, configured self-liberation strategies within the mined terrain of slave-trade suppression worldwide, keeping Africa as an ongoing referent for Brazilian political history.[63]

A Different Geography of Freedom

Freedom's Horizon unfolds according to the themes that Africans and Afro-descendants deemed relevant to their struggles against slavery. The book has a range of protagonists usually counted out of abolition's public sphere: africanos livres, runaway slaves, quilombolas, freedpersons, and free people of color living on the margins of Brazilian society. The chapters follow the horizon of freedom as it moves across Brazil's continental territory, without the intention of being exhaustive. Moving back and forth from the Atlantic coast to the country's interior, the study decenters the narrative of abolitionism from nineteenth-century hubs of political power, such as Rio de Janeiro. I explore slave conspiracies in Amazonian riverine plantations, in northeastern port cities, in the hinterlands of Minas Gerais, and in small towns along Brazil's disputed borders with Uruguay, Paraguay, and Argentina. My analysis of black abolitionism draws on a variety of Brazilian, British, and US archival sources, including police records, trial transcripts, travel accounts, newspapers, letters written by Afro-descendants, diplomatic correspondence, and war veterans' memoirs.

My point of departure in Chapter 1 is the experience of africanos livres and the unresolved nature of recaptivity in Brazil. Liberated Africans embodied the country's first experience with gradual emancipation, which led to the creation of a special category of unfree laborers who occupied a liminal space between slavery and freedom.[64] Often working alongside the enslaved, africanos livres sought protection from re-enslavement at British consulates, escaped to foreign ships or quilombos, and sought advice from British officials in cases of mistreatment and forced removal to Africa, the Caribbean, and distant regions of Brazil itself. Over time, their precarious status translated into a platform of direct action that demanded Brazil's cooperation with

British suppression efforts while sketching out tentative notions of human rights for Africans and their descendants.

Chapter 2 revisits the context of Anglo-Brazilian conflicts over the suppression of the slave trade between the 1840s and 1860s to examine a tradition of insurgent abolitionism expressed through a recurring theme: that of British military support for abolition in Brazil.[65] A series of conspiracies reveals that black visions of an international order under British hegemony intersected with antislavery efforts of all stripes and origins. In 1848 rebels invoked alliances with the French, the British navy, and Latin American republics in the Paraíba River valley, the very heart of the hegemonic Brazilian coffee economy. In 1856 others conspired alongside Swiss and German sharecroppers revolting against planter abuses at the Ibicaba plantation in São Paulo, a forerunner of Brazil's experiments with free labor. In 1863 enslaved communities in various parts of the empire rose up in response to the diplomatic imbroglio known as the Christie Affair. On the last day of 1862 the British envoy William D. Christie ordered a naval blockade of the port of Rio de Janeiro, bringing Brazil and Britain to the brink of war. Black insurgents and quilombolas seized the moment, radicalizing British gunboat diplomacy to mean a decisive alliance for the end of slavery in Brazil.

The resistance politics of enslaved communities continue to drive the chapters that follow, showing how an often-told American story can also be understood as part of Brazilian abolition. In Chapter 3, I explore little-known armed confrontations between Union and Confederate vessels along the Brazilian coast as well as slave flight to North American ships on both sides of the conflict to understand how the US Civil War changed the context of black freedom struggles in Brazil. When they passed through Brazilian ports, either to refuel, land prisoners, or pursue enemy ships, Union and Confederate steamers inspired enslaved people to imagine their captivity being undone. As Afro-descendants found inspiration in US history to strike out for emancipation in Maranhão and Santa Catarina, they brought together the trajectories of the Lusophone and Anglophone Atlantic, advancing the cause of immediatism at a time when Brazilian elites considered abolition impossible.

Chapter 4 explores how the circulation of print increased the opportunities for enslaved people in Brazil to become familiar with the US Civil War. In 1864 the rebels from Serro and Diamantina in Minas Gerais probably learned about the war from the newspaper O Jequitinhonha, edited by the Brazilian writer Joaquim Felício dos Santos, and believed they had been freed by the Emancipation Proclamation. In 1865 enslaved people conversant with press coverage of the war launched a rebellion on a Carmelite-run sugar plantation on the outskirts of Belém, in the northern province of Pará. Their experiences invite us to consider literacy as a crucial component of a diasporic imagination that positioned Afro-descendants to emerge as a dangerous political force in nineteenth-century Brazil.

The book culminates with a study of the emancipation politics of quilombolas during the Triple Alliance War. From 1864 to 1870, marronage escalated across the Brazilian landscape as the Empire of Brazil allied with Uruguay and Argentina against Paraguay in the first case of total war in South America. Chapter 5 focuses on the Brazilian home front, where a troop mobilization campaign that included the recruitment of freedmen and growing opposition to the imperial government opened space for black activism to flourish. Amid a vacuum in local policing, slave flight soared and quilombolas joined forces with army deserters to challenge the slaveholders' peace. Focusing especially on the quilombos of Minas Gerais and Maranhão, I show how escaped slaves combined literacy with grassroots diplomacy to enact wartime emancipation on the ground in the late 1860s.

Ultimately, in *Freedom's Horizon* I search for worlds of meaning and possibility capable of expanding current understandings of black activism and its role in bringing about social change, especially abolition. Thinking with the protagonists of the book, I am convinced that their struggles belong in the history of democracy in Brazil for, alongside abolition, a black political consciousness also came into being. In the nineteenth century, despite the horrors of slavery, blackness functioned as a concept capable of producing a range of identities that often challenged the liberal definitions of selfhood and national citizenship championed by Brazilian elites. It provided a blueprint for action based on international solidarity that now stands as a legacy for Afro-descendants in Brazil.

CHAPTER 1

African Lives and Grassroots Diplomacy

On the afternoon of March 19, 1854, João knocked on the headquarters of the British legation in Rio de Janeiro. Having just escaped abuse at the home of Antônio Luiz da Costa, he still bore the marks of a severe whipping and the tight grip of iron shackles on his body. João, then twenty-nine years old, introduced himself in perfect English to Consul John J. C. Westwood, saying that he was a freedman who had been emancipated in the Cape of Good Hope, a British colony on the southern tip of Africa. In the vocabulary of British suppression, he was a "liberated African," that is, someone recaptured from a slave ship as part of Britain's campaign to ban the transatlantic slave trade after ending its own participation in 1807.[1] In Brazil, João was an *africano livre*, or literally "free African," a rather ironic nineteenth-century expression that juxtaposed free status with the term most associated with the experience of enslavement in the country.[2] Legally freed from bondage in Africa, João had been re-enslaved in Rio de Janeiro, where he had to navigate the uneasy coexistence of Brazilian slavery and British imperial policies. As an African man on Brazilian soil, he had to prove that he was not a slave.[3]

After a preliminary examination at the consulate, João met with Henry Howard, the British envoy extraordinary and minister plenipotentiary to the Empire of Brazil, to whom he gave a detailed account of his ocean crossings. Born in Benguela, a port city on the coast of present-day Angola, João had been kidnapped as a child in the 1830s and placed on a slave ship bound for Rio de Janeiro. Once in Brazil, he was sold to Antônio Augusto de Oliveira, who rechristened him as "Joaquim." A slave trader himself, Oliveira eventually took João aboard the Portuguese schooner *Congresso* on a voyage to the western coast of Central Africa in 1837, when a British cruiser intercepted the ship and dragged it all the way down to the Admiralty Court of the Cape of Good Hope.[4] At the Cape, João became a liberated African when the *Congresso* was found to be in violation of international conventions on the slave trade.[5] He worked under the tutelage of Judge Mansell and the colony's governor, Ker B. Hamilton, for eight years, and decided to seek work back in Brazil upon completing his apprenticeship term. In 1851, João sailed as a passenger on the British ship *Black Squall* to Rio de Janeiro, where he again faced the challenges of being a freed African in a country pondering the future in the wake of its government's decision in 1850 to ban the transatlantic slave trade.

Once in Rio, João lost his claim to freedom when someone he considered a "comrade" stole the emancipation certificate "that was delivered [to him] by Mr. Field at Cape Town."[6] Unable to prove his status to the police, he was arrested as a runaway slave on Saúde Beach and handed over to Antônio Luiz da Costa, a friend of his former master Oliveira. Costa illegally claimed João as a slave and put him up for sale in Arrozal, a town located one hundred miles away from Rio in the coffee-growing region of the Paraíba River valley.[7] Thus in 1854 the freedman João stepped onto the auction block at the house of a certain Captain Barreto but deliberately thwarted the transaction. Speaking in English to an audience of coffee planters, he recounted his Atlantic journey to emancipation, bringing to light an experience in the world of illicit trafficking that his listeners would rather not see publicized. Outraged that he had not "hidden his story and knowledge of the English language," Costa sent João back to Rio de Janeiro. Ultimately, João's attempt at self-liberation resulted in the severe punishment that led him to seek the protection of the British.

Henry Howard believed João's version of the facts from the outset because Ker B. Hamilton of Cape Colony was an acquaintance of his. Moreover, João was fluent in English and Dutch, and his case integrated a litany of other re-enslavement claims brought to the attention of British officers throughout the Brazilian Empire.[8] Howard's intervention in the case prompted José Mattoso de Andrade Câmara, Rio's chief of police, to summon Antônio Luiz da Costa for questioning. At the police station, Costa claimed to have purchased "Joaquim" from his friend Antônio Augusto de Oliveira Botelho in either 1836 or 1837, only to see him run away shortly thereafter. In 1852 "Joaquim" was returned to him by a slave catcher to whom Costa paid sixty thousand réis.[9] Only after his alleged slave spoke up, Costa maintained, did he learn that "Joaquim" claimed to be free "due to having been to England and traveled on English ships."[10] It appears that, having lost his certificate of emancipation, João held on to the claim of having stepped on free soil. Costa was never able to produce a bill of sale and eventually had to give up his property rights over "Joaquim." Henry

Figure 1. View of the Prainha and Saúde neighborhoods, Rio de Janeiro, where the africano livre João was arrested as a runaway slave. Photograph by Marc Ferrez, circa 1893. Acervo Instituto Moreira Salles, Brazil.

Howard found passage for João aboard the British ship *Juno*, which brought him back to the Cape after the three-year ordeal in April 1854.

Like many of the stories that fill the pages of this book, João's is set in the disputed terrain of Atlantic history, at a moment of dramatic historical change for those who sought to ensure that slave-trade suppression actually led to the liberation of Africans. Emancipated by British intervention yet trapped in the webs of seigneurial power in Brazil, João had, in effect, to free himself by creating a narrative of the abolitionist world that made his story credible. Black liberation depended heavily on the recaptives' ability to force compliance with the international terms of abolition and expand the meanings of what both Britain and Brazil conceived as a gradual transition out of bondage. Despite its inflammatory rhetoric against the trade, Britain never ceased to contribute to the reproduction of slavery in Brazil, practicing a version of antislavery that looked at every turn for economic opportunity and geopolitical influence in South America.[11] Alongside the work of suppression, the British owned slaves in the Brazilian Empire and often used their labor to exploit the country's mineral wealth.

This chapter focuses on africanos livres' critical engagement with the geopolitics of slave-trade suppression in nineteenth-century Brazil.[12] Positioned at the center of Brazil's first experience with emancipation, Africans shaped abolitionism from the bottom up by crafting strategies of liberation in the context of the so-called English or Anglo-Brazilian question, that is, the conundrum posed by British antislavery efforts in a country economically dependent on Britain yet determined to consolidate itself as a slaveholding empire.[13] Africanos livres' precarious status translated into a platform of direct action that influenced black activism for years to come, with João being just one among several other freed and enslaved persons who ran away to British consulates over the 1850s and 1860s in Brazil. Individually and collectively, africanos livres pressed for visions of freedom that went beyond the legislative intent of antislavery treaties or ordinances, often seeking legal redress for their grievances. The alliances sought, which ranged from the intimate to the broadly political, as well as the political readings they made and sometimes recorded in the archives of slavery, paved the way for abolitionist activism in the Atlantic world.

Receptive mothers in particular, and sometimes grandmothers, invoked abolitionist principles as they challenged the customary rights of slaveholders to their children and pushed both Brazil and Britain to accept family ties forged across lines of legal freedom. Many, in fact, anticipated the terms of the emancipationist debates in the 1870s over freedom of the womb and wrote directly to the authorities to plead their case against forced removal to Africa, therefore resisting family separation and elite efforts to "de-africanize" Brazil. Ultimately, africanos livres fashioned black abolitionism through what I call "grassroots diplomacy," the quotidian practice of nonstate actors who relied on networks of strategic alliances to challenge slavery. In the collective history of slave-trade refugees, I seek to distinguish an abolitionist imagination capable of piercing through dominant projections of slave power with African geographies of hope.[14]

The "Anglo-Brazilian Question"

João was part of a larger receptive Atlantic diaspora spanning the 1807 abolition of the slave trade in Britain to the end of human trafficking to Cuba in 1867. Africans released from illegal slaving made up the third largest group of coerced migrants to cross the Atlantic Ocean during the nineteenth century, after only those disembarked in Brazil and Cuba as part of the legal stream of the slave trade. Over five decades some 180,000 receptives worldwide found their lives caught up between the activities of anti-slave-trade naval squadrons and the domestic laws of receiving countries in Africa and the Americas. Brazil is estimated to have been the final destination of roughly 11,000 recaptives, although numbers continue to be revised upward by historians.[15]

While in Rio de Janeiro, João earned his definitive emancipation certificate— the third one—on May 9, 1854.[16] His case can be counted among the few that enjoyed a quick turnaround time in the hands of Brazilian authorities, probably as a result of the first wave of compliance with the Imperial Decree of December 28, 1853, which emancipated all africanos livres who had already completed fourteen years of apprenticeship in the hands of private hirers, if they so requested.[17] The Brazilian minister of justice, José Tomás Nabuco de Araújo, decided in August not to indict Antônio Luiz da Costa for the crime of keeping a free African in bondage. Nabuco considered Costa's guilt dubious "because there is no Law in the Country that directly considers free slaves escaped to foreign territory, later returning to the Empire."[18] Therefore, although aware of João's testimony, Nabuco saw him as a runaway and preferred to uphold the authority of his enslaver's version of events.

Such was the tone of affairs in a slave society where the ill-treatment of Africans vexed Anglo-Brazilian relations until the end of the nineteenth century. That the work of suppression was being done by Brazil's most important economic partner since colonial times created an almost unsolvable diplomatic puzzle. Newspapers, politicians, and Brazilian citizens referred to it as the "English" or "Anglo-Brazilian" question, evoking the tightrope along which Brazil walked as a nation committed to slavery in the era of abolition. On the one hand, the British Foreign Office coordinated a network of diplomats, naval officers, judges, commercial attachés, and mixed commission court bureaucrats to force the country into compliance with bilateral treaties. On the other, Brazil systematically evaded diplomatic commitments that threatened the stability of its slaveholders' rights to own people. In Brazilian political parlance, then, the notion of a "question" carried a conservative undertone: it communicated elite resentment of British interference in domestic affairs or the threat that antislavery posed to Brazilian economic foundations and national security.

Despite their disagreements over the slave trade, however, Britain and Brazil had much in common. In the nineteenth century, they both rejected African demands for unconditional emancipation and participated in the construction of new forms of racialized governance through apprenticeship schemes throughout the Atlantic. What the historian David Eltis has called

the "ambivalence of suppression" was evident in the actions of British subjects in Brazil; antislavery activity required the uneasy balancing of the ideo-
logical mainstays of British political life—the rule of law, respect for property,
and laissez-faire economics—with the need to enforce international agreements in a country within its informal imperial orbit.[19] British suppression of
the slave trade, however, provided a powerful argument for those committed
to the cause of black freedom; it signaled a break in the power of slaveholders
and a direct foreign threat to the Brazilian slavocracy's claim to sovereignty.

British influence in Brazil was both a legacy of the country's colonial
experience and a liability to its newfound independence since 1822. Brazilian elites secured political autonomy from Portugal by reaffirming Britain's
privileged position, along with an Anglo-Brazilian treaty signed in 1826 to
abolish the slave trade within the next four years. By this time, the slave trade
had already been abolished in most of the Spanish American mainland, often
under considerable British pressure. The debates surrounding the drafting of
the Spanish Constitution of 1812 in Cádiz included discussions about ending the transatlantic slave trade and taking steps toward gradual emancipation, but it was left to the newly independent republics of South America
to implement abolition over the following decades through their own internal legislative processes. Venezuela and Chile abolished the slave trade with
independence in the 1810s, anticipating British recognition, but the interests
of slaveholders, many of whom commanded liberation armies, prevailed in
other parts of the continent at least until the mid-1820s. In the case of Cuba,
the Anglo-Spanish Treaty of 1817 prohibited Spanish subjects from taking
part in the slave trade north of the equator. After 1820, trading in persons
south of the equator was banned, but trafficking continued until 1867. Spain
ranked as the fourth-largest slave-trading power in the Atlantic world, and
slavers under its flag disembarked over one million Africans in the Americas,
two-thirds of them in the nineteenth century.[20]

As for Brazil, its parliament finally passed the country's first bill to over-
turn the importation of enslaved Africans in 1831. The November 7 law stated
that all enslaved people entering Brazil would henceforth be legally free and
determined reshipment back to Africa of those illegally trafficked as a solution to counter the large influx of Africans. Its second article enshrined in
legal text the principle of "re-exportation," that is, the Brazilian version of
a colonization scheme based on the assumption that Africa, defined very
broadly, should be the final homeland of all refugees from the slave trade.
The 1831 law required that slave traders pay for the expenses regarding the

deportation of Africans illegally introduced in Brazil "to any part of Africa; re-exportation to be made effective by the Government as soon as possible, contracting with African Authorities to provide them asylum." Article 7 completed the proposed sealing off of Brazilian borders by forbidding any African freedperson to disembark in the country's ports under the penalty of immediate deportation.[21] Brazilian planters were anxious to avoid the presence of any "emancipating" black people whose influence they considered detrimental to the enslaved. Yet africanos livres did just that.

Although the imperial government hailed the 1831 law as a milestone against the slave trade to Brazil, subsequent disregard for its provisions turned the law into an endless source of Anglo-Brazilian hostility. Failing to define how the deportation of africanos livres should be carried out, Brazil claimed jurisdiction over a growing number of recaptured men and women in spite of the shared mandate of Anglo-Brazilian courts. Instead of returning to Africa, africanos livres were subjected to the supervision of the Ministry of Justice, which held them at the House of Correction of Rio de Janeiro, Brazil's first penitentiary, and then distributed their services to either private hirers or public and philanthropic institutions across the empire.[22] Moreover, the 1831 law did not eradicate human trafficking from Africa, with numbers surging especially after the rise of conservatives to power in 1837, who at times advocated for the repeal of anti-slave-trade treaties and laws.[23] Brazilian ships continued to trade under the Portuguese or American flags to avoid capture, while both the West African and South American squadrons established by Britain lacked the necessary number of ships to stem the flow of enslaved people bound for Brazil.[24] Between 1831 and 1856 nearly 760,000 Africans arrived in the country as a result of smuggling.[25]

By tying the suppression of the slave trade to the removal of Africans, the 1831 law foreshadowed decades of debate over plans for black colonization. In 1835 the Brazilian Ministry of Foreign Affairs presented its Portuguese counterpart with a proposal to buy part of the Portuguese holdings in Africa in an attempt to enforce "re-exportation."[26] The idea became especially popular after the serious African Muslim rebellion in Bahia, where the provincial assembly even proposed that Brazil establish a colony in Africa to receive African freedmen.[27] In 1850 Brazil again negotiated with the Portuguese government but also sent a special envoy to Liberia to inquire whether the local authorities would be willing to receive some Africans freed by Anglo-Brazilian mixed commissions.[28] Brazilian minister of justice Paulino de Souza went as far as reaching out to British envoy James Hudson to require that Africans captured by British cruisers be sent to Portuguese colonies in Africa rather than to Brazil.[29] Lord Palmerston frustrated Brazilian wishes, though, contending that "negroes so sent, instead of becoming free . . . would in all probability be reduced in those colonies to a state of slavery" and "fall again into the hands of slave traders."[30]

In the end none of the Brazilian colonization attempts bore fruit, and africanos livres gradually adapted to life in South America. Forced to remain in Brazil under the constant threat of deportation, they were assigned a number (*matrícula*) and a Christian name, along with an uncertain future. After being held on confiscated slave ships, in port warehouses, or simply in jail, most of the recaptives endured compulsory apprenticeship periods beyond the fourteen years required by the 1831 law and were subject to constant state surveillance. Provision by private guardians or the state continued to require proof of place of residence, good behavior, and stable employment.

When Emperor Pedro II came to power with the restoration of the monarchy in 1840, he and his government inherited a thorny legacy of unfulfilled promises to the British and scandalous evasion of the 1831 law abolishing the slave trade. By the time it entered what became known as the Second Reign, Brazil already had years of experience as a country legally obligated to prevent the smuggling of Africans yet socially shaped by widespread contraband.[31] The political change at the top of the monarchy brought little innovation in foreign policy, and the imperial government continued to rely on the economic capital of an agrarian elite with long-standing ties to West and Central Africa to thwart the advance of abolitionism.

In 1845 Brazil came close to withdrawing all compliance with British suppression policies. As the 1817 regulations for the mixed commission courts expired, Britain's right to search ships suspected of dealing in slaves also ended. It responded with the Aberdeen Act, which authorized one-sided admiralty courts to clear up ship seizures and adjudicate those believed to participate in the illegal trade.[32] Lord Aberdeen, then the British foreign secretary, insisted that Brazilian slave traders should be treated as pirates and thus fueled the hostile rhetoric that would drive British policy toward increased coercion over the next decade. The Brazilian government viewed the act as a hostile measure in peacetime and protested in the name of national sovereignty. Nevertheless, the empire's unwillingness to uphold the 1831 law left the country in a weak position, as its accusations of British interference translated into the impunity of far too many slave traders and the tacit endorsement of slave owners' customary rights to smuggled labor.[33]

In the midst of uninterrupted illegal trafficking to Brazil, British diplomatic pressure gave way to intervention. The Royal Navy escalated its campaign by seizing even smaller vessels employed in the Brazilian domestic slave trade and, in June 1850, entered Brazilian ports to flush out suspected slavers, burning vessels and exchanging fire with Brazilian fortresses. In the province of Rio de Janeiro, hundreds of people watched British vessels force entry past the fort of Cabo Frio, firing at Brazilian guards who denied passage to armed British officials.[34] Soon the "whole City" of Rio de Janeiro knew that, according to Chief of Police Antônio Simões da Silva, "in the afternoons of the 6th and 7th day of this month, after news of the facts carried out by English cruisers spread, a kind of resentment manifested, because they were considered insults to our Nationality, then some groups of people armed with sticks went to the Largo do Paço [Palace Square], Cais Pharoux."[35] Some citizens gathered in front of the British consulate over the evening, yelling at British sailors and throwing stones at their ships docked in the port.[36]

Popular discontent turned into calls for a war against Britain, and Brazilian authorities rallied to condemn their adversary's conduct as imperious and arbitrary. Nevertheless, in August 1850, the Brazilian Parliament, dominated by the Conservative Party, finally passed the country's second anti-slave-trade legislation. After months of political debate, mostly in secret, the law, named after Justice Minister Eusébio de Queirós, focused on suppressing contraband at sea and the landing of Africans on the Brazilian coast. Vilified by Liberals as the product of British pressure rather than conservative humanitarianism, the 1850 law failed to address the problem of widespread illegal enslavement and ignored criminal acts on the ground, as if counting on the continued inability of Brazilian authorities to enforce the 1831 provisions. The new legislation appointed Navy Auditors (Auditoria da Marinha) as judges of seized ships and reinstated that Africans captured aboard slavers were to be deported in the near future at the expense of the government. In the meantime, these Africans were to be distributed to public institutions and frontier projects throughout the Brazilian territory. In other words, the 1850 law prohibited the concession of recaptured Africans to private guardians but refrained from setting up a concrete scheme for their resettlement in Africa, keeping recaptives under direct control of the government.

In addition to its aggressive antislavery campaign, Britain expanded its economic presence in the Brazilian Empire during the nineteenth century. Up to 1850, the British supplied Brazil with 50 percent of its imports—especially but not solely textiles—ranking the country as the third-biggest foreign market for English goods in the world, after the United States and Germany. British commercial houses, established primarily in Rio de Janeiro, fielded a large part of the Brazilian agricultural production abroad, exporting, for example, at least half of the coffee harvested to the United States and Europe. Britain also played an important role as the prime financer of the Brazilian public debt. Loans contracted in London funded the development of mining, early industrialization efforts, and the construction of Brazilian railways such as the one linking the coffee-producing hinterland of São Paulo to the port of Santos, known as A Inglesa (The English).[37] Needless to say, the coffee transported on English trains was produced by enslaved workers.

Britain supported the continuation of slavery in Brazil. In addition to their subjects' direct ownership of enslaved persons, British merchants with connections to commission houses in Birmingham, Leeds, Liverpool, and Manchester supplied Brazilian slaving voyages with goods specifically destined for the African market. British joint-stock banks financed the sprawling coffee plantations of São Paulo, underwriting all sorts of economic transactions secured by human collateral. Furthermore, British consuls routinely administered the estates of deceased British enslavers, and many were reported by the British and Foreign Anti-Slavery Society as subjects of the Crown acting in direct contradiction of Britain's abolitionist policy.[38] British liberalism remained compatible with coerced labor in South America because it viewed Africans as unfit for freedom and therefore in need of tutelage. Upheld as an ideal, free labor functioned as a brand of British imperialism by providing a language for the British to challenge the pro-slave-trade inaction of governments like those of Brazil or Spain (regarding Cuba) while solidifying their position within the global economy. Asserting freedom as a positive right for the illegally enslaved would be the undertaking of those most affected by the experience of dislocation and loss in the bowels of slave ships. Africanos livres were among the first historical actors to push Brazil and Britain to reckon with the contradictions between abolitionist thought and the codification of race in the Atlantic world.

Radicalizing British Antislavery

Slave-trade suppression profoundly influenced the emancipation politics of Africans and their descendants in the Americas. The trade ban added another layer to black understandings of the unfolding of emancipation, inviting speculation about the long-term implications of the imbalance of power between Brazil and Britain. In this context, africanos livres embodied the contradictions of the abolition era, at once symbolizing British antislavery ideals and the limitations of a liberation process controlled by governments on both sides of the Atlantic committed to racial domination.[39] The uneasy partnership between Britain and Brazil placed them in an almost impossible position. Emancipated as human cargo yet indentured as apprentices, africanos livres labored alongside the enslaved, formed families whose status were even less clear than their own, and lived under the permanent threat of being racially or ethnically profiled as escaped captives. Their terms of apprenticeship frequently expired without a change in their legal condition and, when change did occur, Africans were thrown into a society that denied them any path toward citizenship—a condition that was similar to that of the African freed person (*liberto*). Ultimately, they stood as living proof of Brazil's refusal to alleviate what, over time, became an escalating humanitarian crisis.

In the 1850s, when the Queirós Law that abolished the African slave trade to Brazil finally took effect, africanos livres could be officially divided into two groups: those recaptured by the British at sea and emancipated by Anglo-Brazilian mixed commissions in Rio de Janeiro before 1845, and those apprehended by Brazilian authorities and manumitted through Brazilian judicial procedures. Far more numerous, however, were the Africans who were brought to Brazil in violation of the 1831 law but who were never rescued by either British or Brazilian authorities. They numbered in the thousands, blurring the lines between slavery and freedom throughout the Brazilian Empire. Until 1864 there was simply no legislation in Brazil that granted known recaptives the unconditional right to freedom. Both the 1831 and the 1850 abolition laws made emancipation conditional on more than a decade of apprenticeship or removal from the country, and the 1853 decree that freed those who had completed their service in the hands of private hirers emancipated only africanos livres who could legally petition the government for manumission.[40]

Thus the nature of recaptives' freedom remained unresolved for most of the nineteenth century, opening up space for African activism in Brazil. Such dynamics had been prominent in other parts of the Americas, as during the La Escalera conspiracies in Cuba. In 1844 a wide uprising connecting enslaved people, free people of color, and white abolitionists broke out in the province of Matanzas. Enslaved Cubans acted on the belief in British solidarity with black liberation, and in fact, Spanish colonial officials accused the British consul and superintendent of liberated Africans David Turnbull of inciting a movement that launched one of the bloodiest crackdowns in history on Cuba's population of color. If we decenter the official accounts of La Escalera, however, it is possible to consider how the enslaved interpreted Turnbull's work on behalf of recaptives, drawing on British suppression to destabilize colonial systems of power.[41]

In the case of Brazil, the most notorious collective attempt by africanos livres to seek some form of redress from the British for mistreatment took place while the imperial government was debating its second and final law to abolish the slave trade. Between 1849 and 1851 more than 850 recaptives attempted to meet in Rio de Janeiro with British envoy Robert Hesketh, who wanted to compile a registry of Africans under tutelage of the Brazilian government.[42] In doing so, Africans reinterpreted the protective role that the British Crown had invoked at least since the Abolition of the Slave Trade Act of 1807. British diplomats expected to have supervisory rights over the emancipated population in the Americas, but they repeatedly encountered resistance from the Brazilian government to account for their fate. As they did in Cuba, British officials inundated the Brazilian Ministry of Foreign Affairs with formal complaints about the welfare or illegal detention of recaptured Africans. Such complaints, however, often were prompted by africanos livres themselves.

In 1849, for instance, an unnamed apprentice of one Damásio Antônio de Moura, who had suffered the amputation of a leg while working at the Custom House, and the africano livre Estevão obtained British aid. Their pleas against cruel treatment prompted the British Crown to call for "a List of the Africans who are entitled to their Liberty by action of the late Commission Court."[43] British envoy Robert Hesketh set out to compile the registry by first seeking information directly from imperial authorities. After being denied access to reliable lists, he resorted to spreading the word of his endeavor among the Africans who often appeared at the British consulate in Rio de Janeiro.

The result of African mobilization was outstanding, considering the degree of surveillance to which they were subjected. At the height of a wave of nationalist sentiment against the actions of British cruisers in Brazilian waters, guardians and enslavers closely monitored the actions of black workers in general. Several recaptives were able to appear in person only "by stealth" or not at all. Some of those who were unable to present themselves before the British sent written petitions, such as the africanos livres imprisoned in the House of Correction, who appealed to the British as a paternalistic authority.[44] Those who managed to show up, Hesketh reported, spoke "of their unprotected condition, and of the unjustifiable treatment to which a portion of them have been doomed," including women with unregistered births and "deceased comrades" who had died from barbaric treatment. A few africanos livres regretted especially "not even having the safeguard of being held as their Masters' property," in a clear reference to their de facto enslavement.[45]

Hesketh eventually produced a list of 856 people, the vast majority of whom lived in Rio de Janeiro, a dismal fraction of the total number of emancipated Africans in Brazil. The methods he used to compile his register, however, left a lasting impression on africanos livres, who continued to seek British protection in the years to come. In 1850 alone, as the Brazilian Parliament debated the ban on the slave trade, more than five hundred Africans walked through the doors of the British consulate. Many believed the British were their last hope of achieving any meaningful form of freedom, while others wished to be transferred elsewhere as part of the British African emigration scheme. British suppression in Brazil dovetailed with the policy of securing a steady supply of indentured laborers to plantation colonies in the West Indies. Recaptives were embarked from Brazil involuntarily from slave ships supposed to be adjudicated in Rio de Janeiro. Emigration started in 1838 and ended in 1852, involving the transfer of approximately 2,552 recaptives from Rio de Janeiro to British Guiana and Trinidad.[46]

Africanos livres framed their political identities within a transnational context that included Brazil, the Caribbean, Europe, and Africa. In many instances, British suppression was the thread that connected their varied Atlantic experiences and, as such, allowed them to slowly build up a considerable challenge to the legitimacy of Brazilian slavery. Black activism became ever more threatening when coupled with the British condemnation of the ubiquity of illegal enslavement in Brazil. Each time an africano livre presented his or her case to British diplomats, he or she pushed the boundaries of British advocacy to include a different kind of ethics. British envoy Henry Howard's writings about the Brazilian decree of December 28, 1853, are a case in point.

Howard learned about the shortcomings of the 1853 decree at the British consulate in Rio's Botafogo waterfront district, where Africans came to report their difficulties in accessing proper legal channels and the financial burden of bearing all the costs of seeking final emancipation. In a note to Brazilian minister of foreign relations Antônio Paulino Limpo de Abreu in

1854, Howard offered Cláudio as an example. Apprenticed to a private hirer, Cláudio had sought assistance from Consul John J. C. Westwood to leave Rio de Janeiro on a British ship. We don't know what arguments Cláudio used to convince him, but Westwood went to great lengths to find a British captain who would take Cláudio on board. Before leaving Brazil, Cláudio requested his emancipation certificate from the Curator of Liberated Africans M. H. Figueiredo, who in turn asked him to prove that he had sufficient means to travel abroad. Cláudio then received a letter from Consul Westwood certifying that a British captain was willing to vouch for him. However, Figueiredo refused to accept the letter and demanded that Cláudio instead obtain an affidavit signed by said ship captain and authenticated by the British consulate.

After spending several weeks trying to produce and pay for the necessary documentation, Cláudio finally received the certificate from Curator Figueiredo and applied for a passport at the Foreign Relations Ministry. In the words of Henry Howard, Cláudio had displayed "more perseverance and energy than generally found among Africans," yet his case showed clearly that the 1853 decree still posed too many obstacles to africanos livres in search of legal freedom.[47] Here was another crucial point of disagreement between the Brazilian and British governments: while the former insisted that the wages paid to free Africans were a form of aid to support their relocation to Africa, the latter assumed that such income could be used at the earner's discretion since repatriation plans had never materialized.[48] In other words, Africans had to pay to leave Brazil of their own free will.

Howard's repeated pleas for official explanations forced Minister Limpo de Abreu to elaborate on what he felt better left unsaid: the narrowness of the 1853 decree was due to the need to contain black activism in Brazil. "According to Your Excellency's explanation," wrote Howard, the bureaucratic loopholes kept untouched in 1853 followed "considerations about the public order, on what I very much agree with Your Excellency, with the goal of preventing the inconveniences that could occur in the event of the sudden and tumultuous emancipation of a large mass of Africans." That did not explain, however, why the imperial government continued to avoid the gradual emancipation of Africans. In Limpo de Abreu's view, Howard failed to grasp the distinction on which the status of africanos livres rested. Echoing what had been implicit in Brazil's handling of the end of the slave trade, Limpo de Abreu reminded the British diplomat that emancipation and freedom were not the same thing. In Brazil, Africans illegally imported into the country had only

the right to the former, to a life under the tutelage of the government, a condition comparable to that of orphans, colonists, soldiers, and sailors.[49]

Henry Howard disagreed. In his view, Africans employed in public works
shared none of the free will with which colonists signed contracts to leave
their homelands or the temporary status of recruitment of sailors and soldiers.
"Having been declared free is in all else a slave, and his emancipation is post-
poned and dependent upon re-exportation."[50] Moreover, reiterated Howard
in 1854, removal was an uncertain prospect when one considered that close
to twenty-three years had already passed since Brazil declared its intention of
sending away the Africans illegally introduced into the empire after 1831.

Despite Limpo de Abreu's criticism, Howard's understanding of Brazilian
law was quite accurate and actually closer to that of Africans like Cláudio.
Howard articulated the most dangerous turn yet in British abolitionist foreign policy. Under the influence of instructions sent by Lord Palmerston in
1851, British diplomats connected the cases of Africans emancipated by the
Anglo-Brazilian Commission to the liberation of Africans illegally imported
into Brazil under the 1831 law. Britain even proposed a convention for the
creation of a new mixed commission court that would examine "the cases of
all negroes entitled to freedom by reason of having been illegally imported"
and order their emancipation.[51] The Brazilian government refused to sign
such convention, in keeping with a long tradition of maintaining illegality
as the basis of slavery in the country. Beginning in the 1870s, however, abolitionists such as the black lawyer Luiz Gama would use this very contradiction to mount their challenge to enslavement and win the emancipation of
hundreds of Africans.[52]

Africanos livres escalated their struggle for freedom as they increasingly
watched their apprenticeship terms expire without any change in their conditions. Authorities sometimes acknowledged the abuses committed by concessionaires but constantly blamed receptive activism on Africans' alleged
sense of entitlement and inappropriate work ethic. In 1852, for example, the
president of the province of Maranhão, Manoel de Souza Pinto de Alves,
advocated for full emancipation to all africanos livres as a strategy to curb
their rebelliousness. "Aware of being free," explained the president, "they subject themselves of ill will to the work to which they are forced, and here it
follows that either their concessionaires abandon them for not being able to
take advantage of them or they punish them and they run away."[53] Even the
language to identify receptive resistance was the same used for the enslaved.
In the same year, the president of Piauí apprehended two Africans at the

event of their illegal sale and pleaded with the imperial government to transfer them to the capital or to a different province. "Taken by ideas of freedom,"
argued President Saraiva, Africans refused to work in the provincial institutions and usually ran away only to be enslaved again.[54]

African activism borrowed from experiences of being kidnapped into
slavery in the Atlantic. In June 1856, Sam—or Benjamin, as he was known
in Brazil—requested an appointment with Henry Walter Orendon, a British
consular official assigned to the province of Maranhão. As João and so many
others had done before him, Sam claimed to be a British subject who had
been stolen while working on board the English ship *Desert* off the coast of
Africa in 1841.[55] Two men called Caetano and Honório had snatched him
away from the ship while sailing from Sam's native Sierra Leone to Bissau and
then forced him to embark with other Africans to the province of Maranhão, in the Brazilian northeast. Sam was sold to Captain Josué Jansen Muller,
who employed him for many years on the streets of Maranhão's capital, São
Luís, until Sam spoke to a British consul for the first time. This appeal for
help resulted in him being "dragged to the countryside" to be stationed with
his master during the liberal Balaiada revolt (1838–41), an experience that
probably inspired Sam to later denounce his illegal enslavement.[56] Only after
Muller's death did Sam return to São Luís to live with his mistress Theresa,
Muller's wife, working again as a slave for hire.[57]

Henry Orendon found Sam's account trustworthy because his English
"although not pure, shows that he spoke it before learning Portuguese, as well
as that he has forgotten his native language."[58] Orendon's plea to the Brazilian
government brought international pressure to bear on Sam's case, prompting the intervention of Maranhão's chief of police. When interrogated in São
Luís, Sam and Theresa offered different versions of his time with the Mullers.
Theresa portrayed her alleged slave Benjamin as an incorrigible runaway who
had never put his training as a ship's caulker to good use. Instead of applying
himself to bonded labor, he often escaped to work as a stevedore on the ships
of a man named Sampaio, among other black people "who like Benjamin
also spoke English."[59] Theresa claimed that Sam already spoke Portuguese
when her husband bought him, as if to assure the authorities that he was
not involved in the illegal slave trade. Sam, on the other hand, remembered
everything about his capture in Africa and denied knowing Portuguese upon
his arrival in Maranhão. He mentioned that the people "from his homeland"
knew him as Sam, not Benjamin, and that before setting foot on the coast
of Brazil during the administration of "President Lima" he had never been

a slave.[60] On the contrary, he had worked for wages on board British ships, traveling to the ports of "London, Liverpool, Glasgow, Dublin, and other places in England and the coast of Africa."[61] Theresa Muller had no bill of sale to prove Sam's slave status. Her claim of ownership rested solely on her late husband's will, which bequeathed her a slave named Benjamin, and historical sources do not provide us with a final determination on his fate.

Bridging the realities of slave-trade suppression in Sierra Leone and Brazil, Sam's case highlights how Africans shaped political geographies in the nineteenth century. By claiming British subjecthood in English, he elicited the kind of international support inaccessible to Afro-Brazilians. In linking the social dimensions of illegal captivity to Anglo-Brazilian unequal power relations, Sam modeled for enslaved communities a new avenue of protest that implicated the Brazilian state in the geopolitics of Atlantic abolition. British agents, it is true, prompted a reckoning with the unlawful operation of slavery in Brazil that meant a great deal to black people. Nevertheless, their defense of recaptive rights echoed the Brazilian distinction between emancipation and freedom. British diplomats argued for the individual rights of British subjects within the liberal logic of antislavery imperialism. Survivors of the slave trade, in turn, articulated demands for black freedom that channeled larger diasporic notions of justice and belonging.

Grassroots diplomacy, it is important to note, did not depend on white endorsement of recaptive rights. Africanos livres often combined the struggle against unfreedoms with alliances with the enslaved. In 1854, for instance, Manoel ran away from work at the road being built in Paraibuna, province of Minas Gerais, only to join a quilombo in the outskirts of the city of São João del Rei.[62] Other recaptives employed strategies of resistance very similar to those in conditions of legal enslavement. In 1864 a rebellion of africanos livres broke out at a property of the Mato Grosso Mining Society in Diamantino, a town in the Center-West of Brazil. African miners rose up after decades of mistreatment at the hands of abusive superintendents, unhealthy working conditions, and "the behavior of the company's subaltern employees toward the cited Africans," according to the president of the province of Mato Grosso.[63]

On March 10, 1864, seventy-four africanos livres along with eleven enslaved men from the same mining society seized the moment when summoned to meet the new *agente* (administrator), Bartolomé Bossi, in the town of Vila Maria. Coming from Rio de Janeiro, Bossi bragged about being a close friend of the Baron of Mauá, one of the company's directors, and vowed to transfer the workers from the harvesting of *poaia*, an indigenous root known for its medicinal properties, back to diamond mining in Diamantino.[64] The africanos livres, however, opposed the move. Custódio, of the Cabinda nation, a middle-aged man who acted as the group's spokesperson, insisted on demanding "their *alforrias* (freedom letters) or emancipations." He explained that his comrades saw themselves as workers hired by the Brazilian government whose contracts had already expired. In fact, instead of the ten years stipulated on paper, more than twelve years had already passed. Custódio confronted Bossi in his yard and pondered that "if they were slaves, he should give them order to go find their masters and, if they were africanos livres, that they requested their emancipation."[65] Along with Porfírio Cabinda, Anastácio Congo, Isidoro Congo, Teresa Conga, and Teresa Cabinda, Custódio was eventually arrested and taken by a police official for questioning in Cuiabá, the capital of Mato Grosso.

The chief of police Firmo José de Matos accused Custódio and Porfírio of being the heads of what Bossi called a "revolution of africanos livres that can have an echo among the slaves." In their testimonies, the two Teresas further explained their complaints. They claimed to have risen up because they were tired "of always walking with bundles of clothes on their backs," a likely reference to the constant transfers they were subjected to.[66] Matos reprimanded the insurgents for halting the transference of power within the mining company but did little to challenge the allegations that Bossi's cruelty led to worsening working conditions in the mines. In any case, he denied the africanos livres' claim to emancipation and sent them back with the administrator to the Mindáo mines in Diamantino.[67] On the way back, protest broke out again when one of the Africans demanded the release of Custódio and Porfírio, who had been left behind in prison. In response, Bossi punished him with a hundred lashes, as a master would have done to his slave.

The government of Mato Grosso upheld the chief of police's decision against the insurgent recaptives, based on the fact that, having been assigned to the mining society on December 28, 1851, they still had a year of apprenticeship left to fulfill. Nevertheless, that was not the end of the imbroglio. In October 1864, soon after the passing of the decree granting emancipation to all africanos livres in Brazil, fifteen of them ran away from the Mindáo mines to seek protection from the police, where they again complained of mistreatment by Bossi.[68] In Cuiabá, chief of police Firmo de Matos finally ordered the prosecution of Bartolomé Bossi for attempted murder and assigned the africanos livres to work in the military arsenals. African political activism—a "state of complete anarchy," in Bossi's words—contributed to the demise of the Mining Society of Mato Grosso, which could not survive the chaos caused by mismanagement and the loss of its main labor force.[69]

Writing Family into the Diaspora

For recaptives, abolitionism also meant negotiating the gendered terrain of slave-trade suppression in Brazil. African women had to navigate the intimacy of apprenticeship, where physical proximity and dependence on their employers combined with slavery-like labor. Women's struggles for emancipation were often multigenerational, since concessionaries of their services tended to appropriate their reproductive lives by enslaving their freeborn children (legally defined as *ingênuos*, or born of a free womb). Africanas livres thus experienced a rather precarious iteration of motherhood at the intersection of gender and racial exploitation, which also generated appeals for British protection. The affirmation of black families was a site ripe for the exercise of grassroots diplomacy.[70]

Maria Luiza Rebolo was one of these women who risked losing custody of her relatives to a concessionary who did not recognize her free status. Rescued by the British from the slave ship *Angélica* in 1836, Maria petitioned for her final emancipation in 1857, seven years after the legal expiration of her apprenticeship term. A washerwoman, Maria Luiza accused Francisco da Rosa Quintanilha of literally stealing her labor power and threatening her with imprisonment for rebellion. This was a common strategy among private hirers of africanos livres, and Quintanilha was said to have already sent the African Marçal to the House of Correction, renouncing his services because of theft and alcoholism.

Francisco Quintanilha considered Maria Luiza's petition for emancipation as an act of extreme ingratitude. Borrowing from the paternalistic logic of slave ownership, he resented the fact that for the past six years she had gone out at all hours of the day without justification, worked more for herself than for his household, and showed no respect for him as an authority figure. Moreover, whenever confronted, Maria Luiza would go "to the kitchen screaming so loud that I can very well hear all kinds of things spring out of her mouth, giving me the epithet Thief of her services, and I know she does so in whichever tavern she goes to."[71] In a complaint sent to Rio's police commissioner, Quintanilha noted that the only thing preventing him from renouncing Maria Luiza's services was the bond he had developed with her two sons, whom he claimed to have raised as part of his own family. The eldest, Firmino, had been educated by Quintanilha's son, the priest Francisco do Coração de Jesus Quintanilha, who "taught him the Christian Doctrine" and had apprenticed Firmino to a master tailor. Men like Quintanilha routinely used the language of affect to describe domestic work performed in the context of coercion.[72]

It was not only male employers who abused Africans. Sometimes, for the recaptive woman, motherhood meant surviving the physical violence of female hirers who prevented her from carrying a pregnancy to term. In March 1860, for instance, the africana livre Victorina walked naked into the city of Jaicós, in the northeastern province of Piauí, after spending nearly fifteen years in captivity on the Tamanduá plantation. She showed signs of torturous punishment at the hands of Honória Maria de Jesus Lima; scars and worms covered her slender body from head to toe, and her fingernails were torn from being repeatedly beaten with a ferule. One could still see bloody wounds and the obvious effects of starvation, although it would have been hard to tell that Victorina was pregnant.[73]

Upon her arrival in Jaicós, Victorina met an elderly woman who convinced her to seek the protection of the public prosecutor and judge of orphans, Captain Belisário José da Silva Conrado. Given her "deplorable state" and the repeated pleas of the elderly woman, Belisário Conrado interrogated Victorina in front of local witnesses and requested a forensic medical examination.[74] Victorina's body was indeed "covered from top to bottom with scars left by a scourge (*azougue*), the fingernails of her hands all swollen from the punishment of slapping them on a table, where she says she has lost some blood, and finally she is so badly beaten by punishment, hunger, and nakedness that it is unbelievable to anyone who has not seen her." On March 21, 1860, Judge Conrado placed Victorina under the care of the priest Claro Mendes de Carvalho and immediately informed the president of Bahia, Diogo Velho Cavalcante de Albuquerque, that he would proceed to criminally prosecute Honória for mistreatment.

Victorina recounted that she was kidnapped off the coast of Angola and taken to Salvador, Bahia, in 1845, "in the age of puberty." There, slave traders dressed her up as a man and forced her to accompany them by foot to the interior of Piauí, another Brazilian province located 490 miles to the north. Victorina's fate would have been a quite common one for Africans illegally enslaved at the time, were it not for what happened next. Once in Piauí, traders motivated by what Victorina called "thirst for gold" sold her to a slave of Constância Maria de Jesus—more than a few enslaved people owned others in Brazil—adding a new layer of illegality to her case.[75] The woman immediately delivered Victorina to her mistress, Constância, as payment for her manumission. Baptized on November 1, 1845, as an enslaved twelve-year-old Creole woman (Brazilian-born), Victorina then became a captive in the eyes of the law. Upon her death, Constância's will maintained Victorina's status and designated her as the property of Honória's brother, Carlos, at a price of 300$000 réis.[76] When Carlos died, Victorina became Honória's property.

Despite having a clear case of "reducing to slavery a free person," Belisário Conrado's actions were blocked at every step by the networks of patronage that had protected illegal slavery in the plantations of Piauí for decades. Victorina lived in the Ribeira do Canindé, a rural region where most wealthy families owned Africans who had been illegally imported into Brazil after 1831. In 1860 Judge Conrado requested provincial authorization to take her children into police custody since Victorina was already a mother of four: Romualdo; Ana; Balbina, who belonged to Inácio Fernandes de Lima, the executor of Constância Maria de Jesus on the Capuano plantation; and Francisco, who was held by Coleto Vieira de Sá in the city of Jaicós. The Lima family and their neighbors tried to stall the petitions for Victorina's release and publicly threatened to use violence if their "slaves" were freed. These "improvised masters" feared that word of her right to emancipation would inspire other Africans to seek legal help from the authorities.[77]

Three months of inactivity in judicial custody prompted Victorina to act again. In a final bid for her freedom, she appealed to the emperor for clemency in July 1860, fifteen years after she had been trafficked to Bahia. Although illiterate, Victorina drafted a petition to Emperor Pedro II with the assistance of a literate intermediary. She presented her complaint orally to substitute judge Hermenegildo Lopes dos Reis, who drew on her experience of abuse, legal protocol, and traditional notions of Christian morality to craft a compelling case. The petition begins in the first person, with a direct appeal to the emperor's intervention as the "common Father of Brazilians and Protector of a destitute person like me." Calling herself "the victim of the most unjust and atrocious barbarity," Victorina recounted her illegal enslavement by Honória Maria de Jesus Lima and justified her escape from the Tamanduá plantation: "This woman, Sir, who has only the appearance of a human being, enraged that I had the weakness of giving birth to a child with her brother, inflicted on me the most barbaric and atrocious punishments, and mistreating me considerably with hunger and thirst, I would have perished in the prison in which I was kept, if Divine Providence, to whom I begged for everything, had not facilitated the means of my escape."[78]

This personal story is followed by a list of attached documents and an angry denunciation of the corruption that threatened her safety in Jaicós. "How am I to prove in the face of such documents that I am African, free, when the individuals who own my unfortunate brothers belong to the Family of Judges who have to judge my case?," asked Victorina. Her plea for emancipation was clearly based on the bet that imperial authority could prevail over local planters, and it combined legal language with details of her ordeal as an abused woman. "Pregnant as I found myself by the brother of that beast, I aborted in this Village, and would have died if my guardian, the vicar Claro Mendes de Carvalho, had not rescued me, treating me not as a degraded wretch but as a daughter."[79]

The seven-page petition ends with the same indignant yet humble tone of an ordinary litigant accusing an implacable mistress of inhumanity. Here, the wording follows traditional formulas from petitions for clemency and slave lawsuits that position the emperor as the highest and most impartial arbiter of disputes involving those deemed miserable.

> In this state of affairs, tired of suffering the most unjust persecution, which I have placed at your feet, I turn to Your Imperial Majesty to ask you, by the objects that are most dear to Your Majesty on earth, by the Souls of Your Majesty's August Parents, of Glorious Memory, by the Wounds of Our Lord Jesus Christ, to deign to provide that the Judge of my causes may be an unsuspecting person . . . so that my freedom may not be undermined, and finally, so that all of Your Majesty's Justice may protect me, no matter what the big bosses may say against it.[80]

Embedded in Victorina's petition to Pedro II is a critique of illegal enslavement that highlights the role of literacy in the history of abolitionism in Brazil. Reading and writing were present in the oral cultures of the illiterate poor. Victorina was a writer-dictator able to make her suffering legible through writing and to articulate a sense of collectivity in relation to the enslavement of free black people like herself. She portrayed her mistress Honória as less than human, ironically reversing the logic of racial violence at the root of her case. Moreover, aware of her legal subjectivity (the right to litigate), Victorina spelled out the threat africanos livres posed to slaveholders' rule. Grassroots

diplomacy depended on those like her who produced emancipationist jurisprudence whenever they pressed the Brazilian state to recognize a claim to
freedom thwarted by seigneurial power. Africans inscribed freedom into the
everyday practice of the 1831 law in Brazil, bringing abolitionism to life in
word and deed.[81]

The outcome of Victorina's petition for imperial intervention is unknown.
In August 1860, the Ministry of Justice revealed with rare clarity that, ten years
after the abolition of the slave trade, Brazil still erred on the side of caution in
cases of illegal slavery, choosing to uphold the customary rights of enslavers,
that is, the custom of forcing free Africans into bondage. Despite all of Victorina's documentation and the fact that the people of Jaicós recognized her as
an African, the Ministry recommended that the local government buy her out
of slavery rather than go through the motions of emancipating Victorina as an
africana livre. It was apparently safer to undermine the weight of what passed
as abolitionist legislation. By the end of the year, the status of Victorina's four
children also remained unclear. Romualdo, Ana, Balbina, and Francisco appear
in court documents as being "in the hands of" two planters from Jaicós.[82]

Literacy and the international politics of abolition also intersected in
the lived experiences of the africana livre Marcelina and her daughter Luísa
Leocádia in Rio de Janeiro. Born in Quingolo, a region of Angola, Marcelina had arrived in Brazil in 1839 on board a slave ship intercepted by British
cruisers. Upon emancipation by the mixed commission court in Rio, she was
placed as an apprentice with Joaquim Luís Soares, a Portuguese businessman residing at the busy Rua Direita, the imperial capital's main commercial street. There, Marcelina worked as a *quitandeira* (street food vendor) for
fourteen years, probably carrying baskets of fruit on her head with Leocádia
in tow. In May 1854, she petitioned for her final emancipation and arranged
her return to Africa, as mandated by the 1831 law. Soares, however, apparently
refused to relinquish custody of Leocádia for he saw her as his property. The
businessman had baptized the girl as his slave in her infancy, thus reconfigur-
ing relations of servitude to his advantage despite Leocádia's right to freedom
at birth. Scheduled to board the ship *Josephina* for Bahia in the early days
of May 1864, Marcelina sought police assistance to resolve the imbroglio. In
a desperate attempt to avoid further prosecution, Soares baptized Leocádia
again, this time as a free person, but the case found its way to the desk of
Henry Howard at the British consulate.[83]

Consul Howard openly championed Leocádia's story as evidence of the
mounting wave of illegal enslavement of free people of color in Brazil. After

his intervention, Marcelina regained custody of Leocádia and organized their departure for the African Mina Coast (a stretch of coastline between present-day Togo and southwestern Nigeria). As we have seen, in the letter of the 1831 law, the Brazilian Parliament intertwined gradual emancipation with black removal without devising a concrete plan for the deportation of those expelled from the empire. As a result, africanos livres had to choose between the lesser of two evils: paying for their own trip back to Africa with the salaries they were owed as apprentices, or living under constant surveillance in a country that denied them any prospect of citizenship. That meant that africanos livres such as Marcelina, like other libertos, were to remain stateless in Brazil, lacking at once the legal protection of the political entities from which they had been uprooted and any aspiration to become part of the emerging Brazilian national community.[84]

Excluded from the Brazilian body politic, africanos livres then faced the uncertainty of "re-exportation." Africa occupied as complicated a space as did Brazil and Britain in their imaginations. For emancipated Africans forced to remain in Brazil for at least fourteen years of apprenticeship, deportation meant leaving behind family and community ties that they, like the libertos, had built under great duress in the context of their slavery-like experiences. For African mothers in particular, returning to Africa meant negotiating the future of freeborn children whose status in Brazil was even more ambiguous than their own. Although originally from Angola, Marcelina seems to have come to terms with leaving for the Mina Coast after marrying José Manoel, a freedman of Yoruba descent.

Amid all the turmoil of her mother's deportation, Leocádia, then twelve years old, decided to act. Unwilling to go to Africa, she wrote an appeal to Joaquim Luís Soares, the same man who had illegally enslaved her for more than a decade. Here, in the role of literacy, lies the key to a very important if underappreciated feature of black life in nineteenth-century Brazil. Enslaved, freed, and free people of color experimented with literacy as a set of cultural and social practices that helped them engage with—and sometimes challenge—the primacy of slaveholders' customary rights. Through the written word, Leocádia made herself heard and asserted her status in Soares's household. Her letter was not an insignificant appeal from a young teenager at odds with her mother's authority. On the contrary, Leocádia carefully conveyed the emotional urgency of her predicament, deliberately playing on paternalistic sentiments to negotiate her way out of forced removal from Brazil:

My dear Master,

I hope you and everyone in the house are doing well. My dear Master, I ask you to please make sure I don't go home with my Mother because if I go there with her, she will not come back here. For the good you wish your mother make sure I don't go; don't pay attention to what I talked about yesterday because as you very well know I am a child, because I regret it, for the good you wished the deceased Mistress, because my Mother is fond of Me going with her.

Your slave, Leocadia d'Almda Soares.[85]

Using all the tropes of conventional letter writing, the girl addressed her mother's hirer as "my dear Master" and opened her letter with greetings to him and his family.[86] Then, in a deferential yet direct tone, Leocádia pleaded with Joaquim Luís Soares to prevent Marcelina from taking her away from his home. Her argument was embodied not only in the content of her messages but also in the style of spelling and punctuation. Composed by someone with a unique perspective on writing, her misspelled words and strained sentences resembled the transcription of a live conversation. Leocádia strung sentences together as if she were personally enumerating thoughts, expressing herself to an imaginary audience that may have included several readers. The dynamic interplay between the oral and the written shaped both the production and reception of ordinary people's writings in imperial Brazil, which were aimed at interpretive communities with varying levels of reading competency. In Leocádia's case, caught as she was in the disputed context of africanos livres' emancipation, the trait of literacy was in itself a symbol of agency, even as it was used to claim a place under Soares's tutelage. She was a writer for whom putting ink to paper was a means of negotiation, a tool of self-assertion that allowed her to reconcile a yearning to remain in Brazil with Soares's intention to keep her under his power.

Despite Leocádia's best efforts, Soares refused to allow her back into his home after the police intervened in the case. Determined to stay in Rio de Janeiro, Leocádia felt the need to write again. This time, she resorted to a strategy very common among Afro-descendants. She wrote a letter to José da Silva Mafra, a Liberal senator from the province of Santa Catarina and an old friend of Joaquim Luís Soares, urging him to lobby for her return to Soares's house.[87]

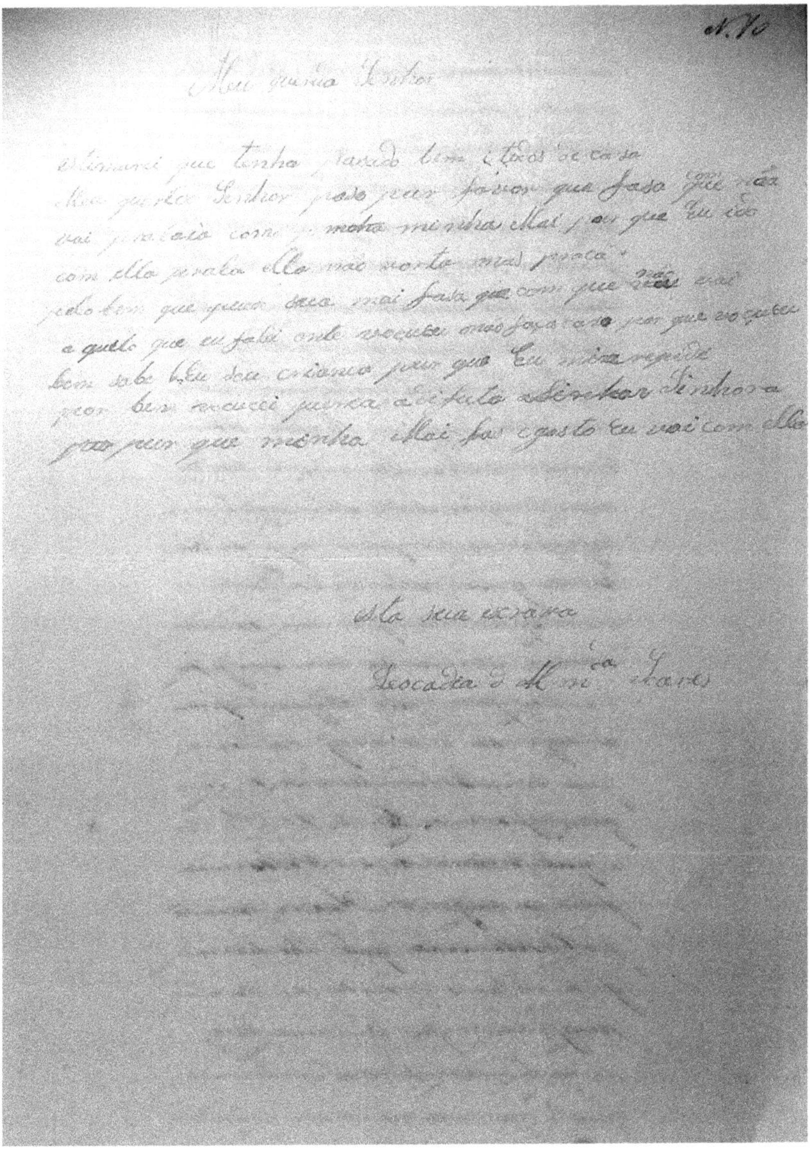

Figure 2. A rare material remnant of black women's literacy in Brazil. Letter handwritten by Leocádia d'Almeida Soares to Joaquim Luís Soares, Rio de Janeiro, 1854. Arquivo Nacional, Brazil.

Marcelina, now convinced that it would be better for her daughter to remain in Brazil if she so desired, personally delivered the note to Senator Mafra. It read:

My Dear Master of my Heart,

I hope you and my Mistress Dona Luiza have been well, to others kindness. My Master, I am sending for you to ask you to speak to Master [Soares] so that I can go there; Because my Mother is going to Bahia; because Master handed me over to her yesterday, because I don't want to go with her because I am fond of My Master. Yesterday he came to pick me and my Mother up and there they asked me if I wanted to go with My Mother to Bahia; I said yes after I left; Because I regretted it as I thought of My Master; Now, I thought of my aunts now send for Mistress or Master to ask for the fondness had for the deceased Mistress, to ask Master that I go to my Master's house, greetings from Me and My Mother,

Your most esteemed,
Leocadia de Almeida Soares.[88]

Leocádia recounted the whole imbroglio with Soares, insisting that she no longer wanted to travel with Marcelina to Bahia and then to the Mina Coast, a conventional route to Africa since the days of the slave trade. She mentioned the senator's wife and her sentimental attachment to the white women in Soares's household ("her aunts"), literally casting herself as part of Soares's family and implicating others in the resolution of her case.[89] Determined to make her plan work, Leocádia then ran away to Senator Mafra's house with the help of a free black woman who worked for him. In this way, she was finally able to secure her stay in Rio. On May 8, 1854, Marcelina sailed to Bahia with her husband, José Manoel, after dropping the girl off one last time at Soares's house.[90]

Encouraged by the British consulate, the chief of police of Rio de Janeiro opened a wider investigation into the illegal enslavement of Leocádia after Marcelina's departure to Africa. Henry Howard characterized the case as a typical attempt by "people in the highest positions to reduce free blacks to slavery" in Brazil.[91] Summoned to the police station for cross-examination, Joaquim Luís Soares and Leocádia placed literacy at the center of their cases, albeit with very different agendas. Soares, who was sixty years old at the time, gave the police Leocádia's letters as proof of her education and thus of his patronage in raising the daughter of an emancipated African woman to whom he had no blood ties. He swore that an old governess of his had mistakenly baptized Leocádia as a slave in his absence and that he had publicly declared Leocádia to be free many times. Soares treated Leocádia's enslavement almost like a slip of the tongue or an acceptable gaffe, based on widespread assumptions about the children of africanos livres in Brazil. From a legal standpoint, however, he was forceful enough to use the language of property, if only to convey a sense of continuing obligation between emancipated women and their hirers. Soares emphasized that Leocádia had always received good clothes and shoes, and that "he had even sent her out to learn how to read and write." As proof, he presented an affidavit signed by four distinguished gentlemen from Rio de Janeiro who could speak of his character as a humanitarian guardian.[92]

In her testimony, Leocádia maintained the image of Soares as a benevolent father figure, thus confirming the content of her letters. She compared him to her stepfather, José Manoel, whom she accused of abusing her and Marcelina. When asked how she knew she was a free person, Leocádia replied that she had always been treated as such by "Master Soares," who spent many nights caring for her when she was young and sick. She added that Soares made sure she learned how to read and write, gave her good clothes and shoes, and had even sent her out to a private school when she was young.[93] Leocádia's testimony highlighted the elements of her experience that could be seen as attributes of freedom. After all, enslaved children were not allowed to be rocked to sleep by their masters, did not wear shoes, enjoyed at most two changes of clothes a year, and were almost always illiterate.

At first glance, the deferential tone of the letters to Joaquim Luís Soares and Senator Mafra seems to indicate Leocádia's resignation to the domestic realities of patriarchy and bondage. Why else would a black girl turn to someone who had taken away her freedom in terms of affection? It may be that Leocádia did so to implicate both men in a certain understanding of slavery as a system of reciprocity.[94] By addressing her guardian as a protective father, she employed the same domestic language that enslavers used to assert mutual rights and obligations with the black and white members of their households. Leocádia included Soares in her larger sentimental community because she understood how her life was entangled with his. In doing so, she communicated the standard by which she expected to be treated, and it was not as an enslaved person.

Writing intersected with separation from loved ones in the lived experiences of other africanos livres in Rio de Janeiro. Another example comes from Cyro, a father of two employed by the Brazilian government. Rescued from illegal enslavement in a Bahian sugar mill in 1835 along with many other men from West Africa's Mina Coast, Cyro spent fourteen years in the Naval Arsenal of Salvador before rising up with some of them in 1848 to demand a change in status. According to Beatriz Mamigonian, he was then placed in the care of Dionísio Peçanha, a high-ranking bureaucrat in the Ministry of the Navy in Rio de Janeiro, who employed him as a muleteer for hire in Rio's coffee trade.[95] During his stay in the imperial capital, Cyro married Luiza, a freedwoman also from the Mina Coast, with whom he had two sons, Gregório and Pedro.

In 1854, Cyro petitioned the government for his final emancipation following the passage of the 1853 decree. While awaiting liberation, however, he became the victim of Peçanha's ill will, who disapproved of his use of the legal system and accused him of inciting fellow Africans to seek their emancipation. Thanks to his contacts in the upper echelons of the imperial bureaucracy, Peçanha had Cyro arrested for rebellious behavior and sent to the House of Correction. By then a widower, Cyro saw his two orphaned sons—Gregório, six, and Pedro, three—also placed under the tutelage of the police. Dionísio insisted that Cyro be transferred to the state of Amazonas, or even to Africa, but eventually secured his transfer to a prison ship docked at the Rio de Janeiro Naval Arsenal.[96]

Considering the separation from his sons untenable, Cyro wrote an ultimatum to Dionísio Peçanha in 1856, asking to be reunited with his children. Cyro opened his letter with a greeting to Peçanha's family, similar to Leocádia's, and then used to his advantage the ethnic identity often invoked to discredit West Africans as unruly. Noting that the letter was the third in a series of unsuccessful pleas, he directly threatened to show Peçanha "what a black Mina is" if he didn't secure his sons' release within three days. Signing as "your slave, Chiro Pisanjes, Africano livre," Cyro concluded his ultimatum with the formal tone of a petition, perhaps anticipating Peçanha's angry response to the threat.[97]

Not even a handwritten note from Cyro could dispel Dionísio Peçanha's degrading view of recaptives, which conveyed a common racialized understanding of illiteracy in nineteenth-century Brazil. "This African is resentful and vindictive, like those of his race in general," Peçanha wrote in his response to the Ministry of Justice. He went on to claim that he believed his existence was "exposed to the treacherous knife of a barbarian African, fierce and savage with no morals nor religion, an illiterate, who only breathes ven-geance."[98] Despite Peçanha's accusations, the imperial government granted Cyro emancipation, stating that he deserved custody of his sons since he had even managed to send the older, Gregório, to school. As with Leocádia, edu-cation was considered proof of responsible parenthood even if it threatened those who opposed black liberation.

The stories of Cyro, Leocádia, Victorina, and Maria Luiza reveal the legal and social precariousness of the lives of africanos livres in Brazil. Even for those who succeeded in petitioning for full emancipation, the process was tortuous, sometimes multigenerational, and subject to the networks of patronage that guaranteed white privilege in the country. If she had not convinced Joaquim Luís Soares to welcome her back into his household, Leocádia could very well had ended up at the House of Correction like Cyro's sons, deprived of both her family and her freedom. She mastered the elements of the paternalistic logic that framed her relationship with her mother's hirer, transforming guard-ianship into protection when she found herself at a crossroads. More than examples of ordinary communication in a slave society, Leocádia's, Cyro's, and Victorina's letters were emotional objects in themselves, artifacts whose mate-riality defied the racial stereotypes that defined their illegal enslavement.[99]

If literacy was the quintessential symbol of rationality and racial superi-ority in imperial Brazil, in the hands of africanos livres it became irrefutable proof of their skill in manipulating the rules of a white-dominated world.[100] By asserting the emotional values that removal denied her and Marce-lina, Leocádia sought to transcend the limitations that slavery and tutelage imposed on their lives. Through the agency of people like Cyro, artifacts of literacy became seminal instruments of change, pushing the boundaries of transatlantic abolitionism in Brazil to include the perspectives and writings of Africans. Such letters also complicate one-sided narratives of British slave-trade abolitionism. In the mid-nineteenth century, international politics—and, within it, the politics of abolition—were made and remade through different kinds of knowledge produced by nonstate actors who radicalized British diplomacy in Brazil.

*   *   *

Africanos livres were part of a transatlantic conversation about slavery and its abolition that was never homogeneous or linear. In Brazil, they struggled for decades to ensure compliance with an abolitionist version of slave-trade suppression. Their efforts at grassroots diplomacy cast British pressure on the Brazilian government in a different light, that is to say, British intervention was often rooted in African-initiated attempts to secure international protection. The intervention of foreign diplomats, however, was only the beginning of a long process of negotiating a way out of enslavement that influenced and intersected with the struggles of the enslaved for self-liberation. British antislavery never lost its imperial and conservative bent in Brazil, as diplomats continued to champion the preservation of political and social hierarchies through policies of mutual rights of search, mixed commission courts, naval cruisers, and compliance with bilateral treaties. Grassroots diplomacy, on the other hand, revolved around personal trajectories of transnational migration that linked Brazil to a broader debate about the fate of Africans in the modern world.

In his 1868 report, the Brazilian minister of justice José de Alencar painted a bleak picture of the experience of africanos livres who had survived that far into the 1800s: "It has still not been possible to destroy the dreadful effects of the slave trade with the emancipation of all africanos livres." Of the 11,008 recaptives listed in a government survey carried out in the 1860s, more individuals had died (3,871) than had received freedom letters (2,534) in Brazil. Another 191 Africans were marked as missing, a staggering 3,308 were unaccounted for, and only 748 individuals had been repatriated to the African continent.[101]

Brazil's first experience with gradual emancipation all but failed recaptives and their descendants, but it also paved the way for the development of antislavery activism in the country. In other words, black abolitionism in Brazil was also African. Africanos livres insistently contested the pace of emancipation, the length and working conditions of apprenticeships, the idea of forced relocation, state policies of surveillance and social control, family separation, and the meaning of abolition. Ultimately, they challenged the very notion that their destinies should be controlled by British or Brazilian officials involved in rescuing them from the Middle Passage or on the mainland after they disembarked. And in their experience, literacy in multiple languages also functioned as a tool of abolitionism.

CHAPTER 2

Insurgent Abolitionism

Enslaved people in Brazil expected much from cooperation with a self-proclaimed global abolitionist power. As Britain intensified its repressive policies against Brazilian participation in the slave trade throughout the 1840s, many felt even more emboldened to speak of emancipation as an urgent goal to be achieved in cooperation with British forces.[1] As far as black insurgents were concerned, the British campaign against the transatlantic slave trade counted as a step in the process of eradicating slavery itself. Thus, from the southern provinces of Brazil to the eastern frontier of the Amazon, they acted on rumors of British advocacy on behalf of africanos livres, raised toasts to freedom and England, and debated whether the presence of British ships along the Brazilian coast signaled the possibility of an invasion of Brazil. For the enslaved, if abolition was to be a process imbued with a sense of justice, it was only natural that the most powerful player on the international stage would join in.

The notion that Brazilian slavery could be destroyed by a slave war fought alongside a foreign power surfaced forcefully in 1848, during one of the largest cycles of black rebellion ever to hit the country.[2] On the eve of the abolition of the slave trade, the idea inspired struggles for freedom in the Paraíba River valley, the heart of the Brazilian coffee economy. In the region that connects the hills of Rio de Janeiro to the eastern part of São Paulo and southern Minas Gerais, the primary site of what some scholars call "second slavery," enslaved people reinterpreted British suppression policies to challenge slavery amid a coffee boom that buried any belief that the institution was on its way out in Brazil.[3] In the county of Indaiatuba, province of São Paulo, the African Francisco provided so much detail about an alliance with the British in 1848 as to win the nickname of "Tático," or "strategist" in Portuguese.[4] Enslaved by the priest Bento Dias Pacheco, Tático belonged to a group of rebels who planned to rise up on Independence Day, September 7, for they were in agreement that "the English or the French should come to help" them become free.[5] Some of his co-conspirators claimed that Emperor Pedro II or even São Benedito, patron saint of slaves, would also intervene on behalf of black emancipation.

Whispers about Britain's role as a strategic ally of Afro-descendants circulated beyond Brazil, rallying insurgent black communities throughout the Americas. Examples abound. In 1823 the enslaved rebelled in Demerara, believing that local plantation owners refused to obey British orders to free them. Likewise, several enslaved rebels in Cuba joined the La Escalera uprisings of 1844 "because the English were coming with ships to wage war on the whites of this land." In 1861 the freedman J. H. Banks reiterated the point, mentioning that African Americans "hear it said that although England was the first to introduce slavery into America, she has abolished it in the West Indies; they, therefore, look upon her as the friend of the colored race. It is a common opinion among the slaves that slavery will be terminated by a war between England and the United States."[6] Insurgent narratives of British antislavery embodied black ideologies of struggle against slavery and colonialism all over the hemisphere, and after France abolished slavery in its colonies in 1848, it too came to populate narratives of emancipation.[7]

Since the late eighteenth century, France had been part of the political imagination of Afro-descendants as a bearer of principles of freedom and racial equality.[8] By the 1840s, however, French antislavery usually appeared alongside mentions of British abolitionism and, from the slaveholders' perspective, conveyed a dual threat to Brazilian slavery: the possibility of prompting another Haitian Revolution and spreading socialist ideas among the enslaved.[9] Be that as it may, Haiti endured as a referent for black freedom struggles in Brazil. In 1846, even before the second French abolition, the free black preacher Agostinho da Silva Pereira was accused of inciting the enslaved to rebel in Recife, Pernambuco. The "Divino Mestre," as he was known by his literate followers, all freed or free people of color, was a military veteran of the Confederation of the Equator in 1824 who preached a black version of Christianity in one of the empire's most important Atlantic cities. When police raided Agostinho's home, they found a Bible with Old Testament passages about freedom highlighted. More important, officers seized two pages of handwritten verses that linked criticism of Brazilian slavery to the Haitian Revolution and emancipation in British colonies. A stanza of the poem praising the "Moreno [brown] race" read: "Oh! Great is the blindness / of these Brazilian people; They don't look at Haiti / and at English America."[10]

It is this actionable knowledge of the nineteenth-century world of reform that I call insurgent abolitionism in Brazil. I refer to the steady undercurrent of black resistance and hope that fed on fragments of news about international politics and looked at every conjuncture for abolitionist opportunity. Across the Brazilian empire, black political communities connected seemingly scattered elements—like British naval reprises, Pedro II's trips to the provinces, African cosmologies, and popular Christianity—through a common quotidian praxis into emancipatory worldviews. Insurgent abolitionism developed in part as an early iteration of black internationalism that grew out of slave rebellion, as we will see in cases where insurgency intertwined with British and French antislavery.[11] In the 1850s, it also expressed a growing critique of the experiences of forced labor that followed on the heels of global abolition, approximating the enslaved to africanos livres or even to ill-treated contract laborers brought from Europe to work in the coffee fields of Brazil. In 1856, for instance, class and racial conflicts shaped a landmark event in the history of immigration to Brazil, the Revolta dos Parceiros, or Sharecropper's Revolt. Swiss immigrants who challenged their treatment as "white slaves" at the Ibicaba plantation in Limeira, São Paulo, and the enslaved in pursuit of emancipation conspired to rebel in the hope that British forces would intervene on behalf of workers' freedom.

In the 1860s black uprisings signaled historic change in imperial Brazil. Although enslaved people had long rebelled against masters who were eager to dismiss abolitionism as a foreign phenomenon—and, especially as a British threat—the context of freedom struggles changed. As a war over slavery raged in the United States and emancipation became a reality in most of the Americas, the enslaved accelerated the pace of insurgency to demand immediate abolition in Brazil. When Brazil and Britain came to the brink of war in early 1863 during what became known as the Christie Affair, cries of "viva os ingleses, viva a Liberdade" (hail the Englishmen, hail Freedom) erupted across the country, exacerbating the interstate crisis over Brazil's mishandling of an internationally sanctioned process of slave-trade suppression. Threatening to ally with the British forces that laid siege to the port of Rio de Janeiro, enslaved and freed people pushed authorities and white vigilantes to confront black activism as a real threat to Brazilian sovereignty.[12] In the long run, and from the perspective of those in bondage, Brazilian abolition was hardly a peaceful process. Insurgency was part of the crisis of slavery, and much of it had to do with black efforts to continually reposition a slave empire in relation to the global history of abolition.

Ending the Slave Trade, Ending Slavery

In the timeline of black struggles for freedom in Brazil, 1848 was remarkable. That year a great cycle of slave conspiracies hit the Brazilian Center-South, expanding the meaning of the Anglo-Brazilian question to include the abolition of slavery in the French colonies. In February insurgents in Lorena, east of São Paulo, were so convinced of the threat to chattel slavery posed by the British that they did not hesitate to claim it.[13] Their call for rebellion echoed far and wide, encompassing the neighboring municipalities of Guaratinguetá, Queluz, Areias, Cunha, Silveiras, and Parati, in the province of Rio de Janeiro, and Baependi, in the province of Minas Gerais. The freed Creole blacksmith Agostinho; Vicente, a slave of Faustino Xavier de Morais; and the African Francisco, a slave of Maria Pereira da Guia, invited their peers to revolt on either Saint John's or Saint Peter's Day, a time of religious festivities at the end of June. Lorena and Baependi planters, however, discovered the uprising in the making and quickly arrested more than thirty suspects.

Rebels vowed to "take up arms with the aim of getting their liberties by force, for which the Englishmen would help, since Brazil is very entangled with that Nation of England and all the more because the slave trade has ceased."[14] They swore to act alone but faced authorities convinced of the influence of foreign agitators intent on undermining the slaveholders' peace. At the insistence of police commissioner José Rodrigues de Souza, Vicente pointed out a French peddler and another "Swiss or French" man "named Jacob or Jacques" who were talking about emancipation in the county of Silveiras. Jacques Troller, one of the opinionated outsiders, was a French planter of republican leanings who had formed a friendship with Antônio Gaspar Martins Varanda, Agostinho's former master, over the ten years of his residence in Brazil.[15]

On Varanda's plantation, antislavery ideas spread as people like Agostinho, then an enslaved domestic worker, engaged in the collective reading of newspapers. Troller often read the *Jornal do Commercio* aloud, including "foreign news without reserve," and would "make remarks about the current state of affairs in Brazil, condemning slavery and pondering the consequences that could follow similarly to those in the Island of S. Domingos."[16] Although insurgents were careful enough never to make direct mention to Saint Domingue or Haiti, the literate Agostinho was said to exchange correspondence with Troller.[17] Lorena authorities also suspected the existence of "statutes" written by a Frenchman guiding the activity of slave "clubs" in the coffee plantations of the Paraíba River valley. The enslaved, however, referred solely to the British.

From the outset, the vice president of São Paulo, Bernardo José Pinto Gavião Peixoto, blamed the 1848 conspiracy "on the skillful thoughts" stirred among the enslaved by "a hidden hand" that planned to extract concessions from the Brazilian government.[18] Peixoto spoke of "the evil spirit of some Foreigner" and, more specifically, of the power of "suggestions hatched by some Gregorian Society or agents of the abolitionist principles of slavery" against planters in São Paulo.[19] He referred to the abolitionist ideas of the Catholic priest Henri-Baptiste Grégoire (1750–1831), a French revolutionary who openly championed the Haitian Revolution.[20] A judge in Guaratinguetá, in the vicinity of Lorena, also speculated about the formation of a "Saintsi-monian" society in the region, that is, a black association influenced by the thought of the French utopic socialist Henri de Saint-Simon (1760–1825).[21]

Thus, in 1848, Jacques Troller emerged as a typical *haitianista* in the eyes of law enforcement authorities, that is, as someone who dangerously swayed the enslaved to republican and abolitionist causes. With a pejorative connota-tion, "hatianism" was part of the political vocabulary of those seeking to dis-qualify opponents—either black or white—as instigators of slave rebellion in Brazil. Found in the press, parliamentary debates, and police reports, the term embodied white fears of black unrest in independent Brazil, as Haiti continued to intersect with Atlantic abolitionism throughout the nineteenth century.[22] The threat posed by Troller became even more acute after the revolutionary wave that overthrew the monarchical government of Louis-Phillipe in Feb-ruary 1848 and ushered in the Second Republic in France. In April 1848, as abolition followed regime change in the French colonies, the country again entered the repertoire of black insurgents in Brazil. Nevertheless, as a planter in the town of Silveiras, Jacques Troller hardly represented a radical figure of the French Enlightenment. Rather than an inciter of slave rebellion, he would be better described as a mediator of the meanings of transatlantic abolitionism in Brazil.[23] At Varanda's plantation, Troller brought up the importance of Haiti as a telltale for those who wanted to avoid a black revolution, so it took some-one like Agostinho to infuse what he heard with a subversive purpose. Rumors of freedom were born of such subaltern acts of political interpretation, which expressed efforts to make sense of the asymmetrical power relations that struc-tured master-slave relations in Brazil. A form of rebel communication, rumors were the language enslaved, freed, and free people used to build political bonds with others, to understand change, and to transform their realities.

Lorena's police commissioner, José Rodrigues de Souza, resented more than the influence of an outspoken Frenchman in eastern São Paulo. He bemoaned the echoes of insurrection reverberating across the country due to "the most unmeasured ambition, selfishness or envy and jealousy that Brazil incites in some Nations."[24] In his analysis of insurgent discourse, Souza highlighted the role of British naval policing; citing the toll it took on the *paulista* coffee business, he accused the British of wanting a war against Brazil under the pretext of freeing the enslaved.[25] Though blind to the internal dynamics of black abolitionism, Souza watched with concern as the enslaved combined the suppression of the slave trade with various strands of antislavery activism.

In 1848 conspiracies like the one in Lorena sprung up simultaneously in the provinces of Rio Grande do Sul, Rio de Janeiro, and Minas Gerais.[26] In Pelotas, Rio Grande do Sul, black rebels forged a powerful alliance: that of enslaved West Africans (known as Minas) who worked in the local *char-queadas* (establishments where beef jerky was made) and Blanco militiamen from the embattled Republic of Uruguay, nominal enemies of the Brazilian empire who supported the Colorado Party. Black insurgents planned to wage a war against the whites and then run away to Uruguay, where slavery had been abolished in 1842. Attentive to the way Minas communicated by shaving their heads as a sign of adherence to the uprising, the police filled the jail of Pelotas with over fifty free and enslaved suspects whom they thought had been "trained in the insurrections of Bahia."[27] That February, ten Africans died under the lash without ever confessing to the names of their alleged abettors.

John Morgan, the British consul in Rio Grande do Sul, attributed the Pelotas' plot to the presence of secret agents coming from the River Plate region. He maintained that "there can be no doubt that there is a spirit abroad amongst the slave population of this Province that sooner or later their emancipation will come through the medium of the neighboring Republican states." In other words, Morgan connected the activism of the enslaved in Brazil to the Uruguayan Civil War (1839–51), in which Manuel Oribe headed the Blanco Party against the Colorados, the faction supported by the Brazilian government. The consul identified "Spaniards" who worked as overseers at the charqueadas of Pelotas as the "master hand" behind the uprising, just as José Rodrigues de Souza had done with the French in Lorena. Morgan claimed that Spaniards enlisted slaves to rebel "by promising them that they would be taken to the Banda Oriental where freedom awaited them in the ranks of General Oribe's Army."[28]

As we can see, British diplomats also ascribed black dissent to outside influence but not to their own. What foreign and domestic authorities in Pelotas struggled to articulate was the fact that the enslaved exploited divisions fostered by the uneven advance of abolition worldwide to construct a politics of self-emancipation. And when they did so, sometimes it sufficed to look at republican experiences that sat just over the horizon in South America. On Brazil's southern borders with Uruguay and Argentina, international escapes were as common as the risk posed by kidnapping networks headed by Brazilian slave catchers.[29] Brazil's northern border with French Guiana was equally porous, and information about emancipation constantly traveled from Cayenne to Amapá, then part of the Brazilian province of Pará.

In September 1848, enslaved men from Brazil claimed their freedom in French territory. After foundering at sea while en route from Pará to deliver a cargo of live cattle, the crew of the Brazilian ship *Águia* took to a thin boat to reach Cayenne. Three enslaved people died of starvation on the journey to port, but another three ultimately reached land and "refused to leave the Colony on the grounds of considering themselves free on French soil." They knew that France had passed an abolition decree on April 27, 1848, as did so many black communities throughout Brazil in that year.[30] Acting on a request from the ship's master Francisco Solano da Fonseca Junior, the president of Cayenne sent an armed party to arrest the recalcitrant Brazilian fugitives, placing them by force on board of the brig *L'Anna* "at the disposal of Fonseca Junior to return them under the custody of the French Flag to slavery."[31]

Perceptions about French and British antislavery informed the prosecution of "the French or Swiss" Jacques Troller in Lorena. Ultimately, his participation in the slave conspiracy was never proved and he walked free in 1848. The freedman Agostinho broke out of jail but turned himself in to the police a year later, when he was sentenced to five hundred lashes and use of an iron collar for three years. Vicente and Francisco sustained the brunt of exemplary punishment: each received 1,400 lashes and wore an iron collar for three years. The conspiracies in Lorena and Pelotas dovetailed with several others throughout Brazil, bringing illegally enslaved Africans together with their Brazilian-born descendants to influence the course of slave-trade suppression in the empire.

In August, Tático's rebellion plan came to light in Indaiatuba, with branches in Itu, Rio Claro, and Campinas, some of the most important coffee-producing counties of western São Paulo. This time, rebels mapped insurrection onto ideas of royal sponsorship of abolition and black rule in distant lands. Tático invoked a belief common among the enslaved that visits by the Bragança imperial family to the provinces signaled imminent state action in favor of emancipation.[32] In 1846 Emperor Pedro II did indeed visit Indaiatuba but left his wife, Teresa Cristina, in the capital, São Paulo. From her absence, Tático and his peers Jacinto, Pedro, and Gabriel inferred that a division within the ruling ranks in Brazil had created an opening for rebellion: "We are all getting ready to become free, and this was because the King had argued with the Queen, because the Queen wanted the captives to be free, and the King didn't want it, and so the Queen distanced herself from the King, till the King decides to free everyone, and that's why the king came here for a visit, and since they were already living apart, only the King came, to see if he could free everyone, and because he could not, they live apart to this day and now it is necessary for all the captives to get together and apply force to become free, and the whites captive, and when this happens the King and the Queen will be reunited."[33]

That was quite an effort of imagination. Tático also alluded to the plight of africanos livres, saying "that the negro meia-cara [half-face black] is already free, and that is why the White at first did not want to buy, but afterwards started to buy yet could not baptize, and that is why now they should all get together to become free."[34] His statement revealed a remarkable awareness of the mechanisms of illegal enslavement in Brazil. Africanos livres, after all, were not supposed to be traded and much less baptized as someone else's property.

Narratives among the enslaved about British suppression bridged black experiences throughout the South Atlantic, showing that, rather than a static origin for Afro-American cultures, Africa continued to be the source of dynamic connections, both material and imaginary, with Brazil. As carriers of news about the workings of emancipation around the world, Africans themselves kept African history alive as an ongoing reference for freedom seekers in Brazil.[35] Tático recalled learning from Joaquim at their senzala about "a land where there were whites and blacks and where, being all the whites in the church one day, the blacks laid a siege and ended them all" so that "today only the black govern." His testimony prompted the Indaiatuba police commissioner to conduct several cross-examinations among enslaved men at the local jail. In the presence of Tático, Joaquim denied ever telling a story about a church siege, saying instead, "I only told a story about the Moçambiques in that same land."[36] Diogo added that "when Piriquito passed through this Parish in 1842, he said that now this land would go to the English, and that white and captive would all go to another land, and the English will take charge of this land."[37] In this scenario, Diogo alluded directly to the possibility of a British conquest of Brazil.

Black geopolitics often combined very different events and cosmologies into an original version of abolitionism. In 1848, religiosity also provided a significant cultural medium for the articulation of slave rebellion. Indaiatuba insurgents interwove popular Catholicism with African spirituality, yielding insight into how projections of emancipation often depended on modes of prophecy, circular temporalities, and divine intervention. Pedro, Rafael, and Luísa invoked, in a millenarian tone, the authority of Brazil's most well-known black saint to explain their decision to rise up in Indaiatuba: "São Benedito had been buried in the mud in Itu, and the Saint ought to reappear in São Paulo, and from there he shall come to free the captives and, therefore, they should all be ready for the occasion." Born enslaved in 1526 to North African parents sold to Sicily, Benedict was freed at birth along with his parents and became a Franciscan friar in Palermo, Italy. Since colonial times, he had been revered in Latin America for his holiness, humility, and miracles. Enslaved, freed, and free black people built many chapels in honor of the saint throughout Brazil. In Itu, a confraternity existed at least since the beginning of the nineteenth century.[38]

When asked about when the uprising would take place, Pedro and Rafael also recounted the story about the king and the queen first recited by Tático, adding a secular dimension to their understandings of the movement. Despite the richness of enslaved people's testimony, José Mendes Ferraz struggled to believe what he heard from Indaiatuba rebels and left much of their thoughts off the record. "It is necessary to caution, that the confessions of the blacks are in excerpts," he told the president of São Paulo, "being true that the essential answers are *ipsis-verbis*, but, in order to say anything, they tell such long tales that are beside the point that, for being tiresome, I did not order written."[39] Distrustful of the insurgents' understanding of abolition's relationship to history, Ferraz edited slave depositions to suit the theme of foreign indoctrination. In his dispatches, he fitted the political imagination of the enslaved into a kind of counterinsurgent prose meant to curb the power of freedom stories.[40] Discontinuous, derived, and erratic, such records read mostly as a reflection of the racialized assumptions of the police officer. Yet enslaved voices shine through.

The interrogation of the rebels at the Indaiatuba police station resembled an intercultural encounter marked by divergent understandings of dissent in the world of slavery. While the authorities operated in a time of exception and emergency and viewed black rebellion as a spontaneous outbreak, the enslaved offered evocative narratives of the motivations behind their quest for change.[41] In representing the many horizons of emancipation, their reasons for insurrection were not always immediate. Stories of black redemption traveled orally across space and time, inspiring activism many years after events happened. Insurgents like Diogo, who talked about the visit of a Brazilian soldier in 1842, or Tático, who recalled an 1846 imperial visit to São Paulo, wove reminiscences into their testimonies. They digressed to give concrete context to ideas of historical rupture. Details that appear in tension with the factual tone of police reports, I would argue, are moments of black authorial voice in the archives, just as they deviate from official temporalities to give the rebellion some depth in time. In Indaiatuba, the rebels presented a unique version of the process of slave-trade suppression, constructed through specific events imprinted in their collective memory over time.[42]

This explains, in part, how religion intersected with British antislavery in almost every place where the enslaved rebelled in 1848. Insurgents typically synchronized uprisings with sacred dates in the calendar to multiply the odds of victory, but religion gave them more than extraordinary favor; it directly influenced decision-making and organizational strategies. Religious days punctuated the quotidian of slavery with a sense of possibility as rituals shaped war-initiation practices and strengthened bonds of solidarity, ethnicity, and diasporic identity during moments of interruption in work routines.[43] When linked to insurgent abolitionism, Catholicism, Islam, Candomblé, and other religions practiced by the enslaved served as sources of political legitimacy that differed from Brazilian authorities' perception of abolition as a largely secular pursuit.

The 1848 conspiracies in the province of Rio de Janeiro revealed their hybrid roots in Bantu spirituality and devotion to Saint Anthony. Drawing simultaneously from Kongo/Mbundu cultures and Atlantic abolitionist currents, the plot in Rio symbolically articulated the worst fears of the Brazilian elite. Under the direction of a secret Kimpasi society, the insurgents were to be divided into circles composed of fifty people each in rural estates, presided over by a chief called "Taté." As in Lorena, on St. John's Day, "all the Chiefs were to meet, receive their orders and instructions and proceed to the slaughter, beginning with the poisoning of their Masters by the *Mocamos do Anjo*," as enslaved domestic workers were called. Finally, when all whites were dead, one of the local "Tatés" would rise to become king.[44]

White fears led to the formation of a special committee in the provincial assembly of Rio charged with gathering information to inform the imperial government of the uprising. After a lengthy investigation, deputies wrote a report on the activities of "Secret Societies of Africans" in Brazil's Center-South. Confirming that the impetus for slave rebellion had once again come from an outside source, the lawmakers exchanged information with the British consulate in Rio de Janeiro. Enslaved insurgents were likely led by "a superior intelligence," the report stated, because their superior organization and "other peculiarities do not correspond to the weak intellectual resources generally observed in the Negro race." The deputies believed that the imperial capital was the center of financing and recruiting operations that radiated into the interior of the province, where emissaries "under the pretext of selling various objects" planned to "transmit instructions and animate the negroes, by saying that so many negroes ought not to be subject to so few whites."[45]

Thus the 1848 conspiracy appeared to elites to be a consequence of black numerical superiority in Brazil, that is, the direct result of the country's continued reliance on the transatlantic slave trade. For our purposes here, it is important to note that when the deputies spoke of "foreign agitators," they also meant Africans. In fact, they accused the Brazilian government of endangering public safety through its handling of the recaptives, echoing with clear purpose what Tático had observed in Indaiatuba. "It would have been much better if these slaves had been re-exported or even handed over to their respective captors," the deputies pondered. They suggested the "deportation of the Foreigner who may be considered as dangerous to the public order, and in this number to be considered the africanos livres."[46]

Two years before the final prohibition of the Atlantic slave trade to Brazil, overlapping black conspiracies exposed the precarious balance on which the largest wave of illegal slave importation in the Americas rested.[47] The issue was not only numerical but political; what enslavers experienced as the threat of "Africanization" included the political calculations of Africans and their descendants, who mixed tradition and rebellion to chart a different course for emancipation. After the cessation of trade in 1850, enslaved activism would continue to intersect with the plight of recaptives and the complexities of Anglo-Brazilian relations, extending the era of suppression far beyond its legal limits. For years to come, black communities would read into British accusations of illegal enslavement the impossibility of achieving freedom through legal means.

Insurgents adapted meanings of freedom to the twists and turns of the global order as they interacted with newly arrived Africans and even those charged with suppressing the illegal slave trade. In 1852, for instance, the brig *Camargo* broke through British surveillance on the coast of Rio de Janeiro and landed some 540 men and women from Mozambique at Angra dos Reis. The ship docked on a beach adjacent to the Santa Rita do Bracuí plantation, a notorious haven for slave smuggling owned by José de Souza Breves, one of the largest slaveholders in the Brazilian empire, if not the largest. From Bracuí, the Africans went up the Serra do Mar to be employed in the coffee plantations of the Paraíba River valley, and one group ended up in the town of Bananal.[48]

The illegal disembarkation at Bracuí became a national scandal in 1852, filling the pages of newspapers and government reports. Under British pressure to show that it intended to uphold the 1850 ban on human trafficking, the Brazilian government sent army troops to search the plantations in Bananal. Rumors of a slave uprising, reminiscent of the events of 1848, soon began to spread in the region where the three provinces of São Paulo, Rio de Janeiro, and Minas Gerais met. This time, soldiers fanned the flames by promising emancipation, money, and other rewards to enslaved people who revealed the whereabouts of smuggled Africans. The raids galvanized the São Paulo press on the side of the planters, leading some Bananal residents to attribute the growing tensions between the masters and the enslaved to the subservience of the imperial authorities to British interests. "Who to obey England has been inciting the slaves to denounce their masters?"[49] Among the enslaved "who reside in the city, and even more so among those who reside in these large plantations to which research and searches have reached" reigns the conviction "that the government protects their intended right to Liberty."[50] In Minas Gerais, the same dynamic took place. In 1853, eighty enslaved people escaped from plantations in São João del Rei and Presídio to report their masters to the police as "owners of recently imported Africans." However, their intention was not to act as mere informers; the fugitives demanded freedom for themselves "and for their African comrades."[51]

Black conspiracies following the "Bracuí Case" rekindled white fears that the suppression of the slave trade could plunge Brazil into a race war. In the *Correio Mercantil*, a letter signed "Of the Nation" linked the efforts to capture recently imported Africans to the circulation of emancipatory rumors that preceded the Haitian Revolution. "[The imperial government] makes the same mistake that in 1790 the French government made. The reason is clear: the siege and raids of these plantations bring slaves into contact with soldiers;

and the slaves hear from the soldiers dangerous revelations." The author feared that the very act of testifying against their masters would give the enslaved access to subversive information. "To this day we have relied on the proverbial stupidity of black Africans, but say: is it not to be feared that this stupidity will yield strength to the influence of contact with men who will necessarily speak to them about matters of slavery? And much more: won't these slaves have a few moments of reflection to realize that the authority that defends with such effort their partners from the African Coast should also defend them, in every way equal to the newly arrived?"[52]

The unnamed correspondent pointed to the military and the process of quelling slave revolts as sources of news for those seeking freedom. The widespread rumors of rebellion in southeastern Brazil in 1848 and 1853–54 suggest that enslaved people also read the world through the structures of oppression that enslaved them and did not remain passive in the face of illegal enslavement. Black activism would also bear the implications of Brazil's first experiments with free immigrant labor. Embraced by some liberals as an economic and civilizational project to address the shortage of black labor and the degradation of social relations attributed to African slavery, white "colonization" would further expand the scope of antislavery critique in Brazil.

The Cosmopolitan World of Forced Labor

"Not only is there an antipathy between free and forced labor; but the latter, so to speak, pours on the soil such baneful seeds as to drive off the first. There is no way to unite them; they mutually repeal each other. And so it is that, to promote colonization is to seek to extinguish slavery."[53] The opinion published in 1849 on the opening pages of the antislavery newspaper O Philantropo sums up the worldview of most self-styled progressives on labor issues facing Brazil at the end of the slave-trade era. In the 1850s a proslavery consensus still dominated national politics, but even among a planter class protective of the privileges it had enjoyed since colonial times, the debate over alternatives to African labor was gaining momentum.

Like the editor of O Philantropo, some planters in the coffee provinces embraced the promotion of European immigration—known locally as "colonization"—as both a measure to avoid labor shortages and a step toward nation-building. The influx of free immigrants, they hoped, would counteract slavery's degrading influence on worker productivity while curbing black demographic majorities that posed the threat of slave revolt. Although Brazilian elites saw European peasants as a substitute for enslaved black people, reality proved to be very different from the planters' dreams of an uneventful transition.[54] In São Paulo, coffee growers with enough capital to invest in contract labor responded to the slave-trade crisis with the tools of oppression they knew. Instead of a fundamental "antipathy" separating different labor regimes, free settlers and enslaved black people often ended up toiling together in lands where bondage made freedom precarious for all.[55]

European immigration dates to the reign of the Portuguese king João VI, but colonization efforts only consolidated in the 1840s along with debates over a land law and the cessation of the transatlantic slave trade. The Lei de Terras, passed in 1850, allowed private companies or associations to purchase and settle unoccupied land through immigration, always with some funding from the imperial government. In its first stages, immigration programs took two different forms: state-sponsored settler colonies (colônias) characterized by small family farms in frontier regions, and private outposts staffed by immigrant indentured laborers in the coffee plantations of São Paulo. In the latter, Portuguese, German, Swiss, and, to a lesser extent, Belgian immigrants learned firsthand that sharecropping in a slave empire rarely led to economic autonomy. Despite elite enthusiasm, Brazil's first experiments with free labor mostly failed due to resource scarcity, diffuse state control, and labor abuses.[56]

Abolitionist geopolitics was also made in the thrust of encounters within the world created by such global migration schemes. On plantations organized around the rhythms of extensive coffee cultivation and large-scale production in the Paraíba River valley, European immigrants came across the continual arrival of enslaved workers either as a product of contraband or through the northeast to south flow of the internal slave trade. As colonos, they crossed paths with the enslaved, for example, at Ibicaba, the famous coffee plantation of Nicolau Pereira de Campos Vergueiro, a lawyer, slave trader, regent in the 1820s, many times senator, and one of the richest men in the province of São Paulo.[57] Most contemporaries regarded Vergueiro as a visionary entrepreneur who presided over the transformation of an export economy deeply affected by the rising cost of slave labor. His workers, however, would expose the gaps in this narrative, making Ibicaba a center of labor activism in the 1850s.[58]

Vergueiro first experimented with Portuguese immigration in 1841 and, in 1846, he was invited by the imperial government to expand his investment in private colonization.[59] Vergueiro & Cia, the company he founded with his sons Luís and José, had offices in Santos and Hamburg, in addition to emigration agents in Portugal and the Swiss Confederation. The company's success in attracting rural settlers to Brazil owed much to Nicolau Vergueiro's political capital and experience as a slave trader. By 1843, for instance, he owned three US-built ships that he used to supply his plantations with enslaved Africans as well as Portuguese and German immigrants.[60] In January 1844, however, Vergueiro had his activities foiled by British anti-slave-trade patrols. The British cruiser *Frolie* interrupted the flow of workers to Ibicaba by capturing the Portuguese brig *Caçador* on the Bertioga River in São Paulo, with six hundred Africans on board. According to a complaint filed by the British legation in court, "the notorious slave trader Vergueiro" used his political power over the São Paulo authorities to participate in slave smuggling. Consul Hamilton alleged that the planter had obtained a license from the president "for the steamships, under Vergueiro's agency, to pass by the fortress of Santos without being visited by the local authorities, this smuggler thus having easier means of taking the slaves to the port and from there taking them *ad libitum*."[61]

Nicolau Vergueiro was, ironically, minister of justice when he founded the Colônia Senador Vergueiro, an immigrant village located next to a pre-existing plantation worked by 215 enslaved people in Ibicaba, many, perhaps most, of whom had been brought into the country illegally. Since 1847, the colônia had operated under the *sistema de parceria*, a sharecropping system in which European immigrants worked under contractual conditions rarely seen in Brazil. The *parceria* delineated labor arrangements very differently from slavery, but the immigrants passed through some of the same spaces known to Africans in Brazil. After agreeing to pay in advance for transportation, taxes, housing, and settling expenses, the sharecroppers endured nearly two months at sea from Europe to Santos. Upon arrival at the port of Santos, they were kept in the slave-trade warehouses at the docks while they waited to be taken up the mountain to Limeira. Once, while greeting a group of colonos in Santos, José Vergueiro said to the Reverend James Fletcher, a US Presbyterian missionary who eventually visited Ibicaba: "They breathe the air of freedom here, sir—as they never breathed in their homeland."[62] After several days in transit to Limeira, the colonos settled at the Colônia Senador Vergueiro, a cluster of thatched one-room huts surrounded by subsistence plots and sprawling coffee fields. According to Swiss consul Carlos Perret-Gentil, the enslaved participated directly in the construction of housing for the arriving European families, and were also responsible for "preparing new lands for the settlement of new *colonos*."[63]

Immigrant families in Ibicaba could hardly call themselves self-sufficient. Although allowed to grow a few basic staples, they had to buy everything else from the plantation's expensive store.[64] Managers tightly regulated their mobility, and permission from the colônia's director was required for incursions into Limeira or travel to other districts. In their contracts, the colonos gave the Vergueiro family responsibility for selling the coffee harvest in the market and, in lieu of a salary, agreed to receive half of the net proceeds of their harvest after annual payments for expenses incurred. All sharecroppers' debts were subject to a minimum interest rate of 6 percent, and the duration of the contracts was indefinite, to be inherited by their families in the event of death. Sharecropping contracts also allowed for the transfer of colonos to other employers regardless of their will, a practice that many likened to the renting and resale of enslaved people in Brazil.

Over time, the sistema de parceria proved to be highly susceptible to abuse, ranging from overcharging for goods and services to violations of sharecroppers' civil rights, permanent indebtedness, obstruction of correspondence, and physical violence. In the first decade of its operation, Ibicaba experienced a real crisis in labor relations. The colonos tried to direct the course of justice officially and extrajudicially by appealing to the Swiss consulate in Rio de Janeiro or also by running away and organizing strikes. Many wrote to European newspapers, accusing Brazilian landowners of turning to "white slavery" after the end of the African slave trade.[65] Two very different visions of colonization were at stake in western São Paulo: while the Swiss immigrants saw themselves as independent peasants working toward land ownership and economic autonomy, the Vergueiros regarded them almost as indentured servants, nominally free but subject to all kinds of social coercion.

Although they worked and lived on different sides of Ibicaba, in practice colonos and enslaved people often met, whether on dirt roads or in the terreiro, the large walled terrace where coffee beans were cleaned, dried, and processed. Nicolau Vergueiro combined landscape management with social control of his workforce: the buildings surrounding the terreiro ensured the surveillance of all workers, while the sparse vertical planting of coffee trees in the hills allowed for constant observation of the enslaved. While the colonos harvested their own coffee at the colônia, the enslaved were solely responsible for all processing tasks, using steam-powered machines at the terreiro. Senzalas, the plantation's chapel, and a machine house completed the compound, in the center of which a clock tower regulated the rhythms of all work, slave and free. The terreiro was the heart of the economic and social

Figure 3. Ibicaba plantation; enslaved peoples in the terreiro with the senzalas and the clock tower in the distance. Carlota Schmidt Memorial Center, Álbum José Vergueiro, Acervo Dra. Lotte Köhler, n.d. 52.

life of Ibicaba and the primary place where different ideas about slavery and freedom circulated.

Labor tensions in Ibicaba came to a head at the end of 1856. That year, the Swiss schoolmaster Thomas Davatz (1815–88) emerged as an organizer among the disaffected immigrants of the Colônia Senador Vergueiro. A political leader from the village of Fanas in the canton of Graubünden, Davatz was drawn to Brazil by the promise of economic prosperity. In 1854, in a semiofficial capacity, he traveled to Ibicaba with a commission from the cantonal authorities to report on local labor conditions. Davatz did just that, as tensions escalated over a sharp drop in sharecroppers' incomes despite a spectacular coffee harvest in 1856.[66] In December, colonos critical of the speculative dimension of the sistema de parceria met in his home, where the makeshift school of Ibicaba was operating. They drew up a list of grievances and an appeal to Swiss diplomats to open an investigation into abuses. Members of eighty-five Swiss families claimed that they had been treated as "real slaves" by the Vergueiros, and presented their petition to João Adolfo Jonas, administrator of the colônia.[67]

On the night of December 24, 1856, as news of the petition spread, Nicolau Vergueiro called Thomas Davatz to his home. Jonas acted as an interpreter at the meeting, which was also attended by Luís Vergueiro, Nicolau's son, and the colônia's doctor, Mr. Gattiker. Soon an argument between Nicolau

Vergueiro and Davatz could be heard, and some Swiss colonists waiting outside assumed that the schoolmaster was being held at gunpoint. The men and women, equipped with firearms and tools, rose up to rescue their leader, firing two shots as a warning. Yet no direct confrontation ensued. The immigrant uprising materialized in the form of armed negotiations for contractual changes throughout 1857. In February, two months after this tense meeting, the Vergueiros expelled Davatz from Ibicaba, but the Swiss consulate continued the investigation requested by the colonos. The diplomats uncovered such grave labor abuses in the coffee fields of Limeira that the Swiss Confederation eventually embargoed immigration to Brazil, as Prussia had done in 1859 with the Heydt Edict. The colono uprising was thus largely successful.

The Revolta dos Parceiros has been memorialized as a turning point in Brazilian labor history. Most historians follow the classic interpretation of Sérgio Buarque de Holanda, who described the revolt as the first struggle over the nature of free labor that preceded Brazil's better-known experience with European immigration at the end of the nineteenth century.[68] Absent from the official narrative of the revolt, however, are the enslaved people of Ibicaba, who also planned an uprising in 1856 that spanned the counties of Limeira, Rio Claro, Constituição, and Campinas. As masters sought to control the changing landscapes of labor in the Paraíba River valley, the immigration schemes they devised as solutions to the "labor problem" expanded the circulation of abolitionist ideas among the working classes.

The 1856 slave conspiracy had its roots in a longer tradition of black activism in Ibicaba. In September 1848, José Vergueiro visited the neighboring county of Constituição (now Piracicaba), where he heard rumors that French jewelers were inciting the enslaved to revolt; he immediately returned to the Colônia Senador Vergueiro to press his workers for information. Two German colonos pointed to one Alberto de Neubern, a former sharecropper who had left Ibicaba a few years earlier without paying his debts. The colonos accused him of inviting others "to incite an uprising of the slaves, which, as he said, united with Indians he knew, offered no small advantages to their greedy eyes." According to Neubern, "one day, he was going to present himself as the head of these people, and then he would be rich."[69] Frustrated with his chances of economic success in Ibicaba, he would have turned against the local planters and gestured toward enslaved and indigenous people.

Alberto de Neubern was a veteran of the French army in Africa who had traveled from Germany to Brazil on a sharecropper's contract. According to José Vergueiro, "he has spent many years in the United States, is Hebrew by religion, short, very blond, pleasant physiognomy, lively in his conversation, and speaks French and English." Vergueiro also suspected an unnamed Frenchman who had visited the senzalas of Limeira and Rio Claro armed with a club. In 1848, as we have seen, slaveholders were attentive to the circulation of emancipatory news and people coming from France and its colonies, especially in a plantation like Ibicaba, where so many Africans had arrived after the prohibition of the slave trade in 1831. In the end, the rumored conspiracy involving Neubern was disbanded, but the police arrested three enslaved men from Limeira during raids in western São Paulo.

Almost a decade later, Thomas Davatz elaborated on the same kind of alliances in his testimony on the Revolta dos Parceiros. Speaking to H. Ullman in 1857, he asserted that "they [the colonos] can count on the other Swiss of this province, numbering perhaps 5,000, to defend their rights with a weapon in their hand," and "according to the assertions of many of their compatriots, they can count on the blacks, slaves on the farms, who are anxiously awaiting an uprising." Engaging with the geopolitical imagination of the workers of Brazil's Center-South, Davatz added that the colonos "agree that the naval forces of France and England are not gathering in Rio de Janeiro for nothing." According to him, "a trustworthy man and a very sincere friend of the Swiss" had told them "that these two nations are only waiting for a reason or a pretext to invade Brazil in order to abolish slavery, both of the blacks and of the white slaves (as they call themselves)." Thus it was not only the enslaved who counted on British or French intervention to abolish forced labor. The idea seemed to be part of a kind of subaltern abolitionism that bridged the cosmopolitan worlds of labor in the nineteenth century.

Davatz's words reveal that slavery provided free and enslaved people with a common language to contest oppression in nineteenth-century Brazil. In Ibicaba, the hope that liberation would come through partnership with British and French forces brought black and white immigrants closer together, even as race continued to divide them. In his account of the Revolta dos Parceiros, published in Chür in 1857, Davatz appealed to European abolitionist sensibilities to highlight the plight of Swiss immigrants in Brazil. With eyes trained on the slave trade's naturalization of forced labor, he argued that men like Nicolau Vergueiro offered colonos "the same contempt" reserved for black slaves and were blind to the kind of freedom sought by Swiss abroad.[70]

Like so many antislavery reformers of his time, Davatz viewed chattel slavery as a barbaric institution and professed his faith in the civilizing power of free labor. His critique of the *parceria* system affirmed the biblical rationale for African susceptibility to enslavement. He attributed the "innate subjugation of Africans to whites" to the curse Noah placed on the descendants of Ham and portrayed the "black inhabitants of Brazil" as people "conscious of being victims" yet unaware of their power. If it were not for their willingness to submit, the Swiss teacher argued, "it would be easy for them, given their considerable numbers, to take revenge on their traffickers and oppressors. But as far as I know, this has never happened, at least not on a large scale."[71]

The residents of Limeira also described the Revolta dos Parceiros as a movement articulated among several local immigrant communities "in order to form an independence, in uniformity [*sic*] with the slaves." Those of Rio Claro considered it undeniable that "Swiss colonos of the Colônia Senador Vergueiro had organized themselves under the direction of a secret society, had armed themselves, corresponded with other colônias, and counted not only on their cooperation but also on that of slaves and discontented Brazilians; they talk about forming a Free State."[72] Authorities pointed the finger in particular at the Swiss J. J. Oswald, a piano teacher suspected of communist leanings who lived in the city of São Paulo.[73] Minister of Justice José Tomás Nabuco de Araújo speculated that insurgent colonos intended to establish a republic with the support of all the Germans, Swiss, and slaves of the province.[74] He expected Oswald to "shout the cry of freedom in São Paulo" and create a new state backed by Anglo-French troops.[75]

These versions of events, it is true, convey both fact and fear. Brazilian planters and authorities perceived Swiss colonos as yet another incarnation of the foreign threat to domestic slavery, as "intelligent" hands tainted by French socialism and British abolitionism that would lead the enslaved to rebel against the laws of the land.[76] Be that as it may, the fact that the enslaved envisioned freedom as an opportunity to become independent farmers and small landowners is significant. Some of Davatz's strategies for confronting the Vergueiros were quite like those traditionally employed by Afro-descendants in their quest for emancipation. If forcibly expelled from Ibicaba, for example, the schoolmaster planned to leave his debts unpaid and lead all the immigrants from the Paulista colonies to a patch of virgin land that could be successfully defended against invasion.[77] Afro-descendants would have found this ideal refuge to be very similar to a fortified quilombo.[78]

Thus, rather than trying to prove at all costs that the enslaved were involved in the revolt, it may be worth asking why so many of their contemporaries considered the prospect of a general workers' uprising feasible. As we have seen, the enslaved and colonos had joined forces in struggles for better living conditions since the 1840s. Frustrated by the odds of becoming free in imperial Brazil, the enslaved of Ibicaba carefully interpreted what colonos negotiated with their masters. In 1856 they may have been interested in realizing their emancipation within a novel political entity, as some Swiss insurgents expected that Emperor Pedro II would grant them lands to establish a colônia under imperial protection in either São Paulo or Rio Grande do Sul. Afro-descendants shared with European immigrants an emancipationist view of Brazil's relations with France and Britain, since the contested nature of slave emancipation never allowed for a clear-cut transition from bonded to free labor in the nineteenth century. In Brazil, a cosmopolitan and diverse group of workers for whom Atlantic abolition mostly accentuated the coercive nature of global capitalism met, opening space for the development of complex antislavery imaginaries. Despite white denial of the agency of the enslaved, black geopolitics thrived precisely on the cross-pollination of ideas with the radical traditions of their time.

In the end, Nicolau, José, and Luís Vergueiro could not muster the political force necessary to impose the kind of labor exploitation that could make their sharecropping system profitable and secure without slavery. The Colônia Senador Vergueiro never fully recovered from the 1856 crisis and subsequent difficulties in recruiting colonos in Europe. When Nicolau Vergueiro died in 1859, his son José took over the management of his estate but eventually became disillusioned with privately sponsored immigration.[79] In 1865 Vergueiro & Cia declared bankruptcy and offered part of Ibicaba's production over the next few years as collateral for the debt. At that time, the estate produced more than 100,000 arrobas of coffee, harvested by 1,100 colonos and slaves. In 1877 Ibicaba was mortgaged to the London and Brazilian Bank—the British again—and the government of São Paulo had to send fifty troops to enforce the mandate in Limeira. The enslaved people of Ibicaba planned another rebellion after they saw the soldiers arriving by train, allegedly at the request of the British. This time they spoke of the possibility that "powerful nations will impose the decree of their sovereign will on the imperial government."[80] Enslaved peoples' belief in British support for abolition was at the heart of Ibicaba's insurgent abolitionism and only escalated after 1862, when black communities throughout the empire radicalized the Anglo-Brazilian crisis.

Rethinking the Christie Affair

On the last day of 1862, a feat of gunboat diplomacy in Rio de Janeiro sounded the bells of war across Brazil. Acting on British envoy William Christie's recommendations, Admiral Richard Laird Warren initiated a five-day naval blockade of the imperial capital's port. At the dawn of the new year, the warship *Stromboli* seized six Brazilian vessels as they approached the port, sparking widespread popular outrage in the streets of Rio.[81] Christie meant the show of force as a response commensurate to Brazil's refusal to apologize and compensate the British Crown for two otherwise unremarkable events: the sacking of the *Prince of Wales*, a British ship wrecked in 1861 off the coast of Albardão, province of Rio Grande do Sul, and the mistreatment of three British officers from the frigate *Forte*, who were arrested by Rio de Janeiro police for disorderly conduct in June 1862.[82] The unspoken subtext of the dispute, however, was known to all: Brazil and Britain continued to argue over the status of africanos livres, disputing the terms and pace of their emancipation.

British cruisers had captured ships in Brazilian waters before, and even exchanged fire with the Brazilian navy in 1850. But 1863 was different; never had Brazil and Britain come so close to a full-scale war over the future of slavery, a telling parallel to what was happening in the United States. After the Marquis of Abrantes, then foreign minister, dodged Christie's ultimatum for reparations in December 1862, Brazilians surrounded the British consulate in the imperial capital to demand an explanation and eventually prepared for war.[83] Citizens enlisted in volunteer battalions, donated monthly wages to the national treasury, and conducted local subscriptions to fund the state's purchase of arms.[84] The navy took up bullet casting at coastal arsenals while the Ministry of War ordered a survey of the state of Brazil's fortresses. The engineer and later abolitionist André Rebouças, for example, was appointed, along with his brother Antônio, to inspect the fortresses of Santa Catarina.[85] Some women showered the imperial flag with flowers at public gatherings, and the mainstream press echoed the call to prepare the spirits for battle.[86] Even Pedro II rushed into the streets of Rio de Janeiro to assure his subjects "that he would cease to be emperor of Brazil the day he could no longer uphold with dignity the national honor and independence of his homeland."[87] The scene was immortalized by the artist Victor Meirelles in his famous 1864 painting *Estudo para a Questão Christie*.[88]

By the time the Royal Navy blockaded Rio's port, Brazil was already adept at resisting British pressure, but William Dougal Christie was no small critic

Figure 4. Victor Meirelles, *Estudo para a Questão Christie*, oil on canvas, 1864. In the lower right, at the Market Square of Rio de Janeiro, the urban black population engages with news of the Christie Affair. Caught up in the heat of demonstrations against the British siege of the city's port, they listen attentively to Emperor Pedro II, who is depicted standing in the middle of the crowd. Museu Nacional de Belas Artes, Brazil.

of Brazil's neglect of bilateral treaties and the 1831 law. From his arrival in Rio de Janeiro in 1859, he worked with fellow diplomats across the empire to map the illegal enslavement of an estimated one million Africans. With the support of the liberal press, Christie eventually reignited debates about the status of africanos livres and strengthened British antislavery policies in Brazil, despite the more cautious tone encouraged by the Foreign Office. His mercurial personality combined with the unfolding of the US Civil War to push the Brazilian state into a firmer defense of slavery through the language of nationalism. Far from being an imaginary fear, the prospect of direct conflict with England mobilized all sides of the slavery debate. While the enslaved yearned for British invasion, slaveholders objected to British suppression activities with a sense of duty.

The patriotic fervor unleashed by the Christie Affair echoed official perceptions of Anglo-Brazilian relations, which were an affirmation of how enslavers and statesmen framed the history of slave-trade suppression in

Brazil. Its description as an interstate matter that invoked popular support at a critical juncture in the formation of the Brazilian nation ignores how hundreds of recently trafficked captives and black communities with a long tradition of activism seized on international affairs to press for the end of slavery. In the lower right-hand corner of Victor Meirelles's painting, one can catch a glimpse of how the black population of Rio de Janeiro would have learned about the "English question." Live debate in the streets interrupted the workday of male porters and female food vendors, inviting commentary on whether Christie's ultimatum challenged the political order that upheld bonded labor in Brazil. In 1863, while most citizens spoke of war as the only way to defend Brazilian sovereignty in the face of British aggression, several enslaved communities prepared to fight alongside the British, often plotting amid the very fireworks that commemorated the monarchy's refusal to capitulate to Christie's demands.

Black perceptions of the Christie Affair were rooted in the slaveholders' ongoing demonization of foreigners but, more important, they also stemmed from lived experiences both at sea and in the Brazilian mainland. Many Afro-descendants were sailors themselves or had encountered the British as interceptors of slave ships bound for the empire. In the maritime provinces of Brazil, enslaved people often escaped onto British ships that were about to sail to lands free of bondage, which they viewed as an integral part of transatlantic routes to freedom.[89] Or they met British subjects in the "public houses" and taverns along the docks. In the interior, Africans and Afro-descendants toiled for British masters in gold mines or shared their geographical knowledge of the country with British engineers and industrial experts engaged in building railroads.[90]

This is not to say, however, that abolition was the cause of every British subject living in the tropics. Throughout the nineteenth century, British citizens and companies owned enslaved people in Brazil, despite the penalties imposed by an 1843 act that made it "unlawful for any British subject, wherever he or she might be, to deal, trade in, purchase, sell, barter, or transfer a slave or slaves, except in cases whereby the Act itself special exceptions were made to the general prohibition."[91] British slave owners were also the unlikely protagonists of scandals over the illegal enslavement of Africans.[92] The St. John d'el Rey Mining Company in Morro Velho, Minas Gerais, is a case in point. The largest British slave-owning organization in Brazil faced a lengthy court battle in 1879 for unlawfully holding three hundred africanos livres in slavery for twenty years. The case, taken up by the Brazilian

abolitionist Joaquim Nabuco, forced the St. John d'el Rey Mining Company
to come up with a justification in true slaveholding fashion. The company
revealed that its silence about the Africans' right to emancipation was rooted
in fear of a general uprising in the mines of Morro Velho.[93] Ironically, diplomatic disputes aside, the British shared with the Brazilian government the
view that emancipation should be a process controlled by the slaveholding
classes.

In February 1863, the work of black liberation intertwined with British antislavery in the hills that connect the neighboring provinces of Rio
de Janeiro and São Paulo. From the port city of Angra dos Reis, one of the
main outlets for coffee bales from the Paraíba River valley, rumors spread
that a black society had set out to "proclaim Freedom" in the aftermath of
the Christie Affair. The newspaper *Liga Constitucional* reported that enslaved
people belonging to a "secret association" called S. Domingos (present-day
Haiti) "are convinced that the Englishmen are their fathers [*pais*], that they
are coming to liberate them, and that we, their enemies, are against it; this is
the language they use."[94] Echoing the dynamics that characterized the 1848
rebellions, the enslaved spoke of British suppression as a full-blown abolitionist pursuit, something that exceeded British intentions in Brazil.

Soon after, rumors of a black uprising spread amid Carnival celebrations
in the district of Campinas, São Paulo. On the first Saturday before Lent, the
slaves of Antônio Januário Pinto Ferraz hosted an evening of *batuques* and
tambaques (drumming sessions) on the grounds of the Atibaia plantation.[95]
Ferraz had traveled with his family to enjoy the Christian holiday in the city,
leaving his property in the care of an enslaved overseer. As the night wore
on, the crowd grew to include at least sixteen other enslaved people from
nearby plantations who danced together to the sound of a viola.[96] Despite the
informal atmosphere filled with music and chatter, tensions soon seeped into
the air. Benedito, long an enslaved worker at Atibaia, arrived at the gathering
in great distress, announcing that he intended to kill Ferraz's son, the plantation administrator, upon his return from town. His motives would have been
obvious to most of those present: Benedito's body still bore the scars of the
twenty-five lashes he had received after breaking into the plantation's main
house with the intention of "entertaining libidinous purposes with a mulatto
woman."[97] Although an integral part of the intimate lives of the enslaved,
such encounters were not so readily sanctioned by masters. The harsh punishment for a transgression like Benedito's fueled the sense of injustice out of
which transformative claims for emancipation were made.

Benedito's enslaved peers rushed to contain his outburst. They questioned not the justice of the grievances but the timing of his plan; Ferraz Jr.'s assassination could very well derail an uprising organized for the Holy Week in anticipation of British armed support. Once briefed on the details, Benedito relented and joined the Atibaia insurgents in shouts of "*viva os ingleses*" and "*viva a liberdade*," revealing how the work of memory, music, and storytelling had rekindled black hopes of liberation from bondage. Insurgents were the guardians of a long tradition of black protest that dated back to 1832 in Campinas. In that year, when the city was still called São Carlos, Antônio Ferraz Sr. himself sat through the interrogations of Brazilian-born and Congolese insurgents from fifteen plantations along the Atibaia River. Freedom intersected with African religiosity and knowledge of two milestones of abolition in Brazil at the time: the passage of the anti-slave-trade law of 1831 and the prohibition of indigenous slavery in São Paulo. The Central African healer and diviner Diogo Rebolo coordinated recruitment efforts at meetings where he distributed herbal preparations to soothe enslavers and protect the bodies of rebels like Francisco crioulo, who openly spoke about the 1831 law. In 1832, he asked the enslaved blacksmith Joaquim: "Now, Uncle Joaquim, the Emperor [has decreed that] blacks are no longer coming to Brazil, wouldn't it be fair to give us our freedom too? To which Joaquim replied that something like that was bound to happen."[98]

A *carapina* (mixed-race man) who played the viola at the slave gathering on the Atibaia plantation in 1863 told a friend about the rebels' plan, and the friend informed the Campinas sheriff. Within hours, the police had rounded up several enslaved people for questioning. One of the insurgents revealed that "the concerted plan was to rise up around the Holy Week, raid the plantations, loot the money, and team up to raid the City, given that they would count for sure at this time on Englishmen."[99] After the discovery of the conspiracy in Campinas, a local officer lamented that "no other nation could do us more harm with a declaration of war than England. It is not so much her piracy and the havoc it can wreak in our ports that is to be feared, but the disorder that can arise among the internal enemy."[100] Likewise, the deputies who met in secret sessions at the provincial assembly attributed the upsurge in black protest to the demographic changes the internal slave trade had brought to the region. In their view, there were simply too many new and unruly captives from the Brazilian northeast who could not (or would not) adapt to the rhythms of São Paulo's coffee culture. "In fact, since the possibility spread that the British wanted to wage a war against us to ensure that we pay for the value of the bodies of some sailors thrown on the beaches by a shipwreck, an extraordinary haughtiness, a joy has developed among the slaves. They are convinced that the war has the sole purpose of freeing the slaves."[101]

In 1863 enslaved people, steeped in the political cultures of the Afro-Atlantic world, drew a strategic lesson from the Anglo-Brazilian crisis. Like so many before them, insurgents wove together a story about racial conflict that linked Brazil, Europe, and Africa. Their ideas spread through personal contact and rumor, with a temporal imprecision that allowed modes of thought to persist over time. In Campinas, seditious talk about the British blockade elicited a militarized response from white citizens. "The occurrences in Rio de Janeiro with the British Minister, the probability of a rupture with England, and the knowledge I have about the meager number of foot soldiers and the Corpo de Permanentes which guards this Province," remarked magistrate Vicente Ferreira da Silva Bueno, inspired locals to establish the Sociedade Patriótica Campineira (Campinas Patriotic Society), an armed vigilante group.[102] The unit was tasked with supplementing the Brazilian military and the National Guard in the event of war with Great Britain.

Silva Bueno (1815–73) was a lawyer, born and educated in the city of São Paulo, who throughout his life served as sheriff and judge in many municipalities of the province. In the late 1860s he was appointed chief of police, bringing with him a wealth of experience in the suppression of black activism.[103] Having sat through several interrogations at the Campinas jail, he considered guarding against slave rebellion a way of maintaining Brazilian sovereignty and feared that the provincial forces were small, poorly armed, and untrained to put down an eventual uprising. Thus, despite Bueno's direct reference to the British threat, the Sociedade's true raison d'être was to empower white citizens in the fight against their "internal enemy," the enslaved.[104] Another group agreed with Bueno's assessment of the 1863 crisis. On March 7, the president of São Paulo received the statutes of the União dos Voluntários Alemães (Union of German Volunteers), a sixty-man battalion, led by Antônio Exel, "established in Campinas to assist the government in the defense of the same city in the event of an aggression or insurrection."[105]

In explaining the intentions of the Sociedade Patriótica and asking for more troops to be sent to Campinas, Silva Bueno conjured up a valuable map of the world of slave communication through which the debate over the Christie Affair took place: "After the Sociedade was created, rumors popped up here and there with respect to these slaves and at that shop about others, and on that road they said this and that and on the bridges, wells, and fountains where they [the slaves] customarily gather and talk, they said (reportedly) whatever it is about an uprising, the Englishmen, etc., for it is a fact that they either count on their protection, or at least there is reason to fear some hostile manifestation on the part of the slaves in case of a break with England."[106]

Preventing rebellion depended on documenting the insurgents' motivations, allies, and strategies, even if it meant dismissing them. The narrative offered by Silva Bueno refers only to rumors, but taking his version literally strips the past of much of its explanatory power. The enslaved spoke of "Englishmen" everywhere, and the list was not short: on the streets they walked to and from work, at the wells where men and women collected water to supply their masters' residences, and on the bridges that connected rural and urban spaces in Campinas. Insurgents occupied strategic spaces of the public sphere, where they managed to come together as a political community by crafting a language of insurgency against injustice.

Interrogations followed largely the same script in nineteenth-century Brazil. The crime of "insurrection," as defined in Article 113 of the Criminal Code of 1830, required proof of the participation of twenty or more enslaved people, its manifestation "by external acts" and the beginning of its execution, and, in the case of an attempt, proof that it did not take effect due to circumstances independent of the insurgents' will.[107] These guidelines informed the cross-examination of rebels in Campinas and, in the absence of surviving transcripts, we can only reconstruct what Silva Bueno would have heard from the questions often asked of the enslaved accused of similar crimes over the 1860s.

Enslaved people could not directly represent themselves in judicial proceedings and were assigned curators when they were brought to court. However, interrogations in local jails were sometimes conducted without the presence of a mediator. Local slaveholders often watched such questionings, contributing to the coercive dominance of police officers who displayed their readings of black people as volatile, irascible, and intellectually inferior. As a result, enslaved insurgents appear in the archive as thoughtless purveyors of a violent threat to white society, as racial subjects of inferior intellectual power susceptible to all manner of indoctrination. Nevertheless, when subjected to a critical reading, even Silva Bueno's words point to rumor as the key to black geopolitical thought. An act of political representation rather than a vehicle for misinformation, it was a central artifact in the development of black emancipation politics in the Americas.

When taken collectively, rumors constituted the closest thing to the existence of a public opinion among the enslaved. Through them, Africans and

Afro-Brazilians interpreted current events, connected them to local politics, and acted on the daily realities of enslavement. Silva Bueno thus cared to highlight the "repugnancy slaves demonstrated in recounting what they talked about" yet mapped their conversations; he sought to blame British agents for fomenting rebellion, yet he admitted that "the English" were an important element of popular thought in Campinas. The magistrate's account of the conspiracy inadvertently recorded the social geography of insurgent abolitionism, where an internationalist vision of emancipation was taking shape.

In March 1863, another slave conspiracy emerged, again at the Ibicaba plantation, about thirty-five miles from Campinas. One evening, the German administrator of the Colônia Senador Vergueiro invited all the workers—colonos and captives—to a dinner where he spoke about slave emancipation and "gave *vivas* to the Englishmen, telling them [the enslaved] that the latter would soon come to liberate them." The administrator allegedly advised enslaved participants "to stop working for the owner of the property because they were as free as their Masters."[108] Shortly thereafter, unrest intensified among enslaved workers who witnessed the Vergueiro family's preparations for war. Offended by the "unspeakable aggression of the English legation against our nationality," José Vergueiro offered the Brazilian government the workshops of Ibicaba to repair defective weapons and attempted to form a corps of volunteers in the port city of Santos to fight England.[109] Coffee plantations like Ibicaba and Atibaia were learning spaces for those interested in the destabilizing geopolitics of the 1860s.

Black networks of rumor and oral transmission also connected British antislavery to the world of print in São Paulo. Benedito, a man enslaved by Joaquim Policarpo Aranha in Campinas, offered what is perhaps the most surprising insurgent version of the Christie Affair in 1863. On the Sunday before Carnival, he stopped by the shop of the enslaved man Benedito Taques to collect a debt and learned that "being him [Taques] in Aparecida, *he had heard a newspaper read* [emphasis added] in which it was said that the Englishmen had demanded a large sum of money from all Slaveholders." Taques explained that, in case masters did not give the money, "they [Englishmen] would make a revolution to give freedom to the Slaves, because the same Englishmen had a Princess who was already twenty-one years old and who could not be baptized unless all the Slaves were freed."[110] And so, slave rebellions could also be fought to save the soul of a British princess.

The two Beneditos carried out the work of black liberation far beyond the boundaries set by the Brazilian cultural elite. Presumed ignorant, the enslaved often shared what little access they had to literacy to make politics through speech and sometimes through writing. Although the reference to the British princess is unclear, it is possible to discern that, for the enslaved of Campinas, Britain's demand for reparations in 1862 had the potential to be a revolutionary act. Hence the need for the Atibaia insurgents to take up arms and determine the outcome of the Anglo-Brazilian crisis by taking over the city, "since at that time they would certainly count on the English."[111] Benedito Taques, for his turn, envisioned rebellion at the intersection of diplomacy and a highly Christianized framing of emancipation that manifested, for example, in the idea that a princess could not at once embrace the Christian faith through baptism and support chattel slavery. His reasoning was also an expression of enslaved people's moral reading of the world.

Interrogations in Campinas, where an estimated six thousand enslaved workers lived in 1863, confirmed that the conspiracy also had branches in the counties of Belém, Amparo, and Indaiatuba.[112] Silva Bueno advised enslavers "to forbid entrance in their properties of these *latoeiros* [tinsmiths], peddlers, jewelers && who can very well be emissaries, for the British Government ought not send Englishmen."[113] Once Holy Week celebrations concluded without incident, authorities declared the region safe from revolt yet remained vigilant because "there have been among the *colonos* and even among our people some who have perversely incited slaves to rise up in the hope that they will take advantage of the plunder."[114] The chief of police, Luís José de Sampaio, agreed that the hope of imminent emancipation had not faded among the enslaved: "It is certain that, in general, they did not hide their hope of having their freedom restored through the intervention of the English, whom they were ready to help as soon as the war began, which they believed would be soon."[115]

The British entered the cognitive world of the enslaved through the same channels of public life that mobilized patriotic responses to the prospect of foreign invasion. In Piracicaba, a town about thirty-nine miles to the west of Campinas, commentary on the Christie Affair appeared in the press. In a letter to the newspaper *Correio Paulistano*, headlined "The exalted slave insurrection and the Anglo-Brazilian question," a planter denounced the harmful effects of the publicity given to the incident.[116] He recalled in detail one of the street rallies held in his hometown, where representative Costa Pinto offered a corrective to those, like one Captain Bento Francisco de Mattos, who believed that Brazil could emulate the United States in its "glorious victory over the British" in 1776. In line with the concern demonstrated by the anonymous planter, Costa Pinto recommended that citizens should invest their time in the arming of the National Guard, "for what we have to fear is the enemy who lives among us . . . [here the orator lowers his voice], we should fear and prevent a slave insurrection!" He almost whispered so that the enslaved could not hear his voice.[117] In the first half of 1863, the government of São Paulo sent dozens of troops to police the coffee districts of Rio Claro, Constituição, Piracicaba, and Campinas.[118]

Other black conspiracies developed outside São Paulo in 1863. In Pelotas, near where the *Prince of Wales* had been wrecked, Sebastião Maria, a free man of color, participated in "gatherings of many other blacks" where he insulted Emperor Pedro II and spread ideas of an imminent British invasion. Sebastião urged free and enslaved Afro-descendants to side with the English in the event of war, arguing that "it was that nation that they should help, because they are the protectors of the class of black folk."[119] The words that led to his arrest conveyed a sense of disillusionment with the imperial state. Sebastião's position differed, for example, from that of João Ferreira Dério, who in 1858 told enslaved people in the province of Paraná that the Brazilian crown had signed an edict of abolition to be delivered by a British ship.[120] Here, perhaps, we can see the Anglo-Brazilian question rephrased from the perspective of Afro-descendants. Emancipation seemed to require some mediation in Brazil, where it had been stalled by the protracted standoff over the slave trade and again in 1863 by enslavers' nationalist response to the British naval blockade. For black communities, there was more to an alliance with the British than state reform. They speculated on the possibility of a historic rupture, that is, of turning the "English question" into an opportunity to accelerate the uncertain course of abolition in Brazil.

William Christie asked for his passport and returned to England in March 1863, citing Brazilian negligence in the case of the *Prince of Wales* and the Brazilian government's deaf ears to his pleas for guarantees of freedom for *africanos livres* as reasons for his departure. As he packed his bags to return to London, three enslaved men from Rio de Janeiro's Carmo Parish "said publicly in conversation with other comrades, that the English were resolved to free the enslaved in Brazil, and that they should help her on the ground."[121] Rebellion plans were also uncovered in Mar d'Espanha, a county on the border of Rio de Janeiro and Minas Gerais, where more than three

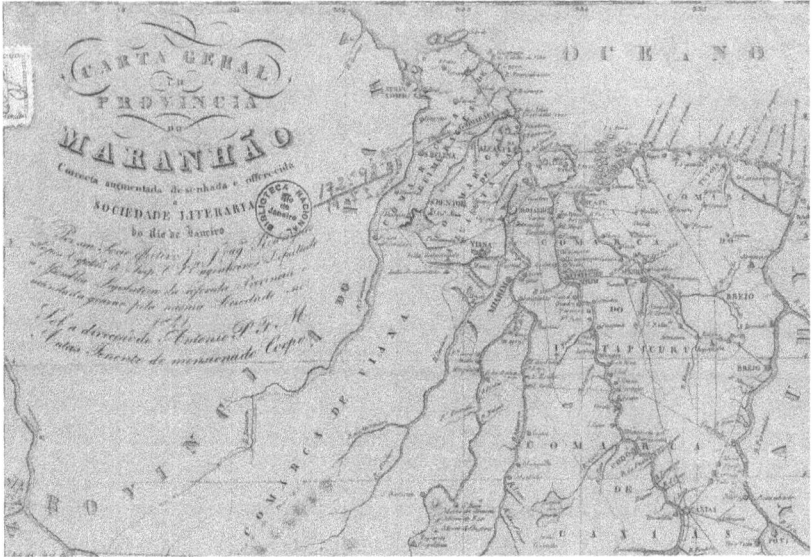

Figure 5. Detail of the Atlantic coast of Maranhão by José Joaquim Rodrigues Lopes, 1841. Montes Áureos was located in the Gurupi River region, on the top left on the border with Pará. "Carta geral da província do Maranhão: correcta e augmentada desenhada e offerecida a Sociedade Literaria do Rio de Janeiro," Biblioteca Nacional, Brazil.

hundred enslaved people ran away from plantations in the vicinity of the suspension bridge that connected the two provinces in Sapucaia. Anticipating the insurgents' intention to cross the bridge to Rio, local citizens guarded the entrance on their side of the Paraíba do Sul River and organized evening patrols to catch armed rebels. Conspiracies also surfaced in Petrópolis, Magé, Cantagalo, Paraíba do Sul, Nova Friburgo, and Estrela, in the province of Rio de Janeiro.

In the gold-bearing lands of the northeastern province of Maranhão, quilombolas imagined fighting an emancipatory war on the side of the British as well. The area of dense equatorial forest on the eastern edge of the Amazon basin was home to some of the largest quilombos in nineteenth-century Brazil. In late 1857, the British-owned Montes Áureos Gold Mining Company tapped into their knowledge of the location of gold deposits and routes of informal trade to explore the "mines of Maracassumé," in the Turiaçu forest.[122] The company's manager, Gustavo Julio Gunther, sought the loyalty of the quilombolas by offering to buy them from their enslavers in exchange for

work in the Montes Áureos mines. Gunther's actions had unintended consequences, however, as the quilombolas understood their interactions with the
British in the context of the Anglo-Brazilian crisis.

In May 1863, quilombolas simply took over the recruitment of local
enslaved workers to Montes Áureos, with the promise that the English would
emancipate them.[123] The director of the neighboring military colony of Gurupi,
one of the outposts established by the imperial government to oversee the
interiorization of the state in Maranhão, reported hearing "that some wiser
crioulos [Brazilian-born slaves] say that since Brazil is at war with England,
these fugitives have to present themselves at the Company to take up arms."[124]
Slave flight became a widespread practice that challenged the local plantation
economy and generated much commentary about British men with "ambi-
tious and evil dispositions against Brazil."[125]

A year after the Christie Affair, a priest from Pará took his grievances
to the government of Maranhão. Luís da Anunciação, vicar of the town of
Viseu, sixty miles north of the Maracassumé mines, accused the British of
inciting both indigenous and enslaved people to rebel in the Alto Gurupi
region, leading to confrontations that resulted in several deaths. Anunciação
feared British imperial ambitions in Brazil, echoing a recurring concern since
the 1840s. "Did not the arrest of disorderly civilians and the shipwreck in
the deserted coasts of Albardão serve as a pretext for unprecedented attacks
and exorbitant demands by the English government against us?" In his esti-
mation, Montes Áureos was like a British fortress from which a territorial
takeover could begin.[126]

In November 1864, the Brazilian Ministry of Justice finally criminalized
Gunther's practice of "seducing" quilombolas with the promise of emancipation, curtailing what the Turiaçu police commissioner deemed "a very
sad business for slaveholders and a good one for the British."[127] It is unclear
whether any of the fugitives who sought British assistance in Montes Áureos
ever obtained their manumission, but they played a crucial role in shaping
the local political climate in the 1860s. Their networks of trade and escape
routes served as communication channels through which antislavery news
reached other Afro-descendants. By attaching particular significance to the
British presence in Maranhão, quilombolas thwarted state attempts at internal colonization and asserted their claim to a remote part of Brazilian territory precisely by connecting it to the larger Atlantic world.

*   *   *

CANTA O MOLEQUE.
Vai-se embora enfadadinho
Sem um adeus me dizer;
As saudades que me deixa
Por dez réis posso vender.
(Alvíçaras ganhas pelo *Diario* de 6 do corrente mez.)

CORO DOS MOLEQUES
Lé cambeta uaravé,
Caravé uaringa,
Lord Cristi com cerveja,
Vai batatas curiá

Figure 6. On the cover of *Semana Illustrada*, the official depiction of the Christie Affair is on full display. *O moleque*, a character created by the illustrator Henrique Fleiuss to represent the editor's sidekick, waves goodbye to William Christie on the docks of Rio de Janeiro, encouraged by a group of enslaved boys. The moleque sings a song: "Go away bore, without saying goodbye; the heartache you cause me, I can sell for 10 réis." The boys' choir responds in unintelligible verse inflected with African languages, as if chanting in corrupted Portuguese. As a racist representation of black youth in Brazil, the cartoon assumes the existence of a consensus against the British in Brazil. In 1863, however, black insurgents turned the official narrative of the Anglo-Brazilian question on its head by claiming British support for the abolition of slavery in the country. *Semana Illustrada*, no. 114, February 1863. Biblioteca Nacional, Brazil.

Brazil and Great Britain finally resumed diplomatic relations in 1865, after the British presented an official apology to Emperor Pedro II in Uruguaiana, Rio Grande do Sul. Just as the two nations resumed relations, William Christie published his famous treatise on the decades-long British campaign against the transatlantic slave trade to Brazil. He offered his *Notes on Brazilian Questions* as a corrective to the "cloud of misrepresentation" that had surrounded British naval reprisals. The former British envoy blamed both the Brazilian press and government for poisoning public opinion against him and creating a misleading picture of British diplomacy overseas.

Portrayed by Brazilian newspapers as the unreasonable paladin of exorbitant British claims on an independent country, Christie became the symbol of undue British interference in domestic affairs throughout the nineteenth century. A rather controversial figure, he seems to have stolen the limelight from other historical actors who were pushing against the resilience of Brazilian slavery in the 1860s. For if emancipation was everyone's problem in the nineteenth century, freedom was the compelling issue that the enslaved chose to address. In the context of the Christie Affair, insurgent abolitionism became an even more disruptive force that forced the imperial government and white citizens to react, signaling an important moment in the long struggle through which slavery in Brazil slowly lost its legitimacy. The fact that the grammar of insurgency seemed to have remained the same since the 1840s—evoking a succession of geopolitical allies like France and Britain as well as Swiss and German colonos—should not obscure the transformation of its subtext. If, in the 1840s, Africans and Afro-descendants entered the realm of abolitionism to radicalize the process of slave-trade suppression, in the 1860s they seized on the political atmosphere of a crucial decade in the history of hemispheric warfare to demand the end of slavery in Brazil.

The enslaved knew that neither French nor British subjects were a homogeneous bloc, and images of antislavery powers ready to take up arms for abolition coexisted with experiences of enslavement by British and French masters in Brazil. Nevertheless, the subversive dialogue associated with foreign intervention served specific functions in insurgent communities: it defined loyalties, the terms of alliances with whites, and the timing of rebellion. Beyond resistance to slavery, insurgent abolitionism drew on and produced geopolitical knowledge: it opened a sphere of discourse about the responsibilities of rulers over black subjects; the multiple subaltern experiences of unfreedom; Brazil's ongoing connections to Europe, the Caribbean, and Africa; the interdependence of oral and written cultures; and the broader linguistic terrain of black abolitionism. An act of world-making, insurgency extends traditional accounts of interstate politics to include a cast of characters engaged in grassroots diplomacy. In the 1860s, it also developed in dialogue with the staging of US history in Brazil, to which we now turn.

CHAPTER 3

A Forgotten Battleground of the US Civil War

On September 6, 1861, as warfare raged across the United States, the CSS *Sumter* arrived at the roadstead outside the port of São Luís, the capital of the northeastern province of Maranhão. In this cosmopolitan island community located just two degrees below the equator, nearly a third of the population lived in bondage alongside a sizable free population of color that crisscrossed the narrow streets daily, as if stitching together the city's economic and social life.[1] Africans and Afro-descendants steered vessels, labored in residences, sold food, transported cargo, and, if enslaved, were themselves placed on ships as part of the internal human trade that supplied the coffee plantations that flourished in southeastern Brazil. Amid the vibrancy of waterfront life, black seafarers would have been the first to spot the CSS *Sumter* in port. The "American vessel" was the first Confederate cruiser to escape the federal blockade at the mouth of the Mississippi River and aggressively descend into the South Atlantic, capturing Union ships in Cuba, Trinidad, and Surinam.[2]

By this time, Emperor Pedro II had already declared Brazil's neutrality in the US Civil War, seeking to align the empire with the European policy of respecting Lincoln's blockade but granting the Confederates "belligerent" status.[3] Thus Brazil maintained diplomatic relations with the Washington government yet sought to reconcile impartiality "with the duties of hospitality which humanity demands" whenever a Confederate cruiser reached its shores.[4] Confederate ships often secured provisions and fuel in coastal towns, where Brazilian authorities struggled to adhere to a neutral stance when confronted with North Americans' polarizing views on the slavery issue. They opted instead to tread carefully along the divide between an abolitionist North and the slave South with which Brazil had so much in common.

On September 7, 1861, accompanied by fireworks and canon salutes performed by the Brazilian navy in commemoration of Brazil's Independence

Day, the CSS *Sumter* finally hoisted the Confederate flag above the waters of São Luís, fully equipped for war and with nearly two hundred men on board. Less than two weeks passed before another US vessel, this time the steam frigate USS *Powhatan*, entered the port on September 22, proudly floating the Stars and Stripes from her peak. Directly embroiling Brazil in the politics of wartime, Captain David Porter threatened "to capture the *Sumter* and drag it away under the purview of Brazilian fortresses and war ships," but it was too late.[5] The Confederate cruiser had already drawn away to sea, leaving behind streets overflowing with impassioned talk about the war in the United States. Disillusioned by what he described as a lukewarm reception given to the *Powhatan*, Porter diagnosed "the people of Maranhão from the President down" as having gone "*Sumter* mad." According to the Union captain, "Brazilians sympathize almost to a man with the secessionists, under the impression that the South was fighting the battle of Brazil—fighting to protect their property in slaves."[6]

Among those who had gone "Sumter mad," but in a quite different way, were the enslaved and freed people of São Luís. Upon seeing the *Sumter* in port, they gathered in secret under the leadership of *libertos* to discuss the US Civil War, eventually channeling political commentary from the seaside of Maranhão to inland *senzalas*. At one of these September meetings, Agostinho heard about the presence of North Americans and rushed back to Anajatuba, a small town sixty miles south of the capital, to alert other enslaved people to the fact that freedom was on the way, for "they only waited for the war steamer to disembark her troops."[7] Agostinho believed in a US commitment to abolition in Brazil and further "told his peers that they would all be free, for he had heard so from several blacks at the capital."[8]

It may sound odd to us today that the *Sumter*, a ship belonging to the proslavery republic in rebellion against the United States, led the enslaved to imagine their captivity undone in Brazil. Afro-descendants at Atlantic seaports had geopolitical cause to favor the Union, no doubt, but their interpretations of the meanings of secession remained elusive in 1861. When the *Sumter* docked in São Luís, even Maranhão authorities were surprised to learn of the existence of "two United States" and their different flags, a notion first explained to them by Captain Raphael Semmes.[9] Throughout the 1860s, enslaved and freed people used to probing the points of contact between Brazil and the world tended to follow the US Civil War with hope, picturing North Americans as their all-powerful allies, undivided in the struggle for liberty at home and abroad.

The near miss between the *Sumter* and the *Powhatan* in 1861 was the first in a series of maritime encounters that transformed Brazil into a battleground of the Civil War over the 1860s. Confederate cruisers and Union merchant ships bombarded each other on the Brazilian waterfront, routinely landed prisoners or sought provisions in port cities, captured and towed war prizes at their convenience, recruited crew members, and even engaged the Brazilian navy in the crossfire of sectional clashes. In the process, several North American lives were lost, and ships set ablaze on Brazilian shores in clear violation of international law. In the sway of these naval incidents, insurgent abolitionism continued to develop in the provinces of Maranhão, Pará, and Santa Catarina.

That the enslaved assumed that North Americans had come to Brazil to support their emancipation suggests that the histories of the lusophone and anglophone Atlantic were much more entangled than historians have cared to notice.[10] Much has now been written about the global impact of the US Civil War, but very little of this new transnational historiography is informed by sources in Portuguese. In Brazil, the US conflict has garnered much attention among social historians for helping ignite the political debate that culminated in the passage of the country's Free Womb Law in 1871.[11] Those who have chronicled the emergence of the modern Brazilian state and its international economic position in the nineteenth century have also studied the war as a fatal blow to proslavery policies carefully crafted by the conservative political leadership after 1850.[12] The role of the US Civil War in catalyzing discussions over the future of slavery in Brazil is not in dispute here. The conflict clearly destabilized the general inertia of the Brazilian government with regards to emancipation, giving Liberal politicians the moral high ground to steer reform along a moderate path. The impact of the war on black emancipation politics, however, still deserves scrutiny, for Afro-descendants carved out a place for the United States in the radical chronology of abolition they crafted for Brazil. Taken together, the stories that fill the pages of this chapter illuminate the hemispheric crisis of slavery in the 1860s by showing that Afro-descendants in Brazil interpreted the Civil War as another chapter in the struggle for black freedom throughout the African diaspora.

Of Ships and Freedom

US consul William H. Grath immediately accused the CSS *Sumter* of piracy as it approached the coast of São Luís in early September 1861. Unhindered by

Grath, however, Raphael Semmes secured an audience with the president of Maranhão, Francisco Primo de Aguiar. In his first interaction with a Brazilian official, Semmes introduced himself as an officer in the Confederate navy and played on the weight that the South's commitment to slavery carried abroad to elicit sympathy from his host.[13] Acting as a quasi-diplomat broadcasting ambitions of an alliance with Brazil that could strengthen the South against both Northern military forces and British abolitionism, he explained to President Aguiar that the war in the United States "was in fact a war as much on behalf of Brazil as of ourselves, and that if we were beaten in the contest, Brazil would be the next one to be assailed by Yankee propagandists."[14] Semmes shared with Brazilian slaveholders the belief that antislavery was a foreign menace that ought to be contained. The Confederate captain even offered to salute the Brazilian flag upon entering São Marcos Bay, but President Aguiar "delicately insinuated" that he would prefer that the *Sumter* avoid any gesture that could be interpreted as a formal recognition of the Confederacy as a friendly nation.[15]

In 1861 David Porter and Raphael Semmes embodied very different facets of the United States abroad. Born in Pennsylvania, Porter was the son of a naval hero of the War of 1812 who followed in his father's footsteps when he joined the US Navy during the Mexican American War (1846–48). In the 1860s, while on blockade duty on the Mississippi, he helped recapture the USS *Mary Bradford*, the first prize ever taken by the *Sumter*. From the crew on board, Porter learned about the *Sumter*'s next movements and secured permission to chase the privateer down the South Atlantic. Whenever in foreign waters, Porter purported to wield the national power of the United States and condemned what he saw as international compliance with the Confederate's predatory warfare methods.[16]

Semmes was also a veteran of the Mexican American War but had been born into a slaveholding family from Maryland and gone on to become an enslaver himself in Mobile, Alabama. In 1861 he abandoned the US Navy and received a letter of marque from the very hands of Jefferson Davis, president of the Confederate States of America (CSA). Semmes then set out to sea aboard the *Sumter* with a firm conviction that, to win the war, the South needed to internationalize the conflict by attacking the Northern merchant navy abroad.[17] His proslavery beliefs took full effect in both discourse and practice. On board the *Sumter*, Ned served as his cabin slave and cook but ran away the day before the cruiser left Suriname for Maranhão and disappeared ashore among the colored population of Paramaribo. Semmes blamed the

Figure 7. CSS *Sumter* coaling at the Dutch island of Curaçao, in the Caribbean. Line engraving from a photograph by S. J. Nathans. *Frank Leslie's Illustrated Newspaper*, August 24, 1861.

escape on the interference of the US consul in the city and again expressed his distaste for the presence of "Yankees" throughout the Atlantic.[18] Semmes's affinity with Brazil was moderated by his belief, left unstated at the time, in Anglo-Saxon superiority, which led him to later reminisce about the "set of half-breeds" whom he encountered in Maranhão.[19]

The Brazilian press reported extensively on the arrival of the CSS *Sumter* in Maranhão. The official newspaper of the province, *Publicador Maranhense*, had been printing correspondence and political debates on the issue on its front page since the beginning of September. The *Jornal do Amazonas*, published in the neighboring province of Pará, offered colorful commentary on the "great commotion" caused in São Luís by a war vessel "with manifest and flag of the Confederation" said to have "taken and destroyed eight American ships, and three more after leaving Cuba." The newspaper closely followed Semmes's intentions, as he was said to be waiting in port to capture the *Maria*, a cargo brig outfitted in New York.[20] Rumors also circulated about the existence of two Union warships hiding near the Santana lighthouse, but the *Sumter* was able to leave Maranhão on September 15, unharmed by Union fire and replenished with ninety-four tons of coal.

Both Porter and Semmes denied the existence of Brazilian neutrality on the ground, pointing out that Confederates were quite popular in the empire. Lodged at the Hotel do Porto in São Luís, Semmes routinely ran into ordinary Brazilians who enjoyed talking about the Civil War. He commented on the "excited imaginations of the townspeople," marveling that "the whole town is agog discussing our affairs."[21] Porter, for his part, translated his inability to catch up with his enemy into distrust of the Brazilian government, adding to the racial storytelling that emerged from the US presence in Brazil. He noted that President Aguiar did not grant him an official visit and carelessly left all communication with his crew to lower-level black officials. "The *Powhatan*, in the eyes of these people, represents the cause of slave emancipation," Porter argued.[22] Be that as it may, he duly agreed to accept 270 tons of coal from the provincial government of Maranhão.[23]

Like Semmes, Porter memorialized his racialized impressions of Brazil and, in so doing, registered how Afro-descendants interacted with North Americans. He recalled an exchange with "an insolent negro pilot" on board the *Powhatan* when the ship reached the entrance of the São Luís harbor. The man had seen the *Sumter* out a few days earlier and was surprised to learn that the *Powhatan* was able to navigate the shoals leading into the harbor without damage to the embarkation. The unnamed pilot mentioned that "even the little *Sumter* struck coming in and came near to leaving her bones among them." Porter reacted with anticipation, imagining the enemy still within his reach in Maranhão, but "the negro laughed and replied impudently: 'No, you can't catch her, she is miles away—she sailed four days ago.'"[24] After the *Powhatan* crew came ashore to procure supplies, again "a black officer with an aide of the same complexion" came on board to demand that the ship stop taking coal. By that time, the *Sumter* had already reached the Cape of São Roque, where Semmes expected to intercept Union vessels coming back from ports south of the equator.

The mere presence of US warships forced Brazilians to grapple with the implications of Northern antislavery and Southern proslavery internationalism at a time when immediate abolition remained firmly off the official political agenda. As news spread quickly in Maranhão, tensions between fearful masters and enslaved people familiar with the winds of abolitionism challenged the fallacy of Brazilian noninvolvement. Information about war traveled, for example, on waterborne trading routes like the Mearim River, which linked the Atlantic seaboard to the Center-West of Maranhão, a region that would benefit from the global economic realignment sparked by the Civil

War.[25] In 1861, this was probably the path taken by Agostinho, who spread the word about war steamers among the enslaved of Anajatuba. A small settlement of 3,205 inhabitants, of which 751 were enslaved, Anajatuba spread out along four streets that centered on the Rosary Church. Cattle ranching, sugar, cassava, and tobacco as well as cotton dominated its surroundings, which stretched seventy-eight miles west toward Viana, a more significant town on the edge of the Turiaçu forest, on the Amazonian borderland with Pará.[26] With a population of 8,397, Viana was at the center of a network of old quilombos, and one in four of its inhabitants was enslaved.

Agostinho was the Brazilian-born slave of a retired schoolteacher and cattle rancher named Cristóvão de Santiago Vieira, who developed a cosmopolitan abolitionist worldview without ever leaving Maranhão. He was probably a slave for hire, or *escravo ao ganho*, who embodied a covert system of knowledge production and conveyance that overlapped with the local infrastructure of slavery. The *ganho* system required enslaved people to contract with masters for a reasonable amount of money to be delivered at the end of the day or week as the result of their labor.[27] Such an arrangement allowed them to work without direct supervision and to keep earnings in excess of what was owed to the master. Thus escravos ao ganho had more control over their daily lives than their peers on the plantations and this often confused authorities, who could hardly differentiate them from free people of color, especially if they were Brazilian born. Mobility allowed workers like Agostinho to interact with people of different social positions and across geographic, social, and cultural boundaries.

Escravos ao ganho were often the initiators of streams of conversation that connected rural villages to the larger urban systems on the Brazilian coast. Insurgency also emerged from their geopolitical literacy, as imagined geographies were a critical element in the development of allegiances, identities, and projects for the future. Agostinho may also have gathered information about the United States through print. At the very least, we know that he worked with older, literate enslaved people who had access to press coverage of the *Sumter* incident.[28] In August 1862, for example, his master, Cristóvão Vieira, offered a handsome reward to anyone who would return Raimundo, a mixed-race tailor who "wishes to pass as white saying that he has patent because he knows how to read and write, presents himself as a lawyer . . ."[29] Like Raimundo, Agostinho resisted bondage by constantly challenging his condition; he spent almost more time in prison than working for Vieira. After his arrest for leading the 1861 slave conspiracy, he was arrested at least three more times over the next six years on charges of drunkenness, violating the evening curfew, and participating in street fights.[30]

In November, on the outskirts of São Luís, the enslaved rejoiced again in the certainty of freedom. This time, they talked about "a liberty that had been granted to them by an American warship that, not being able to free them the first time, will be back soon, and then freedom will be posted by announcement on the door of the church."[31] This news quickly spread to the quilombos of western Maranhão. In Viana, the police commissioner José Cândido Nunes cracked down on insurgent gatherings that had nearly escaped his control: "When I entered in the exercise of the functions of police commissioner, I already found the idea spreading in this City, the slaves so ungoverned, gathering in evening sessions at home where they made arrangements about the expected freedom; when they did not have sessions at home, they met at night in groups of four, six, and eight on the streets. Finding things in this state, I terminated these sessions."[32] Nunes was particularly worried about the increase in the flight of enslaved people to the forests of Turiaçú, where a quilombo had developed in the last five years. In the town of São Bento, in late 1861, those still "inspired by the news of events in America" planned to revolt alongside the quilombolas of São Vicente do Céu, the community that became the largest focus of insurrection in a province aflame with talk of a war over slavery in the United States.[33]

Located to the south of Viana, the quilombo of São Vicente do Céu was founded in 1856 by enslaved workers who had been forced out of the gold mines of Maracassumé to establish the Anglo-Brazilian mining company Montes Áureos.[34] These quilombolas, then, were the same ones who acted on rumors of British antislavery, as discussed in the previous chapter. The quilombo was situated in lands that spread along three river systems—known as the Gurupi, the Maracassumé, and the Turiaçu—along which nature-carved groves and hamlets attracted Afro-descendants escaping slavery. Just as sailors on the Brazilian coast, quilombolas acted as privileged carriers of information about "the Americans" and played an important role in shaping the political climate in Maranhão. Nearly four hundred people were said to live in the settlement, a typical Brazilian quilombo that thrived in close proximity to local plantations. Its trade networks and escape routes ran through the Santa Bárbara plantation, owned by the Baron of Turiaçú, and extended to the outskirts of the towns of Santa Helena and Viana.[35]

In January 1862 fears of a black rebellion inspired by North American naval presence led the provincial authorities to raid São Vicente do Céu.[36]

Runaway communities in Maranhão were so large and resilient that they merited repeated military interventions, along with the recruitment of civilian militias and slave catchers. They constituted important nodes of underground economies and social networks that linked quilombolas to the everyday workings of Brazilian slave society, including planters, indigenous peoples, merchants, and senzalas. In 1862, President Antônio Manoel Campos de Mello dispatched fifty-two soldiers and fifty national guardsmen to São Vicente do Céu under the command of Lieutenant Máximo Fernandes Monteiro, a veteran officer from the military colony of Gurupi.[37] After several days on foot, the group found the quilombo virtually empty. Only two men resisted the armed siege, the quilombolas having been warned by their local trading partners.

Lieutenant Monteiro described the quilombo as a "colossal settlement" located on top of a hill, stretching 601 yards deep and 216 yards wide. São Vicente do Céu was, in fact, an agrarian community of self-liberated people composed of seventy-eight residential houses, one sugar mill, six ovens for the processing of manioc flour, one weaver's cottage, and a big house of worship decorated with a large cross and flowers. Founded by plantation runaways in a frontier region of dense forest and swampland that was difficult to cross, the quilombo had developed a self-sufficient food system capable of sustaining the invading force for weeks.[38] Soldiers found over a thousand chickens, forty-six dogs, sixty-nine pans for mining gold, and fifty cauldrons along with crops of manioc, cotton, rice, and tobacco. As was customary, the raid ended with the burning of all residences—though the troops, mindful of their Christian god, were careful to leave the cross in the house of worship intact—but took few prisoners. The quilombolas of São Vicente do Céu moved to other, smaller settlements throughout Turiaçú, keeping rumors of rebellion alive in northeastern Brazil.

At the end of February 1862, black discontent spilled from western Maranhão to the neighboring province of Pará, "as the two warring parties in the United States unfortunately continue to fight each other."[39] President Antônio Manoel de Campos Mello considered the extermination of the quilombos of Viana as the most important measure to enforce law and order during the US Civil War. "I take this matter seriously," Campos Mello pondered, because the enslaved population "on which the denouement of the war in the South of the American Union is bound to make an impression is still large, since just the coming of the *Sumter* and the wickedness or imprudence of some propagated dangerous ideas."[40]

Campos Mello was right. In the 1860s, the US Civil War changed the context in which enslaved resistance took place, pushing enslaved and free black people to imagine their own struggles against bondage as part of an international conflict fought on multiple battlefronts. As the war raged on, Afro-descendants looked for signs that the end of slavery loomed near and seized opportunities for new alliances. The intricacies of US sectional politics in this case lost importance to a broader assessment of Atlantic geopolitics that fed black insurgency in Brazil.

Sectional Warfare in a Slave Empire

During the nineteenth century, the Brazilian state also consolidated itself through the rebuke of abolitionism. Surviving the threats posed by slave revolts, anti-slave-trade legislation, British gunboat diplomacy, and foreign wars required that those upholding the social order pay sharper attention to the scope of Brazilian sovereignty. Thus, as with the Christie Affair, the issue of national self-determination dominated public discourse on the US naval presence in Brazil, trumping debate on the underlying issue of slavery. In a clear parallel to the Anglo-Brazilian crisis, state neutrality during the Civil War was intended to complement slaveholders' efforts to deny foreign influence over domestic affairs. And when it came to the United States, this meant shielding the enslaved from the circulation of news and carefully navigating the geopolitics of emancipation, which insistently penetrated Brazil's protected slave zone via warships, soldiers, diplomats, and world travelers.

US naval incursions into Brazilian waters, however, made elite concern for noninvolvement in the Civil War into an impossible proposition. As early as September 10, 1861, three days after the *Sumter*'s arrival in São Luís, controversy regarding Confederate presence gained the floor of the Provincial Assembly of Maranhão. The Liberal deputy Gentil Braga, the most vocal spokesperson of the local political opposition, rushed to discredit President Primo de Aguiar for allowing the *Sumter* to fly the Confederate flag for more than twenty-four hours.[41] Citing the equivocal terms set forth by the imperial circular of June 1861, Gentil Braga contended that the gesture equaled an official acknowledgement of the Confederacy as a sovereign nation and expressed concern about the impact of such position on the "commercial body" of São Luís, so used to trading with the Union.[42]

Gentil Braga's opinion on matters of international law echoed the position of the US State Department, which consistently criticized Brazil for recognizing the belligerence of the Confederate states. James Watson Webb, the temperamental and verbose envoy to Rio de Janeiro, displayed such an attitude toward Brazilians. Born in New York, Webb retired early from a military career in the US Army and became the editor and proprietor of the *New York Courier and Enquirer* until his appointment as ambassador to Brazil in 1861. A member of the Republican Party and a friend of Secretary of State William Seward, Webb fervently opposed the proliferation of Confederate cruisers in Brazil. His career as a devout Unionist in a slave empire began with his denunciation of the government of Maranhão for having provided "material aid to rebels involved in the depredation of U.S. commerce."[43] Throughout the 1860s Webb defended the Union's unwillingness to concede the rights of foreign governments to aid the Confederacy and often invoked the Monroe Doctrine to counter fears of a European invasion of the Americas.[44]

In a context in which many expressed concern that Emperor Pedro II might eventually recognize the independence of the South and enter into a proslavery alliance including Cuba, Foreign Minister Benevenuto Augusto de Magalhães Taques explained Brazil's position to the Parliament.[45] Casting the country as a mere spectator of events in 1862, Taques thought it imperative that consular attachés stationed in dissident US states remain neutral and that Brazilian maritime provinces follow certain procedures while the conflict unfolded at sea. He clarified that imperial policy specifically forbade pirate ships or warships carrying prizes from entering Brazilian ports; policy determined that the country's ports should not be used as bases for war operations or for seizing prizes, and it allowed trade with belligerents but recommended that federal warships be assisted in every way possible, except for the provision of ammunition and war supplies.[46]

All these measures, however, did not prevent Brazil from becoming a theater of operations in the US Civil War. For the duration of the conflict, the Brazilian coast remained full of US naval combatants from both sides, which had already been abundant in the previous decade. Consider the capital city of Rio de Janeiro as an example. According to the Brazilian minister of the navy, of all the 8,888 ships that entered the port between 1852 and 1860, the majority sailed under the US flag (2,325), followed by British (1,645) and Portuguese (1,007) vessels.[47] In October 1861, US consuls in Brazil were instructed to require captains of US vessels to take an oath to support the Constitution of the United States. Refusal to do so meant loss of clearance to sail. The measure seems to have been inspired by cases such as the *Sumter's*, when ship masters sailing with US papers either displayed in some part of their rigging the "Rebel Flag of the Southern Confederacy" or instigated Union crews ashore.[48] In 1862, for instance, the US consul in Maranhão received formal complaints about Confederate captains who had "made themselves particularly obnoxious to the numerous loyal Americans now sojourning here, by the expression of treasonable sentiments."[49] Brazil had become a site for the staging of US wartime politics.

Outraged by President Primo de Aguiar's leniency toward the *Sumter*, James Watson Webb warned Minister Taques that the very survival of the Brazilian empire seemed to be at stake. The downfall of the American Union, Webb argued, would "inevitably be followed, sooner or later, by the decline and fall of every independent nation on this continent, which must, in that case, become once again a theatre for the ambition of European Powers."[50] Whenever possible, Union representatives in Brazil played up the threat posed by Southern filibustering and couched their concerns about European intervention in terms of the French invasion of Mexico and the Spanish capture of Santo Domingo in 1861.[51] During the 1860s, the threat of a French protectorate was particularly real in Ecuador. In 1864 Peru nearly went to war with Spain after seizing the Chincha Islands, while Paraguay's Solano Lopez courted European support for his imperial ambitions in the Rio de la Plata region before the Triple Alliance War broke out in 1864. The Lincoln administration adopted a cautious policy toward the revolutionary governments of Venezuela, Colombia, and Bolivia, wary of setting a precedent that might open the door to recognition of the Confederacy. Nevertheless, Confederate officials also counted on the vitality of South American nationalist traditions formulated during wars of independence to find allies in their struggle for sovereignty.

In addition to the sheer threat of recolonization, Webb also sought to ensure Brazilian loyalty to the Union through military and economic arguments. He asserted that the *Sumter* did not deserve to be treated as a "man of war" and warned Brazil that "rebel sailors" had permission from their commanders to attack Union ships in international waters and could expect cash prizes for capturing Union citizens.[52] Hoping for compliance, Webb reminded Brazilian authorities that the United States was one of the most powerful nations in the world and that the Union consumed more than half of Brazil's coffee production.

Ironically, coffee was one of the commodities that linked the Union to the center of the Brazilian slave economy—the Paraíba River valley.[53] In the mid-nineteenth century, Brazil sold most of its coffee to the United States, importing some cotton textiles and codfish from New England, wheat flour from Maryland and Virginia, and charcoal. Commercial ties between Brazil and the United States were much more salient than accounts of British primacy in South America have yielded. After England, France, and Cuba, Brazil was the fourth most important source of US imports in the antebellum period as well as a node in the circuit of knowledge production that linked the Upper South to the Brazilian southeast. Industrial experts hailing from the South, like the Virginians Richard Morton and Matthew Fontaine Maury, played a major role in early railroad projects in Brazil, helping to integrate new coffee-growing areas to global industrial modernity.[54]

More than half of all disembarkations of enslaved persons in Brazil during the illegal period (1831–50) involved some form of US participation, a rarely told spin-off tale from the golden era of North American shipbuilding. US-built ships accounted for about a thousand voyages, or 58.2 percent of the 1,789 slave voyages organized between 1831 and 1850. The US merchant houses Maxwell, Wright & Co. and James Birckhead, with offices in Rio de Janeiro, sold and chartered many of the ships used on slave voyages to Africa. Following passage of the Eusébio de Queirós Law in 1850, US companies turned their attention to Cuban markets and US individual brokers filled in the gap. Men like Joshua M. Clapp—the "go-between of the man-stealers of Rio de Janeiro," in the words of a British consul—and George Marsden then took up the sale of vessels to be engaged in the African-related trade.[55] The voyages of the *Mary E. Smith*, the *W. H. Stuard*, the *Vickery*, and the *Manchester* have been well documented.[56] In the first half of the 1860s, of 170 slave-trading expeditions carried out in the Atlantic, at least 117 are believed to have sailed from North American ports to feed the contraband markets in Brazil and Cuba.[57]

The Union's participation in the Brazilian slave economy, however, did not prevent Webb from requesting a remonstrance in the *Sumter*'s case. His imperious attitude typified the general tone of Washington diplomats in their dealings with South American governments. At the direction of Secretary Seward, men like Webb sought to convey to other nations that the greatness of the Union cause lay in its combined defense of the end of slavery, the preservation of democratic principles, and the protection of the Americas from foreign (i.e., European) intervention.[58] The Union's antislavery and democratic arguments carried little weight in Brazil, though. Webb's portrayal of the "Southern Rebellion" as a movement to create another slave country had little chance of resonating with Brazilian authorities, who presided over an empire built on the enslavement of Africans.

In 1862, Brazilian minister Taques reminded Webb that secession was not a unique event in world history. "It is not the first time that a portion of an Empire is found in rebellion against the legitimate and recognized government or sovereign. The United States of America from 1776 to 1783 and Brazil from 1822 to 1825 were found in these circumstances." Directly equating the global position of both countries at the time of their independence, Taques added, "it would have been the greatest good fortune for England in 1776 and for Portugal in 1822, that all civilized nations should cruise against American and Brazilian ships as against pirates and malefactors. But this was not the case."[59]

Ultimately Seward accepted Brazil's affirmation of neutrality in the *Sumter* incident. However, he cautioned the Brazilian envoy to Washington, Miguel Maria Lisboa, that the US government still considered harmful the acts of any foreign government (referring specifically to Britain, Spain, the Netherlands, and France) that recognized the Southern insurgents as belligerents, and that he would not acquiesce in them.[60] In April 1862, Seward even suggested that all maritime nations that granted belligerent rights to insurgents were somehow conspiring against the United States, but he soon retreated from his harsher stance against Brazil. In mid-1862, the Brazilian Foreign Ministry approved the Maranhão president's actions and considered the Sumter controversy settled.[61]

A year later, Raphael Semmes returned to Brazil at the helm of the CSS *Alabama*, reigniting tensions with the Union government. Built in Liverpool, the Confederate ship sailed with British cannons and several veteran *Sumter* officers aboard.[62] Arriving in the empire in mid-March 1863, the *Alabama* captured and burned at least eleven Union ships off Brazilian territorial waters, leaving the president of Bahia, Antônio Coelho de Sá e Albuquerque, with the task of dispelling any accusations of Confederate sympathies.[63] Mindful of what had happened with Primo de Aguiar in Maranhão, Albuquerque assured the minister of foreign affairs that this time "all had gone well so that we are neither committed to the English nor to the Americans from either North or South."[64]

After stopping in Bahia, the CSS *Alabama* veered toward the island of Fernando de Noronha, far off the coast of Pernambuco, to meet her tender, the *Agrippina*. Carrying the *Louisa Hatch* in tow, the ship made port on April 9, 1863, and spent five days in the penal colony of Noronha to complete coaling. Semmes sent all his prisoners ashore, and sixty-two of them were later taken to Recife aboard the Brazilian schooner *Sergipano*. Forty-four prisoners remained on the island awaiting transportation along with a crew composed mostly of British sailors. Brazilian newspapers reported on the conditions faced by Union crews captured by the *Alabama*: "The prisoners, except for captains, are put in irons as long as they are on board, are left with no money, and are subjected to the most rigorous searches. All papers belonging to the ship are taken and sealed. Those sailors who wish to remain on board are received, and on this account eleven English seamen of the crew of the *Kate Cora* [*sic*] remained."[65]

At the end of his stay, Semmes burned two whalers, the *Lafayette* and the *Kate Cory*, setting off next to Bahia with eighty-four prisoners on board.[66] This time, once informed of the assistance provided to the Confederate brig in Noronha, the Brazilian government promptly fired its commanding officer on the island.[67] The *Alabama* continued her raids, though, burning the *Union Jack* and the Boston clipper *Sea Lark* in the waters of Bahia. In all, Semmes destroyed twenty-nine Union merchant ships during the summer months of 1863.

Imprisoned sailors acted as disseminators of stories from both sides of the sectional divide. In their public ordeals between ship gallows, prisons, and consulates, these seamen—some of whom were African American—built foreign relations on the ground.[68] In May 1863, at the request of the US consul in Recife, the president of Pernambuco allowed the crews captured by the CSS *Alabama* and the CSS *Florida* to be held in the warehouses on Pina Island. During the transfer, the sailors waited in the streets of Recife, causing great commotion among the local population. The *Diário do Rio de Janeiro* described the area around the US consulate in the city as a kind of "refugee camp" where "prisoners from the Confederate ships coming from Fernando Island were waiting for their fate to be decided." Among them were North Americans, Portuguese, Spaniards, Malays, Indians, and even Brazilians from the province of Santa Catarina, who sat among piles of boxes, mattresses, bundles, and bags of clothes. The prisoners were a fascinating sight, reported the *Diário*, "in which here and there groups of storytellers were the highlight, surrounded by a growing crowd of curious passers-by, who perhaps listened attentively to the tall tales, but no less enjoyed them."[69]

Although Brazil officially forbade the acceptance of prizes in its ports, concessions were often made for the landing of prisoners by Confederate ships. In April 1863, while passing by Bahia, the *Alabama* landed eighty-four prisoners from the USS *Oneida*, and the CSS *Georgia* landed twelve men from the ships *Anice* and *Clarence*, along with their baggage, provisions, and stories. All prisoners were said to have been captured beyond one league from land. Semmes enjoyed watching news of the war spread by word of mouth in Recife. He recalled that "the landing of so many prisoners amid so small a population has created a very great stir, and the excitable Brazilians are discussing among themselves and with the Yankee captains the question of the American war with great vehemence."[70]

The CSS *Florida* anchored off Fernando de Noronha a day after the departure of the CSS *Alabama* for Bahia on April 28, 1863. Captain John Maffitt landed thirty-two prisoners from his latest captures but soon received an ultimatum from the commanding colonel at the island's fort, Antônio Gomes Leal, to withdraw from Brazilian waters within twenty-four hours. Maffitt met with the president of Pernambuco, João Silveira de Souza, and was surprised by "his undisguised fear of the Federal Government." President Souza, anticipating the arrival of three Union ships in a few days, asked Maffitt to leave because he could not offer him protection from violence. Maffitt laughed off Souza's suggestion, remarking that the Confederates did not need Brazilian protection and that "the influence of the United States is very great here, but I think the majority of the citizens sympathize with the Confederacy."[71]

The CSS *Florida* eventually got permission to set anchor in June 1863 in Fortaleza, the capital of the province of Ceará, where it disembarked the remaining eleven prisoners. Once out in the high seas, the brig finished its first trip to Brazil with the capture of the bark *Clarence*, which sailed with a cargo of coffee from Rio de Janeiro to Baltimore under Captain Brown, a Northerner "full of biblical lore on slavery."[72] Articles taken from prisoners were peddled on the streets of Pernambuco. In the words of a prominent local merchant, the province had become "a mart for the sale of goods taken by Pirates out of American vessels almost within sight of the port." Only the US consul to Shanghai, also made a prisoner of war, managed to save a few dollars by shoving them inside his boots.[73]

Still in 1863, the CSS *Alabama* returned to Bahia, where Semmes sent more prisoners to safety "under the official wings of the American consul."[74] Allowed to walk on the streets of Salvador, Confederate officers enlivened the waterfront promenades with their uniforms, being closely observed by local shop owners and maritime workers. While in port, the CSS *Alabama* witnessed the arrival of the CSS *Georgia*, led by Captain Lewis F. Maury, and received news that the CSS *Florida* was also on her way to the Bay of All

Saints. For one of Semmes's crew members, the moment was nothing short of historical. "We can straighten up now and put on airs, boast of the 'Confederate squadron of the South American station,' and await the arrival of any vessel of the enemy's navy in perfect security." With three Confederate raiders within reach, Arthur Sinclair could not "avoid the feeling of pride and satisfaction that our struggling little Confederacy has actually been able to overmatch the enemy in cruisers" and hoped for British intervention on their behalf.[75]

In Salvador, Bahia, North American naval presence inspired the naming of two opposing newspapers between 1863 and 1864: *O Alabama: Periódico Crítico e Chistoso* and the short-lived *O Mohican: Jornal do Povo e Para o Povo*,[76] whose only declared goal was to "be in pursuit" of the political commentary published by the *Alabama*.[77] The USS *Mohican* was a steam sloop ordered in 1862 on a special mission to hunt down the CSS *Florida* and the CSS *Alabama* throughout the Atlantic. Captain O. S. Glisson arrived at the helm of the vessel in Bahia on June 25, 1863, thus missing the Confederate raiders by a couple of days.[78]

In an inversion of the Confederate cause, the CSS *Alabama*, for its part, named a newspaper edited by the Afro-Bahian editors Aristides Ricardo de Santana, José Marques de Souza, and Francisco Alves da Silva Igrapiuna. Printed at the Interesse Público press, the satirical paper chronicled the daily life of Salvador from 1863 to 1890, with temporal gaps and editorial changes along the way. Domingos Guedes Cabral was its typesetter, a man recently released from imprisonment on charges of press crimes. Maybe for that reason, the first edition of the *Alabama* published on December 21, 1863, offered almost a disclaimer on its first page, along with a cheeky reference to the Confederate navy: "The Alabama is not a thief; it is a staunch enemy of thieves. Cosmopolitan, it has no regard for nationality, political party, or any other kind; where there are thieves, there it will be found. . . . So prepare yourselves, for the Alabama is on a journey inland. Poor of those who meet her."[79]

Despite the rhetoric of victory, the Confederate navy experienced conflict during its time in Brazil. The *Alabama* master-at-arms, for example, a James King of Savannah, deserted the ship while in Bahia despite antecedents "proving his devotion to the Southern cause."[80] Meanwhile, commanders of Union vessels monitored the movements of Confederate cruisers by communicating regularly by letter with Washington's consuls in Brazilian maritime provinces. The presence of so many "piratical vessels" on Brazilian shores prompted James W. Webb to protest the conduct of the Brazilian government. The Brazilian State Council took up the issue on June 4, 1863,

O ALABAMA

PERIODICO CRITICO E CHISTOSO.

SERIE 3.ª   BAHIA 14 DE ABRIL DE 1864.   N.º 47

Publica-se na typographia de Marques, Aristides e C., a 1$000 rs. por serie de 10 numeros, pagos adiantados. Folha avulsa 120 rs.

O ALABAMA.

EXPEDIENTE.

Cidade de Latronopolis, bordo do *Alabama* 13 de abril de 1864.

Officio ao Sr. commandante das armas, para que mande informar o Sr. official da guarda do commercio d'hontem 12 do corrente sobre um espancamento que soffreu um guarda das mãos d'um africano, a quem o official se negou a prender, quando lhe foi elle apresentado por dous officiaes da guarda nacional, prisão que só effectuou á reclamação dos mesmos, de um seu collega e do Sr. subdelegado da Penha, que lhe extranharam o procedimento pouco honroso para um militar que via ser brutalmente vilipendiada a farda brasileira, no meio das galhofas e dicterios dos insoltantes gallegos que presenciavam a scena.

— Ao Sr. subdelegado de Sant'Anna, partecipando-lhe que no largo da Saúde costumam certas ganhadeiras assar peixe, dando logar a que lh'o vão comprar alguns capadocios que o *petiscam* no adro da egreja, ao som de palavradas, modinhas e toques de violão, no enthusiastico fervor de brindes immoraes; abuso que admira que a policia ignore-o até hoje.

— Ao Sr. subdelegado de Santo Antonio, afim de indagar quaes são as familias, por cujo intermedio foram raptadas na noite de Sexta Feira da Paixão duas moças que residiam em casa de sua mestra, á rua dos Marchantes, das quaes era uma de menor edade; e dar as providencias, para que sejam punidos os criminosos.

— Ao 4.º juiz de paz da Sé, pedindo-lhe que não consinta a continuação de sambas e gritarias que todos os domingos ha por baixo da casa de sua residencia, occasionados por innumeros negros, que fazem dalli um grande terreiro, em que exercitam suas costumadas bruxarias.

and analyzed all the correspondence exchanged over the hostilities involving the *Sumter*, the *Georgia*, and the *Alabama* in Brazil.[81]

The councilors Eusébio de Queirós, the Marquis of Maranguape, and the Viscount of Uruguai ruled that Confederate vessels should be treated according to the law of nations as belligerents and not as pirates, being therefore allowed entry for the peaceful and humanitarian purposes of gathering supplies, making repairs, and escaping life-threatening situations. The Marquis of Abrantes, however, wondered about the lack of a proper treaty or Brazilian law regulating rights of asylum or simply the use of neutral territories by vessels of war.[82] The Councilors reaffirmed as guidelines the principles contained in the 1861 circular, which equated corsairs and war vessels, giving both the same right of entry and supplying in Brazilian waters.[83]

The State Council deemed Webb's request for the capture of the *Alabama* in Bahia "inadmissible" even if it recognized that the president should never have allowed entry to a ship that had violated Brazilian territorial rights so many times. The councilors invoked the authority of US and French experts in international law to base their decisions on the jurisdiction of neutral states, citing especially Henry Wheaton and L. B. Hautefeuille. Eusébio de Queirós was the only one to differ slightly from his colleagues, recommending that Brazil set a limit on coal supplies to Confederate ships, since fuel should be considered an article of war. All in all, the State Council made an effort to minimize the payment of reparations to the United States and said nothing in favor of either party at war. "The section fears that, unfortunately, this struggle of the United States will end up being very expensive to us. Let's see if, at least, it can be rendered cheaper."[84] In 1864, the CSS *Alabama* ended her career near the harbor of Cherbourg, France, where it sank after a battle with the Union war vessel *Kearsarge*.

Despite the intervention of the State Council, the most significant naval incident in US-Brazilian relations would occur in 1864. In October, the Union gunboat *Wachusett* captured the Confederate brig *Florida* in the waters off Bahia after months of tracking it down the West Indies.[85] According to the Brazilian government's version of events, the USS *Wachusett* had been in the port of Salvador for several days when the CSS *Florida* anchored in the area on October 4. Having come from Tenerife, Commander Charles M. Morris requested permission to obtain coal and supplies and to have her machinery repaired at the Navy Yard. Morris had stopped at the All Saints Bay on his way around Cape Horn, from where he intended to launch an attack on the Federal Pacific whaling fleet.

Considering it to be his duty, "in the name of humanity," to aid a vessel that was running very low on supplies and whose engine was severely compromised, the president of Bahia, Antônio Joaquim da Silva Gomes, fixed the term of forty-eight hours for the CSS *Florida* to refit and repair. After obtaining Captain Morris's assurance that no attack on the USS *Wachusett* would be attempted in Brazil, Gomes sent a Brazilian engineer on board to inspect the engine. Additionally, anticipating the possible breakout of hostilities between the two North American vessels stationed in Salvador, he ordered the CSS *Florida* under the protection of the artillery of the Brazilian corvette *D. Januária*.[86]

The US consul in Bahia reacted in disbelief. Thomas Wilson soon alerted President Gomes to his government's censures over the admittance of Confederate privateers by neutral nations and reminded the imperial official that the CSS *Florida* had burned down the Union bark *Mandamis* less than three miles away from Fernando de Noronha in 1863. Consul Wilson then sent letters to Captain Morris of the CSS *Florida*, directly challenging him to fight the *Wachusett*. At about 3 a.m. on October 7, close to the expiration of the forty-eight-hour period given to the CSS *Florida*, Commander Napoleon Collins of the *Wachusett* decided to attack his adversary. On passing across the bows of the Brazilian corvette *D. Januária*, Collins was summoned to anchor but continued to approach the Confederate privateer, firing a gun and some musketry.

The impending attack prompted Gervásio Mancebo, commander of the Brazilian Naval Division, to threaten the USS *Wachusett* with opening fire from the ships and forts under his power, but Captain Collins moved on to take the CSS *Florida* when most of her crew was on shore. Under cover of darkness, the USS *Wachusett* rammed her hull, and with the CSS *Florida* still afloat, Collins decided to tow her away with a long cable. A boarding party secured the surrender of twelve officers and fifty-eight men, as well as all the ship's cargo, but not without a fight. According to the Brazilian press, the battle that ensued in Bahia resulted in many casualties, especially on the Confederate side. One officer was killed with a bullet in the chest and then hanged; Lieutenant S. G. Stone shot himself in the mouth after killing more than six men and finding himself outnumbered; and another officer was killed "by the blows of pistol butts" after stabbing six Union officers aboard the USS *Wachusett*. "Four of the fifteen mariners who jumped overboard into the sea escaped because they were rescued by merchant ships anchored nearby. The other eleven were shot dead by the enemy, who fired at one of

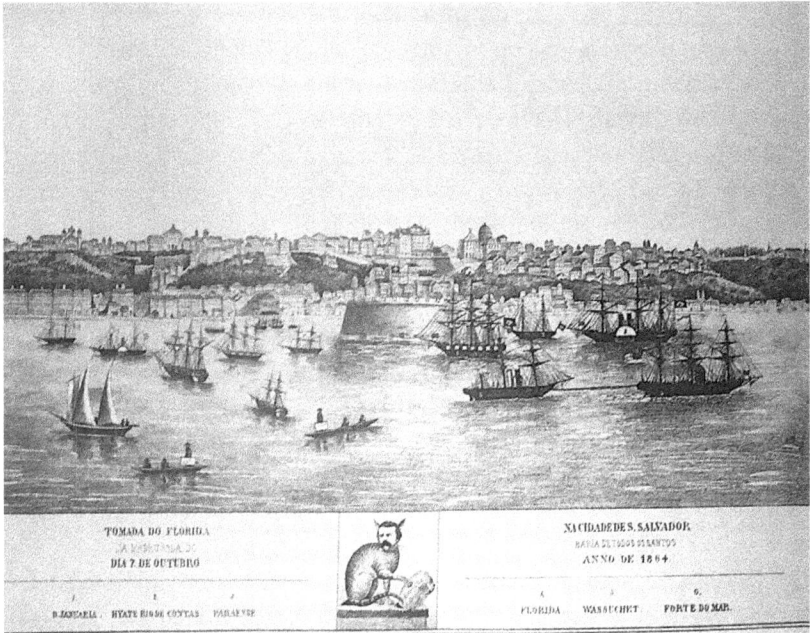

Figure 9. "Seizure of the *Florida* in the early hours of October 7th in the city of S. Salvador, Bahia de Todos os Santos, Year 1864." Anonymous lithograph, n.d. The man depicted as an animal holding a sum of 5,000,000 dollars in the lower center is the US consul in Bahia, Thomas Wilson. Biblioteca Nacional, Brazil.

them nine times!"[87] Among the Northerners, Officer Walter Delany was killed by friendly fire from the USS *Wachusett* while a prisoner aboard the CSS *Florida*. The Brazilian steamers *D. Januária*, *Paraense*, and *Rio de Contas* soon went to sea to pursue the Union ship but were unable to prevent her from sailing north to St. Thomas in the Caribbean. Along with her prize, the USS *Wachusett* also offered refuge to Consul Wilson, who decided to leave his post in Salvador.[88]

A year after the Christie Affair, events in Bahia were reminiscent of the British blockade of Rio de Janeiro. A portion of the Brazilian press framed the sectional confrontation in Salvador as the "American Question," referring this time to the challenge to Brazilian sovereignty posed by a Union warship. The same adjectives directed at British cruisers were now used to qualify the actions of the USS *Wachusett*, in effect reversing the language the Union used to describe the Confederate navy. The Bahian press denounced the incident as a "slaughter" that violated Brazilian independence, a "highly treacherous procedure" and an "act of piracy."[89] The public outpouring of nationalist sentiment even led to the open articulation of sympathy for the Confederacy, as in the case of the newspaper *O Constitucional*: "No reparation will be complete unless the Florida is placed in the anchorage where she used to be, with everything she had inside, and if this does not happen within a short period of time to be determined by our government, it must immediately recognize the independence and sovereignty of the southern states."[90]

Brazil demanded a solemn and public statement from the Union government condemning the actions of the USS *Wachusett*, the dismissal of Captain Collins, the release of the crew of the CSS *Florida*, and the return of the ship to the Brazilian authorities so that the empire could send it back to the Confederates. William Seward responded cautiously, admitting only that the capture had been "an unauthorized, unlawful, and indefensible exercise of the naval power of the United States in a foreign country, in defiance of its established and duly recognized Government."[91] Seward did grant some of Brazil's demands, however: a naval court-martial eventually found Napoleon Collins guilty of "violating the territorial jurisdiction of a neutral power." Consul Wilson lost his post, and the Brazilian flag received the honors reserved for friendly nations.

The incident also made headlines in the United States. The *Times* of New York rejoiced in the Union's "daring naval achievement" in Brazil,[92] while the local chamber of commerce applauded Captain Collins's action. The *Courier des États Unis*, also published in New York, reported that the Richmond Congress had even recommended that the Confederate government send an agent to Brazil to discuss the case of the *Florida* and asked that the matter be submitted to the arbitration of a European power.[93] In his 1864 message to the US Congress, President Abraham Lincoln referred to the events in Brazil. Criticizing the decision of other maritime powers to "grant the privileges of a naval belligerent to the insurgents of the United States," Lincoln spoke of the need to reconcile the grievances created by the naval war in the Atlantic. "Unforeseen political difficulties have arisen, especially in the Brazilian and British ports and on the northern frontier of the United States, which have required, and will probably continue to require, the practice of constant vigilance and a just and conciliatory spirit on the part of the United States, as well as of the nations concerned and their governments."[94]

In the capital of Bahia, news of the North American clashes on provincial territory spread like wildfire in 1864, provoking outrage among the population.⁹⁵ The Bahia chief of police ordered his troops to monitor any threat to the public order, since "emotions were running high after the unqualified insult to Brazilian Nationality by the War Steamer of The United States of America."⁹⁶ Despite his efforts, though, a group of "common people" gathered in protest outside the US consulate located on top of the Ladeira da Conceição in Salvador. Some men pulled the American coat of arms down from the building and tore it into shreds before a cheering crowd.⁹⁷ Later, in front of the customs house, some sailors from the CSS *Florida* tried to seize the Union coat of arms, but outraged Brazilians refused to give it to them. The newspaper *O Alabama* took a humorous look at the escape of US consul Thomas Wilson aboard the USS *Wachusett*. In October 1864 an imaginary conversation read:

> — Such carelessness!
> — What happened, man?
> — It is said that the face of Wilson, ex-consul of the United States,
>   was painted and tied to the body of a dog!
> — But if it were true!
> — No, this is not good.
> — Now, don't be annoying! It should have been gallant. Wish I could
>   have seen him! Whoever commits an ignominy . . .
> — Pi-i! Shut up now! I don't want any international complications.⁹⁸

Despite Brazilian reclamations, the CSS *Florida* was never returned to the empire, having sunk off the coast of Hampton Roads, Virginia, in late November 1864. The Union government reported that the steamer collapsed after being struck by a transport carrier, but contemporaries seemed to agree that the Union navy had sunk the *Florida* to prevent it from returning to Confederate hands. After the Bahia incident, Confederate and Union vessels continued to sail to Brazil in search of harbors of refuge from which to attack each other. The sheer profit Brazilians stood to make from outfitting and supplying North American ships may have led coastal authorities to overlook the formalities of maintaining Brazil's neutral status. On the other hand, captains on both sides of the conflict elicited Brazilian hospitality by relying on long-established subterfuges that seafarers used to overcome imperial rivalries, war, and prohibitions on the slave trade. The Confederates often claimed distress at sea, as earlier slave traders had done, to evade waters protected by antitrade sanctions. Maritime distress was the argument of choice for

Southern privateers who stopped at neutral ports in Latin America during the Civil War.[99]

"Embarking with the Americans"

On June 6, 1865, as the US Civil War drew to a close, the Brazilian government sent out a dispatch to its bureaucrats communicating that the Confederate states should no longer be granted belligerent status.[100] Emperor Pedro II was lenient, however, and gave the Confederate ships that continued to call on Brazilian ports four months to respond to his decision.[101] North American ships in transit along the Brazilian coast continued to expand the geopolitical imagination of Afro-descendants in the years to come. When the United States became a new site of black emancipation in 1865, US ships became an even more attractive destination for people escaping slavery in Brazil. North American presence inspired the maritime resistance of enslaved people especially in Santa Catarina, a Brazilian province located halfway between Rio de Janeiro and Buenos Aires. Bordering Argentina to the west and the Atlantic Ocean to the east, it encompassed both a swath of continental territory and the island where the capital, Nossa Senhora do Desterro (now Florianópolis), was located. In 1855, Desterro had 5,611 inhabitants, nearly 25 percent of whom were enslaved.[102] Through its ports passed ships bound for the bustling markets of Rio de Janeiro, Rio Grande do Sul, and Buenos Aires, as well as Union whalers headed toward Pacific fishing grounds. Desterro's whale oil factories provided lighting for most of Brazil's provinces, and by midcentury it became a hub for Afro-descendants interested in "embarking with the Americans" who stopped there on their way to the American West or the Pacific.[103]

Santa Catarina hardly conjures up traditional images of Brazilian slavery. The province flourished as an important hub in the domestic food market, exporting staples such as cassava flour, sugar, and rum, especially to Rio de Janeiro. Although part of Atlantic commercial circuits since colonial times, the province never developed the kind of plantation regime seen in other parts of the empire. Its diversified economy, however, also depended on slavery, which existed alongside the free labor of European immigrants. Enslaved and free people of color could be easily found on Desterro's streets and wharves working as vendors, stevedores, ferrymen, and artisans. Many arrived in the city by canoe, transporting agricultural products from rural parishes, or hired out their services to contractors associated with the

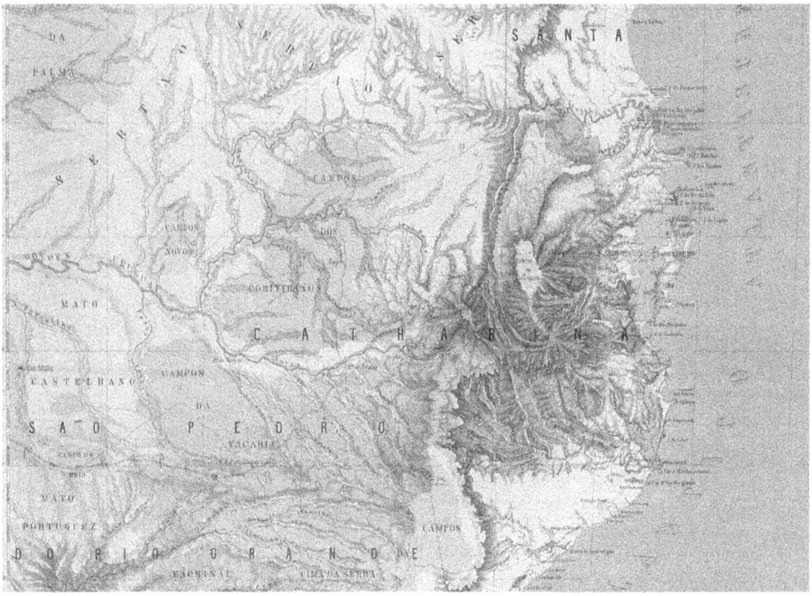

Figure 10. Detail of a map of Santa Catarina's littoral, 1863 with Desterro on the center right. "Mappa da Provincia de Santa Catharina do Imperio do Brasil com as partes adjacentes das Provicncias do Parana e de São Pedro do Rio Grande do Sul/ traçado e desenhado por Woldemar Schultz e completado com os novos trabalhos feitos pelo mesmo e seu companheiro o Barão O Byrn durante as excursões que fizeram nos annos 1859 e 1860," Biblioteca Nacional, Brazil.

intermittent movement of ports and public works.[104] Others had long been linked to the island's whaling industry, historically the largest slave-owning enterprise in Santa Catarina.[105]

The relationship between this part of Brazil and the United States dated back many years. US citizens en route to the gold mines of California in the late 1840s took the province by storm as their ships traveled west by going around Cape Horn, often stopping first in Rio de Janeiro and then in the village of Desterro to refuel or gather provisions. In 1849 alone, for example, eighty-six ships bound for California passed through Santa Catarina.[106] US whalers had also been hunting sperm whales off the coast of Brazil since at least the early 1800s, when Portugal allowed foreigners to fish in Brazilian waters. Sailing out of New England, they plied the South Atlantic for oil and baleen (whalebone), following the migrations of whale populations that typically reached Brazilian waters between June and September. Like other commercial vessels, US whalers stopped along the South American coast for supplies, emergency repairs, or to disembark injured or sick sailors. Brazilian whaling took place primarily off the coasts of Bahia, Rio de Janeiro, São Paulo, and Santa Catarina.

At their height in the 1850s, US whaling expeditions, famous for the perils of the hunt, became even more dangerous during the US Civil War. Confederate cruisers such as the *Alabama* and *Florida* deliberately targeted Union whalers on the high seas, sinking, burning, or hauling ships along as prizes. Despite the dangers of escaping aboard ships engaged in an Atlantic conflict, however, enslaved people in Brazil could not ignore rumors of imminent emancipation. Warfare extended freedom's horizon to the holds of US ships docked in Brazilian ports. At the very least, Union whalers offered Afro-descendants a way out of a slave empire, albeit through participation in the harsh world of maritime labor. In practice, most enslaved people expected to gain free status as soon as they stepped onto US territory, although Brazilian law never ceased to classify them as runaways. They made their way to North American ships by stealing canoes and small boats or by enlisting the help of sympathetic ship captains. In time, such shipboard escapes made them skilled sailors and part of vast networks of escapees that extended inland. Of the steady stream of escaped slaves who left their masters in Santa Catarina, some found new lives as sailors aboard whalers, others reached free soil in the United States, and many more found servitude under new owners elsewhere in the Atlantic.

In taking up maritime marronage, Afro-descendants joined a transatlantic practice that shaped abolitionist politics wherever slavery had existed since the Age of Revolution.[107] In Brazil, there was a long tradition of fleeing enslavement by seeking berths on ships that eventually overlapped with the era of British suppression.[108] In the imperial capital, British ships were popular with those who wanted to leave their masters, a practice reminiscent of africanos livres' pursuit of protection at British consulates. In January 1856, Bento Congo, a man enslaved by José Antônio Oliveira, and Antônio Benguela, enslaved by Tomás Rodrigues, absconded on the HMS *Danube*, a merchant ship carrying materials from England for the construction of the Pedro II Railway in Rio de Janeiro.[109] By March, the number of enslaved people escaping to ships in Rio was so high that a group of slaveholders from the port area petitioned the chief of police to intervene. These local businessmen held the British responsible for conspiring with Brazilian officials to entice slaves to run away. "If in the past, Your Excellency, all these facts and others were committed by English captains of merchant ships, may you not discover, with the insight and illustration that characterize you, that they involve a notorious politician, sharpened by greed and sordid selfishness? In this case, Your Excellency will be doing yet another public service, by revealing to the country a plot hatched against Brazilian fortune."[110]

The enslaved also sought refuge aboard US ships, which had integrated Atlantic maritime escape routes before the Civil War. Once again, they assumed that radical change hinged on their ability to form strategic bonds with foreigners, even if these bonds were temporary and rooted in unequal power relations. In 1857, the US consul in Pernambuco, Alexandre H. Clemente, turned over to Brazilian authorities an enslaved man who had been found aboard the *Timor*, a US ship that had left Rio de Janeiro with a cargo of coffee bound for New Orleans.[111] Escaped slaves claiming foreign ships as safe havens approached the Brazilian coast as an international border shaped by the asymmetrical nature of the laws of slavery and freedom in the Atlantic world. In this environment, their political struggles took on immediate transatlantic dimensions, reverberating in the urban and rural hinterlands they had left behind.

Complaints about slaves escaping to whalers on the Brazilian coast have accompanied the history of US fishing abroad, dating back to colonial times.[112] While anchored in Brazilian ports, some North American whale fisheries hoping to cut costs actively took local escapees on board as crewmen. Facing high rates of desertion and deaths or starting off with just enough men to make it to whale-killing waters, US captains often signed on entire international crews, paying foreigners less than US sailors earned. The fate of escaped slaves was probably more like that of those who had no experience at sea and signed on as unskilled laborers, cooks, or stewards in exchange for clothing or food.[113] Sometimes, though, passage on a whaling ship could mean a way back into the world of the Atlantic slave trade. Whalers sailing south from New Bedford, Nantucket Island, New London, and Sag Harbor are known to have been engaged in illegal slave voyages, often serving as disguises to deceive British cruisers.

The volume of slave escapes to Union whalers led Santa Catarina captains to seek out the press in 1865. Weekly advertisements for fugitives publicized escapes to national and foreign ships and warned sea captains not to aid runaways. Enslavers from Desterro expressed their concerns with rare clarity in a letter published by the newspaper *O Despertador*: "We have long heard complaints of slaves escaping on North American ships docked in the port of Santa Cruz; and the slave who escapes on such ships is lost to his master." They denounced "a barge from a North American ship anchored in Santo Antônio," which took away two men used to maritime work, "the first having declared long ago that he would run away with the Americans." The Desterro slaveholders went on to demand strict surveillance of US ships, suggesting that guards be sent on board "to keep watch during the last days of each stay; otherwise, whoever owns slaves who miss traveling will not be able to sleep in peace."[114]

The allure US ships exerted on Brazil's southern seaports can be illustrated by another episode that took place again in Desterro, shortly after the publication of the Santo Antônio letter. In May 1866, five masters petitioned President Adolfo de B. Cavalcanti de A. Lacerda for the return of six enslaved men who had escaped to the US ship *Marcella*. The whaler had entered the port on April 4, 1866, and was soon accused of seducing the enslaved with "the prospect of being freed from bondage."[115] Desterro owners demanded that the imperial government force Commander Henry B. Chase to either return their slaves or pay reparations if he dared to anchor in another Brazilian port. Along with the petition, they sent a list of the characteristics of the six men they claimed the North Americans had recruited as sailors. Francisco, Luiz, Jacinto, Floriano, João, and João were young, all between nineteen and thirty years old, at the peak of their working lives. President Lacerda immediately wrote to the US consul in Santa Catarina, Benjamin Lindsey, asking him to crack down on the dubious behavior of his nation's whaling ships. Lacerda argued that US captains were in the habit of coming to Desterro to take along slaves "with the intention of changing their condition."[116]

Consul Lindsey, himself a New Bedford native and editor of the whaling industry's weekly newspaper the *Whalemen's Shipping List and Merchant's Transcript*, promised to abide by the president's terms but admitted no wrongdoing on the part of North American skippers. Slave flight, however, continued to increase in 1866. Three men sailed on the USS *John Dowbrou* to the Cape Verde Islands off the coast of Africa, and others were captured on the island of São Miguel before reaching the brigs *Spartan* and *Triton* outside the port of Santa Cruz in 1866.[117] Among those arrested were three field workers who reportedly fled with the intention of boarding "an American ship." When asked why he had run away, the Brazilian-born José explained that he had planned his escape after meeting "the fugitive black man named Ignácio in the backlands of Inferninho, where he lives." Ignácio, enslaved by

Manoel Pacheco, had been away for four months "in search of another master" and agreed to help José find "a place to embark with the Americans"; he
advised him to go to Caieiras, an inland town west of Desterro, to find someone who could negotiate it.[118]

Sprawling networks shaped by the US presence cut across legal status. In
Caieiras, "after some asking around," José learned that "Carlos Americano"
(Carlos, the American), a resident of Estanisláu Beach, was the main link
between local black people and US ships. Carlos Americano immediately
agreed to help José and even encouraged him to bring other enslaved people
along, promising that "all those who go aboard will soon be free." Emboldened by the prospect of emancipation, José returned to his master's property
in Tijuquinha, near Caieiras, and invited Ignácio and Vicente to join him
on the escape. They then returned to Carlos Americano's house and got into
his canoe at midnight after paying a moderate fee and handing over their
personal knives.[119] José, Vicente, and Ignácio boarded a "three-masted fishing
boat" in the harbor of Santa Cruz that same evening.

After speaking "in a language they could not understand," Carlos Americano turned the three enslaved men over to Captain Chase, who hid the
stowaways behind barrels and lumber. Two days later, expecting a visit by
local authorities, Chase took the men to Pontal Beach, promising to come
back in a few nights. Ignácio described Pontal as a place akin to a quilombo,
populated by black runaways who were just waiting for an opportunity to
sail away from slavery in Brazil. Since Captain Chase never returned to land,
Ignácio, Vicente, and José set out on their own to another place called Ponta
Grossa, where the police arrested them as fugitives. A man at the port of
Santa Cruz had tipped off the officers, mentioning an encounter with the
enslaved men at the docks, where they claimed to be fishing for shrimp.[120] It
seemed that the vigilance of the authorities in Santa Catarina had finally paid
off after months of raids to uncover black networks of communication organized around Santa Cruz's restaurants, lodges, and drinking establishments.

Nevertheless, as the chief of police disparagingly put it, there was little
hope of preventing US whaling vessels from seducing enslaved people to the
coast "when they could offer the lure of freedom."[121] In 1867, a party sent by
him aboard a US vessel anchored again in the port of Santa Cruz arrested
Adriano dos Santos on suspicion of being enslaved by the Rio de Janeiro
firm of Cassão & Paranhos. In May 1868, Estevão, Paulo, Joaquim, Geraldo,
Domingos, Gregório, and Manoel escaped on the whaler *Highland Mary* of
Sag Harbor, New York, a ship flying British colors. In the name of Estevão's

owner, Luiza Maria Sabino, a certain Carlos Duarte Silva placed several advertisements in Desterro newspapers in early May publicizing his escape and anticipating Estevão's plan to "embark as a freeman on one of the North-American ships that usually call at the port of Santa Cruz."[122] Authorities finally learned of the escapees' plan from a Portuguese seaman named João Cardoso Jacques, who had deserted the *Highland Mary* after being severely punished by its captain A. B. French. Jacques revealed that the captain had hired Fructuoso as his chief recruiter on the coast of Santa Catarina. Fructuoso, a man enslaved by João José da Cunha, as we have seen, had escaped by sea from Santo Antônio three years earlier and boarded the *Highland Mary* in the United States at the height of the Civil War.

Upon learning of the joint escape, President Lacerda sent the Brazilian warship *Henrique Dias* in pursuit of the *Highland Mary*, but the whaler successfully sailed out of Santa Cruz harbor shortly before her arrival. The incident sparked outrage in the local press, which condemned Brazil's weakness in the face of the United States. This time, however, Captain French was convicted in absentia of stealing enslaved men, a rare instance in which the Brazilian government prosecuted a foreign national for threatening property rights in the empire.[123] It is impossible to determine whether any of the enslaved Brazilians who embarked on New England whalers ever received their de facto freedom. The men who traveled on the *John Downsen* became true Atlantic wanderers. Others were smuggled as captives by foreign privateers. With their manumission never formalized, escapees faced the risk of re-enslavement or even legal prosecution for past crimes whenever they returned to Brazil. Such was the case of Fructuoso, who despite spending three years at sea, including a passage through the United States, had to hide aboard a Union whaler to avoid capture by Santa Catarina police officers. Nevertheless, enslaved people continued to escape on ships, transforming the world's oceans and port spaces into contested sites of abolitionism.

Well into the 1870s, slave flight to British ships docked in Brazilian ports remained a point of contention between the two countries. The problem was so widespread that, on August 10, 1876, the British Foreign Office sent a final version of the *Instructions respecting reception of fugitive slaves on board Her Majesty's Ships* to the secretary of the Admiralty. The fugitive slave circular, addressed to all masters, captains, and commanding officers of the Queen's ships, was a new iteration of the instructions originally published in July 1875 and was soon rescinded after receiving heavy criticism from the British abolitionist press.

The circular set out the conditions under which ship captains could offer the protection of the British flag to fugitive slaves. "In any case in which you have received a fugitive slave on board your vessel and taken him under the protection of the British flag, whether within or beyond the territorial waters of any State, you will not admit or entertain any demand made upon you for his surrender on the ground of slavery." The 1876 circular departed from the cautious tone that abolitionists had called too lenient in the face of "the vested interests of slavery," by allowing captains to take enslaved people on board regardless of the risk to their lives. Decisions to aid those held in bondage, in violation of treaties with Great Britain, were to be guided not by local enslavers but by "considerations of humanity."[124]

When the new text of the instructions reached Brazil, the imperial government reacted with great discontentment. The State Council advised Emperor Pedro II to protest directly against the measure and recommended the creation of a police force to prevent the escape of enslaved people through Brazilian ports. Such a force, however, was to be mustered only in the event of a British attack on Brazilian sovereignty, since the councilors feared that patrols would "awaken or advise slaves" to the refuge they could find aboard British ships.[125] It was clearly too late for that. The admonition came after decades of surging maritime marronage to British and US ships.

*　*　*

The enslaved in Brazil invoked the hemispheric landscape of antislavery to subvert a system they knew to be transnational and deeply interconnected. Their imagining of North Americans as allies in their rebellions or of international ship holds as pathways to freedom points to the strategic nature of emancipation struggles in the second half of the nineteenth century. In times of rapid change, the Atlantic was an arena of social and spatial struggle, a place constantly evaluated by those attentive to news that slavery had already collapsed elsewhere. Brazil depended heavily on information disseminated through nautical sources. Ships were purveyors of print in the form of newspapers and letters, sites of intercultural encounters and interfaces with foreign people (especially seafarers) and ideas. On their decks, once spaces of the Middle Passage, waterborne elements of abolitionism also took shape. The stories from Maranhão, Bahia, and Santa Catarina show how seafarers, once the largest community of North Americans abroad, internationalized the US Civil War in the 1860s, offering enslaved people the opportunity to set the terms for personal interactions, diplomatic strategies, and the championing of the principle of free soil as a liberating mechanism. By crossing borders at sea, they advanced claims to state-sanctioned free status and rights that challenged the limits of Brazilian citizenship.[126] Fugitives waged a grassroots abolitionist campaign that was broader than Brazil's manumission laws.

Black insurgents, quilombolas, and runaways transformed the terrain of antislavery in Brazil by daring to envision the country as a battleground in a hemispheric war over slavery. A sense of possibility manifested itself in unexpected ways when US ships clashed on Brazilian coastal waters. Like floating embassies, these ships unlocked a new interface with Atlantic geopolitics through which Africans and Afro-descendants wrote themselves into international disputes. Docked in the middle of slave territory, ships offered black geopolitical imagination a degree of concreteness that has yet to be accounted for in narratives of abolitionism in the Americas. Geography, after all, referred not only to a sense of physical materiality but also to different ways of knowing the world.[127] And, for the enslaved, the expansion of print would do just that, bringing the US Civil War closer to black communities in the hinterlands of Brazil.

CHAPTER 4

Reading for Freedom

In the early days of May 1864, fireworks illuminated the narrow streets of the old colonial downtown of Diamantina, a mining village in the mineral-rich Serra do Espinhaço, a mountain range stretching from the center-north of Minas Gerais into Bahia. At 3,654 feet above sea level, the former Arraial do Tejuco sits on the steep side of a rocky valley cut across by the Jequitinhonha River, whose banks yielded enough gold and diamonds in the eighteenth century to make Brazil the most valuable possession of Portugal. The pyrotechnics added color to a landscape of almost lunar quality, dominated by granite foothills that extended as far as the eye could see. Paradoxically, the scenic vista bore an unsettling resemblance to riverbeds degraded by mining operations. The colorful display announced the consecration of a new archbishop, José Antônio dos Santos, and the beginning of the Festa do Divino Espírito Santo, or the Festival of the Holy Spirit, a three-day Catholic celebration of the third person of the Trinity. Such a large festive gathering also disrupted the working routine of slavery in the districts of Serro and Conceição, which, along with Diamantina, formed the administrative region of Comarca do Serro.

Nearly a century after the mining boom that brought global renown to Minas Gerais, Diamantina continued to stand out as the world's prime source of rough diamonds.[1] Local merchants employed enslaved labor to extract these uncut gems, which were then exported to Europe through the port of Rio de Janeiro, a journey of some four hundred miles to the south via the colonial-era Estrada Real. Mining and slavery thus linked the diamond-rich plateau to the Atlantic as the engines of an economy that had grown to include a domestic market for staple foods and a few manufactured goods.[2]

Minas Gerais was no outlier to the expansion of slavery in nineteenth-century Brazil. As the largest single slaveholding province in the empire, it

Figure 11. Bishop's Palace, Diamantina. Photograph by Augusto Riedel, 1868–69. Coleção Thereza Cristina Maria, Biblioteca Nacional, Brazil.

received a massive influx of enslaved Africans during this period. Between 1824 and 1833 alone, 59,040 newly arrived Africans—a staggering 40.7 percent of the 145,158 enslaved individuals who disembarked at the port of Rio de Janeiro—were sent to Minas.[3] Coming mainly from the Congo and Angola, some went to work in the coffee-growing Zona da Mata in the southeast of the province, but others ended up at Diamantina in 1864.[4] Africans and their descendants participated in the sacred and profane rituals that set the tone for the Festival of the Holy Spirit; they helped crown a festival emperor, played music at theatrical dances, and sold goods at improvised market stalls. While joyful revelry filled the streets of Diamantina, the holiday represented more than just a time for celebration. For the enslaved population in the nearby town of Serro, the occasion offered a rare opportunity to plot rebellion.

With their masters away in Diamantina, a group of enslaved artisans convened at the school building on the Sesmaria plantation owned by Francisca de Araújo Padilha, a property dedicated to growing sugar, corn, beans, and cassava for local consumption. They listened intently to the blacksmith Nuno as he laid out an escape plan to the *sertão* (backlands) of Minas Gerais—one he had previously discussed with fellow enslaved men Clementino, Chico, Luís, David, and Adão. Nuno's willingness to flee, however, was tempered by "news in the papers about the war" and the knowledge that "an order had come for the slaves to be freed, and that the whites were hiding this order."[5] He then called on those present to "make a *bagunça* [a mess] at the city of Serro" instead of staging a collective run to the woods.[6]

José Cabrinha and Demétrio, two of Nuno's most attentive listeners, agreed and shared additional information with the group. "According to their reading of the newspapers," said the stonemason Cabrinha, "we saw that the Liberals were tending to the issue of the emancipation of the slaves and, therefore, they [the enslaved] should seek to acquire it with their own hands."[7] Cabrinha referred to debates held at the Brazilian Parliament, where senators like José Inácio Silveira da Motta had recently introduced bills to prohibit the sale of the enslaved in public auctions and the separation of their families. Such amelioration projects channeled an elite version of antislavery tied to the modernizing dreams of white liberals, who conceived of liberty as a legal concept defined within a set of property relations and notions of public order.[8] In Cabrinha's understanding, however, Brazilian liberalism morphed into an invitation to the enslaved to participate in the literate culture where political representation took place.

After the Sesmaria meeting, the insurgents felt emboldened to expand their recruitment efforts throughout the Comarca do Serro. José Cabrinha started at Adão's tailor shop on the Rua das Flores, a popular gathering spot for the enslaved and freed people of Serro. He told Adão, a pardo man enslaved to Ermelinda Cândida Perpétua, that Nuno, Demétrio, and Sebastião—all *parceiros* (pals) at the Sesmaria—had "formed a plan to acquire freedom, because they were reading the papers, and from it, they saw that all the slaves were free, but that the whites were hiding it so that the slaves wouldn't know about it."[9] Adão listened carefully to Cabrinha and decided to make inquiries about the story around town, which confirmed the existence of a "war for the freedom of slaves in another country." Print culture and the vibrant insurgent tradition of the enslaved in Minas Gerais unleashed Adão's imagination to foresee a victorious black rebellion in the context of US abolition.

For insurgents who viewed the US Civil War as a movement kindred to struggles for emancipation in Brazil, rebellion flourished at the intersection of literacy and orality.[10] Though illiterate, Nuno invoked the authority of print at the Sesmaria meeting as if he had skimmed the newspapers. As we have seen, enslaved men like him often experienced written culture indirectly through literate acquaintances who made reading a collective exercise. Some of the 1864 insurgents were probably familiar with *O Jequitinhonha*, the only newspaper published in the Comarca do Serro in the early 1860s. The weekly often reported on the progress of the war, reprinting excerpts from foreign dailies and sharing its editors' impressions in articles such as the one suggestively titled "The United States and Slavery."[11] In the pages of *O Jequitinhonha*, one would learn that chattel slavery had caused the conflict on US soil and now threatened Brazil with a similar fate if the imperial government continued to avoid regulating a way out of it. For the enslaved, though, the combination of a war abroad with amelioration bills at home held out the horizon of black freedom, so much so that it was worth risking their lives in battle to overcome white resistance to emancipation.

Slave rebellions like the one in Serro and Diamantina draw attention to how Africans and their descendants used literacy in its multiple forms to pursue intelligence of the world and educate those excluded from the expanding culture of print. Obscured from the view of contemporaries who condemned and feared the education of the enslaved, black literacy activities happened almost everywhere. Insurgents exchanged letters between mines and cities, brought newspapers to the fields, and discussed imperial politics in small gatherings in their senzalas. In 1865, collective reading was again at the heart of a slave uprising in the Amazonian province of Pará, in northern Brazil. Enslaved people belonging to the Carmelite order rebelled against their overseer at a sugar plantation and demanded government support of their emancipation. This time, authorities found newspapers in the senzalas, suggesting that the rebels were acting on rumors about the US Civil War. In the second half of the nineteenth century, the diffusion of print increased opportunities for the enslaved to situate their activism within hemispheric history, and they did indeed escalate the social insurgency that contributed to the crisis of slavery in Brazil.[12]

Mining for News: Diamonds and Rebellion in Minas Gerais

In October 1864 the call for rebellion, first discussed at the Sesmaria plantation in May, had rallied the support of more than four hundred rebels—including enslaved people, quilombolas, libertos, and even some "men

Figure 12. View of the city of Serro, Minas Gerais. Photograph by Assis Alves Horta, 1953. Instituto do Patrimônio Histórico e Artístico Nacional, Brazil.

wearing ties"—from the *mineiro* villages of Serro, Itambé, Milho Verde, São Sebastião das Correntes, Rio do Peixe, Diamantina, and São João da Chapada.[13] The insurgents planned to gather on the last Sunday of the month in front of the Church of the Rosary in downtown Serro, the most popular place of black devotion; from there they would set fire to the homes of diamond traders and occupy the National Guard headquarters to obtain more weapons.[14] Once fully armed, the leaders vowed to spare no one. To "recalcitrant" slaves, José Cabrinha promised nothing but death.[15]

The conspiracy covered a five-mile radius from its epicenter in Serro, overlapping with black networks of communication that stretched into the senzalas, mines, and quilombos of the Jequitinhonha River valley. Most participants adhered to the movement after coming face-to-face with literate enslaved activists who, like José Cabrinha, wielded the authority of print to call for "a war, or an uprising of the slaves against the whites in order to be freed."[16] The story that expanded the scope of Brazil as a battleground in the US Civil War was powerful enough to prompt the enslaved to arm themselves. Passing by Adão's shop one day, the carpenter Ricardo from Diamantina talked to Cesário about the insurrection and heard that the people from the Barro mine were ready for battle.[17] One Sunday, after stopping to light a cigarette, Alexandre was drawn to a gathering at a senzala in Serro, where he learned about the uprising. Later, when he spoke to Clementino, he discovered that his parceiro had already been walking with a sword attached to his body, just like the quilombolas of Diamantina.

In mid-October, the carpenter Vicente, who had learned of the insurrectionary plot when he overheard the rebels' boastful discussion while repairing a sidewalk in Serro, betrayed the conspiracy to his master. Adão had reportedly proclaimed "as if by grace" at a fountain in town that the enslaved would soon be emancipated because the boys from the Sesmaria plantation "were about to make an uprising in favor of Freedom, according to the news they read in the papers."[18] To dispel police suspicions of his involvement, Vicente testified against his peers and argued that self-purchase was the only honorable means of achieving manumission. Upon hearing the news, his owner, the merchant Francisco Cornélio Ribeiro, convened a secret meeting with local diamond traders, authorities, and planters to devise a timely response to black insurgency. The white population of Serro, grateful for Vicente's denunciation, eventually organized a subscription to free him from bondage.[19]

Police commissioner José Maria Brandão cast the insurgents' plot in stark terms: "We are standing on a volcano that is about to erupt and decimate peaceful citizens, women and children."[20] The image of a volcanic eruption was not that phantasmagoric. To quell the rebellion, President Pedro Cerqueira Leite sent twenty-four cavalry troops from the capital, Ouro Preto, to Serro, recommended vigilance to the police authorities of the entire province, and authorized the assembly of forty cavalry and sixty infantry troops of the National Guard in the center of Diamantina. At his request, even the africanos livres arriving in Ouro Preto, over two hundred miles away, were sent directly into the custody of British mining companies, which the government praised for their disciplinary abilities.

Suppressed in its original form, the 1864 rebellion broke out as guerrilla warfare in the diamond mines of São João da Chapada, a mining hamlet located seventeen miles away from Diamantina. The small settlement of only 2,000 people had been built in the early 1830s at an elevation of 5,700 feet on the plain considered by many to be the highest point in the province of Minas.[21] From São João, slopes led down to the region's most important river basins; the source of the São João stream flowed south into the vast

Figure 13. Barro diamond mine, São João da Chapada, Minas Gerais. Photograph by Augusto Riedel, 1869. Coleção Thereza Cristina Maria, Biblioteca Nacional, Brazil.

São Francisco River, and a little more than five hundred steps to the northeast, the waters of the Duro stream flowed into the bed of the Jequitinhonha. These were also the inroads populated by several small quilombos, where Afro-descendants challenged the elite monopoly over mining by claiming viable territory beyond state sanction. In 1864 the insurgents occupied the village's main diamond mines, the Barro and the Duro, where more than 450 enslaved men worked in the excavation of diamantine veins that cut through both properties. Allied with the quilombolas, they waged war against police authorities and military troops, leading to a long and costly campaign of repression that lasted two months.

São João da Chapada epitomized the changing terrain of labor relations and land tenure in northern Minas. The mining outpost had been at the center of demarcation conflicts since the 1830s, when new legislation ended the colonial-era royal monopoly on diamond mining in Diamantina. Change

came after a severe drought in 1832 destroyed most of the agricultural production in the Comarca do Serro, spreading hunger and dispossession in
what became known as the Ano da Fumaça (Year of Smoke). Recognizing the
precarious nature of life in the region, Intendent João Pires Cardoso granted
poor miners the right to work on allotted diamond-bearing lands while
reserving the richest parcels for state use.[22] The *faiscadores*, as free landless
miners were called, could only mine on previously exploited land, usually
parcels that had been depleted by decades of alluvial mining. More promising "diamantine fields," on the other hand, were to be leased to men with
enough capital to excavate them.[23]

The 1864 rebellion proved to be a flash point in a broader wave of unrest
that swept the diamond mining region from 1840 through the late 1860s.
During this tumultuous period, the Comarca do Serro experienced a succession of invasions and bloody clashes at the mines themselves, largely driven
by dispossessed populations—almost always of color, including faiscadores,
quilombolas, and enslaved people—in pursuit of viable livelihoods. Land was
a pressing issue throughout the empire, and its regulation related directly to
elite anxieties about the supply of labor for Brazil's agro-exporting regions
after the abolition of the slave trade. In Diamantina, the phasing out of the
trade coincided with reforms that accentuated land concentration in the
1850s. New requirements for demarcation and registration of property, as well
as the policy of bidding for vacant land, led to intense conflict throughout the
rest of the century, as faiscadores and quilombolas in particular struggled to
assert their own politics of place.

In 1852, for instance, a new law replaced an 1845 decree regulating the
demarcation of diamond districts in Minas Gerais. Diamond-bearing lands
continued to belong to the state, with the Inspetoria da Administração e
Extração Diamantina, a kind of specialized office subordinated to the Provincial Treasury, as the state agency responsible for supervising the leasing
of parcels for diamond mining. The 1852 legislation, which favored miners
who already occupied land, eliminated the need for public auctions for new
leases, set a high price for measuring and leasing parcels, and stipulated that
each bidder could purchase no more than two of them. Wealthy miners were
able to get around the restrictions, however, by using middlemen to lease
different lots in their names and ensure control of the diamond trade. Only
land that had already been explored but remained vacant was required to be
auctioned. To maintain public order, the 1852 law also stipulated that some
sixty guards should remain at the disposal of the general inspector in the city

of Diamantina. The options for faiscadores were therefore limited. Since they had to pay a mining license to have access to the exhausted fields demarcated for their collective use, many decided to become day laborers in the service of slaveholders.[24]

In 1853, Antônio Correia Braga took advantage of the privatization of land to divide his large dig at São João da Chapada and create the Barro mine. Given the depth of the diamond reserves, two mining companies were created to manage the operation: the Lavra de Cima, led by merchants Rodrigo de Sousa Reis and Francisco José de Almeida; and the Lavra de Baixo, owned by Maria Antônia de Amorim and Felisberto Ferreira Brant, who would soon explore it exclusively with his children. Brant was a lieutenant in the National Guard who lived in São João, where he also had a pharmacy. Known for his prominent role as a member of the Liberal Party and for sponsoring a famous band of enslaved musicians, he also took on the role of *procurador fiscal* (tax attorney) in Diamantina, amassing a large fortune in diamonds, enslaved workers, and land.[25]

Since the 1850s, new diamond discoveries had stimulated migration to São João. Typically found ninety feet into the ground, diamonds required a great deal of scaffolding and effort from workers who scooped out and washed the stones out of the mineral-rich soil. Brant and Reis pioneered the use of British steam engines to pump water from nearby rivers and divert all that hydraulic power for excavation of the Barro and Duro mines. The pumps allowed them to increase the pace of work and keep the digs open all year long. The so-called modernization of diamond mining transformed the Barro and Duro into highly profitable enterprises without doing away with the dependence on slave labor. On the contrary, machines made the work regime even harsher by circumventing the seasonality of mining activity, so that enslaved people spent more time in the mines or in the final stages of washing rather than being moved to other activities during the rainy months. Work-related accidents and illnesses continued to occur, as well as sustained slave flight from the steam-powered mines.[26] Much like the more famous Paulista coffee plantations, which have been memorialized as crucial sites of "second slavery" in Brazil, diamond mines functioned as spaces for the entrenchment of bonded labor and the development of subaltern politics.

It is not difficult to imagine, then, how São João became a hotbed of both slave rebellion and agrarian conflict at midcentury. In 1863, authorities estimated that twelve thousand people worked in mining activities throughout the county of Diamantina, two-thirds of them enslaved.[27] In May, a bloody conflict involving faiscadores, enslaved people, and the police foreshadowed some of the tensions that would resurface in 1864. In the midst of a legal dispute over property rights between the former partners Felisberto Brant and Luiz Antônio Homem, six hundred faiscadores invaded the Duro mine. Claiming that Homem wanted to distribute his share of the Duro to landless miners, the faiscadores took up position on the left bank of the Duro River, facing more than a hundred troops lined up to "maintain the security of the property threatened by the *povo* [people]."[28] Bullets fired by police, civil militias, and the National Guard left six faiscadores dead and a dozen wounded, including enslaved persons.[29] After Vicente's betrayal of the slave insurrection in 1864, the Duro was again devastated, and a group of eighty slaves from the neighboring Barro mine escaped to join forces with the quilombolas of Diamantina.[30]

Mineiro elites framed the 1864 rebellion in the racialized language they often used to dismiss regional class and land conflicts. Provincial deputy José Joaquim Ferreira Rabello, whom the insurgents had chosen as one of their first targets, blamed the uprising on the lack of vigilance toward the free black population that had occupied the mines of São João da Chapada. In a letter to Cerqueira Leite, he concluded that slaveholders' negligence had dovetailed with the effects of the war unfolding in the United States:

> We have reason to believe that this revolt is being instigated by free people of color, members of the low classes, who perhaps guided by the horrible hope of profiting by lootings and armed robberies do not fear to drown themselves in the blood of their fellow citizens. Unfortunately, some circumstances that went unnoticed during the peace and tranquility in which we lived, today become vehement indications. Being it *the education of some slaves who read about the development of the Civil War in the United States only to pass the news on to those who don't know how to read* [emphasis added]; the purchase of firearms by the more daring ones; the state of excitement among them; the meetings and groups of four or more individuals, and the figurative and enigmatic conversations. We have few or no means of stopping these.[31]

Rabello emphasized (and criminalized) the connections between free and enslaved people through which black political consciousness was forged in Minas Gerais. Although he insisted on the theme of outside indoctrination of enslaved rebels, Rabello touched on the important relationships that dispossessed people built across the boundaries of slavery and freedom. Perceptions of the Civil War that began in print took on other meanings in the everyday lives of enslaved persons who often mined side by side with libertos, collected firewood in the forests, transported goods, and spent nights together in the mining barracks of Diamantina. Sometimes, they attended the same churches and brotherhoods—like the one devoted to Our Lady of the Rosary—or shared kin. Police authorities found this socializing dangerous and were especially weary of free black people acting as *falas* (literally a derivation from the verb "to speak" in Portuguese) or informants for the quilombos of the Jequitinhonha River valley. Quilombolas maintained close commercial ties with local senzalas and relied on falas for information about the proximity of slave catchers to survive in hiding. Their massive participation in the 1864 uprising was also a response to military expeditions and/or wealthy miners encroaching on their lands in the outskirts of Diamantina.

In Deputy Rabello's account of what had transpired in 1864, black education appeared as an issue of public safety.[32] He argued for a ban on black gatherings because these allowed literate people to verbally disclose powerful written narratives of emancipation to the enslaved. In addressing the sociability of reading as a seed of revolt, Rabello tapped into a peculiarity of semiliterate cultures. The penetration of print into the lives of Africans and Afro-descendants was not only a function of literacy but also depended on their desire for information in writing and on occasions when printed material could be conveyed through the spoken word. Written culture did not exist at the expense of orality in nineteenth-century Brazil; on the contrary, it traveled through speech to reach listening audiences that were often far removed from the original ideas on paper.[33]

Another example of the authority of print among the enslaved comes from the *engenhos* (sugar plantations) of Muribeca, province of Pernambuco, in 1862. That year, some enslaved workers met repeatedly at local *fábricas*, as the mills and boiling houses where sugar was refined were known, to organize an uprising that would span the Guararapes, Conceição, Santana, and Recreio plantations.[34] Insurgents expected to "march" over to other engenhos carrying "flags" that would signal to masters that the enslaved only wanted their emancipation. Recife's chief of police, José Antônio Vaz de Carvalhaes, referred to them as armed rebels convinced that either the Brazilian government or England would support their endeavors.[35] The African Januário Rebolo joined the conspiracy precisely because he believed that all the enslaved "had been freed by the Government, and that their masters had to pass on their letters." Such ideas about freedom, he explained, "were published by blacks who read newspapers aloud for others to listen."[36]

Januário referred to the oral dissemination of text as an act of publication, leading us back to a world in which print and oratory were mutually constitutive. The metaphor says much about the relationship between enslaved people and the newspapers; reading aloud released news for distribution within communities of learners concerned, for example, with the issue of black emancipation. Joaquim, a Brazilian-born slave, confirmed their access to the press in 1862: "Due to the newspapers that were read to many slaves by people whose names he did not know, the news spread that they were all free."[37] Geraldo, also Brazilian-born and enslaved, echoed Joaquim's sentiments, revealing that the insurgents were planning to "gather by the Formoso River with the purpose of obtaining their freedom, because Miguel, Constâncio and David read a newspaper and told them that the Government would protect them in their action."[38] In Brazil, perhaps we can imagine the existence of another public sphere, one that invokes print but also voice, embodied collectivity, and the lived experience of enslaved people.[39]

Atlantic abolitionism has placed a premium on printed discourse. The idea of fostering antislavery sentiments among the reading public or instigating literary discussion as a means of advancing the cause of freedom into the public sphere remains prevalent in accounts of abolitionist movements in both the United States and Latin America. In the 1860s, however, when the abolitionist movement was at best incipient and antislavery publications had limited circulation in Brazil, enslaved people found ways to reinterpret mainstream news and printed materials through the lens of their own experiences and political aspirations. By engaging in communal reading practices and oral transmission of news, they effectively expanded and transformed the meanings of these texts, laying the groundwork for a reading public that was attuned to the cause of abolition. When claiming ownership over the interpretation of news, the enslaved asserted their intellectual autonomy, even in the face of publications produced by and for a public that was complicit with the institution of slavery. Unlike the bourgeois public sphere, where the freedom of assembly and expression enabled open discourse, the enslaved had to operate under constant threat of punishment or violence. Their efforts to reinterpret information occurred clandestinely and precariously, marred by surveillance and the criminalization of black dissent.

As the examples from Pernambuco and Minas Gerais show, newspaper reading gave insurgents symbolic capital, as Afro-descendants often equated printed news with legality and government action. In March 1866, enslaved workers at Pernambuco sugar plantations organized another uprising to demand that authorities produce their manumission papers. Insurgents from the Belém and Condado plantations, along with quilombolas from the district of Pau d'Alho, prepared to "take part in a war to proclaim [shout out] the freedom of the slaves." They expected to "yank the Freedom paper" from the hands of Lieutenant Luís de Albuquerque Maranhão, whom they accused of hiding valuable information.[40] Government agents served as rallying points for abolitionist demands because the enslaved understood that the state could act as a counterweight to the power of their masters. Dreams of freedom found support not only in news of Atlantic emancipations but also in the domestic rhetoric that sudden changes in the condition of the enslaved in Brazil would turn the world upside down. Warnings that radical abolition would destroy the country's agricultural organization, that abolitionist propaganda endangered property rights, or that gradualism was all the imperial state could afford nurtured insurgent abolitionism.

Although reading hardly generates material products, traces of this elusive practice can also be recovered from legal sources. As arrests and interrogations progressed in Serro and Diamantina in late 1864, authorities discovered that the insurgents had varying levels of literacy and had exchanged letters since May.[41] Of the nine enslaved men singled out as leaders of the rebellion, five showed some familiarity with the written word. The artisans Adão, José Cabrinha, Demétrio, and David testified to their ability to read and write, while the enslaved domestic worker Sebastião affirmed that he "could hardly read the *letra redonda* [round letter]," probably referring to round hand.[42] The freedman Herculano Manoel de Barros, Adão's brother, revealed that "he could read and write poorly."[43] José Cabrinha was by far the most prolific author of letters sent to his parceiros through enslaved domestics who worked on the Sesmaria plantation. Leonel took notes to Adão about the loyalties of the enslaved in Diamantina; Timóteo delivered them to Nuno at the Liberdade plantation, the property of Serro's police commissioner.[44] Adão also sent letters from Serro to David and Francisco in Diamantina. To my knowledge, none of these letters have been archived by authorities in Brazil.

Writing, on the other hand, had long been associated with black rebellion in Minas Gerais. In 1848, Evaristo organized a conspiracy by distributing written scraps of paper to other enslaved persons in the Angahi da Ayuroca plantation, in the county of Baependi. "To each of his associates, he would give a kind of password, a *papelinho* [small piece of paper] slightly larger than a 3-pataca stamp, with the name of the slave who received it written on one side and the name of the slave's master in the middle." Evaristo told his peers that "not only were they free in their land, they were even more so by declaration of the Emperor, when he abdicated; and for this reason it was necessary to make an effort in the interest of having the freedom that belonged to them."[45] He pointed to the abdication of Brazil's first emperor, Pedro I, in 1831, the same year that Parliament passed the Feijó Law, which abolished the transatlantic slave trade to Brazil. Thus, Evaristo had ample reason to believe that emancipation had been a reality for quite some time. In fact, when he was arrested in 1848, he had a bag full of scraps of paper with him. Each of the other eleven insurgents captured that year also hid a *papelinho* in their clothing.

With few exceptions, almost all the Serro and Diamantina insurgents were born in Minas Gerais and had worked for the same owners since birth. Of the forty enslaved men indicted, twenty-one revealed their place of birth: Faustino was from Africa, sixteen other men were from local mineiro villages, and four were generically described as Brazilian-born black people (Creoles). Police officials diligently classified most in racial terms, demonstrating the extent of the Brazilian color spectrum: eight were described as *crioulo*, eight as *cabra*, three as *pardo* or mulatto, and one as *preto* or black, a term used to describe Africans. Within the local racial hierarchy and shades of blackness, people called *cabra* were the most devalued because of their unclear ancestry between black and racially mixed. Creoles were often the sons and daughters of African-born slaves and had darker skin than the cabras.

Despite their low status within the local racial landscape, the cabras José Cabrinha, Nuno, and Adão rose to leadership positions thanks to their occupational mobility and literacy skills. They belonged to a class of skilled craftsmen employed in various trades who circulated widely between Serro and Diamantina. Among the 1864 insurgents were tailors, stonemasons, muleteers, blacksmiths, shoemakers, joiners, and carpenters, whom the rebels considered "the most capable of motivating" the people to revolt.[46] Men like Cabrinha, in particular, demonstrated a remarkable ability to disseminate political knowledge by placing rumors, snippets of conversation overheard in masters' houses, and news on paper in an interpretive context that spoke to the conditions of enslavement.

Repression fell heavily on the black communities of Minas in 1864. Nine enslaved men were tried in November, and most were subjected to excruciating corporal punishment. None of the insurgents were sentenced to death, and for reasons still unknown, none of the Diamantina miners were even taken to court. José Cabrinha, considered by the police to be the supreme leader of the rebellion, received eight hundred lashes while waiting for the trial in Serro and was finally condemned to twenty years of forced labor (galés). Nuno, Demétrio, Adão, Leonel, and Sebastião were all sentenced to public floggings ranging from two hundred to nine hundred lashes each, followed by the use of an iron rack around their necks for periods varying from two months to one year. Nuno suffered a heart attack in prison but survived to complete his sentence. The enslaved miner Antônio and the quilombola Vitória, the only woman arrested in 1864 (see more about her in Chapter 5), were scheduled for trial but somehow escaped from the Serro city jail. Alexandre, José Cabrinha's brother, the freedman Herculano Manoel de Barros, and Faustino, the only enslaved African ever interrogated, were all acquitted. The tailors David and Francisco, who had recently been sold from Serro to Diamantina, testified, but only David was punished by being drafted into the army.

In 1866, José Cabrinha began his sentence in Ouro Preto and reappears in the Brazilian archives a year later. Having failed to have the ruling overturned by the Court of Appeals, his mistress, Francisca de Araújo Padilha, petitioned the emperor for pardon in 1867.[47] Padilha argued that Cabrinha had been the first insurgent to be put on trial in 1864 and had been made an example of undue justice in light of the terror that had gripped the Diamantina jury. An exclusively male punishment, the galés were reserved for prisoners over twenty-one years old and under sixty, and required the use of shackles on their feet attached to an iron chain. Convicts worked either alone or in groups on urban sanitation or public works projects. Despite the favorable opinions of imperial advisors, Padilha had the petition rejected in 1867 due to the exceptional circumstances of war in Brazil. On April 5, 1873, however, José Cabrinha managed to escape his sentence while on a work assignment in the town of Mariana. Along with fellow galés Ireno, José Gregório, and Joaquim Silvério, he vanished from the Mariana City Council during the day while being watched by two guards.[48]

The 1864 rebellion produced quite unusual information about the underworld of ordinary literacy practices that underpinned insurgent abolitionism in Minas Gerais. Trial records contain signatures of the enslaved, traces of networks of literate slaves, and direct references to the authority of press discourses over those concerned with the future of emancipation in Brazil.

Black abolitionism bears the imprint of these lettered and unlettered insurgents who enlisted the newspapers as another ally in their struggles against slavery.

"May Some Personality Be Given to Things": Antislavery in Print

"Books and magazines being still rare and expensive, the newspaper is the staple of literary *pabulum* throughout Minas," Sir Richard Francis Burton concluded. "In every shop from early dawn the master or his men may be seen wasting time—foreigners call it—over the periodicals. As the citizen of the United States, so the Brazilian finds amply sufficient enjoyment in a glass of water, here not iced, and a cigar, there a quid or chaw, accompanied by a newspaper."[49] This is how Burton, a British explorer and diplomat, described the print culture of Minas Gerais in the 1860s. Newspaper reading combined leisure and sociability, bringing people of all conditions and classes together in public spaces.[50] In a shop in Serro or Diamantina, "the master or his men" could pick up a paper, listen to active commentary on the news of the day, or perhaps just glance at the front page of *O Jequitinhonha* to get a taste of the political life of the country and the rest of the world. Though aimed at a white readership able to afford a subscription, newspapers achieved a wider reach through collective reading practices and oral communication networks that, as we have seen, extended into the senzalas.[51]

Burton, however, barely noticed the black population of Minas. A Victorian explorer experienced in traveling in the Middle East and Africa, he arrived in Brazil in 1864, when the British Foreign Service assigned him as consul to the city of Santos, on the coast of São Paulo. In 1867, he organized an expedition to the interior of the country, navigating over 1,500 miles of the São Francisco River from Sabará, in Minas Gerais, to the Paulo Affonso rapids, on the border between the provinces of Bahia and Alagoas, where the river turns towards the Atlantic Ocean. In 1868, his interest in the mineral wealth of Brazil led him to an overland diversion to Diamantina, where he spent ten days on muleback surveying the diamond washings of the Serra do Espinhaço. Burton described the landscape as "a fracas of Nature, a land of crisp Serras stripped to the bones, prickly and bristling with peaky hills and fragments of pure rock separated by deep gashes and gorges." In short, he concluded, "the land is also illiterate, and it is wild."[52] Despite such dismal impressions of the region, Burton's account of the diamond mines of São João da Chapada, including the Duro mine of Felisberto Ferreira Brant, who hosted him during his stay in Diamantina, occupies four chapters and sixty pages of the second volume of his *Exploration of the Highlands of the Brazil*.

In these supposedly "illiterate" diamantine highlands, the process of ending slavery in the United States lent itself to multiple interpretations in the press, which evolved along with the crisis of the Brazilian slave system. From an important element of the reformist rhetoric of liberal emancipationists in the 1860s, the Civil War went on to influence the terrain in which political actors finally approved Brazil's first emancipation law in the 1870s, and then reappeared in the work of Brazilian abolitionists like Joaquim Nabuco as a cautionary tale against the radicalization of abolitionism in the 1880s.[53] In the pages of *O Jequitinhonha*, the US war served as an ominous reminder of the need to implement at least some ameliorative policies in Brazil. Following in the footsteps of their national counterparts, mineiro liberals favored gradual and state-controlled abolition as the only mechanism to prevent a race war in the country.[54]

News of the latest battles fought in the United States arrived in Diamantina by print and word of mouth each time a merchant ship docked at the port of Rio de Janeiro to transport Minas's diamonds to Europe. *O Jequitinhonha* reprinted information gathered by Brazilian diplomats abroad or letters sent from correspondents in London, who in turn gathered news from US and European newspapers. With no reporting on the ground, the paper often published opinion pieces signed by one of its founders, Joaquim Felício dos Santos (1822–95). A writer, lawyer, professor, and journalist, Felício dos Santos graduated from the São Paulo Law School and returned to his native Diamantina in 1850. Ten years later, together with Giraldo Pacheco de Mello, he founded *O Jequitinhonha: Folha Politica, Litteraria e Noticiosa*.

The paper published both information and literary content. In his weekly column titled "Pages of Brazilian History Written in the Year 2000," Felício imagined conversations between a viscount and an emperor to offer comment on current political events. Between 1861 and 1862, he also published the chronicles of colonial life in the Comarca do Serro that would become his classic book *Memórias do distrito diamantino*.[55] The book offered a history of diamond mining and a critique of Portuguese rule in the region since the eighteenth century. Influenced by the work of the Liberal politician Teófilo Ottoni, Felício was a critic of Emperor Pedro II and, in 1871, he openly declared his republican sympathies.[56]

O Jequitinhonha began its coverage of the US Civil War in April 1861 in the context of a rejected ban on the sale of enslaved people at public auctions proposed in Congress by Senator Silveira da Motta. The paper denounced the maintenance of such enduring symbols of slavery as an attack on religion and civilization, in clear contrast to the "noble and humanitarian sentiments" of the Union, which promised to emerge victorious in the war.[57] Later that year, in a front-page editorial titled "Slavery in Brazil," it criticized the imperial government's passivity in the face of what it called "an institution from the pagan era." *O Jequitinhonha*'s editors called for the repeal of the 1835 law that shortened trial and sentencing procedures while increasing the number of crimes committed by the enslaved that were subject to the mandatory death penalty in Brazil.[58] It was imperative to "consider the slave as a man" and not as a "thing," the editors proclaimed, by giving him a measure of legal protection. "Brazil crosses its arms, and glances with a stupid gaze at the great struggle taking place in the United States; . . . it does not see that it is time, that it symbolizes the human spirit, or civilization itself."[59]

Articles like these drew the ire of conservative forces in Minas, who accused journalists of inciting slave rebellions in the Comarca do Serro. Especially during the electoral season, public figures like representative Cruz Machado called on liberal writers to answer accusations of preaching the end of slavery in print. Nevertheless, *O Jequitinhonha* continued unabated in its campaign to prepare Brazil to "inevitable historical changes." In December 1861, the paper reaffirmed its commitment to reform. Viewing slavery as a necessary evil, Joaquim Felício argued for legislative measures to improve the condition of the enslaved until more could be done. "We want abolition, it is true, but may it proceed cautiously, as all stable and lasting progress should be."[60] In line with the dominant antislavery currents of the time, he went on to advise readers of the need to prepare the enslaved for freedom and rescue them from the "moral degradation" of bondage that threatened society at large. Felício proposed, for example, a new law to encourage the religious education of enslaved people and even the granting of manumission to enslaved women who, after bearing many children, "distinguished themselves in the zealous performance of maternal duties."[61]

Brazilian newspapers were arenas of political controversy that very often revolved around slavery but relied on the exclusion of the enslaved from the public sphere. Print journalism was a relatively recent phenomenon dating back to 1808, when the Portuguese royal family moved to Rio de Janeiro to escape Napoleon's invasion of Portugal. Until then, the Portuguese crown had banned printing precisely because it feared the subversive potential of news in a colonial society. The debate over the circulation of newspapers had been political from the beginning, as Portugal wanted to avoid the spread of information in Brazil about the American, French, and Haitian revolutions.[62] For the most part, nineteenth-century newspapers normalized slaveholding ideology by printing advertisements for runaway slaves, notices of slave auctions or sales, and by portraying the enslaved as law-breaking individuals involved in a variety of crimes.[63] This was the case in O Jequitinhonha, which routinely supported mineiro slaveholders who invested in the capture of runaway slaves and the decimation of regional quilombos.

Throughout 1862, O Jequitinhonha followed with interest the debates taking place in the US Congress, believing that the war would at least influence the passage of a law declaring free those who escaped slavery in the South and managed to cross to free soil in the North. In June the paper published the latest news on emancipation in the District of Columbia, praising the Union Senate for linking abolition with financial compensation for masters and the distribution of funds for African Americans who wished to emigrate to Haiti or Liberia. "It would be great if the Brazilian government followed this example," the editors opined, and outlawed slavery at least in Rio de Janeiro, the capital of the empire, while it "could not heed the demands of humanity and reason, which it continues to violate with draconian slavery laws."[64] As the war progressed, President Abraham Lincoln also became a regular feature in the news, receiving increasing praise for his willingness to prevent the expansion of slavery in the Southern territories acquired during the conflict.[65]

At times, O Jequitinhonha published quite bold statements on the issue of emancipation, revealing that the genealogy of its liberal views went back to the tumultuous decades of 1820 and 1830. Although always fearful of the leveling potential of ideas of popular sovereignty and representative government, some Brazilian liberals argued at the time of independence in 1822 that slavery weakened the Brazilian economic system and exerted a destructive influence on the newly emancipated social body. O Jequitinhonha, always suspicious of the centralizing tendencies of Pedro II, used the liberal language of political emancipation to reaffirm its commitment to natural rights and religious philanthropy.

An editorial commemorating the fortieth anniversary of Brazil's independence in 1862 argued that "September 7th is a more memorable day for the dynasty of D. Pedro than for the nation; it elevated a family to a new empire, but when it comes to Brazilian emancipation, it was an incomplete act." The paper added that "in the act of independence we should also have proclaimed the emancipation of all Brazilians in order to be coherent with this great principle; . . . The least we should have done was to declare free every womb, to declare free every man who came to see the light of day for the first time on Brazilian soil."[66]

The mineiro newspaper's call to action resonated beyond Minas Gerais. In October 1862, *Actualidade*, an opposition periodical published in Rio de Janeiro, transcribed Joaquim Felício's equation of Brazilian political emancipation with abolition and denounced the silence that had so far characterized the imperial government's response to the upheavals taking place across the Atlantic. Anticipating the arguments of conservative critics wary of any public debate on the issue of slavery, the editors argued: "But fear not. We do not want to see slavery decisively abolished overnight. . . . We want respect for the rights of masters, but also respect for the human rights represented by the poor slave. We therefore call for the slow and gradual emancipation of slaves."[67]

Rio de Janeiro's newspapers, such as *Actualidade*, had covered the US Civil War since 1861 in relation to the diplomatic positions of England and France. Coverage continued as the conflict progressed, but press commentary eventually waned after 1862 under pressure and censorship from the imperial government. Because the Civil War required journalists to take a position on slave emancipation, they often faced backlash from the authorities. Proslavery writers preferred to ignore controversial issues and sought to silence critics of the institution who attacked it with their words. They feared that inflammatory accounts would trickle down to the enslaved and incite rebellion in Brazil. The conservative press was particularly adept at suppressing news of slave revolts, making newspapers such as the semiofficial *Jornal do Commercio* complicit in the idea that slaveholders held absolute power over their property in persons.

US emancipation first appeared in the pages of *O Jequitinhonha* in November 1862 in a brief passage about the defeat of the Confederates in Virginia: "President Lincoln has decided that from January 1, 1863, the slaves of the States remaining in rebellion shall be declared free without compensation."[68] Curiously, the issue did not generate much comment until mid-1863, but news of the war's turn toward the Union appeared frequently in the paper, sometimes alongside correspondence denouncing the growth of quilombola crime in Diamantina.

In 1863 the "Anglo-Brazilian question" also came to preoccupy the residents of Serro and Diamantina. *O Jequitinhonha* published William Christie's correspondence with Brazilian authorities, taking a patriotic stance on the side of the imperial government, which it usually criticized. On January 24, the headline "English Pirates" announced the topic that would occupy the entire front page of the paper. Felício blamed Britain's "unspeakable violence" against Brazil on the effects of the US Civil War: "Unfortunately, poor Albion is in a sad state of misery due to the lack of cotton. If the government of the gracious Queen Victoria does not resort to piracy, it will not be able to satisfy these waves of workers who are invading the great capital and dying of hunger."[69] In Diamantina, where the city council had convened a special session the day before to discuss the Christie Affair, the commitment of the press echoed that of civil activists. On February 1, the Sete de Setembro Association held a commemoration of Brazilian independence and led nearly two thousand people in a parade through the streets of Diamantina to the sound of a military band playing the national anthem. As elsewhere in the empire, no one in the region would have missed the talk of a war against Britain, also popularized at the Santa Isabel Theater by the sold-out play *John Bull or O Pirata Inglês*, written by Joaquim Felício dos Santos.[70]

Anglo-Brazilian relations dominated print discourse for months. It was not until June 1863 that Joaquim Felício returned to the analysis of the US Civil War. In a two-page article entitled "The United States of America and Slavery," he equated the horrors of Southern slavery, as described by a M. Bandim in 1857, with the reality of bondspeople in Brazil, whose masters insisted on treating as "irrational property." Moreover, Felício defined the war as a warning to the Bragança monarchy about the limits of Brazilian legislation on slavery, which was based on Roman law tempered by Christian ideals. "It enshrines the principle that the slave is a thing [*res*], a principle that has many consequences and that justifies, according to the law, all the actions of the masters with regard to their rational property; but does it justify them according to reason?"[71]

Despite all his judicious criticism, Felício's final policy prescription was gradualist and respectful of property rights, which differed sharply from the interpretation it received among the enslaved of Serro and Diamantina in 1864. Noting the difficulty of the press in discussing "so delicate a question" as slavery, he preached to readers: "May some abuses be prevented; may some degrading spectacles be forbidden among us; may the ground be prepared for the time of complete regeneration; may each one of us make a small sacrifice. May we not horrify the foreigner who treads our soil; in one word, *may some personality be given to things* [emphasis added]: this is what we ask for, this is what we demand in the name of humanity and reason."[72]

O Jequitinhonha's coverage of the Civil War ended in November 1863, when Joaquim Felício left Diamantina for a seat in the Brazilian Chamber of Deputies in Rio de Janeiro. The last word on the conflict was that the separatist forces were close to exhaustion and had therefore resorted to the "organization of a formidable army of blacks."[73] Before its demise, the periodical reported in vivid color the murder of a white man committed by runaway slaves in the locality of Pinheiro, on the outskirts of Diamantina. The editors' tone left little to the imagination when it came to local racial perceptions; the crime represented nothing less than "a photograph of heinous types. It is the infernal project of enslaved Africans" who had no sympathy for hard-working families. The "perverted maroons," blinded by their "savage instincts" and "cannibal ferocity," were, in their view, a blatant symbol of how slavery was corroding Brazilian society from within. Even among self-styled progressive liberals, antislavery had nothing to do with racial egalitarianism; rather, it was a matter of enlightened principle, a tool used to influence the debate over Brazil's political future. As the 1864 insurgents demonstrated, it was up to them to wage a war to ensure that the futures of Brazil and the United States intertwined in the pursuit of black freedom.

Literacy and the Geopolitical Imagination

Wartime events in the United States continued to open new spaces for the development of an internationalist imagination after the 1864 rebellion in Serro and Diamantina. On July 4, 1865, enslaved people from the northern province of Pará struck out for freedom in hopeful anticipation of the abolition of slavery. They worked on the Pernambuco plantation, an estate located upstream from the capital city of Belém on the banks of the Guamá River, which flows in the mouth of the Amazon. Managed by Carmelite friars, the property was located on flood plains not far from the Atlantic Ocean, where slave labor was used to produce cacao, sugar, rice, manioc flour, meat, and hides.[74] The rebellion broke out on the morning of the fourth after the overseer ordered the punishment of some enslaved workers during their daily lineup.[75] The rebels took up arms and forced him to leave the estate in a canoe before fleeing to nearby quilombos. The overseer rowed directly to the Carmo convent in Belém and met with his superior, Friar Francisco da Natividade Azevedo, who reacted with great distress to the news of an uprising on a plantation notorious for its workers' disobedience.[76]

Friar Azevedo pondered that the Carmo slaves "had for so many years been in possession of a *de facto* liberty, indolence, and demoralization that it was even difficult to describe it."[77] Since the Cabanagem revolt (1835–40), one of the largest liberal revolts in Brazil involving peasants and the urban poor during the regency period, the enslaved had at times refused to work, disappeared into the forest, or defied direct orders from the Carmelites. According to Friar Natividade, the Pernambuco plantation was "more a heaven for deserters and assassins than an agricultural establishment," reflecting the state of decay in which many religious properties found themselves in imperial Brazil.[78] Once one of the richest orders in the empire, the Carmelites had lost much of their wealth by the 1860s due to mismanagement, debt, and, as some bishops noted, the "secularization of the friars," who were more concerned with the economic maintenance of the order's property than with religious activities.[79]

When the president of Pará, José Vieira Couto de Magalhães, was alerted to the massive escape of slaves from the Pernambuco plantation, he contacted the Ministry of Justice, considering the uprising "of some importance" because "the war in the United States" had spread the "belief" among Pará's slaves "that they would all be emancipated."[80] Many suspected that President Magalhães had already signed a manumission decree but refused to communicate it to local masters. Initially optimistic about the quelling of the uprising, Magalhães sent a steamship from the Companhia do Amazonas with eighty soldiers to lay siege to the Pernambuco plantation and capture the insurgents on the run. Officers had orders to arrest all enslaved males between the ages of twelve and sixty and bring them to Belém for imprisonment.[81] They knew that black activism in the region relied on alliances between senzalas and quilombos, which formed either within the boundaries of large estates or extended deep into the rainforest.

Written accounts of the war in the United States brought to the surface underlying tensions over labor rights that had long existed in the Carmelite properties in Pará. In 1860, at the end of an apostolic visitation to the Diocese of Belém, Friar Joaquim José da Silva Costa lamented the state of the three plantations administered by the Carmo convent. At that time, the Pernambuco, Engenhoca, and Cabresto plantations had a total of 203 enslaved workers, although their production was barely enough to meet the basic needs of such a robust workforce. The order's dire economic situation contrasted with the opportunities for black autonomy offered by the forest: "In general, the slaves do not offer blind obedience, as in the south of the Empire, and they work because they want to, and because of the resources and wild fruits they can find in the forest, in the quilombos, and in the neutral nations on the border, which treat them as if they were free." Given the impossibility of disciplining the enslaved, Friar Costa thought that the best solution was "to live fraternally with them, being even more convenient to liberate them."[82]

Fearing that the Pernambuco plantation could become "the nucleus of a general slave uprising" in 1865, President Magalhães sent a second military expedition to the property on July 10 under the command of José Geraldo Barroso da Silva. The lieutenant left Belém aboard the steamer *Tabatinga* and anchored the next morning at the Carmelites' property with orders to raid all the quilombos he could find along the Guamá River. With the assistance of the National Guard, Barroso set up a camp outside the embattled plantation and, from there, sent search parties into the forest in hopes of spotting the rebels. He also surveyed the Engenhoca and Cabresto sugar mills, where enslaved people were believed to be aiding the rebels with food, weapons, and information.[83]

Within a week, Barroso's troops had gathered enough intelligence to raid the quilombos of Maracanã, Guajarámirim, and Jacareconha, all of which were accused of supporting the uprising. Soldiers burned a total of nineteen dwellings and several ovens used to make manioc flour in Jacareconha. They shot and killed two quilombolas and also destroyed fourteen slave huts built in the woods within the Pernambuco plantation.[84] After the destruction of the quilombos, some escapees turned themselves in to Lieutenant Barroso, complaining of hunger and fear of further reprisals. Of the fifty-four quilombolas, twelve remained at large. The soldiers eventually brought twenty insurgents to Belém, including the alleged leaders Joaquim and Marcos, to whom Friar Natividade added another fifty captured by private parties.[85]

Despite the large repressive campaign of guerrilla warfare and the deployment of nearly two hundred troops, the propertied classes of Belém still feared for their lives at the end of July 1865. After the return of the *Tabatinga* to the capital, some merchants moved out, taking everything they had on board ships docked in the port of Belém.[86] The specter of a provincial rebellion hovered so ominously over Pará that in August President Magalhães petitioned the imperial government for a special credit line to finance the crackdown on the enslaved. He described the uprising on the Pernambuco plantation as "a bad example rooted in the spirit of the greater part of the bondsmen of the Province, who envision their imminent emancipation in the facts taking place in the United States." The Ministry of Justice soon committed and authorized the allocation of 10.000$000 réis to Pará from the so-called secret appropriation funds, that is, an emergency account usually reserved for cases of insurrection, war, or sedition.[87]

The slave rebellion of 1865 was representative of a larger phenomenon in northern Brazil. In early 1864, the authorities in Codó, Maranhão, received a complaint about the fact that at "a dinner organized by slaves, and attended by some free men, they gave *vivas* to the Republic, to Freedom, and to the American war."[88] Later that year, the situation foreshadowed in Pará led local authorities to stockpile arms and ammunition in anticipation of uprisings throughout the province of Maranhão. In Viana and Turiaçu, where the passage of the CSS *Sumter* had inspired a slave conspiracy in 1861, they expected nothing less than "an invasion" by the quilombolas (see Chapter 5).

Taken to the Belém jail, the Pernambuco insurgents were charged, and their presence sparked rumors that President Magalhães planned to auction them off. The *Jornal do Amazonas* published the story, fueling a lengthy dispute between secular authorities and the Catholic Church over the placement of "rebel slaves." The bishop of Pará, Antônio Macedo da Costa, challenged the authority of the provincial government to dispose of the sacred property of a religious corporation, claiming that the enslaved—like all other Church "assets"—belonged to and should first benefit God and the poor. Citing the rulings of the Council of Trent and the role of Emperor Pedro II as patron of Catholics in Brazil, he fiercely criticized President Magalhães in the press, all the while portraying the Carmelites as excellent slave masters.[89]

In an outraged response to Bishop Costa's tirade in the press, President Magalhães criticized the Catholic Church's lax treatment of its enslaved workers. Defending his initial response to the uprising on the Pernambuco plantation, Magalhães remarked: "If, instead of giving the order to sell the slaves and exchange their value for bonds, I had given the order to free them all, Your Excellency would have responded with the thunderbolt of excommunication!"[90] In addition, President Magalhães, referring to the role of the press in fomenting popular discontent in Pará, warned the bishop of the cumulative nature of the problem at hand:

Shaken by fear, the population witnesses with increasing horror the theft of a police canoe and the escape of twenty slaves on May 9th, and the escape of another twenty from Lieutenant Colonel Lima on June 24th, and finally the rebellion of those of the Carmo Convent on the 4th of this month; in this progression against which I struggle in the midst of such difficult circumstances as the current one, you would advise me to resort to the only means I had to destroy this terrible den that answers to the name of Pernambuco Plantation.

I am burdened, Bishop, with the terrible responsibility of ensuring public safety and tranquility. . . . It is believed among the bondsmen of Pará, and those belonging to the Carmelites play in it the greatest part, that they have all been recently freed, and that I am the one who withholds their emancipation Decree. *The Carmo slaves also have newspapers.*[91]

Enslaved insurgents in Pará had found reason in the local press to believe that their emancipation might well have become a historical imperative. In 1865, it should be noted, the US Civil War overlapped with the outbreak of the Triple Alliance War, and both conflicts combined to underscore the political urgency of the slave cause in Brazil.

Those living between Pará and Amapá, an adjacent territory disputed by Brazil and France, also heard the message. The minister of justice, José Tomás Nabuco de Araújo, feared that more than four thousand of them, "ill-inspired since the war of the United States," were preparing to flee to Amapá, hoping to find freedom at the French Guiana.[92] More than seventy enslaved individuals took this route in May, and another forty-four, accompanied by sixteen freedmen, escaped from Cintra to Amapá in August 1865.[93] The issue of international slave flight reached the State Council in early 1866, prompting an interesting response from the councilors José Antônio Pimenta Bueno, the Viscount of Uruguai, and the Viscount of Jequitinhonha. Reflecting on the aid to fugitives allegedly provided by the French government, they mused: "Slavery is an immoral institution, and the country which has the misfortune to possess it should not count on the aid of those who do not. Evasion shall progressively increase at the borders of Brazil; it is one of the many symptoms of fermentation that this shameful institution reveals, and that undoubtedly requires the vigilant attention of the Government."[94]

Brazilian elites feared both the geographic advance of abolition and the symbolic capital that literacy afforded Afro-descendants in the 1860s. Reading for freedom was at the heart of the major slave rebellions of the decade. In November 1865, the minister of foreign affairs, José Antônio Saraiva, decided to censor the publication of articles from the *New York Times* and the *New York Herald* for containing mentions of President Lincoln's defense of emancipation.[95] By then, it was clear that the enslaved in Brazil, drawing on a long tradition of internationalism that included the radicalization of British antislavery and the US Civil War, saw freedom as something to be conquered rather than gradually granted.

Understanding how literacy and black abolitionism intersected requires moving beyond linear and progressive notions of cultural process as the correct way to conceptualize learning. Old divides such as oral versus literate only mask the complexity of black life in Brazil.[96] The surprise at finding enslaved people in Belém linking events recorded in writing to concrete struggles for freedom, for instance, dissipates when we address the misconception that news, once printed, carried an unambiguous message. Effective communication did not depend on the ability to remember things—such as newspaper words—in any precise form.[97] For the oral sectors of semiliterate cultures, perfect linguistic transmission over distance simply did not exist. Each time an enslaved person read newspapers aloud to others, he or she compelled the formation of new meanings by listeners. This practice made Atlantic abolitionism truly transnational as the enslaved applied the meanings of their own experiences to events happening beyond their immediate lived experience.

Africans and their descendants in Brazil followed multiple paths to literacy at varying ages. Self-education at home by overhearing lessons of slaveholders' children or by interacting with literate visitors led many to become familiar with reading and writing. The abolitionist lawyer and writer Luiz Gama (1830–82), one of the few freedmen to forge a career as a public intellectual in Brazil, famously recounted his experience of learning his "first letters" at age seventeen from a guest at his master's house in São Paulo. Then a domestic servant to the merchant Antônio Cardoso Ferreira, Gama formed a friendship with Antônio Rodrigues do Prado Júnior, a law student from Campinas who seems to have introduced him to reading. Gama was the son of a freedwoman of color from West Africa, Luisa Mahin, and a Portuguese merchant who sold him into slavery in Bahia when he was only ten years old. Around 1848 and thanks in part to his newfound literacy, Luiz Gama gathered enough evidence to prove his illegal enslavement (he was the son of a freedwoman and, therefore, free at birth) and guarantee his manumission.[98]

Gama further honed his literacy skills by consulting the barracks' library during his time in the Brazilian army and by working as a scribe for Counselor Francisco Maria Furtado de Mendonça, São Paulo's chief of police. In Furtado's office, Gama recalls being given "lessons in letters and civics" and being introduced to the world of legal knowledge.[99] Counselor Furtado was also the director of the library at the São Paulo Law School and may have facilitated Gama's access to the materials that allowed him to become a practicing lawyer, litigating freedom suits on behalf of illegally enslaved people. Gama once said that "he had no parchments, because intelligence repeals diplomas, like God repeals slavery."[100] He went on to work as a clerk and copyist in São Paulo police stations, the very places where he wrote his book, *Primeiras trovas burlescas de Getulino*, a collection of satirical poems published in 1859.[101]

Although his later trajectory as a self-taught attorney, journalist, and Freemason set him apart, Luiz Gama's educational experiences reflected the possibilities open to enslaved and free people of color in Brazil. For them, education often took place beyond the school environment in private settings, often by chance or through the demands of work itself. Enslaved people were part of the daily life of Brazilian typographies, for example, where they worked mostly in logistical roles but also benefited from a kind of vocational training that happened in the workplace. The journalist Max Fleiuss, son of the famous nineteenth-century cartoonist Henrique Fleiuss, claimed that "the first Alauzet machine that printed the *Jornal do Commercio* was operated by six black men, some of them slaves of the same newspaper, who turned its large 2-meter diameter wheel. Two of them were not only printers but also compositors of the daily."[102] Francisco de Paula Brito (1809–61), one of Rio de Janeiro's leading publishers and himself a free man of color, also employed enslaved workers in commercial printing.[103]

Britto's career complicates any simple portrait of the relationship between literacy and race in Brazil. Born a year after the establishment of the country's first printing press, Paula Brito wrote verse, published more than twenty-eight newspapers, promoted the literary work of authors such as Joaquim Maria Machado de Assis, and helped shape a national publishing market that grew alongside the Brazilian state. Raised in a family of educated freedpersons—artisans, freedwomen, and members of pardo battalions—who valued the connection between literacy and social mobility, he learned how to read from his sister on their cassava farm. In time, he went from apprentice printer to publisher, setting the standards of taste and cultural production in the imperial capital. Paula Brito's success embodied the contradictions of the slave society in which he flourished. Literate and a slaveholder himself, he deflected criticism of his racial identity with the phrase "virtue has no color," yet he embraced the civilizational project of the Brazilian slaveholding elite.[104]

Black literacy also intersected with print culture when notices of an enslaved person's ability to read and/or write appeared in the classified sections of newspapers. Slaveholders considered literate slaves valuable, dangerous, and more adept at evading capture. Examples abound. In 1855, the middle-aged José ran away from the plantation of Joaquim Lourenço Baeta Neves in Queluz, Minas Gerais. A blacksmith with white hair, he knew how to read and write.[105] The same was true of Hipólito, a twenty-four-year-old shoemaker who escaped from his master in Recife two years later.[106] Gabriel was rented out to work in the typography of the newspaper *O Paiz*, in São Luís, Maranhão, but escaped to build a new life in Pará or Lisbon. A young man of twenty years of age, his master advertised, he "can read, write, understands some French and draws."[107]

Sometimes literacy acquisition took place in the quilombos. In 1839 the liberto Cosme Bento das Chagas created a school for the alphabetization of runaway slaves in the community located at the Lagoa Amarela plantation in Brejo County, Maranhão. From there, under the title of "freedom's tutor and emperor," Cosme organized more than three thousand Afro-descendants to fight alongside the peasants during the Balaiada Revolt (1838–41).[108] In 1861, during a police raid on a quilombola ranch in Nova Almeida, Espírito Santo, primers, pamphlets, a spelling book, and manumission letters were found. The unnamed quilombola, authorities discovered, had been teaching the indigenous woman Maria Genoveva to write and was said to be learning the formalities of letter writing to better understand the process of purchasing emancipation.[109]

The enslaved navigated space mostly through oral communication but often with reference to authoritative written documents: passports, emancipation letters, laws, and news. Nineteenth-century Brazil was paradoxically a legalistic and semiliterate world where workers had to contend with a deeply notarial culture inherited from the Portuguese colonial state.[110] Ordinary people and elites alike learned to seek authentication and recording of all kinds of mundane transactions. Thus, for most enslaved people, the written word carried the weight of an official document. Nevertheless, the power of speech balanced the proliferation of print. Practices of oath taking, testimonies, proclamations, speeches, and recitation filled their daily experience.

Some texts, especially newly enacted laws, were only effective when read aloud in public places or churches.[111]

An example from 1852 illustrates the relationship between literacy and the law. At the beginning of that year, two related imperial decrees issued in 1851 came into force. One mandated the establishment of a civil registry (Imperial Decree on the Registration of Newborns and the Deceased) throughout Brazil, and the other scheduled the collection of data for a national census for the months of June and July. The massive government effort in information gathering provoked a strong popular reaction that led to the suspension of both decrees by the end of January.[112] The public announcement of new legislation was usually the responsibility of local priests, who read the decrees aloud at Sunday Mass to bring their congregations up to date. In 1852, churches and messengers became the target of an angry populace intent on preventing all correspondence from reaching the priests. Armed groups invaded churches in northeastern Brazil and threatened local magistrates charged with collecting data for the civil registry. In Pernambuco, Alagoas, and Paraíba, authorities counted scores of dead and wounded from the popular uprisings.

But why all the excitement about the propagation in writing of new laws? Two years after the end of the transatlantic slave trade, many believed that the civil registry and the census had been designed by the imperial government to count and subsequently enslave free people of color. Afro-descendants even nicknamed the decree requiring the registration of newborn and deceased persons the "Law of Captivity" (Lei do Cativeiro).[113] For our purposes, it is interesting to note how the fear of enslavement prompted a widespread, albeit decentralized, rebellion to prevent the verbal reproduction and textual dissemination of the law. Africans and Afro-descendants knew that the acts of recording and publishing someone's status (even if orally) were deeply political. Throughout Brazil, they threatened to tear up edicts posted on doors, confiscate books and papers, attack local scribes, and even kill anyone who read "the slavery paper" in public.[114]

Few have counted the enslaved as readers or writers in imperial Brazil, and yet they sometimes were. For those in bondage, literacy implied an alternative kind of logic, a specific engagement with power relations rooted in the contingencies of everyday life. By exchanging letters or participating in information circuits in which literate people read newspapers aloud, Afro-descendants developed a sense of trust in the written word and imbued messages with specific meanings around which practical resistance to enslavement could coalesce. In Serro and Diamantina or in Pará, collective reading practices about a war in print combined with the quotidian violence of slavery to allow insurgents to emerge as interlocutors in the emancipation process.

*   *   *

Slave activism challenges preconceived notions of how Brazilian society must have functioned in the past. Although denied citizenship under Pedro II, bondsmen like José Cabrinha and Nuno of Minas Gerais or the enslaved from the Pernambuco plantation in Pará helped shape an increasingly contested political terrain in which the future of slavery was at stake. Using their own channels of communication, they educated themselves about the first emancipationist projects being debated in the Brazilian Parliament and the US Civil War, and decided to push for immediate abolition through rebellion. In the 1860s, the collaborative nature of literacy played a key role in advancing diasporic visions of abolition and interweaving insurgent communities engaged in abolitionist praxis. Print helped the enslaved express the historic significance of their struggle by offering analogies with distant events.

Black literacy and the activism it spawned also invite us to rethink a master narrative of abolition that emphasizes legislative landmarks and the boundaries of the nation-state. Scholars of Brazil have written the broad story of how the Civil War reshaped the debate over slavery within the Brazilian state, but they have rarely stopped to fully consider the enslaved as part of the process. The rebellions examined in this chapter hopefully add diverse voices to the debate by showing how newspapers enabled enslaved people to navigate the country's political landscape in the terms of a transnational sense of belonging. Afro-descendants produced a distinctive narrative of emancipation in the 1860s, one that included notions of imminent abolition, land conflict, black hemispheric solidarity, and international pressure against slaveholding in Brazil. From their perspective, the US Civil War was part of the history of those still struggling for freedom, from the Serra do Espinhaço in Minas Gerais to the heart of the Amazon rainforest in Pará.

Black insurgency also highlights an important aspect of grassroots abolitionism that went beyond challenging the institution of slavery. These movements represented a broader threat to the hegemony of wealthy landowners in Brazilian society. By raising the possibility that dispossessed people of color, especially those from quilombos, would become an autonomous peasantry with control over the means of production, uprisings posed an enduring challenge to the existing economic and social order. Black abolitionism was, at its core, not merely about the legal abolition of slavery but rather a larger struggle for economic empowerment, land redistribution, and the dismantling of the systems that perpetuated racial oppression. Although often marked by internal tensions, quilombos played a crucial role in such abolitionist practice. Through the establishment of semi-independent communities, quilombolas engaged in a powerful act of repossession—reclaiming ownership over their bodies, land, and labor. In doing so, they linked the struggle for black liberation to the wars of the 1860s and to Brazil's broader agrarian history, intertwining the fight for land access with the pursuit of racial justice, as the next chapter will show.

CHAPTER 5

Quilombos and the Politics of Emancipation

Emancipatory work demanded strategic thinking, and one would be hard pressed to find savvier tacticians than quilombolas. A political force since colonial times, they continued to expose the seams of slave society in the second half of the nineteenth century by engaging in the larger struggle against racial oppression and economic exploitation in Brazil.[1] As members of either enduring rural polities or itinerant groups of men, women, and children on the run, fugitives from slavery relied on close relationships with senzalas and the marginalized poor to exist beyond the reach of their masters. Spread throughout the entire country in urban, mining, and rural areas, quilombolas needed economic partners, environmental expertise, and information to circulate undetected in a society that made no room for their integration. Theirs was a social world shrouded in secrecy, constant dislocation, and drawn-out resistance to slaveholder violence in which geopolitical literacy was a requirement for survival.[2]

In the 1860s, quilombos proliferated across the Brazilian landscape as wars became the signal issue of the decade. Fugitives from slavery lived globally enmeshed lives from which they gleaned insights to assess the possibilities of migration, rebellion, or retreat. Each emerging conflict advanced their understanding of abolition's relationship to history and prompted a realignment of political alliances and insurgent geographies. Though Brazilian authorities deemed these self-liberated communities unlawful (because existing outside their control), quilombos were not marginal to abolitionism. Rather, they were a driving force of hemispheric black politics propelling emancipation forward by rendering it obvious that neither the enslavers nor the imperial government could control the energies of subaltern resistance in the country. And when conflict erupted on the western border with Paraguay in late 1864, the last in a series of international influences on abolition, quilombolas seized the opportunity to reshape the struggle for freedom on the home front.[3]

The largest interstate war in South American history, the Paraguayan War or Triple Alliance War (1864–70) plunged Brazil into political turmoil while devastating Paraguay (which lost over half of its population in the conflict).[4] Brazil had long sought territory and political power in the River Plate region, sometimes claiming parts of it as an extension of its southern frontier. In 1825, it declared war on Buenos Aires over control of the Cisplatine Province (or Banda Oriental, invaded by the Portuguese in 1816). The conflict resulted in the independence of the República Oriental del Uruguay from Brazil in 1828, yet approximately one third of properties in the north of Uruguay remained in the hands of Brazilians. Again in 1851–52, Brazil formed an alliance with Uruguay and the Argentine provinces of Entre Ríos and Corrientes against Buenos Aires to support the defeat of Juan Manuel de Rosas. Throughout the decade, the imperial government faced sustained pressure from the cattle ranchers of Rio Grande do Sul who wanted to protect their interests across the border with Uruguay. Brazilians made up 10 percent of the neighboring country's population, and the region's political instability complicated the geopolitics of abolition, which was advancing in South America despite Brazil's attachment to slavery.[5]

The Platine region (encompassing parts of present-day Argentina, Uruguay, and Brazil) had developed as a crossroads of slavery on the transimperial border between Spain and Portugal in the Americas. Between 1777 and 1812, when the Buenos Aires government outlawed the slave trade, most enslaved people who entered the region did so through Brazilian ports, mostly Rio de Janeiro and Salvador.[6] Black social networks also developed along these trade routes, further connecting South America during the national era. Beginning in the 1810s, fugitives from slavery who crossed Brazil's southern borders with Platine countries regularly complicated diplomatic relations between territories ravaged by civil wars, social unrest, and gradual emancipation.[7] This was the case, for example, of fugitives who came to Montevideo when the Colorado government proclaimed the abolition of slavery in 1842, making freedmen eligible for military enlistment, or when the Blancos did the same in 1846, effectively turning Uruguay into free soil.[8] Competing national policies on slavery also created complex dynamics around the status of free black communities, who became vulnerable to re-enslavement and kidnapping by Brazilians.

In 1864 a Platine political crisis brought matters to a head. In April Brazil sent a diplomatic mission to Uruguay to demand payment for damages suffered by Rio Grande do Sul cattle ranchers in border disputes. Uruguayan president Atanásio Aguirre of the National Party refused to comply, rekindling fears of a Brazilian intervention along the lines of what had happened in the 1850s. On October 12, 1864, Brazil invaded Uruguay to overthrow Aguirre and the Blancos in alliance with the Colorado opposition and with the support of the Buenos Aires government. Fearing that his country would be next, Marshal Francisco Solano López ordered that the Paraguayan navy capture the Brazilian merchant ship *Marquês de Olinda* as it sailed up the Paraguay River on November 11, 1864.[9] Channeling the rivalries that had torn the Rio de la Plata basin since decolonization from Spain and Portugal, López declared war on Brazil on December 13 and invaded the province of Mato Grosso. Further offensives into the Argentine province of Corrientes and in Rio Grande do Sul escalated a conflict that few expected to last long. By 1866, López's offensive had ended and was replaced by a brutal siege of Paraguay waged by the allied forces of Brazil, Argentina, and Uruguay.

Paraguay's geography, with extensive swamps, marshes, and wetlands, presented an unfamiliar and challenging environment for Brazil's inexperienced army, which was still developing as an institution. The troops suffered from malnutrition, poor preparation, and rampant epidemic disease. Despite eventually achieving victory, the government of Pedro II dragged the country into economic exhaustion, with further indebtedness to Britain, and created a social environment where slavery faced new criticism. The conscription of a barely professional army to form the bulk of the allied forces fighting alongside Argentines and Uruguayans provoked domestic opposition, especially among popular sectors suspicious of military service as an instrument of social control.[10] Ultimately, the imperial authorities had to rely on the mustering of existing police forces, the National Guard, and the recruitment of freed slaves, a wartime policy that energized debates over the pace and timeline of emancipation.

The protracted and costly military endeavor in Paraguay provided new momentum for black abolitionism in Brazil. Often betting on the empire's defeat in the conflict, quilombolas took the lead in weaving together the geopolitical meanings of the Triple Alliance War. Subverting elite discourses in defense of national sovereignty, they seized the opportunity to act on information about "freedom, Lopez of Paraguay and many other dangerous things" amid a weakening of law enforcement in Brazil.[11] Local authorities were still struggling to quell black rebellion in Minas Gerais, for example, when they uncovered a large quilombola network in the outskirts of Diamantina in 1865. Vitória da Costa Pinheiro, a freedwoman who had "disappeared into the bushes for a long time to live with the *negros do mato* [bush negroes or quilombolas]," told the police that they believed that, with the outbreak of war, "they were about to be free and rich, and the whites poor." Along the Jequitinhonha River valley, many were ready to rise with scythes, knives, and firearms.[12] Sparked by news of the US Civil War, the 1864 uprising lived on in the defiant actions of escaped slaves like Vitória, who resided in a province threatened by Paraguayan invasion in May 1865.[13]

In Mato Grosso and Maranhão, the war also emboldened the abolitionist voices of quilombolas, who posed an ever-larger problem of governance as troop mobilization continued to undermine domestic policing. In Maranhão, the inhabitants of São Benedito do Céu, a quilombo that had prospered in the Turiaçu region over the 1860s when Anglo-American abolitionism hinted at the possibility of emancipation in Brazil, took up in arms in 1867. In July they descended on the sugar plantations of Viana, the same county set ablaze by the sightings of US ships in the port of São Luís in 1861. The quilombolas raided nearby towns by the hundreds, killing whites, shutting down sugar production, and daring to negotiate freedom by letter in one of the largest quilombola uprisings Brazil has ever seen.[14] It was no coincidence that these same black communities had engaged in acts of rebellion throughout the 1860s; their activism expressed the construction of a kind of emancipatory politics that linked war to the abolition of slavery.

The Paraguayan War, as it is popularly known in Brazil, occupies a powerful place in the national memory, but quilombolas are hardly a part of it. The conflict produced the military heroes of modern Brazil, immortalized in statues, street names, and textbooks that continue to educate the public in a rather masculine and elitist version of nineteenth-century state-building. When it comes to slavery, the war is usually portrayed as a catalyst for abolitionism because it strengthened military sectors critical of the monarchy and empowered black veterans returning from a victorious campaign abroad to a society that used to enslave them. The end of the conflict is credited with bringing the issue of slave emancipation back into the government's agenda, leading up to the passage of the Free Womb Law in 1871. This chapter explores a distinct facet of the Triple Alliance War by drawing attention to the grassroots politics of fugitives from slavery on the home front. I argue that, in the late 1860s, quilombolas emerged as an insurgent force that rejected the path of incremental emancipation pursued by the Brazilian government. Instead, they relied on literacy and the politics of place to position themselves directly as subjects in the process of abolition.

We begin our examination of quilombolas' politics of emancipation by reconstructing the social worlds of fugitives in Diamantina. Their experiences reveal how training for life at a quilombo began in bondage, with the enslaved running away for short periods of time, negotiating some degree of autonomy with masters—in the form of garden plots or trading in Sunday markets, for example—and creating relationships of trust and trade with surrounding communities.[15] Senzalas, as slave quarters are known in Brazil, were the cradle of the social, cultural, and political arrangements that gave birth to fugitive communities in the first place, and they continued to shape how these communities interpreted the currents of warfare that defined the 1860s.[16] Next, the wave of black conspiracies that followed the outbreak of war with Paraguay brings different wartime experiences into view. Enslaved people both resisted military service by hiding in quilombos and escaped slavery to present themselves as army volunteers in search of freedom. Quilombolas attacked troops sent to capture them in the Brazilian hinterlands and took advantage of military training offered by disgruntled national guardsmen to defend their livelihoods.[17] The late 1860s were, therefore, an important moment in the radicalization of black politics, which found expression in the quilombola rebellion of Viana, Maranhão, in 1867. That year, hundreds of fugitives waged war on provincial troops and forced an overseer to write a letter outlining the terms of their peace. Presenting themselves at once as writers-dictators and soldiers of their own war for emancipation, these quilombolas subverted their disenfranchisement to become the interlocutors of a society—and of a national historiography—that has consistently denied them a voice.

Information Gatekeepers:
The Social World of the Quilombolas

Slave rebellions were often open-ended processes rather than one-time events. Although authorities sought to establish a fixed timeline of incidents to declare the threat extinguished with the arrest of alleged ringleaders, black activism endured as enslaved rebels evaded capture, organized hit-and-run attacks on villages, and regrouped in quilombos, where they continued to mobilize for freedom for years to come.[18] The Serro and Diamantina uprising of 1864 was one of such long-lived movements, surviving into 1865 as the Triple Alliance War provided the backdrop for continued activism.[19] Quilombolas played an important role in shaping this subaltern culture of transgression, which also drew on women's struggles to remain masterless despite the gender and racial inequalities that held them in check in Brazil. They were often the keepers of information and economic circuits that structured the social lives of enslaved and poor people in places like Diamantina. And for these underground networks of trade and protection to endure, loyalty oaths were crucial.

In June 1865 quilombolas launched a daring attack on the home of Francisco Leandro Pires, a merchant in Farinha Seca, a mining village some five miles from Diamantina. A correspondent for *O Voluntário*, the local newspaper founded to cover the war against Paraguay, made the connection the slaveholders feared: "This fact is a consequence of that insurgent spirit that recently threatened the public tranquility of Serro. It is the breath of that slave hatred that signals its passage with robbery and murder."[20] Elected "emperor" of the Holy Spirit Festival, Francisco Pires had traveled to participate in the festivities, leaving his wife and her sister at home. On the night of June 8, the "pardas" Maria Rosa Pereira and Silvéria Maria Pereira had dinner with the cattle rancher Joaquim Alves da Calçada in Farinha Seca. Just before going to bed, at around ten o'clock, they heard someone knocking at the door. Joaquim asked who was calling so late and a male voice answered from outside: "It's me, I want to buy some *cachaça*!" The man was told that there was no sugar cane rum for sale, but the quilombolas suggested that they were used to negotiating with Francisco Leandro Pires. The voice from outside insisted: "There is cachaça, one of our comrades here bought it today and drank it. Open the door Mr. Chiquinho that I want to talk to you and I am a slave of Raimundo Pires."[21]

Silvéria vividly described what happened next. After the windows of the house were broken, "a voice from outside shouted: shoot! and at the same moment a big shot went off, or two at once; at that moment my sister, already mentioned here, fell and cried out: Our Lady of Sorrows, I'm dead!" Silvéria embraced Maria Rosa and, as they both fell, she heard another shot, "which was fired at her friend Joaquim Alves who was screaming at the same time: I'm dead!" She then saw two black men rush into the house while many others stood guard outside with rifles pointed at the window. Silvéria, the only person who survived that night, stayed under her sister's body, and pretended to be dead until the next morning.[22] Joaquim also resisted for a while before succumbing. He was lying injured on the ground when a man turned to him and asked: "What money have you got, devil?" Joaquim gave him everything he had in his pocket—some diamonds and money to pay a bill—and watched as the man took other items from Francisco's house: more diamonds kept as savings, gold dust, copper, money, wax, gunpowder, fireworks, boxes of dishes, and clothes.

It is unclear whether Joaquim knew the quilombolas, but his family certainly did. In early 1862, his sister Carolina Alves da Calçada had her tongue cut off by the same group of runaways for exposing the location of their quilombo on the outskirts of Diamantina. Carolina was ambushed, severely beaten, and left for dead in a ditch near the place known as Moinho do Choro. She had hired mercenaries to arrest an escaped slave who had been hiding in her house and collect the reward offered by his master.[23] Another one of her brothers found her at a "crumpled place which showed that there had been a fight there," with several traces "of people that seemed to be barefooted; people stepping with the tips of their feet, and barefoot, and there were in this place some drops of blood that followed until a channel behind the hill where there was a greater amount of blood."[24] The footprints of barefooted people (the enslaved did not wear shoes in Brazil) incriminated the members of the nearby quilombo. Carolina later confessed that two men "held her behind the gills" and "one of them said to the other (give me the handkerchief) and tied her eyes and said: you want to trick us, lost you will be."[25] Remembered by locals for decades, the attack revealed that quilombola life depended on systems of justice capable of ensuring the absolute loyalty of members and allies.

In 1865, building on previous knowledge about the quilombo, the Diamantina police dispatched a force to search all the houses adjacent to that of Francisco Leandro Pires, where they found stolen property and loaded guns.[26] On their way back to Diamantina, the officers arrested Tiago and Maria, a Brazilian-born couple enslaved by Joaquim José Simões, who had been missing for twenty days. Tiago was one of the quilombolas who had killed Joaquim and Maria Rosa. A twenty-four-year-old field worker, the son of the African Silvéria, he had tried to pass as a free and married man in Farinha Seca, asking "for shelter for the love of Our Lady of Mercês, because they were very tired."[27] At the time of her arrest, Maria was about twenty years old and carried two letters that suggested the couple's motivation for fleeing. One was signed by an uncle of Maria's master, who asked his nephew to forgive her "for a certain fault she has committed." The second letter was penned by a Joaquim Severiano de Aguilar, who refused to buy new slaves, citing a lack of money. It seems that Maria, faced with the threat of being sold to another owner, asked for the mediation of her master's uncle, who could not find another buyer for her. Illiterate herself, Maria chose to run away to the quilombo with Tiago, keeping the letters as leverage for an eventual negotiation.

The investigation into the murders of Joaquim and Maria Rosa led slave catchers to a place known as Buraco do Facho on August 18, 1865. An armed expedition, much like the ones leaving the province for Paraguay, stormed the quilombo at 4 a.m., killing the enslaved man Francisco while most of the quilombolas fled into the forest under heavy fire. The militiamen were only able to capture the women who stayed in place: Vitória, Praxedes, Eva, and Rita.[28] They were all libertas, or freedwomen, whose precarious existence underpinned political decisions to resort to marronage. Emancipationist politics in Minas Gerais also relied on the lived experiences of women like them rather than depending solely on spectacular acts of violence perpetrated by their fellow enslaved men.[29]

The female quilombolas of Diamantina come to life in the archival record as the fighters, seamstresses, cooks, traders, and informants who performed most of the logistical work behind the quilombo's longevity. Praxedes Padilha de Araújo was a thirty-year-old widow born in the city of Serro who "lived off her work" in Curralinho, a diamond district east of the city. Like Vitória, she told the police that enslaved men had taken her to the quilombo against her will. Francisco and João Rainha would have kidnapped her the week after Kings' Day (January 6) while she was working at a diamond mine. Praxedes went first to "a quilombo in the place called Ferreiro, and then to another quilombo not far from José Ferreira's house," and lately to a third quilombo "beyond the Mendanha, near the Jequitinhonha River, where there were three quilombola huts."[30] The three quilombos were the iterations of the same fugitive community, which kept moving in order to evade capture.

Praxedes accused her male peers of committing the Farinha Seca murders. She saw João Rainha, Francisco, and Jerônimo return to the quilombo the next morning "carrying the spoils of the robbery they had carried out at the house of Francisco Leandro Pires, such as wax candles, a sack of gunpowder, *chita* (cheap cotton cloth), a scythe, and a machete, all three with blood-stained clothes, and more stolen clothes, bloody, as well as the candles and the sickle that she and her companions had washed." According to her, the real targets of the attack were Maria Rosa and Silvéria, who had confided to a woman called Emília Carlota that they had a sword and a rifle ready in case the quilombolas dared to come after them. Like Carolina, the sisters had defied their authority and stood ready to respond if attacked. Shortly before arriving at the scene of the murders, the male quilombolas indeed passed by Emília Carlota's house and left "irritated by the stories she had told them." On their way back to the quilombo, they made a point of returning to Emília's house to give her "some stolen candles to light at the feet of Saint Rita, so that they could come out of it happy."[31]

Tipped off by Praxedes, the police arrested Emília Carlota along with the French merchant Antônio (Antoine) Richier. Emília Carlota de Oliveira, a woman in her forties, lived with her family in a place in Diamantina called Chica da Silva. A notorious *fala* or informant of the quilombolas, she earned a share of whatever they produced or stole in the villages while providing a facade for the fugitives who lived off "killing cattle they caught in the fields, making dried meat and selling it."[32] The forty-six-year-old Frenchman Richier owned a grocery store and, conveniently, also a gunpowder factory on the Caminho do Palha, where he had lived for nearly ten years. He exchanged dried meat for weapons, ammunition, and information on a weekly basis with the quilombolas. In 1868, the diplomat Richard Burton almost met Richier at his ranch during a visit to Diamantina. "I failed to find him at home, but thumbing through his photographic manuals showed an interest in something civilized," Burton wrote. Little did he know that Richier traded with the "Quilombeiros of Mendanha," the "maroon settlement within a league of the village" that had threatened the town with a "mutiny" in 1865.[33]

Arrested for the second time in 1865, Vitória referred to the same riverine geography drawn up by Praxedes, recalling that the quilombolas had lived first on the banks of the Teotônio stream, then at "the Ferreiros behind José Ferreira's house," and finally at the quilombo located upstream from the Buraco do Facho, where "Joaquim was no longer present, because he had quarreled with Francisco, and Modesto." She accused Emília Carlota of inciting her male companions to commit the Farinha Seca murders and explained that the alliances between the quilombo and Richier extended to his enslaved men. The quilombolas counted on the loyalty of Raimundo, for example, who had recently bought a double-barreled rifle for Jerônimo "on behalf of his master." In turn, they refrained from stealing what belonged to Richier as long as he kept quiet about their thefts.[34] The group also relied on Vitória's husband, João Pinheiro, who, in 1865, was accused of disposing of the products of the robbery at Francisco Pires's house and of supplying the quilombo with cachaça and tobacco.[35]

Constructions of gender figured prominently in the accounts the libertas gave to the police about life in the quilombo.[36] They portrayed their intimacy with enslaved men as forced and raised the issue of control over women as an important factor in the insurgents' political power. Rita Pereira dos Santos recalled that, while staying at the ranch of an "old black" over Christmas, João do Dó, João Rainha, and Jerônimo took her "by force" to the quilombo in the backyard of Father Januário's residence, where they sold dried meat to the priest's slaves.[37] Rita was a twenty-four-year-old single woman who "lived off her work." The daughter of Maria Tereza da Costa, she was from "the forest of Rio Vermelho" in the municipality of Serro.[38] Eva Francisca da Conceição was a twenty-two-year-old single woman from Diamantina who had worked as a washerwoman and seamstress; "after moving to the quilombo, she did nothing."[39] Eva also described the social organization of the quilombo along gender lines. She recalled that João Rainha, Jerônimo, and Francisco shared all the money stolen in Farinha Seca before arriving at the quilombo. Enslaved males brought back only a barrel of Geneva [gin], a sack of salt, a man's shirt, a few pieces of Americano and Morin (fabrics), and a bushel of flour.[40] Eva confirmed the role Antoine Richier played in the informal economy of the quilombolas. "Every week they would steal three or four cows, make dried meat and sell it to the foreigner Richier, at four thousand réis an arroba, and that this foreigner was the one who would administer the salt to salt the meat."[41]

By the end of August 1865, the evidence against Emília Carlota was so strong that she didn't even try to hide her involvement with the quilombolas, attributing the "favors" she received from them to the fear of reprisals.[42] The only woman who escaped being charged as an accomplice in the Farinha Seca crimes was Joana Francisca das Neves, a twenty-six-year-old liberta. She also accused Francisco, João Rainha, and Jerônimo of kidnapping her at the end of July from the Caruru mine to the Buraco do Facho, where they gave her no chance to escape.[43] Stories of noncooperation probably responded to and reinforced police assumptions that rebellious acts were primarily carried out by male figures. The invaluable roles quilombola women played, ranging from supporting male insurgents to engaging in covert subversive efforts themselves, remained simply invisible to authorities. The women of Diamantina helped sustain quilombola communities not only through their hidden labors but also through their participation in the information-sharing

circuits that allowed fugitive slaves to receive news, weapons, and goods from
the outside world.

In September 1865, Tiago, Jerônimo, Francisco, João Rainha, and Joaquim, all men enslaved by the main diamond miners of Diamantina, were
charged with the murders committed in Farinha Seca, although most of them
remained on the run.[44] Vitória and Emília Carlota were named as accom-
plices, "the former for having accompanied the accused authors, aiding and
abetting them in the commission of the crime, and the latter for having instigated and advised them, making her house available for the robbers to meet,
both of them later participating in the stolen property."[45] Richier was also
accused of participating in the robbery but was eventually acquitted. At the
end of the year, the Triple Alliance War inspired a push to pack the local jail
with outlaws, but with troops few and far between, the crackdown on crime
did nothing to quell the constant talk of slave rebellion in Diamantina. The
town echoed the atmosphere of white fear that had gripped the province of
Minas Gerais. In the southern village of Congonhas, for instance, authorities
rushed to repress an insurrection at the British-owned Morro Velho mining company. More than two thousand enslaved people who allegedly corresponded with miners of Diamantina just waited for the National Guard to
leave for Mato Grosso to rise up.[46]

The larger threat to slaveholder's peace gave the Diamantina authorities an excuse to retaliate against the population of color. In April 1866,
they finally caught the quilombola João Rainha when he pulled a knife on
a policeman in Mendanha. Brazilian-born João was then twenty-two years
old and belonged to Vicente José da Trindade.[47] His arrest breathed new life
into the investigation of the Farinha Seca murders, which João blamed on the
instigation of Emília Carlota. When questioned again, Emília invoked the
memory of Carolina's lost tongue to defend herself against João's accusations.
"She was afraid that they would make good on their threats to kill her and
cut out her tongue, as they had already done to a woman." The reference to
quilombola violence earned her an acquittal from the jury.

Eva, Praxedes, Rita, and Vitória were also asked to give new testimony
in 1866. Although they shed little light on the deaths of Joaquim and Maria
Rosa, the libertas offered many details about daily life in the quilombo and
their relationships with the enslaved women Luzia, Carolina, Raimunda,
Mariana, and Maria, who also lived there. After the murders of 1865, Francisco distributed the money that Jerônimo had stolen from the Oratory of
St. Anthony only to the male quilombolas. To the women, he gave trousers,

a coat, a petticoat, two used men's shirts, a cup sword, a woman's skirt, and a sheet. Since women were responsible for household chores at the quilombo, they also received several pieces of china, three table knives, and two pointed knives "for use in the kitchen."[48] Some of the remaining items were kept under a rock and then sold by the men to their informants.

A male quilombola also watched over the women to prevent any escape from the Buraco do Facho. Rita claimed to have invited the others to run away several times, but they always gave up because of the "vigilance in which they were kept."[49] Vitória, on the other hand, managed to escape twice by taking advantage of her companions' drunken state, only to receive death threats upon her return "because of the relations she made during her escape."[50] Rita worked as a cook in the quilombo, preparing "meat from the cattle that the blacks stole, cornmeal, flour, and other supplies that they bought in exchange for meat, at the house of Richier and others."[51] She resented her position because, as a cook, she "was mistreated by them, and did not enjoy the same favors as the other women because, unlike them, she did not have someone to carry her bag, and that is why they got in the way of her escapes, so much so that they tried to get rid of her by killing her."[52] In other words, Rita may have been the only single woman in the quilombo. With testimonies filled with details of internal tensions, Rita, Praxedes, Vitória, and Eva were eventually acquitted.

In August 1866, the Baron of Arassuaí turned the quilombolas' leader Jerônimo over to the municipal judge, stating that he no longer wanted to be responsible for "a *cabra* who had been on the run for years and had been involved in other crimes."[53] Then forty years old, Jerônimo had resisted capture at a ranch along with four other runaways.[54] The group had been living there with the consent of Joana, an old acquaintance who traded provisions for dried meat with the quilombolas. Jerônimo and Frutuoso were hiding under the bed when Joaquim, Joana's son, opened the door to the police. "They immediately started shooting under the bed of Dona Joana, where he and his comrade were." Fructuoso was killed by one of the shots he received, and Jerônimo, coming out from under the bed to surrender to the corporal, was then also hit on the head, and arrested.[55]

Jerônimo confessed that the quilombolas were mining for gold and diamonds in the rivers of Diamantina. He also testified that he beat Praxedes because she tried to hit him with a scythe. Jerônimo and his companions left Buraco do Facho because an enslaved worker had discovered the trail leading to the quilombo after they had stolen a heifer.[56] Before joining the quilombolas, he had been on the run for six years "with a girl of Lieutenant Colonel Felisberto Brant," owner of the Barro mine.[57] The confessions of the quilombo leaders showed that the rebels sometimes fought each other more than they fought the system.

In his last attempt to avoid the death penalty, João Rainha denied being the other head of the quilombo and referred to Jerônimo and Francisco as leaders, of whom he and Joaquim were "slaves."[58] However, on October 10, 1866, he was sentenced to prison at hard labor. Two days later, Jerônimo received the same sentence.[59] Of the thirty-one members of the quilombo known to the police, three were dead, two had escaped prosecution for the crime of robbery followed by death, and five had been acquitted, but twenty-one remained at large. An indication that the community survived the 1860s can be found in the arrest of the last quilombola accused of participation in the Farinha Seca killings. Joaquim Cassange, enslaved by Misael Felicíssimo de Aguilar, was captured in October 1874 in Leopoldina, southern Minas Gerais.[60]

To the volatile years of the Triple Alliance War, quilombolas brought a tradition of insurgency that mapped the meanings of freedom onto a context of land dispossession, economic precarity, wartime instability, and racial violence that was ripe for explosion. Brazilian elites thus believed that they were fighting a multifront war, not only against rival Paraguay but also against Atlantic antislavery forces and their own enslaved population actively seeking emancipation through insurrection. Anti-quilombo campaigns were also a response to the spread of abolitionism in Brazil, which thrived as quilombolas practiced freedom and place-making by creating a subaltern economy of survival at the margins of slavery.

On the Home Front of the Triple Alliance War

The mobilization of troops to fight against Paraguay began in earnest with a government appeal to citizens in the name of Brazilian honor, a call reminiscent of the nationalist vigor displayed during the Christie Affair.[61] An imperial decree of January 7, 1865, created the Voluntários da Pátria, a corps of volunteer soldiers entrusted with meeting Brazil's manpower needs in the River Plate region. Combining patriotic fervor with government benefits, the force was tailored to address the country's long-standing aversion to military service among working-age men. Traditionally, army recruitment did not rely on conscription but rather on episodic efforts at impressment that fell on the shoulders of the poor. Given the overall composition of the Brazilian population, most of the soldiers pressed into service were Afro-descendants.[62] Enlistment also occurred through the judicial system, serving since colonial times as a form of punishment for vagrancy and disorderly conduct. Thus the Voluntários da Pátria offered extra advantages to potential soldiers: besides receiving better pay than regular troops, volunteers would serve only as long as the war lasted (as opposed to nine years), and could receive a bonus and privileged access to land grants in government colonies at the end of the conflict.[63]

In addition to organizing a volunteer unit to supplement the regular army, the government of Pedro II called the National Guard to the front lines, extending to guardsmen the benefits enjoyed by volunteers.[64] Founded in the 1830s as a civilian militia, the guard assisted the army and police in maintaining public order and defending Brazil's borders in times of peace. Income requirements determined eligibility to serve, but only men of property could be elected as officers. Landowners controlled enrollment in the National Guard, dipping into networks of patronage and political influence to trade posts for loyalty and votes. In 1865 the guardsmen became even more indispensable as the travails of troop mobilization escalated with the invasion of Brazilian territory.[65] Paraguayan troops took over the Coxim region of Mato Grosso in April, entered Rio Grande do Sul in May, and soon threatened to invade Minas Gerais from Santana do Parnaíba, a village that marked the border with Mato Grosso.[66] Nevertheless, even in the face of aggression by a wartime enemy, enthusiasm for defending Brazilian sovereignty quickly waned among a population accustomed to associating military service with social degradation.

Over time, the Triple Alliance War became synonymous with disdain for combat, draft evasion, and the disorganization of local patron-client networks in Brazil. For example, Minas Gerais, a province of 1,600,000 people, was expected to muster 6,000 guardsmen in 1865 to form an expeditionary party to fight López's forces in Mato Grosso, but only 1,100 reported for duty. Local commanders blamed resistance, political rivalries, and precarious transportation routes for the meager numbers.[67] Throughout Brazil, however, the situation was similar. Soldiers were supposed to be free citizens eager to defend the nation, but even the poor looked with contempt to the ill-prepared regular troops, who often lacked the necessary training, ammunition, food, and logistical conditions necessary to succeed on the swampy battlefields of Paraguay.[68] In 1865 and 1866 alone, deserters accounted for 36 percent and 43 percent of the sentences handed down by the Supreme Military Council.[69]

In the sway of widespread discontent, black conspiracies spread throughout Brazil. In Cariacica, Espírito Santo, enslaved insurgents expected that "the
war of the Republics of Uruguay and Paraguay with the Empire is aimed at
freeing the slaves."[70] Chief of Police Eduardo Pindaíba de Mattos reported in
February 1865 that "some slaves in the belief that the war against the Republics of the River Plate means freedom for all slaves in Brazil, showed themselves in some points of this province willing to carry out an insurrection."[71]
Some had been seen walking the streets of Camboapina with guns and saying
that they were just waiting for the troops and guardsmen to leave so that they
could go into action.

In Minas Gerais alone, twenty-five black conspiracies surfaced in 1865. In
São João d'el Rei, enslaved and freed people sponsored religious meetings at
a ranch called Córrego d'Areia, where Inocência, "an old black woman who
calls herself a freedwoman," led what authorities described as "witchcraft" rituals in which participants cheered a red flag with green borders and the freedom of the slaves.[72] In nearby Mariana, some enslaved people "were sure that
the present war was for their freedom,"[73] while others referred to the fact that
"the Blancos wanted to free them," in direct reference to the Uruguayan civil
war.[74] In Caeté, the police commissioner Caetano de Souza Telles Guimarães
reported "that some slaves were talking, and saying, that the current war was
in their favor, that if our opponents won, and the Brazilians lost, the slaves
would be freed, and the whites of Brazil would be made captives. . . . Perhaps
some foreign emissaries have spread such rumors among the slaves to cause
us difficulties at this time. This is an assumption of mine."[75]

Other plans for rebellion were later discovered as the war approached
southwest Minas. In May, another slave uprising was expected to break out
in Serro, and in Juiz de Fora authorities spoke of "hidden emissaries," especially Italians and Jews, sowing the seeds of insurrection among the black
population.[76] In Conceição, near Serro, slaveholders, perhaps mindful of the
collective reading practices that inspired the 1864 slave rebellion, complained
that newspaper coverage of the Triple Alliance War had become dangerous.
They spoke out against the Rio de Janeiro press, which "perhaps imprudently,
has published about the kidnapping of Brazilian-owned slaves by our enemies
from Paraguay, and Uruguay." They worried that such news "may in some way
contribute to the exaltation of these people, who abound in this city . . . and
prudence advises that not only all the precautions be taken, but that we be on
guard, so as not to be surprised by any insurrection."[77] Literacy was important as a means of disseminating intelligence about the possibilities of crossing

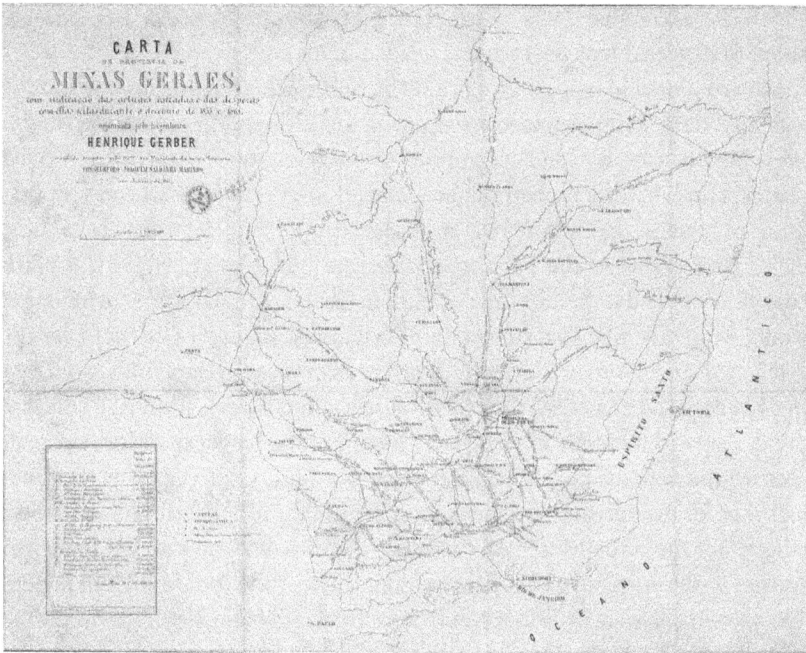

Figure 14. Map of the province of Minas Gerais by Henrique Gerber, 1867. "Carta da província de Minas Geraes: com indicação das actuaes estradas e das despesas com ellas feitas durante o decennio de 1855 e 1865. Rio de Janeiro, RJ: Imperial Instituto Artistico, 1867," Biblioteca Nacional, Brazil.

to free soil and the shifting balance of power in the Southern Cone. For the enslaved, strikes against Brazil were tantamount to attacks on chattel slavery.

In São Francisco das Chagas do Campo Grande, Santa Bárbara, Parai-buna, Rio Preto, Barbacena, and Lavras, the enslaved walked around armed in anticipation of revolts.[78] In Taquaraçu, emancipation was brought up during nightly drumming sessions, where a liberto who served as king of the Brotherhood of the Rosary proclaimed that "they [black people] would soon rule." In Caeté, enslaved men discussed together the implications of a pos-sible Brazilian victory over Paraguay. An enslaved woman named Rita over-heard a group of them mention that "the boys are tight, they are all going to war, and when they go we will take care of the white and mulatto girls." Race and gender inversions were part of imaginings of emancipation on the part of both black activists and the police. The black woman Paula even played on gender norms to pass bullets to enslaved men. Upon meeting one on the street, she exclaimed: "It is all right, man, if you are to marry her, you are about to be free. I have just what is needed in my bag."[79]

International kidnappings, slave flight, and black conspiracies marked the war in Brazil's southernmost province of Rio Grande do Sul, which shares borders with Uruguay and Argentina. At the battlefront, enslaved and freed people who had long probed the geopolitical implications of an uneven abolition process in South America experienced the Platine conflict in its most vivid connections to the horizon of freedom.[80] In November 1864, a black conspiracy linked to Brazil's intervention in Uruguay signaled the turmoil that would define the first year of war. In the village of Taquari (a district near the provincial capital of Porto Alegre), a group of enslaved insurgents planned to meet at the local cemetery, turn the iron fence into spears, attack the city, and then escape to freedom in Uruguay.[81] Joaquim, the leader of the movement, accused the national guardsman Bernardo dos Santos Praia of being the main recruiter for the uprising and the mentor behind the idea of training "slave battalions" for the battlefields.[82] All the police could determine was that Praia had spoken to the enslaved about the war raging across the Rio de la Plata region. The movement was, in fact, a black conspiracy, probably based more on the impressions of a liberto who had recently returned from Uruguay to meet with two enslaved brothers involved in the plot. Rumors of rebellion reached the capital, Porto Alegre, in December and escalated in early 1865 when Montevideo's ruling faction, the Blancos, invaded the Brazilian town of Jaguarão in anticipation of Paraguayan support.[83] On January 27, the cavalry, commanded by Basílio Munhoz, general-in-chief of Uruguay's vanguard army, confronted imperial troops allied with the Colorados, ultimately losing to Brazil.

As several foreign officers would do in the years to come, Munhoz invaded Jaguarão after issuing a provocative proclamation that played on the weaknesses of a slave empire:

> Soldiers! Let us set foot on the territory that the Empire of Brazil has usurped from us, it is necessary that with your valor and patriotism we reconquer its dominion, making our flag flutter on it, and give freedom to the unfortunate men of color who groan under the yoke of slavery, which humanity reproves. Compatriots! Our mission is to fight for the independence of our country, threatened by the Empire of Brazil, and for freedom; to this end we will only fight the slaves of Pedro II, until we make this ambitious monarch understand that we Orientals will never be slaves of his infamous crown, but free and independent.[84]

The enslaved of Rio Grande do Sul heeded such calls as they echoed in the charqueadas and ranches of the province.[85] Many knew Uruguayans who encouraged them to flee to their armed forces or across the border to free soil. On February 4, in Piratini, insurgents again expected assistance from the Blancos in an uprising against slavery. Deciding to wear a white ribbon on their hats to signal the outbreak of the rebellion, the enslaved planned to raid the town of Piratini and cross the border into Uruguay, taking some white women with them.[86] The conspiracy gathered more than thirty insurgents from local cattle ranches and resulted in the arrest of Uruguayans who were considered slave seducers. On all sides of the Platine conflict, combatants expected a slave uprising to destabilize Brazil in the war.

The largest black conspiracy in the south of Brazil took place in 1868. In June of that year, the pardo Dionísio, along with Patrício and Teodoro, all enslaved to the merchant Francisco Ferreira Porto, organized a revolt for Saint John's Day (June 24) in Porto Alegre. The insurgents planned to meet up at the property of Captain Manuel Joaquim, who owned a slave from whom Patrício had ordered "twelve dozen spear handles, in which knives and other instruments could be stuck to serve as spears." At the rendezvous point, they would divide themselves into four groups to head toward the city and gather weapons. The separate "divisions" would then take over the National Guard headquarters, the Pyrotechnics Laboratory, and the War Arsenal, with the latter being responsible for freeing the prisoners in the local jail. Before insurgents could gear up for action, however, Antônio Maria, enslaved to Gabriel Francisco de Oliveira, denounced the plot and foiled the rebellion.[87]

The authorities involved in the interrogation of suspects reported that Dionísio defined the uprising as an attempt by "the slaves to obtain their freedom, to which they would give *vivas* when they entered the city."[88] Patrício revealed that the insurgents were counting on the support of Paraguayan prisoners who had recently been transferred to Porto Alegre. He cited conversations with one Gabino Flores, who relayed news of the uprising to Floribio Palácios, Julian Flores, and Miguel Cácere. Once cognizant of the facts, the Ministry of Justice decided to make the informant Antônio Maria an example of loyalty to the "public cause" of the empire, asking his master to name a price for his emancipation. Gabriel Francisco de Oliveira gave an interesting answer. He set Antônio Maria's price at 1:400$000 réis and agreed to free him "as long as the slave was not obliged to enlist for military service, because in that case, he would not sell him, because the slave did not want

to be freed for that purpose either."[89] Antônio was finally emancipated with
money from the secret funds of the province of Rio Grande do Sul.[90]

As wartime mobilization continued to disrupt slaveholders' ability to
fight resistance throughout Brazil, black networks of dissent also intersected
with army desertion to fuel the growth of quilombos. For the enslaved in the
town of Bragança, far north in the province of Pará, "the triumph of Paraguay
over Brazil was discussed as a necessary condition for their freedom, and
therefore that they should all contribute to this end, indicating as the first victims the highest authorities of the place and other noble Citizens."[91] In Mato
Grosso, on the border with Paraguay and Bolivia, troops made up mostly of
poor men impressed into frontier patrolling connected enslaved workers in
the gold mines to the political conflicts of the Platine region. On the river
border between Brazil and Bolivia, the centennial quilombo of Sepotuba
grew steadily during the war and was said to have housed even a captain of
the National Guard.[92]

Army deserters often found refuge among quilombolas, who were eager
to acquire weapons and knowledge about the movements of police patrols.
They were a common presence in Serra Dourada, Mato Grosso, where a network of quilombos existed along the banks of the Jangada, Roncador, and
Manso do Sul Rivers. The latter, near the capital Cuiabá, had been home to
a large maroon community since 1859. In April 1867 newspapers speculated
that the quilombo had close to four thousand inhabitants, including "runaway blacks, deserters and Indians. These people were said to have a city
and a regular form of government, as well as a force to police the city, which
they called Rio Manso. Since there was a shortage of women, the inhabitants
of Rio Manso decided to rob them, and one of the kidnapped women who
managed to escape gave these details."[93] After the war, the president of Mato
Grosso spoke of a settlement of six hundred people who often traveled to
Vila do Diamantino and Cuiabá to trade in precious stones, firearms, knives,
gunpowder, lead, and provisions. During the Triple Alliance War, accounts
about the military organization of quilombos also soared. "It is believed that
they practice their weapons under the tutelage of a deserter from the Second
Artillery Battalion. There are sentries at various points who report any news
to the quilombos, whose agents, unknown except by those who use the stone
exchange to this day, count on impunity."[94]

Army deserters were considered a security problem in Minas Gerais.
Those who ran away from the military headquarters in Uberaba were accused
of spreading "terrible news about military life" in the remotest corners of the

province. The commander of Oliveira, Manoel Soares Fortuna, found appalling "the audacity with which many individuals, some of whom hold positions in the National Guard, are trying to scare people away from enlisting!" If it were not for their desire "to harass the imperial government and Your Excellency, without considering the damage they inflict on the country, with great suffering for the province, I would say that they are emissaries of the dictator of Paraguay."[95] Francisco de Paula Carneiro Campos, military commander in Paracatu, described runaway recruits in much the same way as quilombolas, citing "the aversion that the rural population has to uniforms, preferring the forests, where game, fish, hearts of palm, potatoes and honey are easy to find. . . . Some are burrowed in these forests and within the boundaries of the municipality, and others flee to the province of Goiás, and to neighboring towns, where they necessarily find protection in exchange for work."[96]

By the end of 1866, the magnitude of the Triple Alliance War forced the imperial government to consider the conscription of the enslaved. The ensuing controversy further destabilized the country and sparked debate about the relationship between the war and slave emancipation. Although freed slaves had served in the military during Bahia's wars of independence, the arming of freedmen had always been polemical, especially among planters who feared a social revolution in the wake of war. On November 5, Brazil's State Council convened to discuss whether "it would be convenient to make use of the freedom of the slaves to increase the number of soldiers in the army." In a meeting chaired by Emperor Pedro II and attended by the ministers of war, foreign affairs, finance, and the navy, the councilors discussed which slaves would be "preferable in case of a positive answer": "slaves of the Nation" (*escravos da Nação* or state-owned slaves), those belonging to religious orders, or slaves owned by private citizens.[97] Seeking alternatives to meet the need for recruits without infringing on the perceived rights of slaveholders, the imperial government suggested that the State Council first consider publicly owned slaves. These divisions, however, mattered little to the enslaved, who had always subverted the categories imposed on them by the elites. Any official gesture toward emancipation, however tentative, signaled an opportunity to mobilize for more meaningful freedom for all.

The pulse of black activism during the Triple Alliance War influenced the councilors' opinions on the safest way to expand Brazil's national armed forces. Rather than have the government issue emancipation decrees, most preferred to follow the military practice of requiring owners to manumit slaves as a condition of their enlistment. Black men who joined the war effort were therefore libertos volunteered by their former masters either as replacements or as donations to the state. Councilors who opposed the impressment of the enslaved anyway, such as the Viscount of Itaboraí, warned others of "the excitement that such a measure would cause among the slaves themselves; the hopes it would give rise to, the incentive to seek their freedom; and the insurrections and scenes of bloodshed which might ensue." José Maria da Silva Paranhos also echoed slaveholder sentiment, noting that the enlistment of captives would "arouse in the slave population, already quite excited in recent times by the propaganda of the ideas of abolition, more or less imminent, the natural desire to shake off the yoke of slavery."[98] Even council members who supported the measure, such as José Tomás Nabuco de Araújo, argued for a concerted government effort to buy the enslaved from their owners rather than freeing them directly. For Nabuco de Araújo, military service had a salutary disciplinary effect on freedmen, as the US Civil War had recently demonstrated.

Ultimately, caution would win the day. Four councilors voted decisively against slave recruitment, while six suggested that the government convince slaveholders to sell their slaves in exchange for compensation. On November 6, 1866, imperial decree 3725 emancipated the escravos da Nação able to serve in Paraguay. In 1867 and 1868, the imperial government systematically paid slaveholders willing to free their slaves for enlistment, in effect bolstering an elite version of proslavery nationalism. Controversy over slave recruitment subsided in mid-1867, when Pedro II allayed fears of wholesale expropriation by acknowledging in front of a planter-dominated parliament that emancipation should respect the rights of slaveholders.[99] In the end, around seven thousand freedmen fought in the Triple Alliance War on the side of Brazil, representing only 0.86 percent of the enslaved male population of the empire.[100] Most important, until 1871 manumission remained exclusively a prerogative of masters.

Regardless of what the higher echelons of government decided, the enslaved continued to read the war effort as an opportunity for emancipation. In 1867 the *Correio Mercantil* recorded one of such freedom stories.[101] A long advertisement on the last page offered a reward for the capture of two enslaved men who had escaped from the Três Rios plantation in Barra do Piraí, Rio de Janeiro province. Malachias and Salomé, both Brazilian-born and in their twenties, had ran away to Minas Gerais, where the former had been arrested as a fugitive two years earlier. "It is suspected that they both fled to Minas, where Malachias knows how to get around, and that they only

walk at night because they are quilombolas, or, in fact, that they want to present themselves as *voluntários da pátria*; they went equipped with fine clothes
and mason's tools and took Chile hats."[102]

In Minas, similar trajectories plotted slave activism into written form for
both white audiences and black reader-listeners. Manoel Cesário, an enslaved
muleteer on the run from the Baron of Aparecida for four years, was said to
have changed his name in São José do Além Paraíba. "He calls himself free,
and there are reports, that he has offered himself as a volunteer, and is stationed in some army corps, or province."[103] Custódio, enslaved by Vicente
José da Trindade, owner of the quilombola João Rainha in Diamantina, was
advertised even in the newspapers of Rio de Janeiro. A twenty-two-year-old
"with the habit of staring little at whomever talks to him," he had escaped
to Ouro Preto "with the purpose of offering himself as a volunteer there."
Rumors had it that Custódio survived by making arrangements with military
commanders as if he were free to escape arrest as a fugitive.[104] At the end of
1869, the enslaved miner Francisco ran away from Milho Verde, a district of
Serro. According to his master, he "wants to be very talkative, but has a thick
African accent, and is very clever." Apparently Francisco "carried fantastic
letters and a fake passport, having paid in money whoever prepared it, can
have enlisted in Ouro Preto, due to some advice he received."[105] He probably
possessed a counterfeit letter of manumission to pass as a freedman.

From the point of view of black insurgents, the Triple Alliance War was
the third military conflict to intersect with slave emancipation in the 1860s. It
was the first, though, to be fought in parts of the Brazilian territory and require
the national mobilization of troops and resources on an unprecedented scale.
Press coverage, veterans' narratives about the front lines, and public debate
over the monarchy's management of the war became features of daily life for
all, turning Brazil into a hotbed of social activism and political opposition.
Although sidelined by a national historiography more concerned, for instance,
with the emergence of a republican movement connected to military cadres,
quilombos were an integral part of the ebullient 1860s. Historical subjects
that transformed along with Brazilian society, they kept the momentum for
insurrection alive by attracting an ever-larger number of freedpeople, military
deserters, convicts, africanos livres, and indigenous people during wartime.
Quilombos were plural communities that embodied not only hopes for black
freedom but also a larger subaltern struggle for some degree of autonomy, land,
and protection from state violence in Brazil.[106] As we will see next in the case of
Maranhão, quilombolas also conceived of abolitionism at the level of agrarian

relations by removing their labor, rebelling against landowners, and securing their own subsistence through the cultivation of alternative food systems. Military mobilization and armed resistance were also part of quilombola activism, allowing them to defend their communities and change, at least temporarily, the power dynamic with the Brazilian slave society.

Emancipation in Writing

As war raged on in Paraguay, literacy continued to fuel social pressure for abolition in Brazil. In São Luís, Maranhão, Vice President José Caetano Vaz Júnior described the phenomenon in no uncertain terms: "There are free blacks who know how to read badly, and to whom the ideas expressed lately in favor of the emancipation of slaves are not new. Similar ideas have been propagated in a confusing and vague manner among slaves in the capital and in the interior." According to Vaz Júnior's informants, "these poor people apparently believe that the current war has some kind of affinity with the cause of their emancipation."[107] Afro-descendants counted themselves as newspaper reader-listeners and produced wartime texts that contradicted the exclusionary politics of the Brazilian mainstream press. Literacy, in other words, played an important role in organizing collectivities of enslaved people during the Triple Alliance War.

Knowledge about the Platine conflict boosted quilombolas' struggles against slavery in Viana, where an uprising started to brew in 1865. Located on the left margin of the Mearim River in the lowlands of Maranhão, Viana stood in the middle of a tangle of rivers and lakes that worked as highways of information for those escaping slavery. In April, the National Guard arrived in time to prevent an invasion of the town by quilombolas, yet mass flights from local plantations, especially in the villages of Codó and Rosário, kept locals on alert.[108] In October rumors of an alliance between quilombolas and the enslaved of Viana ramped up the military response to black activism in an attempt to show rebels that "the government, despite the withdrawal of regular troops, has elements ready to quell any attempt at insurrection."[109] In the midst of the turmoil, the army recruit Silvério Antônio Dutra and his father, Benedito, both freedmen, were arrested for preaching "dangerous ideas tending to the freedom of the slaves."[110]

What was just idle chatter in 1865 blossomed into full insurrection in 1867. The year opened with hit-and-run strikes in rural areas and an upsurge in marronage in western Maranhão. On the evening of January 20, escaped slaves of Raimundo Antônio da Costa Ferreira invaded his plantation in São Vicente Ferrer to start an uprising, but the neighbor Manoel Alves da Costa Ferreira brought his own slaves to stop the quilombolas. Not long afterward, collective flights from the outskirts of the village of São Bento responded to the arrival of a government emissary entrusted with the recruitment of guardsmen. Midway through 1867, the intensification of black activism became a subject of discussion in the Provincial Assembly of Maranhão, where deputies expressed concern with enslaved people "enticed by agents of the numerous quilombos that exist in those municipalities and in Viana, and perhaps influenced by the absurd rumors that have been spread among them regarding the cause of the war with Paraguay and the solution of the servile question."[111]

As we have seen, the Gurupi and Turiaçu river basin had been home to some of Brazil's largest quilombos since the eighteenth century. In this rainforest-covered borderland between two provinces—Maranhão and Pará—enslaved fugitives had staked claim to vacant land and established what already amounted to peasant settlements in the mid-1800s. On July 7, 1867, rebellion broke out as the quilombolas of São Benedito do Céu, one of the oldest runaway communities of Turiaçu, descended on the sugar plantations of Viana.[112] The latest iteration of the *quilombo* on the margins of the Bonito Creek had formed out of the destruction of the São Vicente do Céu, whose members relocated after the 1861 Anajatuba rebellion (see Chapter 3). In 1867, enslaved men and women journeyed east from Turiaçu for five days through the counties of Maracassumé, São Vicente Ferrer, and São Bento to reach Viana. Including some army deserters and freedmen, the group sprang into action as Maranhão coped with the departure of more than three thousand regular military troops, national guardsmen, and volunteer forces to Paraguayan battlefields.[113]

The insurgents marched into the Santa Bárbara, Timbó, and Santo Inácio plantations armed with the same clubs and scythes they used to slaughter cattle and defend themselves along the way. Local police learned of the scale of the invasion in the early hours of July 9, when a convoy of twenty families from Maracassumé personally reported to Commissioner José Gregório Pinheiro that they were fleeing an "uprising of escaped and *amocambado* [marooned] slaves" who had cordoned off the Santa Bárbara plantation.[114] Within hours, Judge Benedito de Barros e Vasconcellos asked the president of Maranhão for more weapons and a suspension of the military recruitment campaign in Viana. He lamented that sugar production had come to a halt in the Maranhense lowlands because "most of those able to pick up weapons in defense of the country" were "tucked in the woods," leaving villages exposed to several quilombos and hostile indigenous groups.[115] With the complicity of the local senzalas, the quilombolas slowly expanded their presence from Viana to surrounding villages such as Vila Nova de Anadia and São Vicente Ferrer. As the uprising spread, the police commissioner of São Vicente remarked: "It reminds me of what happened in Haiti at the time of the French Revolution, that in three days all the white people who existed on that continent were murdered."[116]

What came to pass at Santa Bárbara was indeed quite remarkable. Amid the bloodiest clashes of the rebellion, the quilombolas of São Benedito do Céu decided to write wartime emancipation into being. On July 8 they broke into the administrator's house and overpowered all the plantation's caretakers. After tying the arms of the administrator Plácido Mello dos Santos, the Portuguese overseer Manoel Ferreira, and three other men, the rebels dragged them outside and tied them to poles on the dirt road that ran alongside Plácido's house. When the quilombolas set out to shoot the prisoners, Joaquim Calisto demanded that Plácido give him the keys to the "prison" where he knew the enslaved men Firmiano and Benedito were kept in chains. Joaquim Calisto was a man convicted of murder in the town of São Bento who had escaped from prison in the early 1860s to live in the quilombo of São Benedito do Céu.[117]

Upon freeing Firmiano and Benedito, Joaquim Calisto returned to Plácido's house, where the rebels gave the administrator of Santa Bárbara a taste of the kind of punishment he had meted out to the enslaved. After a round of flogging, Joaquim Calisto swore Plácido to secrecy by saying "that he would be forgiven as long as he did not whisper a word about it for a week, but if he told anyone about what had happened there, he would inevitably be killed by two or three of them."[118] Plácido and his family remained hostage in his bedroom for the next few days while the quilombolas set out to attack Vila Nova de Anadia. On July 10, 1867, they returned to the Santa Bárbara plantation after hearing that Plácido's sons-in-law were looking for him. It was during this second meeting that Daniel and João, both enslaved by the heirs of Miguel de Araújo, forced Plácido to compose a message to Viana authorities.[119] Written under duress, the letter had the urgent tone of an ultimatum:

Honorable Mister deputy and Commander of the detachment of Viana–

Santa Bárbara, 10 July 1867

I inform your Lordships that we are in the field to handle the issue of the Freedom of the Captives, because we have been waiting for it a long time, and since our desire is to cover everyone, and not to harm anyone, we are waiting for it [freedom] in Santo Inácio, and if it does not appear by the 15th of next month, we will have no choice but to take up arms and go there, and your Lordships can be sure that we have 1,000 firearms and all the bows of the gentiles in our defense and of freedom and we hope you will not take our warning for granted; our deliberations are very serious, and so you should take precautions, and we will wait for a response all day tomorrow.

Yours,
Daniel Antônio de Araujo
João Antônio de Araujo.[120]

Daniel and João, leaders of the quilombo of São Benedito do Céu, framed the struggle for emancipation as the most important war at hand. They presented themselves as soldiers who had gone into the field to obtain a right for which they had waited a long time. In the name of the insurgents, Daniel and João tried to negotiate because they wanted freedom to "cover everyone" without further loss of life. Nonetheless, the quilombolas threatened authorities with an armed confrontation led by black and indigenous people in case emancipation did not take place. They counted on support from the Gamella indigenous people, who had lived in Turiaçu since colonial times.[121] The letter bore the authorship of two escaped slaves who had no legal claim to full names. Daniel and João used the surname of their late master, Miguel de Araújo, to sign the document they dictated to Plácido.[122] In doing so, they signed as if they were already free, following the customary naming practices of libertos. Presenting themselves as legitimate interlocutors of the Brazilian state was, perhaps, their most defiant gesture. Through writing, quilombolas asserted discursive control over their rebellion.

Although what Daniel and João actually said to the Santa Bárbara administrator is not recorded in the archives, it seems that the insurgents wanted to produce a binding document that would justify their war against the

Figure 15. Copy of the letter dictated by Daniel and João during the quilombola rebellion of 1867 in Viana, Maranhão. The copy was produced by the notary Ovídio da Gama Lobo and sent by the provincial government to the Ministry of Justice. Arquivo Nacional, Brazil.

whites. They used Plácido as a notary, that is, someone who would mediate their access to both the written word and the sphere of legal representation. Plácido added to the letter all the elements of official correspondence: honorific pronouns conveying respect for rank, date and place determining provenance, and the enumeration of terms for a truce. A rare material example of grassroots diplomacy at work, the missive was a hybrid document: penned by an educated man committed to enforcing slavery in Viana, it conveyed the quilombolas' understanding of freedom as a claim to justice. Plácido thus embodied the reversal of power sought by the 1867 insurgents; literacy gave the enslaved a chance to procure emancipation in a way that was fundamentally different (or they had one thousand firearms at the ready) from the gradualism underwritten by liberal elites.

Along with the letter, Plácido produced a passport guaranteeing safe passage for Antônio, an enslaved man from Santa Bárbara whom the rebels entrusted with delivery to the authorities in Viana.[123] The note this time had the signature of the administrator:

I beg everyone not to interrupt the bearer,

who will take the letter to the Deputy and the Commander of the regiment.

Santa Bárbara, 10 July 1867.
Plácido M. dos Santos

Although the quilombola uprising in western Maranhão had made local roads unsafe and stopped all postal correspondence by mid-1867, Antônio safely delivered the insurgents' ultimatum in Viana's jail. He left Santa Bárbara before 120 troops entered the plantation under heavy fire coming from insurgents holed up in the sugar houses on the property.

Authorities responded to the quilombolas' letter with great contempt. Interrogated from his bed two days after the siege of Santa Bárbara, Plácido recounted his ordeal to judge Benedito de Barros Vasconcellos, emphasizing the high degree of violence that justified his betrayal of slaveholders' exclusive claim to literacy. Vasconcellos listened with care and later communicated to the imperial government that Daniel and João were enslaved men of "poor intelligence" for whom it was impossible "to seek so effective a means to conceal the purpose of the letter and make it arrive so promptly and safely at its destination." For the judge, the quilombolas could only have been influenced by "a shrewd individual" willing to profit from "the idea of freedom and the natural hatred that slaves have for their masters and, especially, for whites." Perhaps he was referring to Joaquim Calisto, whom Plácido described as the mastermind of the flogging that left him bedridden. The letter, Vasconcellos concluded, was nothing more than an "insane demand for a freedom dictated and sanctioned by them [the enslaved]."[124]

What proslavery authorities considered unthinkable, however, should not be trivialized in historical discourse. In 1867 the quilombolas of São Benedito do Céu created a document of unique value. Similar remnants of the material culture of black abolitionism have either perished or are yet to be discovered by scholars. There is perhaps only one comparable example in Brazilian history, a "peace treaty" drafted by escaped slaves. In about 1789, as historian Stuart B. Schwartz has discovered, a group of enslaved people at the Engenho Santana in Ilhéus, Bahia, rose up, killed their overseer, and ran into the forest to form a quilombo.[125] After surviving attacks by various military expeditions, the rebels decided to negotiate with Manoel da Silva Ferreira, the plantation owner, and sent him a letter through emissaries.

The 1789 "treaty" is a curious document; instead of demanding complete freedom, it enumerates the conditions for the fugitives' return to work or, in their own words, the terms of their peace.[126] "My Lord, we want peace and we do not want war, if My Lord also wants our peace it must be in this manner," wrote the enslaved of Santana. Insurgents negotiated changes in work routines, asked to retain possession of their tools and choose their overseers, argued for more autonomy to cultivate garden plots and trade in the market, insisted on a four-day workweek and, most strikingly, included a demand "to play, relax, and sing whenever we wish without hindrance."[127] The letter, clearly written on behalf of the Creoles, also requested that the most unhealthy and dirty work—such as fishing in the mangroves—be assigned to Africans. If implemented, the insurgents' demands would have made slavery in the Santana plantation meaningless. Ultimately, the letter conveys their view of rural labor, ethnicity, and black life in colonial Brazil in an authoritative tone that directly challenges the power of planters in Bahia but stops short of calling for an end to slavery.[128]

Although there is precedent to rebellious written communication between escaped slaves and enslavers, the 1867 letter from Maranhão stands out for expressing quilombolas' understanding of the right pace and timing for emancipation in Brazil. Some of them explained the need to resort to writing when interrogated in São Luís. For Benedito, Daniel had ordered Plácido to write "a letter concerning war matters to be sent to this City to Mr. Egidio, saying that they thought they were ready for the war they had warned about."[129] Other insurgents claimed that the document was inspired by Solano López's hostility to slavery in Brazil. Martiniano mentioned that López seemed to be "taking care of their freedom" and that Daniel and João had forced Plácido to "make a letter proclaiming the freedom of the slaves." Vicente argued, as if to save himself, that some of his peers had objected to "communicating that they had come to proclaim their freedom" but had complied with Daniel's orders. Joaquim Calisto and Bruno even asked a certain João Borges at the Timbó plantation "about the gazettes that spoke about López and their freedom."[130] Pulcheria, one of the few enslaved women arrested by the police, defined the 1867 rebellion in the clearest of terms: their intention was "to wage war against the whites because of the Law of the Blacks [Lei dos Pretos], that is, so that they could be considered free."[131]

A week after receiving the insurgents' ultimatum, Viana authorities responded with the usual show of force. Judge Vasconcellos mustered 400 men to quell the rebellion, sent armed patrols to Viana's roads, harbors, and river beaches, and halted the departure of all embarkations from local ports. Nevertheless, the insurgents dispersed, armed, to the forests of Itapecuru and Turiaçu from where they kept the movement alive. On July 17, 1867, the police commissioner of Viana led a party of 250 men to the quilombo of São Benedito do Céu, under the guidance of Feliciano Corta-Mato, an enslaved rebel and turncoat who had been on the run for twenty-five years. The troops, gathered at São Bento and São Vicente Ferrer, occupied the quilombo until July 20 but soon showed signs of disobedience and exhaustion. The soldiers had to move through the forest under intense rain, defending themselves from shots fired by the quilombolas, and with very little food.[132] At the end of their stay in São Benedito, they were able to catch only those who could not run quickly enough into the forest: women, elderly men, and small children. Most of the quilombolas fled to another quilombo on the banks of the Parauá River or toward the gold mines of Maracassumé.

The quilombo of São Benedito do Céu lived off gold mining, agriculture, hunting, and the bartering of goods with the senzalas and impoverished inhabitants of Viana. Although quite large, with six hundred to seven hundred members, São Benedito was contemporary to Vitória's quilombo in Minas Gerais, with which it shared many characteristics. In Maranhão, men were responsible for the mining of alluvial gold (as diamonds were mined in Diamantina), which they exchanged for clothing, weapons, and food. Some women and children from São Benedito worked in the fields of nearby plantations for allotments of ammunition and gunpowder.[133] When the quilombo was raided in 1867, soldiers found manioc flour, rice, sugar cane (and milling machines), tobacco, chickens, and reported the burning down of eighty dwellings.[134] Unlike the quilombos of Diamantina, which were located in very rocky terrain, São Benedito had cotton fields and sold cloth to merchants along the Tury River. It was, in other words, a black peasant community with extensive commercial links with nearby villages.

The insurgents named the enslaved man José Crioulo as the "commander" of the quilombo, with "captains" Daniel, Bruno, Feliciano Corta-Mato, and the free man Joaquim Calisto Soares coming just below him. Feliciano recalled that, in July, Daniel allayed his fears of invading plantations by saying "that they could come without fear because the whites had already gone to Paraguay and there was no one to beat them."[135] Militarily organized into battalions of twenty to thirty men, the quilombolas had prepared a makeshift hospital in the bush behind the Santo Inácio plantation to receive the injured, and they stormed the properties where they had informal agreements with the senzalas. Dona Thereza Borges, owner of the Engenho Timbó, heard Daniel say that "he was the commander of those troops" with Joaquim Calisto and Bruno as his "Chief Lieutenants and Officers."[136] José de Colônia, enslaved by Mariana Porfíria Pinheiro, referred to his leaders in the fields as "captains" and "counter-captains" who sought "to enjoy freedom at the *mocambo* where they lived."[137] It seems that 1867 insurgents had the intention of claiming some kind of sovereignty over the forests of Turiaçu through what they clearly envisioned as a military campaign. Tensions in Brazilian imperial society, the enslaved knew, centered on black freedom and land ownership.

After attacking the Viana plantations, most insurgents disappeared into the far west of Maranhão, settling on the border with the province of Pará. At the end of July, judge Joaquim Costa Barcelos of Turiaçu described the mines of Maracassumé as the rebels' main refuge: "It is in this locality, where there are the largest number of quilombos, especially around the mining company of Montes Áureos—which today is a real quilombo, since it is abandoned and contains a large number of spacious houses and large plantations of flour, corn and rice."[138] Another expedition, led by Major João Francisco Regis, camped out in August at what was left of São Benedito do Céu but again failed to capture insurgents, who continued to wage guerrilla warfare from the forest. In October a militia group stormed the old British headquarters at Montes Áureos, killing one guardsman and three quilombolas.

Even after interrogating and indicting dozens of insurgents, authorities in Maranhão refused to believe that the enslaved could be responsible for such a complex uprising. They sentenced Joaquim Calisto to death for the crime of insurrection, assuming that he was the "intelligence" behind the movement and, especially, of the dangerous letter composed at Santa Bárbara. In November 1868, a popular jury in Viana condemned thirty-one slaves, most in absentia, to forced labor for the rest of their lives. The leaders Feliciano Corta-Mato, Bruno, Daniel, João, Sabino, and Joaquim Calisto remained at large and formed other quilombos in the 1870s, like the famous Limoeiro. For them, the 1867 rebellion remained undefeated.

* * *

Abolitionism was made in part in the clandestine paths through which quilombolas moved people, goods, weapons, and information during the Triple Alliance War. Their politics of emancipation grew out of imperfect strategic and economic alliances that hinted at alternative ways of living—even if traversed by gender differences, racial tensions, and the instability of secrecy pacts—that complicated the Brazilian state's endeavors on the home front. It also developed from the multiple strategies the enslaved employed to bring about social change, such as armed insurgency, the formation of maroon families, and recourse to the authority of print and the written word. Quilombolas often perceived opposition to Brazil's war efforts in Paraguay as a potential step toward general emancipation, and their widespread presence also curtailed state encroachment into vast territories, albeit under constant threat of destruction. Existing as quasi-peasant or itinerant communities, quilombos played a subversive political role that would only expand in the 1870s and 1880s.

As Brazilian soldiers fought in the battlefields of Paraguay, quilombolas waged war domestically against more than just slavery. Sometimes they struck out for a world upside down where the enslaved dictated the terms of emancipation and the whites were poor. Other times they fought among themselves to determine the best course of action against slaveholders and the different outcomes of rebellion for men and women. Quilombola activism was so prominent in the 1860s that it entered the war rhetoric in Brazil. When allied forces defeated Paraguayan resistance and advanced on

Asunción in late 1868, Brazilian newspapers portrayed the search for Solano López and his dwindling group of followers as something akin to a hunt for quilombolas: "López is no longer the head of his nation, he's the head of a quilombo!," exclaimed a correspondent from Montevideo.[139] After the takeover of the Paraguayan capital in January 1869, a citizen from São Paulo concurred: "The war will end immediately with the escape, imprisonment or death of López, who will not be able to sustain himself in the quilombo he will form with his few fellow fugitives."[140] In the end of the last year of the war, a correspondent of the influential *Jornal do Commercio* concluded from Asunción: "The question today, therefore, is to limit the expenses of this war, if possible, to our ordinary budget, bringing back to the Empire most of our army, and reducing the forces that remain here to the number strictly necessary to pursue the quilombola with small expeditions, which today can no longer offer any resistance."[141]

For all the power of circulating antislavery discourses, Brazilian abolitionism had yet another point of origin in black activism. The letters exchanged among Serro rebels, those carried by quilombolas like Maria of Diamantina, or the one Daniel and João forced Plácido to write in Viana survive as records of the deliberative voice of the enslaved in the process of emancipation.[142] And so are the powerful actions of quilombolas like the one that caused Carolina to lose her tongue in Diamantina. Following so many conspiracies, the Viana insurgency represented a culmination of the struggles of the 1860s in which quilombolas mapped out political opportunity onto the turmoil caused by the Triple Alliance War. They sought to bring about nothing short of freedom. To 1871, the official marker of Brazil's transition into a state-controlled emancipation process, Afro-descendants brought a long tradition of insurgent abolitionism that relied largely on literacy and a transnational understanding of history that recast what belonging could mean.

How the Enslaved Storied Their World

A year before the end of slavery in Brazil, slave literacy found its way into the visual record of Rio de Janeiro's signature illustrated magazine. At a time of radical polarization between abolitionists and a planter-led conservative countermovement, the October 1887 issue of the *Revista Illustrada* offered a brief glimpse of what enslaved people in rural areas were up to. The tone was ironic and the trace unmistakable. Italian graphic artist Angelo Agostini, the most famous cartoonist in the imperial capital, depicted an enslaved man reading aloud from the newspaper *O Paiz*. The scene was part of a two-page illustrated story entitled "Extraordinary Things," which offered commentary on current events.[1] The satirical sketches clearly communicated the *Revista's* criticism of the slow pace of emancipation, which it blamed on the conservative wing of Pedro II's government. To portray the enslaved as readers, however, Agostini drew inspiration from what the press reported as fact. In early October, the *Correio Paulistano* published news coming from Itatiba of a planter who found his enslaved workers reading the republican-leaning newspaper *A Província de São Paulo*. The reprint from the local *Imprensa Ituana* read: "We are informed: On a farm in the municipality of Itatiba, when the owner went to the fields to check on the work of his slaves, instead of finding them at work, guess what they were doing? Huddled together, they listened intently to one of them read the newspaper *A Província*, which was nothing more or less than a summary of a speech by Councilor Dantas! The naturally surprised master . . . kept quiet."[2]

Agostini had often addressed the issue of slavery. The *Revista Illustrada* was, after all, an important voice in public debates about the future of the institution in Brazil. Enslaved people were often featured in sections such as the recurring "Slavery Scenes," in which Agostini advanced an abolitionist argument by emphasizing the violence of masters and the degradation of

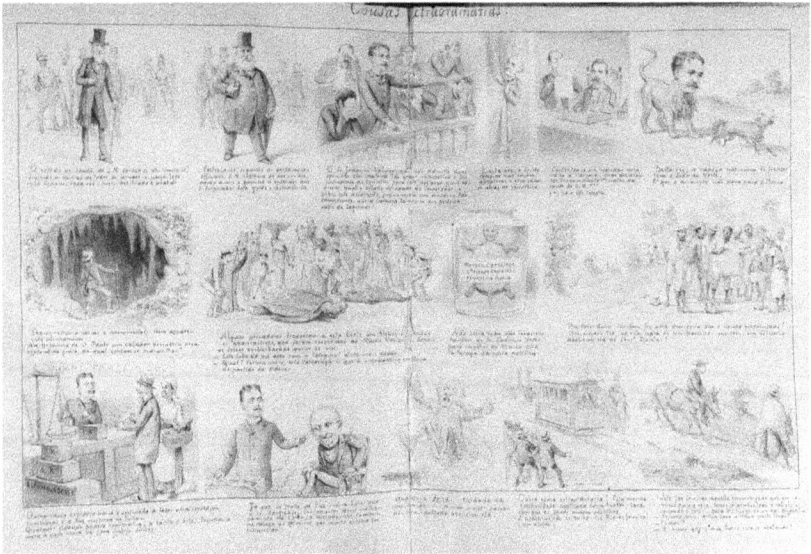

Figure 16. "Extraordinary Things," *Revista Illustrada*, no. 467, October 15, 1887. Fundação Casa de Rui Barbosa, Brazil.

the enslaved under an old-fashioned system set up by ruthless landowners.[3] Although central to his understanding of abolition as a necessary guarantor of Brazil's sovereignty and economic development, Agostini's portrayals of the enslaved often placed them in the role of victims brutalized by a retrograde elite. For him, slavery—and those supposedly stupefied by it—was primarily an obstacle to social progress, a vision very much in line with the nationalist antislavery narrative that dominated the abolitionist press.[4]

Thus "Extraordinary Things" can be confusing at first glance. The series depicts the enslaved in an active yet unthreatening manner, as if inviting the reader to share in a secret moment of their lives. This snippet of black agency appeared in the context of other illustrations on topics ranging from the emperor's fitness to rule to the propagation of electricity in Rio de Janeiro. An image of Pedro II's failing health opened the sequence of images in the first strip, as Joaquim Nabuco, one of the most important national leaders of the abolitionist movement, gestured from the royal chamber to get more news about the emperor from the Baron of Cotegipe, the proslavery chief of cabinet. Suffering from diabetes, Pedro II had fallen ill in public in February 1887, sparking rumors of his declining ability to govern.[5] Cotegipe, the strongman of the regime, hides behind the curtains of the Parliament to avoid catching Nabuco's attention, as if trying to keep a dangerous matter under control.

Next, on the strip below, a turtle and a sea lion, deemed worthy of preservation at the National Museum of Natural History, serve as emblems of the Conservative Party. Cotegipe appears as the antiquated species "Wander Cotegipus," floating in formaldehyde in a glass jar. The third series of drawings concludes the exposé of curious facts in the life of the empire by addressing the arrival of electric power in Rio de Janeiro. Agostini mockingly suggests that Mr. Hargreaves of the Companhia de Força e Luz (Rio's electric power company) use it to illuminate the head of Cotegipe, who is seen jumping from his seat, hair flying, as wires give him an electric shock. The following caption summarizes Agostini's sharp view of the Party of Order: "When it comes to Power . . . careful with its application, if you don't want to pass for an exalted abolitionist!"[6] The entire series reads as a commentary on the conservative backlash that followed the recent Liberal defeat in parliamentary elections.

The "extraordinary fact" that interests us most appears on the far right of the second strip, next to the bottled Baron of Cotegipe, and below a caricature of Joaquim Nabuco as the "Lion of the North" towering over a tiny, fox-like Cotegipe.[7] On what appears to be a coffee plantation, in the middle of a workday, a group of enslaved men, women, and children, all barefoot, gather around a literate peer reading the abolitionist newspaper O Paiz. Attentive to the news being effectively "published," some still lean against the hoes used to plow the land from sunrise to sunset.[8] From behind, a white master wearing a straw hat and a walking stick approaches the group, showing great surprise at what he sees. The caption under the picture reads: "A planter also made a discovery that puzzled him. A slave in the field was reading an abolitionist speech by Conselheiro Dantas for his peers to hear!" The cartoon was a parody of slave literacy, meant to reinforce the notion of elite impotence in the face of the popularity of abolitionism and the disorganization of rural labor in the 1880s. Political news traveled fast, the reader can infer from the illustration, reaching even those least likely to be seen with a newspaper in hand.

The reference to O Paiz was no accident. During the decade of abolition, the daily was a popular newspaper in Rio de Janeiro. In 1887, Quintino Bocaiúva, president of the Republican Party, served as its editor after the brief tenure of the abolitionist Rui Barbosa. Joaquim Nabuco also used the paper as a platform to mobilize readers for the legal abolition of slavery. On

Figure 17. Detail from *Revista Ilustrada*, no. 467, October 15, 1887. Fundação
Casa de Rui Barbosa, Brazil.

August 30, 1888, for example, he contributed an entire article to *O Paiz* about
his encounter with Angelo Agostini at a banquet in honor of the abolitionist
Antônio Bento. Nabuco described Agostini as a brother in arms in the abolitionist campaign, defining his importance as an illustrator: "For twenty years,
his pencil had the unfailing courage to tell the truth to the enemies of national
progress in a language that everyone could understand. His *Revista* was the
abolitionist bible of the people [*povo*] who could not read."[9]

Ironically, *O Paiz* played the same role in the *Revista Illustrada* when in
the hands of the enslaved persons caricatured in 1887. The paper popularized the parliamentary activism of Manuel Pinto de Souza Dantas, a Liberal Party member from the province of Bahia who had presided over the
Council of Ministers in 1884. That same year, his son, Rodolfo Dantas, introduced an emancipation bill that gained wide support in abolitionist circles,
proposing the freeing of elderly slaves without compensation to masters.
Although defeated in its full scope by a proslavery alliance of Conservatives
and Liberals, the Dantas project formed the seed of what became the 1885

Sexagenarian Law, which freed enslaved people over sixty years of age.[10] After the vote, Dantas's cabinet fell, leaving him as the only prominent abolitionist voice in the Senate during the Baron of Cotegipe's tenure as chief of cabinet. João Maurício Wanderley, as the baron was named, a sugar producer and slaveholder also from Bahia, finally passed the Saraiva-Cotegipe Law in 1885 to control the growing progressive wave in Parliament. Until 1888, he worked to defend the interests of the slaveholding elite and suppress popular mobilization for abolition.[11]

Enraged by these developments, abolitionists radicalized the ongoing movement in the streets, plantations, and newspapers of the empire. The dramatic breakdown of plantation discipline between 1886 and 1887 underscores the role that education had long played in the run-up to abolition. The political worlds of the enslaved changed to accommodate the 1885 law, the abolitionist movement's commitment to unconditional emancipation, and the elimination of public flogging as a punishment for crimes committed by enslaved people in 1886.[12] For the first time in Brazilian history, the activism of the enslaved gained a measure of legitimacy as abolitionist leaders turned to clandestine activities to destabilize the power of slaveholders in rural Brazil. In the coffee regions of São Paulo and Rio de Janeiro, Antônio Bento, Quintino de Lacerda, and many others extended networks of protection to escaped slaves, much like the US Underground Railroad, and supported the formation of abolitionist quilombos.[13] In the northeast, alliances also encouraged slave flight in search of free soil, often to Ceará and Amazonas, where provincial abolition had taken place in 1884. Be that as it may, Cotegipe presided over brutal reprisals of radical abolitionism, while Dantas continued to fight for an emancipationist agenda in the Senate. However, Dantas's longstanding sympathy for the "slaves' cause" earned him a reputation among conservatives as the paladin of revolutionary agitation, which he was far from representing.

Agostini's illustration amplified Dantas's leading role in the opposition while suggesting that slave unrest would be the price of inaction on the issue of emancipation. The slaveholder in his drawing was stunned not only to find his captives reading instead of working but also to realize that they were drawn to political debates that threatened Brazil with social revolution. The enslaved appear to be interested parties but are still susceptible to incitement by outside forces. Their collective reading was, after all, an "extraordinary thing" designed to provoke laughter from an audience of white readers. But that should be no laughing matter. Access to literacy remained at the heart of white fears of slave rebellion in 1887. What seems inescapable, however, is Agostini's attention to the role of the press as a vector of information on which all kinds of abolitionism depended, and not only the medium adopted by the formally educated. Newspapers in imperial Brazil had more listeners than readers, and, as we have seen, these included the enslaved.

What Agostini intended as a caricature of the reach of abolitionism in the 1880s takes on new meaning when understood as a metaphor for the subordinate place the enslaved still occupy in the historiography of abolition. Positioned almost as voyeurs of a national or transnational conversation that is about them but not addressed to them, enslaved people remain objects of discourse rather than subjects of historical change. In *Freedom's Horizon*, I have suggested that we shift our attention to the decades before abolitionism coalesced as a national mass movement in Brazil to focus on the people reading the newspaper in 1887. By analyzing the history of a black insurgent tradition in Brazil, I have sought to document black imaginaries of freedom that expose the limits of history writing about abolitionism itself. Even if unintentionally, Agostini's account makes visible the contested terrain in which literacy was linked to individual and collective demands for social justice throughout the century of abolition. Freedom could be a fateful encounter with a printed document circulated orally.

The scene in the *Revista* evokes the strategic and collaborative ways in which the enslaved narrated and acted on the nineteenth-century world. The rumors they gleaned from the newspapers informed an insurgent political geography that placed freedom on the horizon in Brazil. Black abolitionism depended on collective problem-solving, shared memories, foreshadowing of what was to come, and knowledge of the prospects of black insurgency. Although enslaved people never produced an "abolitionist press" per se, as free black abolitionists did, their familiarity with periodicals was a mark of their autonomous participation at a time when print culture was considered a privilege of the white elite. Their politics of emancipation demand that we tell the story of abolition differently.

Insurgent abolitionism did not uniformly propose a Haiti-like solution to slavery even as it legitimized armed struggle as an aspect of black politics. The enslaved often worked in conjunction with parliamentary politics and international actors to ensure the application of abolitionist measures, to free the illegally enslaved, to enforce notions of free soil, to occupy land, or to push the boundaries of conditional freedom. Timing was an essential component of their emancipatory practices. The explosive intersection of national and Atlantic histories gave Afro-descendants a common repertoire of struggle that facilitated the creation of antislavery networks and expanded the meanings of black rebellion. This repertoire simultaneously borrowed from diasporic religions, subaltern cosmopolitanism, and multigenerational battles against the slave trade and re-enslavement. Insurgent abolitionism connected British imperialism in Latin America and Africa, grounded hemispheric history in early iterations of black internationalism, and gave new meaning to a black civil rights agenda in Brazil which is perceived mostly through the lengths of eminent black individuals.

Freedom's Horizon ends where most accounts of Brazilian abolition begin. The book, after all, was born out of a desire to understand how black traditions of rebellion constructed abolitionism as a form of engagement with Atlantic history. Beginning with the rise of grassroots activism in the era of the suppression of the slave trade, it documents the ways in which Africans and their descendants transformed nineteenth-century political and diplomatic conflicts into struggles for black freedom, radicalizing antislavery as they thought comparatively about abolition in the Americas. The personal and collective journeys covered here took place before gradual emancipation became law in 1871, accelerating the social and political crisis that ended slavery in 1888. This temporal focus was intended to honor the timeline of abolitionism that Afro-descendants built from their daily experiences with human trafficking, bonded labor, punishment, and racism.

Moreover, a long-term perspective underscores the fact that the link between slave rebellion and abolition is not to be found in the expediency of direct causation. The politics of emancipation that underpinned black life in Brazil was cumulative, quotidian, and deeply rooted in historical circumstances. In the 1880s, Afro-descendants brought to bear a wealth of strategic knowledge developed over decades of coexistence between slavery and freedom. Thus, to the liberal tenor of the official abolitionist movement, they added a different narrative of emancipation that invoked collective literacy, practices of self-liberation, expectations of land ownership, and grassroots diplomacy tactics borrowed from a transnational runaway tradition. Insurgent slaves collectively broke with abolitionism as a reformist movement that condemned slavery but saw its demise as an object of state policy. Their imagination was necessary to abolition, even if it did not make the dream of unlimited freedom come true.

The Brazilian republic that emerged from the slave empire in 1889 did not incorporate insurgent visions of freedom. These, however, remained alive in the postemancipation period and continue to frame social and political understandings of the unfinished nature of emancipation in Brazil. Where the horizon of freedom once highlighted the interconnectedness of slavery with global geopolitics, it now points to the ways in which racial subjugation has outlived the institution's legal life to thwart equality in the Brazilian present.

NOTES

Introduction

1. Processo crime, insurreição, José Cabrinha (escravo), 9, Arquivo Nacional do Rio de Janeiro (hereafter ANRJ), Corte de Apelação, Serro, 1865.

2. Robert W. Slenes, "Múltiplos de porcos e diamantes: A economia escravista de Minas Gerais no século XIX," *Cadernos IFCH/Unicamp*, 17 (1985): 1–80.

3. Processo crime, insurreição, José Cabrinha, 33, 75.

4. Processo crime, insurreição, José Cabrinha, 12.

5. This data, compiled by the minister of justice Francisco José Furtado, covers the period between 1860 and 1864. "Relatório do Ministério da Justiça de 1865 referente ao ano de 1864, Estatística Criminal," Biblioteca Nacional, Rio de Janeiro, microfilm.

6. Communities of fugitive slaves were originally called "mocambos" in colonial Brazil, a Kimbundo word used to designate "war camps" or "hideouts" in West Central Africa. The word continued in use but eventually gave way to "quilombo" in the eighteenth century, an Ovinbundu term also associated with Imbangala (jaga) warriors and their initiation rituals. Either way, both terms of Central African origin evoke military strategies—encampments—in pre-colonial Africa and/or resistance to slavery in Portuguese territories and may have spread through Portuguese administrative practices. In the book, I stay true to the most common usage in the nineteenth century, that is, *quilombos* and *quilombolas*, the inhabitants of a quilombo. Flávio dos Santos Gomes, *Mocambos e Quilombos: Uma história do campesinato negro no Brasil* (São Paulo: Claro Enigma, 2015).

7. Brazil participated in the transatlantic slave trade for more than three centuries either legally in the colonial and national periods (1550–1831) or illegally (1831–56). Leslie Bethell, *The Abolition of the Brazilian Slave Trade: Britain, Brazil and the Slave Trade Question, 1807–1869* (Cambridge: Cambridge University Press, 1970); Robert E. Conrad, *World of Sorrow: The African Slave Trade to Brazil* (Baton Rouge: Louisiana State University Press, 1986); Rafael de Bivar Marquese, Tâmis Parron, and Márcia Regina Berbel, *Slavery and Politics: Brazil and Cuba, 1790–1850*, trans. Leonardo Marques (Albuquerque: University of New Mexico Press, 2016); José Murilo de Carvalho, *Teatro de sombras: A política imperial* (Rio de Janeiro: Civilização Brasileira, 2003).

8. In approaching the enslaved as agents of abolitionism, I draw inspiration especially from João José Reis, "'Nos achamos em campo a tratar da liberdade': A resistência negra no Brasil oitocentista," in *Viagem incompleta: A experiência brasileira (1500–2000)*, ed. Carlos Guilherme Mota (São Paulo: Senac, 2000), 241–63; Flávio dos Santos Gomes, *Histórias de quilombolas: Mocambos e comunidades de senzalas no Rio de Janeiro, séc. XIX* (Rio de Janeiro: Arquivo Nacional, 1995).

9. On transnational perspectives of Brazilian history, see Keila Grinberg, "The Two Enslavements of Rufina: Slavery and International Relations on the Southern Border of

Nineteenth-Century Brazil," *Hispanic American Historical Review* 96, no. 2 (2016): 259–90; Micol Seigel, "Beyond Compare: Comparative Method After the Transnational Turn," *Radical History Review*, no. 91 (2005): 62–90; Roquinaldo Ferreira, *Cross-Cultural Exchange in the Atlantic World: Angola and Brazil During the Era of the Slave Trade* (New York: Cambridge University Press, 2012); George Reid Andrews, *Afro-Latin America, 1800–2000* (Oxford: Oxford University Press, 2004).

10. João José Reis and Flávio dos Santos Gomes, eds., *Revoltas escravas no Brasil* (São Paulo: Companhia das Letras, 2021); João José Reis, *Rebelião escrava no Brasil: A história do levante dos Malês em 1835* (São Paulo: Companhia das Letras, 2003); Maria Helena P. T. Machado, *O plano e o pânico: Os movimentos sociais na década da abolição* (Rio de Janeiro: Editora UFRJ; São Paulo: EDUSP, 1994).

11. Adom Getachew, *Worldmaking After Empire: The Rise and Fall of Self-Determination* (Princeton, NJ: Princeton University Press, 2019).

12. Thomas Whigham, *The Road to Armageddon: Paraguay Versus the Triple Alliance, 1866–70* (Calgary: University of Calgary Press, 2017); Vitor Izecksohn, *Slavery and War in the Americas: Race, Citizenship, and State Building in the United States and Brazil, 1861–1870* (Charlottesville: University of Virginia Press, 2014); Marlene Daut, *Awakening the Ashes: An Intellectual History of the Haitian Revolution* (Chapel Hill, University of North Carolina Press, 2023), 20.

13. Brazil's first 1872 national census estimated that only 15.75 percent of the total Brazilian population (including slaves) qualified as officially literate. Brasil, Diretoria Geral de Estatística, *Recenseamento da população do Império do Brasil em 1872* (Rio de Janeiro: Leuzinger e Filhos, 1872).

14. This is not a study of the "black literate mind" in Brazil. On black thinkers and men of letters in nineteenth-century Brazil, see André Rebouças, *Cartas da África: Registro de correspondência, 1891–1893*, ed. Hebe Mattos (São Paulo: Chão Editora, 2022); Ana Flávia Magalhães Pinto, *Escritos de liberdade: Literatos negros, racismo e cidadania no Brasil oitocentista* (Campinas: Editora da Unicamp, 2018); Ligia Fonseca Ferreira, ed., *Com a palavra, Luiz Gama: Poemas, artigos, cartas, máximas* (São Paulo: Imprensa Oficial, 2011).

15. Maria Cristina Wissenbach, "Cartas, procurações, escapulários e patuás: Os múltiplos significados da escrita entre escravos e forros na sociedade oitocentista," *Revista Brasileira de História da Educação*, no. 4 (2002): 103–22.

16. The educator Paulo Freire elaborated the issue like few others when articulating the tenets of a democratic and popular pedagogy in the 1960s, a time when half of the Brazilian population was still illiterate: "Reading the world precedes reading the word, and the subsequent reading of the word cannot dispense with continually reading the world. Language and reality are dynamically intertwined. The understanding attained by critical reading of a text implies perceiving the relationship between text and context." I am interested in this intertwining of literacy and the lived experiences of the dispossessed or the notion that reading the world does not necessarily depend on a complete mastery of written culture. Paulo Freire and Loretta Slover (trans.), "The Importance of the Act of Reading," *Journal of Education* 165, no. 1 (1983), 5.

17. Beatriz G. Mamigonian, *Africanos livres: A abolição do tráfico de escravos no Brasil* (São Paulo: Companhia das Letras, 2017); Sandra Lauderdale Graham, "Writing from the Margins: Brazilian Slaves and Written Culture," *Comparative Studies in Society and History* 49, no. 3 (2007): 611–36; Bianca Premo, *Enlightenment on Trial: Ordinary Litigants and Colonialism in the Spanish Empire* (New York: Oxford University Press, 2017).

18. I borrow insights from the scholarship on the history of education in Brazil, the field of new literacy studies, and from studies of African American culture. Marialva Barbosa, *Escravos e o mundo da comunicação: Oralidade, leitura e escrita no século XIX* (Rio de Janeiro: Mauad Editora, 2016); Martyn Lyons, Sofia Kotilainen, and Ilkka Mäkinen, eds., "The Functions and Purpose of Vernacular Literacy," special issue, *Journal of Social History* 49, no. 2 (2015); Martyn Lyons, *The Writing Culture of Ordinary People in Europe, c. 1860–1920* (Cambridge: Cambridge University Press, 2013); David Barton, Mary Hamilton, and Roz Ivanič, eds., *Situated Literacies: Reading and Writing in Context* (London: Routledge, 2000); Janet Duitsman Cornelius, *"When I Can Read My Title Clear": Literacy, Slavery, and Religion in the Antebellum South* (Columbia: University of South Carolina Press, 1991); Elizabeth McHenry, *Forgotten Readers: Recovering the Lost History of African American Literary Societies* (Durham, NC: Duke University Press, 2002); Heather Andrea Williams, *Self-Taught: African American Education in Slavery and Freedom* (Chapel Hill: University of North Carolina Press, 2005).

19. Robert Krueger, "Brazilian Slaves Represented in Their Own Words." *Slavery and Abolition* 23, no. 2 (2002): 169–86.

20. Latin Americanists have played a central role in reinterpreting intellectual history as also the realm of subaltern people. For some examples, see Karen Graubart, *"Pesa más la libertad*: Slavery, Legal Claims, and the History of Afro-Latin American Ideas," *William and Mary Quarterly* 78, no. 3 (2021): 427–58; Corinna Zeltsman, *Ink Under the Fingernails: Printing Politics in Nineteenth-Century Mexico* (Oakland: University of California Press, 2021); Cristina Soriano, *Tides of Revolution: Information, Insurgencies, and the Crisis of Colonial Rule in Venezuela* (Albuquerque: University of New Mexico Press, 2018); José Ramón Jouve-Martín, *Esclavos de la ciudad letrada: Esclavitud, escritura y colonialismo em Lima, 1650–1700* (Lima: Instituto de Estudos Peruanos, 2005).

21. Christopher Hager, *Word by Word: Emancipation and the Act of Writing* (Cambridge, MA: Harvard University Press, 2013), 5.

22. The Golden Law of May 13, 1888, abolished slavery in Brazil without compensation to masters. Angela Alonso, *The Last Abolition: The Brazilian Antislavery Movement, 1868–1888* (Cambridge: Cambridge University Press, 2022); Celso Castilho, *Slave Emancipation and Transformations in Brazilian Political Citizenship* (Pittsburgh: University of Pittsburgh Press, 2016); Jeffrey D. Needell, *The Sacred Cause: The Abolitionist Movement, Afro-Brazilian Mobilization, and Imperial Politics in Rio de Janeiro* (Stanford, CA: Stanford University Press, 2020).

23. Focusing on the thirty years between 1868 and 1878, Angela Alonso has identified the existence of 2,214 abolitionist events and 367 civil associations in 206 cities throughout the twenty provinces of the Brazilian Empire. Alonso, *The Last Abolition*, 11.

24. See, among several other titles, Eduardo Spiller Pena, *Pajens da Casa Imperial: Jurisconsultos, escravidão e a lei de 1871* (Campinas: Editora de Unicamp, 2001); Elciene Azevedo, *O direito dos escravos: Lutas jurídicas e abolicionismo na província de São Paulo na segunda metade do século XIX* (Campinas: Editora da Unicamp, 2010); Maria Helena P. T. Machado, Luciana da Cruz Brito, Iamara da Silva Viana, and Flávio dos Santos Gomes, eds., *Ventres livres? Gênero, maternidade e legislação* (São Paulo: Editora Unesp, 2021).

25. Robert E. Conrad, *The Destruction of Brazilian Slavery, 1850–1888* (Berkeley: University of California Press, 1972), 305–9.

26. Felipe Azevedo e Souza, *Nas ruas: Abolicionismo, republicanism e movimento operário em Recife* (Salvador: EDUFBA, 2021).

27. For a sample of the Brazilian historiography of abolition, see Brodwyn M. Fischer and Keila Grinberg, eds., *The Boundaries of Freedom: Slavery, Abolition, and the Making of Modern Brazil* (Cambridge: Cambridge University Press, 2023); Maria Helena P. T. Machado and Celso Castilho, *Tornando-se livre: Agentes históricos e lutas sociais no processo de abolição* (São Paulo: EDUSP, 2015); Camillia Cowling, *Conceiving Freedom: Women of Color, Gender, and the Abolition of Slavery in Havana and Rio de Janeiro* (Chapel Hill: University of North Carolina Press, 2013); Wlamyra Ribeiro de Albuquerque, *O jogo da dissimulação: Abolição e cidadania negra no Brasil* (Rio de Janeiro: Companhia das Letras, 2009); Célia Maria Marinho de Azevedo, *Onda negra, medo branco: O negro no imaginário das elites, século XIX* (Rio de Janeiro: Paz e Terra, 1987); Hebe Maria Mattos, *Das cores do silêncio: Os significados da liberdade no sudeste escravista, Brasil século XIX* (Rio de Janeiro: Editora Nova Fronteira, 1998).

28. Robin D. G. Kelley, *Freedom Dreams: The Black Radical Imagination* (Boston: Beacon Press, 2002); Julius Scott, *The Common Wind: Currents of Afro-American Currents in the Age of the Haitian Revolution* (London: Verso, 2018); Monique Bedasse, et al., "AHR Conversation: Black Internationalism," *American Historical Review* 125, no. 5 (2020): 1699–739; Brandon R. Byrd, *The Black Republic: African Americans and the Fate of Haiti* (Philadelphia: University of Pennsylvania Press, 2020); Leslie M. Alexander, *Fear of a Black Republic: Haiti and the Birth of Black Internationalism in the United States* (Urbana: University of Illinois Press, 2023).

29. Ada Ferrer, "Slavery, Freedom, and the Work of Speculation," *Small Axe* 23, no. 1 (2019): 220–28; Saidiya V. Hartman, *Scenes of Subjection: Terror, Slavery, and Self-Making in Nineteenth-Century America* (New York: Oxford University Press, 1997); Saidiya V. Hartman, "Venus in Two Acts," *Small Axe* 12, no. 2 (2008): 1–14; Stephanie E. Smallwood, "The Politics of the Archive and History's Accountability to the Enslaved," *History of the Present: A Journal of Critical History* 11, no. 2 (2016): 117–32; Marisa Fuentes, *Dispossessed Lives: Enslaved Women, Violence, and the Archive* (Philadelphia: University of Pennsylvania Press, 2016).

30. For an overview of the history of quilombos in Brazil, see João José Reis and Flávio dos Santos Gomes, eds., *Liberdade por um fio* (São Paulo: Companhia das Letras, 1996).

31. White discourse about outside agitators of enslaved populations has a long history in the Atlantic World. Michel-Rolph Trouillot, *Silencing the Past: Power and the Production of History* (Boston: Beacon Press, 1995), 103.

32. Ranajit Guha, "The Prose of Counter-Insurgency," in *Selected Subaltern Studies*, ed. Ranajit Guha and Gayatri Chakravorty Spivak (New York: Oxford University Press, 1988), 45–84.

33. On works of social geographers and historians concerned with issues of power in the production of space, see Vincent Brown, *Tacky's Revolt: The Story of an Atlantic Slave War* (Cambridge, MA: Belknap Press of Harvard University Press, 2020); Vincent Brown, "Mapping a Slave Revolt: Visualizing Spatial History Through the Archives of Slavery," *Social Text* 33, no. 4 (2015): 134–41; Ernesto Bassi, *An Aqueous Territory Sailor Geographies and New Granada's Transimperial Greater Caribbean World* (Durham, NC: Duke University Press, 2016); David Harvey, "The Sociological and Geographical Imaginations," *International Journal of Politics, Culture, and Society* 18 (2005): 211–55; Phillip Troutman, "Grapevine in the Slave Market: African American Geopolitical Literacy and the 1841 *Creole* Revolt," in *The Chattel Principle: Internal Slave Trades in the Americas*, ed. Walter Johnson (New Haven, CT: Yale University Press, 2004), 203–33; Katherine McKittrick, *Demonic Grounds: Black Women and the Cartographies of Struggle* (Minneapolis: University of Minnesota Press, 2009); Stephanie Camp, *Closer to Freedom: Enslaved Women and Everyday Resistance in the Plantation South* (Chapel Hill: University of North Carolina Press, 2006).

34. Lawrence Hill, *Diplomatic Relations Between the United States and Brazil* (Durham, NC: Duke University Press, 1932).

35. For other examples of how slave flight influenced international legal regimes, see Keila Grinberg, "Illegal Enslavement, International Relations, and International Law on the Southern Border of Brazil," *Law and History Review* 35, no. 1 (2017): 31–52; Keila Grinberg, "Free Soil: The Generation and Circulation of an Atlantic Legal Principle," in *Free Soil in the Atlantic World*, ed. Sue Peabody and Keila Grinberg (London: Routledge, 2014), 1–10.

36. Dale Tomich and a number of historians have used the term *second slavery* to describe how the Haitian Revolution and British industrialization sparked a reformulation of political economies in the Americas, shifting economic gains from old colonial slave zones like Saint Domingue to Cuba, the US South, and Brazil. They argue that the nineteenth century was an era in which direct political domination of colonial riches ceased to represent the obvious path to global dominance. I don't contest this geopolitical realignment but rather explore how the enslaved seized on the contradictions of a changing world to enact a larger challenge to chattel slavery. Dale Tomich, *Through the Prism of Slavery: Labor, Capital, and World Economy* (Boulder, CO: Rowman and Littlefield, 2004); Dale Tomich, ed., *Atlantic Transformations: Empire, Politics, and Slavery During the Nineteenth Century* (Albany: State University of New York Press, 2020); Daniel Rood, *The Reinvention of Atlantic Slavery: Technology, Labor, Race, and Capitalism in the Greater Caribbean* (New York: Oxford University Press, 2017); Roberto Saba, *American Mirror: The United States and Brazil in the Age of Emancipation* (Princeton, NJ: Princeton University Press, 2021).

37. David Brion Davis, *Inhuman Bondage: The Rise and Fall of Slavery in the New World* (New York: Oxford University Press, 2006); David Brion Davis, *The Problem of Slavery in the Age of Emancipation* (New York: Alfred A. Knopf, 2014); Seymour Drescher, *Abolition: A History of Slavery and Antislavery* (New York: Cambridge University Press, 2009). Classic comparative studies published in English approach Brazil as a case of late emancipation enacted through parliamentary reform in the 1880s: Conrad, *Destruction of Brazilian Slavery*; Robert Brent Toplin, *The Abolition of Slavery in Brazil* (New York: Atheneum, 1972); Célia Marinho de Azevedo offered a more nuanced analysis, including slave resistance as a factor in the destruction of Brazilian slavery, in *Abolitionism in the United States and Brazil: A Comparative Perspective* (New York: Garland, 1995).

38. Postcolonial studies inform some of my thinking in the book. Ranajit Guha, *Elementary Aspects of Peasant Insurgency in Colonial India* (Durham, NC: Duke University Press, 1999); Ileana Rodríguez, ed., *The Latin American Subaltern Studies Reader* (Durham, NC: Duke University Press, 2001).

39. On new works of hemispheric history that offer insights into the historiographical implications of fully engaging with the shared context of "American" abolitions, see Alice Baumgartner, *South to Freedom: Runaway Slaves to Mexico and the Road to the Civil War* (New York: Basic Books, 2020); Aline Helg, *Slave No More: Self-Liberation Before Abolitionism in the Americas* (Chapel Hill: University of North Carolina Press, 2019); Magdalena Candioti, ed., "Dossier: Nuevos horizontes en la historia de la esclavitud en América Latina," *Revista Paginas* 13, no. 33 (2021); Marcela Echeverri and Celso Castilho, eds., "Dossier: Ecos atlánticos de las aboliciones hispanoamericanas," *Historia Mexicana* 69, no. 2 (274) (2019); María Verónica Secreto and Flávio dos Santos Gomes, eds., *Territórios ao Sul: Escravidão, escritas e fronteiras coloniais e pós-coloniais na América* (Rio de Janeiro: 7Letras, 2017); Keila Grinberg, *As fronteiras da escravidão e da liberdade no sul da América* (Rio de Janeiro: 7Letras, 2013).

40. On the influence of the Haitian Revolution in Latin America, see Marixa Lasso, *Myths of Harmony: Race and Republicanism During the Age of Revolution, Colombia 1795–1831* (Pittsburgh: University of Pittsburgh Press, 2007); David P. Geggus and Norman Fiering, eds., *The World of the Haitian Revolution* (Bloomington: Indiana University Press, 2009); Laurent Dubois and Julius S. Scott, *Origins of the Black Atlantic* (New York: Routledge, 2010); Marco Morel, *A Revolução do Haiti e o Brasil escravista: O que não deve ser dito* (Jundiaí, SP: Paço Editorial, 2017); Soriano, *Tides of Revolution.*

41. Luiz Geraldo Silva, "Negros de Cartagena y Pernambuco en la era de las revoluciones atlánticas: Trayectorias y estructuras (1750–1840)," *Anuario Colombiano de Historia Social y de la Cultura* 40, no. 2 (2013): 211–40.

42. As Hendrik Kraay argues, popular participation in politics at the time was hardly "about independence narrowly defined; rather it was about the big questions that the Age of Revolutions posed in a society highly dependent on the slave trade (imports averaged nearly fifty thousand per year in the 1810s and 1820s), close to 30 percent of whose population was enslaved, and in which free people of color were the most rapidly growing segment of the population." Kraay, "Slaves, Indians, and the 'Classes of Color': Popular Participation in Brazilian Independence," in *The Cambridge History of the Age of Atlantic Revolutions*, vol. 3, ed. Willem Klooster (Cambridge: Cambridge University Press, 2023), 523. On critical interpretations of Brazilian independence, see István Jancsó, ed., *Independência: História e historiografia* (São Paulo: Hucitec, 2005); Marcus J. M. de Carvalho, "O outro lado da Independência: Quilombos, negros e pardos em Pernambuco (Brasil), 1817–23," *Luso-Brazilian Review* 43, no. 1 (2006): 1–30.

43. During the struggles for Bahian independence, many slaves worked on the front lines alongside their masters or escaped to freedom in the war-torn years of 1822 and 1823. Some reappeared later in Bahia's record of slave resistance, such as Domingos Sodré, an African diviner and healer who was arrested for "witchcraft" in the 1860s. A leading Candomblé figure, the freed Domingos considered himself a war veteran, though he was still a slave in 1823, and he wore his uniform to walk to prison to praise the fight for independence. João José Reis, *Divining Slavery and Freedom: The Story of Domingos Sodré, an African Priest in Nineteenth-Century Brazil* (New York: Cambridge University Press, 2015); Hendrik Kraay, "De outra coisa não falavam os pardos, cabras, e crioulos: O 'recrutamento' de escravos na guerra de Independência na Bahia," *Revista Brasileira de História* 22, no. 43 (2002): 109–26; João José Reis, "Rebeldia, negociação, desencanto: negros na independência na Bahia", *Revista do Centro de Pesquisa e Formação do SENAC* 15 (2022): 78–102.

44. Mundrucu (also spelled Mundurucu in some sources) would have composed the following verse to be sung by the members of his pardo battalion on June 22, 1824: "As I imitate Christophe/ This immortal Haitian/ Eia! Imitate his people/ My sovereign people." Glacyra Lazzari Leite, *Pernambuco 1824: A Confederação do Equador* (Recife: FUNDAJ, Editora Massangana, 1989), 102. On Mundrucu, see also: Vamireh Chacon, ed. and trans., *Natividade Saldanha: Da Confederação do Equador à Grã-Colômbia: Escritos políticos e manifesto de Mundrucu* (Brasília: Senado Federal, Centro Gráfico, 1983).

45. Caitlin Fitz, "Latin America and the Radicalization of U.S. Abolition," *Journal of American History* 108, no. 4 (2022): 701–25; Lloyd Belton, "'A Deep Interest in Your Cause': The Inter-American Sphere of Black Abolitionism and Civil Rights," *Slavery and Abolition* 42, no. 3 (2021): 589–609.

46. E. C. Sena, "Fugas e reescravizações em região fronteiriça—Bolívia e Brasil nas primeiras décadas dos Estados nacionais," *Estudos Ibero-Americanos* 39, no. 1 (2013): 82–98.

47. Rodrigo Wiese Randing, "Argentina, primeiro país a reconhecer a independência do Brasil," *Cadernos do CHDD* 16, no. 31 (2017): 499–524.

48. The Bolivian Constitution of 1826 declared the country free soil for those in pursuit of refuge and forbade the introduction of enslaved persons. It also endorsed the eventual abolition of slavery yet recognized the property rights of slave owners thus far. In 1851 a new constitution finally outlawed slavery in Bolivian territory. Paula Peña, *La guerra de independencia en Santa Cruz de la Sierra según sus historiadores* (Santa Cruz: Imprenta 2E, 2015); Natalia Sobrevilla Perea, Marco Antonio Villela Pamplona, and Maria Elisa Mäder, *Revoluções de independências e nacionalismos nas Américas: Peru e Bolívia* (São Paulo: Paz e Terra, 2010); Alberto R. Crespo, *Esclavos negros en Bolivia* (La Paz: Academia Nacional de Ciências de Bolivia, 1977).

49. Ron L. Seckinger, "The Chiquitos Affair: An Aborted Crisis in Brazilian-Bolivian Relations," *Luso-Brazilian Review* 11, no. 1 (1974): 30; "Devassa procedente da Ouvidoria Geral de Cuiabá em razão de boatos sobre alforria de escravos, chegada de Bolívar e projeto de República," 1826, ANRJ, Supremo Tribunal de Justiça, BR.AN.BU.0.DPP.13/003.

50. Testimony of José Coelho Lopes, Apr. 12, 1826, "Devassa," ANRJ.

51. Testimony of Captain Francisco Xavier da Silva, May 2, 1826, "Devassa," ANRJ.

52. *Piriquito* or *periquito* was a nickname for soldiers of the Brazilian army that referred to the use of green in their uniforms or caps (the usual color of the army uniform was blue). For examples, see Aluísio de Almeida, *A Revolução Liberal de 1842* (Rio de Janeiro: J. Olympio, 1944), 109; Gustavo Barroso, *História militar do Brasil* (Brasília: Senado Federal, 2015), 38. I would like to thank Hendrik Kraay for these references. The term also denominated a specific black battalion that fought the Bahian war of independence and was disbanded to other provinces, but not before they rebelled in 1824. João José Reis and Hendrik Kraay, "'The Tyrant Is Dead!' The Revolt of the Periquitos in Bahia, 1824," *Hispanic American Historical Review* 89, no. 3 (2009): 399–434.

53. In some cases, slavery was even reinstated. Yesenia Barragan has documented the trade in Free Womb children after Colombia's first gradual emancipation law in 1821, and Marcela Echeverri studied the reopening of the slave trade from the province of Popayán to Peru and Panama in the 1840s. Yesenia Barragan, "Commerce in Children: Slavery, Gradual Emancipation, and the Free Womb Trade in Colombia," *The Americas* 78, no. 2 (2021): 229–57; Marcela Echeverri, "Slavery and the Slave Trade in the South American Pacific in the Era of Abolition," *Historia Mexicana* 69, no. 2 (2019): 627–91; Sarah Washbrook, "Independence for Those Without Freedom: Slavery and Manumission in Mérida, Venezuela, 1810–1854," *Slavery and Abolition* 39, no. 4 (2018): 708–30.

54. I refer here to Christina Sharpe's observations about black being in diaspora, that is, the possibility of studying black lives outside of the categories defined by slavery. Thinking blackness "otherwise" means at once the exercise of subjectivity and a form of consciousness which existed "in excess of" enslavers and the state. Christina Sharpe, *In the Wake: On Blackness and Being* (Durham, NC: Duke University Press, 2016), 12, 18.

55. Laurent Dubois, "An Enslaved Enlightenment: Rethinking the Intellectual History of the French Atlantic," *Social History* 31, no. 1 (2006): 1–14.

56. In 2022, circa 56 percent of Brazilians self-declared as Afro-descendants. Brazilian Institute of Geography and Statistics (IBGE), "Censo 2022," https://censo2022.ibge.gov.br/panorama/ (accessed Jan. 2, 2024).

57. João José Reis and Carlos da Silva Jr., eds., *Atlântico de dor: Faces do tráfico de escravos* (Cruz das Almas, Bahia: EDUFRB; Belo Horizonte: Fino Traço, 2016), 16.

58. Lucilene Reginaldo and Roquinaldo Ferreira, eds., *África, margens e oceanos: Perspectivas de história social* (Campinas: Editora da Unicamp, 2021); Luiz Felipe de Alencastro, *The Trade in the Living: The Formation of Brazil in the South Atlantic, Sixteenth to Seventeenth Centuries* (Albany: State University of New York Press, 2018); Ferreira, *Cross-Cultural Exchange*.

59. These are estimates based on slaves disembarked in Brazil, available at the Trans-Atlantic Slave Trade Database, https://www.slavevoyages.org/voyage/database (accessed May 30, 2024).

60. In 1822, half of the Brazilian population, estimated around 4.5 million people, was made up of free and enslaved people of African descent. Either through the law or self-liberation (the country also boasted the highest rates of manumission in the Americas), free Afro-descendants corresponded to 43 percent of the Brazilian population in 1872, almost three times the number of slaves. Fischer and Grinberg, *Boundaries of Freedom*, 8.

61. Luís Felipe de Alencastro, "O pecado original da sociedade e da ordem jurídica brasileira," *Novos Estudos CEBRAP*, no. 87 (2010): 5–11; Sidney Chalhoub, "The Precariousness of Freedom in a Slave Society (Brazil in the Nineteenth Century)," *International Review of Social History* 56, no. 3 (2011): 408; Sidney Chalhoub, *A força da escravidão: Ilegalidade e costume no Brasil oitocentista* (Rio de Janeiro: Companhia das Letras, 2012).

62. Bethell, *Abolition of the Brazilian Slave Trade*.

63. The historian Luís Felipe de Alencastro eloquently describes illegal enslavement as the "original sin" of the Brazilian social and political order, a practice that has shaped the structural nature of racism in the country to this day. Alencastro, "O pecado original." On the archives and black experiences of the illegal trade, see Beatriz G. Mamigonian and Keila Grinberg, "The Crime of Illegal Enslavement and the Precariousness of Freedom in Nineteenth-Century Brazil," in Fischer and Grinberg, *Boundaries of Freedom*, 35–56; Yuko Miki, "In the Trail of the Ship," *Social Text* 37, no. 1 (2019): 87–105; Martine Jean, "The Slave Ship 'Maria da Glória' and the Bare Life of Blackness in the Age of Emancipation," *Slavery and Abolition* 42, no. 3 (2021): 522–44.

64. Mamigonian, *Africanos livres*; Richard Anderson and Henry B. Lovejoy, eds., *Liberated Africans and the Abolition of the Slave Trade, 1807–1896* (Rochester, NY: University of Rochester Press, 2020).

65. Matt Childs, "Master-Slave Rituals of Power at a Gold Mine in Nineteenth-Century Brazil," *History Workshop Journal* 53, no. 1 (2002): 43–72; Flávio dos Santos Gomes, *A hidra e os pântanos: Mocambos, quilombos e comunidades de fugitivos no Brasil (séculos XVII–XIX)* (Rio de Janeiro: Polis, 2005); Courtney Campbell, "Making Abolition Brazilian: British Law and Brazilian Abolitionists in Nineteenth-Century Minas Gerais and Pernambuco," *Slavery and Abolition* 36, no. 3 (2015): 521–43.

Chapter 1

1. *Liberated African* was the term most commonly used by the British to refer to Africans rescued from illegal slave ships and emancipated by a network of naval courts, international mixed commissions, and Atlantic authorities accountable to anti-slave-trade treaties negotiated by Britain. Brazilian authorities preferred the literal translation *africanos livres* or sometimes *emancipados* (emancipated). I use the former in the book to invoke the specific set of decrees that governed the experience of liberated Africans in Brazil, where, for example, they were subjected to fourteen years of apprenticeship after being rescued from illegal slavery.

2. On African recaptives in the Atlantic world, see Robert Conrad, "Neither Slave nor Free: The Emancipados of Brazil, 1818–1868," *Hispanic American Historical Review* 53, no. 1 (1973): 50–70; Anderson and Lovejoy, *Liberated Africans*; Mamigonian, *Africanos livres*; Sharla Fett, *Recaptured Africans: Surviving Slave Ships, Detention, and Dislocation in the Final Years of the Slave Trade* (Chapel Hill: University of North Carolina Press, 2016).

3. João was certainly a cosmopolitan participant of an Atlantic culture that bore the features of the contested encounters of Europeans, Africans, and the peoples of the Americas. Here, however, I prefer not to call him an "Atlantic Creole" and focus rather on his strategic use of language and social identity. Although familiar with cultural codes from Atlantic Africa, João was fundamentally constricted by the violence of enslavement in the heart of the Brazilian plantation economy. For a different view on the topic, see Ira Berlin, "From Creole to African: Atlantic Creoles and the Origins of African American Society in Mainland North America," *William and Mary Quarterly* 53, no. 2 (1996): 251–88.

4. Henry Howard to Antônio Paulino Limpo de Abreu, Mar. 20, 1854, ANRJ, Seção Justiça (hereafter SJ), IJ1-999. According to the Slave Voyages Database, the schooner *Congresso*, coming from Rio de Janeiro, was indeed condemned at the Cape in 1840. João was probably one of the twelve crew members listed. Between 1808 and 1867 the Royal Navy intercepted more than 1,600 slave ships carrying around 160,000 captives bound for the Americas. More than 85 percent of all slave-ship captures happened off the coast of Africa. Robert Burroughs and Richard Huzzey, eds., *The Suppression of the Atlantic Slave Trade: British Policies, Practices and Representations of Naval Coercion* (Manchester: Manchester University Press, 2015), 9.

5. Jake Christopher Richards, "Anti-Slave-Trade Law, 'Liberated Africans' and the State in the South Atlantic World, *c.* 1839–1852," *Past and Present* 241, no.1 (2018): 179–219; C. C. Saunders, "Liberated Africans in the Cape Colony in the First Half of the Nineteenth Century," *International Journal of African Historical Studies* 18, no. 2 (1985): 223–39.

6. Great Britain, Parliament, House of Lords, Accounts and Papers, Slave Trade Correspondence (Class B), *Correspondence with British Ministers and Agents in Foreign Countries, and with Foreign Ministers in England, Relating to the Slave Trade, from April 1, 1854, to March 31, 1855* (London: Harrison and Sons, 1855), vol. 19, 95.

7. Henry Howard to Antônio Paulino Limpo de Abreu, Mar. 20, 1854, ANRJ, SJ, IJ1-999.

8. Dispatch of Henry Howard to Earl Clarendon, Rio de Janeiro, Apr. 13, 1854, British Foreign Office (hereafter FO) 84/910.

9. The *mil-réis* (one thousand réis) was a unit of currency in Brazil until 1942. During the nineteenth century 1,000 réis (singular, *real*) was written 1$000; 1,000 mil-réis was known as a *conto* and was written 1:000$000. According to the historian Hendrik Kraay, despite fluctuations, the mil-réis's value remained close to US$0.50 for most of the century. Hendrik Kraay, *Bahia's Independence: Popular Politics and Patriotic Festival in Salvador, Brazil, 1824–1900* (Montreal: McGill-Queen's University Press, 2019), xiii.

10. Deposition of Antônio Luís da Costa before Rio's chief of police José Mattoso de Andrade Câmara, Apr. 5, 1854, ANRJ, SJ, IJ1-999.

11. Padraic X. Scanlan, *Freedom's Debtors: British Antislavery in Sierra Leone in the Age of Revolution* (New Haven, CT: Yale University Press, 2017).

12. On the cessation of the African slave trade to Brazil, see Bethell, *Abolition of the Brazilian Slave Trade*; Robert E. Conrad, *World of Sorrow: The African Slave Trade to Brazil* (Baton Rouge: Louisiana State University Press, 1986); Conrad, *Destruction of Brazilian Slavery*; Dale T.

Graden, "An Act 'Even of Public Security': Slave Resistance, Social Tensions, and the End of the International Slave Trade to Brazil, 1835–1856," *Hispanic American Historical Review* 76, no. 2 (1996): 249–82; Jaime Rodrigues, *O infame comércio: Propostas e experiências no final do tráfico de africanos para o Brasil (1800–1850)* (Campinas: Editora da Unicamp, 2000).

13. Mamigonian, *Africanos livres*; Chalhoub, *A força da escravidão*.

14. Natalie Zemon Davis, "Decentering History: Local Stories and Cultural Crossings in a Global World," *History and Theory* 50, no. 2 (2011): 188–202; Joanne P. Sharp, "Geopolitics at the Margins? Reconsidering Genealogies of Critical Geopolitics," *Political Geography* 37 (2013): 20–29.

15. Daniel Domingues da Silva, David Eltis, Philip Misevich, and Olatunji Ojo, "The Diaspora of Africans Liberated from Slave Ships in the Nineteenth Century," *Journal of African History* 55, no. 3 (2014): 347–69.

16. Certificate of emancipation signed by José Joaquim de Siqueira, May 9, 1854, FO 84/954.

17. "Decreto n. 1303 de 28 de Dezembro de 1853—Emancipação dos africanos livres que tiverem servido por quatorze anos a particulares," *Coleção das Leis do Império do Brasil (1808–1889)*, Portal da Câmara dos Deputados, http://www2.camara.leg.br/atividade-legislativa /legislacao/publicacoes/doimperio (accessed July 21, 2022).

18. José Tomás Nabuco de Araújo to Antônio Paulino Limpo de Abreu, Aug. 30, 1854, ANRJ, SJ, IJ1-999. Similar decisions were made regarding the case of free black people from Uruguay and Argentina captured on the border and sold as slaves in Brazil. Grinberg, "The Two Enslavements of Rufina."

19. David Eltis, *Economic Growth and the Ending of the Transatlantic Slave Trade* (New York: Oxford University Press, 1987), chapter 7, especially 102–14.

20. Spain abolished the slave trade in 1820, and in that decade, the British made slave-trade abolition a condition for recognizing the independence of all South American countries. Alex Borucki, David Eltis, and David Wheat, *From the Galleons to the Highlands: Slave Trade Routes in the Spanish Americas* (Albuquerque: University of New Mexico Press, 2020), 454. See also Jesús Sanjurjo, *In the Blood of Our Brothers: Abolitionism and the End of the Slave Trade in Spain's Atlantic Empire, 1800–1870* (Tuscaloosa: University of Alabama Press, 2021).

21. Brasil, *Coleção das Leis do Império do Brasil (1808–1889)*, Portal da Câmara dos Deputados, http://www2.camara.leg.br/atividade-legislativa/legislacao/publicacoes/doimperio (accessed July 21, 2020).

22. "Aviso de 29 de outubro de 1834, com Instruções relativas à arrematação dos Africanos ilicitamente introduzidos no Império." Cited by Beatriz Mamigonian, "To Be a Liberated African in Brazil: Labour and Citizenship in the Nineteenth Century" (PhD diss., University of Waterloo, 2002), 300. Construction began in 1834 with the labor of enslaved persons, africanos livres, and convicts, but the House of Correction was not officially inaugurated until the end of the slave trade in 1850. Martine Jean, "Liberated Africans, Slaves, and Convict Labor in the Construction of Rio de Janeiro's Casa de Correção: Atlantic Labor Regimes and Confinement in Brazil's Port City," *International Review of Social History* 64, no. 27 (2019): 173–204. See also: Martine Jean, *Policing Freedom: Illegal Enslavement, Labor, and Citizenship in Nineteenth-Century Brazil* (Cambridge, UK: Cambridge University Press, 2023).

23. This was the case of Bernardo Pereira de Vasconcellos, one of the leaders of the reactionary movement that overtook Brazilian institutions after 1837 (the so-called *Regresso*), who in fact proposed the abolition of the 1831 law in Parliament in 1835. On the Conservative critique

of the 1831 law, see Tâmis Parron, *A política da escravidão no Império do Brasil, 1826–1865* (Rio de Janeiro: Civilização Brasileira, 2011); Jeffrey Needell, "The Abolition of the Brazilian Slave Trade in 1850: Historiography, Slave Agency and Statesmanship," *Journal of Latin American Studies* 33, no. 4 (2001): 681–711. On new interpretations about the enforcement of the 1831 law, see: "Dossiê: 'Para inglês ver?' Revisitando a lei de 1831," ed. Beatriz Mamigonian and Keila Grinberg, *Estudos Afro-Asiáticos* 29, nos. 1/2/3 (2007).

24. David Eltis, "The U.S. Transatlantic Slave Trade, 1644–1867: An Assessment," *Civil War History* 54, no. 4 (2008): 347–78; Leonardo Marques, "A participação norte-americana no tráfico transatlântico de escravos para os Estados Unidos, Cuba e Brasil," *História: Questões e Debates* 52 (2010): 91–117; Leonardo Marques, "Slave Trading in a New World: The Strategies of North American Slave Traders in the Age of Abolition," *Journal of the Early Republic* 32, no. 2 (2012): 233–60.

25. Beatriz G. Mamigonian, "O direito de ser africano livre: Os escravos e as interpretações da Lei de 1831," in *Direitos e justiças: Capítulos de história social do direito no Brasil*, ed. Silvia H. Lara and Joseli Mendonça (Campinas: Editora da Unicamp, 2006), 130. On the general non-compliance with the 1831 law in Brazil, see also Azevedo, *O direito dos escravos*; Keila Grinberg, "Slavery, Manumission and the Law in Nineteenth-Century Brazil: Reflections on the Law of 1831 and the 'Principle of Liberty' on the Southern Frontier of the Brazilian Empire," *European Review of History: Revue européenne d'histoire* 16, no. 3 (2009): 401–11; Chalhoub, *A força da escravidão*.

26. Joaquim Barrozo Pereira to the Portuguese minister of foreign affairs, May 10, 1835, Arquivo Nacional da Torre do Tombo (ANTT, Portugal), MNE, cx. 536. My thanks to Roquinaldo Ferreira for this reference.

27. As João Reis explains, the president of the province of Bahia, Francisco de Souza Martins, also suggested in 1835 that the imperial government negotiate with the United States to have freed Africans sent to Liberia, while the Regency considered Sierra Leone as a possibility. João José Reis, *Rebelião escrava no Brasil: A história do levante dos malês em 1835* (São Paulo: Companhia das Letras, 2003), 484.

28. Dispatch from José de Vasconcellos e Souza, Nov. 29, 1850, ANTT, MNE, cx. 541; Arquivo Histórico do Itamaraty (AHI), 1861, 284-4-10.

29. Protocol signed on Nov. 5, 1851, by James Hudson and Paulino José Soares de Souza, FO 84/847.

30. James Hudson to Lord Palmerston, May 12, 1850, British and Foreign State Papers, v. 40 (1850/1851), 353.

31. The Second Reign refers to the period of Pedro II's monarchical rule from 1840 to 1889.

32. Richard Graham, "Os fundamentos da ruptura de relações diplomáticas entre o Brasil e a Grã-Bretanha em 1863: A 'Questão Christie," *Revista de História* 24, no. 49 (1962): 119.

33. Mamigonian, *Africanos livres*; Chalhoub, *A força da escravidão*; Parron, *A política da escravidão*.

34. Francisco Otaviano de Almeida Roiz to Joaquim José Batista da Motta, June 27, 1850, ANRJ, SJ, IJ1-452.

35. These were the geographical centers of power in downtown Rio de Janeiro. The imperial palace faced the Pharoux Quay at the water's edge in what is today the Praça XV. Antônio Simões da Silva to Eusébio de Queiroz Coutinho Mattoso Câmara, July 26, 1850, ANRJ, SJ, IJ1-998.

36. Manoel Vianna to José Maria dos Anjos Esposel, July 14, 1850, ANRJ, SJ, IJ1-998.

37. Britain's political and economic influence in Brazil has even led some historians to ask whether the country could be considered part of the British "informal empire" during the nineteenth century. Some, like Leslie Bethell, for instance, partially agree with this assertion, describing the end of the slave trade in 1850 as the product of British political intervention in Brazil. Leslie Bethell, "O Brasil no século XIX: Parte do 'império informal britânico,'" in *Perspectivas da cidadania no Brasil Império*, ed. José Murilo de Carvalho and Adriana Pereira Campos (Rio de Janeiro: Civilização Brasileira, 2011), 15–36; Leslie Bethell, "O Brasil no mundo," in *A construção nacional: 1830–1889*, vol. 2 of *História do Brasil Nação* (Rio de Janeiro: Editora Objetiva, 2012), 131–77.

38. Joseph M. Mulhern, "After 1833: British Entanglement with Brazilian Slavery" (PhD diss., Durham University, 2018); Chris Evans, "Brazilian Gold, Cuban Copper and the Final Frontier of British Anti-Slavery," *Slavery and Abolition* 34, no. 1 (2013): 118–34; L. Guenther, "Merchants, Abolitionists and Slave Traders: Brazilian Perceptions of the British in Bahia, 1808–1850," in *Negotiating Identities in Modern Latin America*, ed. Hendrik Kraay (Calgary: University of Calgary Press, 2007), 93–114.

39. David Brion Davis defines the Age of Emancipation as reaching from the 1780s and the postrevolutionary emancipationist impulse in the United States to the 1880s and the abolition of slavery in Brazil. See Davis, *The Problem of Slavery*; Dawne Y. Curry, Eric D. Duke, and Marshanda A. Smith, eds., *Extending the Diaspora: New Histories of Black People* (Urbana: University of Illinois Press, 2009); Rosemary Brana-Shute and Randy J. Sparks, eds., *Paths to Freedom: Manumission in the Atlantic World* (Columbia: University of South Carolina Press, 2009).

40. "Decreto n. 1303 de 28 de Dezembro de 1853." For detailed examples of abuses against African apprentices, see Mamigonian, *Africanos livres*.

41. See Robert L. Paquette, *Sugar Is Made with Blood: The Conspiracy of La Escalera and the Conflict Between Empires over Slavery in Cuba* (Middletown, CN: Wesleyan University Press, 1990); Aisha Finch, *Rethinking Slave Rebellion in Cuba: La Escalera and the Insurgencies of 1841–1844* (Chapel Hill: University of North Carolina Press, 2015).

42. Mamigonian, *Africanos livres*, 253.

43. "List of Persons, and Departments Having Under Their Charge a Portion of the Africans Liberated by Sentences of the Mixed Commission at Rio de Janeiro," FO 131/7.

44. Beatriz Mamigonian transcribed two of these petitions, in which a group of seventy-eight africanos livres made an emotional appeal to Hesketh as "their father and mother for we have no one else," asking to know if "they would be slaves until they die in this House of Correction." Mamigonian, *Africanos livres*, 253–56.

45. William D. Christie, *Notes on Brazilian Questions* (London: Macmillan and Co., 1865), 36–37; dispatch by James Hudson, Dec. 11, 1851, FO 84/847.

46. Beatriz G. Mamigonian, "In the Name of Freedom: Slave Trade Abolition, the Law and the Brazilian Branch of the African Emigration Scheme (Brazil-British West Indies, 1830s–1850s)," *Slavery and Abolition*, v. 30 (2009), 45.

47. Henry Howard to Antônio Paulino Limpo de Abreu, Mar. 3, 1854, ANRJ, SJ, IJ-999.

48. AHI, 1861, 284-4-10.

49. Confidential dispatch from the Justice Department to Antônio Paulino Limpo de Abreu, Mar. 23, 1854, ANRJ, SJ, IJ1-1000.

50. Henry Howard to Antônio Paulino Limpo de Abreu, July 25, 1854, ANRJ, SJ, IJ-999.

51. AHI, 1861, 284-4-10.

52. Lara and Mendonça, *Direitos e justiças*; Elciene Azevedo, *Orfeu de carapinha: A trajetória de Luiz Gama na imperial cidade de São Paulo* (Campinas: Editora da Unicamp, 1999); Azevedo, *O direito dos escravos*; Ricardo Tadeu Caires Silva, "Caminhos e descaminhos da abolição: Escravos, senhores e direitos nas últimas décadas da escravidão (Bahia, 1850–1888)" (PhD diss., Universidade Federal do Paraná, 2007); Ferreira, *Com a palavra, Luiz Gama*.

53. Manoel de Souza Pinto de Alves to José Idelfonso de Souza Ramos, July 20, 1852, ANRJ, SJ, IJ1-221.

54. José Antônio Saraiva to Eusébio de Queiroz Coutinho Mattoso Câmara, Mar. 29, 1852, ANRJ, SJ, IJ1-244.

55. On other examples of black claims to British subjecthood, see Ndubueze L. Mbah, "The Black Englishmen of Old Calabar: Freedom and Mobility in the Age of Abolition in West Africa," *Radical History Review*, no. 144 (2022): 45–75; Scott Heerman, "Abolishing Slavery in Motion: Foreign Captivity and International Abolitionism in the Early United States," *William and Mary Quarterly* 77, no. 2 (2020): 245–73; Richard P. Anderson, "The Diaspora of Sierra Leone's Liberated Africans: Enlistment, Forced Migration, and 'Liberation' at Freetown, 1808–1863," *African Economic History* 41 (2013): 101–38.

56. The Balaiada (1838–41) was a multiracial social uprising that brought together maroons, peasants, and liberal sympathizers against the governments of the provinces of Maranhão and Piauí. Maria Januária Vilela dos Santos, *A Balaiada e a insurreição de escravos no Maranhão* (Rio de Janeiro: Editora Ática, 1983); Mundinha Araújo, *Em busca de Dom Cosme Bento das Chagas, Negro Cosme: Tutor e imperador da liberdade* (Imperatriz: Ética, 2008); Matthias Röhrig Assunção, *De caboclos a bem-te-vis: Formação do campesinato numa sociedade escravista: Maranhão 1800–1850* (São Paulo: Annablume, 2018).

57. *Escravos de ganho* had some autonomy in procuring jobs in the urban space so long as they paid masters a fixed fee at the end of each day or week. These men and women were sometimes able to save enough money to purchase their own freedom, and often lived outside of their masters' home, paying for their own maintenance. João José Reis, *Ganhadores: A greve negra de 1857 na Bahia* (São Paulo: Companhia das Letras, 2019).

58. Memorandum from Henry Walter Orendon, July 4, 1856, ANRJ, SJ, IJ1-1000.

59. Testimony of Theresa Jansen Lima Muller, Oct. 18, 1856, ANRJ, SJ, IJ1-1000.

60. Sam probably refers here to Luís Alves de Lima e Silva, president and commander in chief of the Brazilian Armed Forces in Maranhão during the Balaiada revolt. The future Duque de Caxias was nominated by the regency government to quench the Balaiada revolt in the province, where he arrived in 1840.

61. Testimony of Benjamin/Sam, Oct. 16, 1856, ANRJ, SJ, IJ1-1000.

62. After arresting him at the quilombo, authorities sent Manoel to the Botanic Gardens, where they thought he could be better disciplined. José Ricardo do Sá Rego to Eusébio de Queiroz Coutinho Mattoso Câmara, Apr. 30, 1854, ANRJ, SJ, IJ1-618.

63. Augusto Leverger to Eusébio de Queiroz Coutinho Mattoso Câmara, June 30, 1852, ANRJ, SJ, IJ1-679.

64. Bartolomé Bossi, *Viagem pitoresca pelos rios Paraná, Paraguai, São Lourenço, Cuiabá e o Arinos, tributário do grande Amazonas: Com a descrição da província de Mato Grosso em seu aspecto físico, geográfico, mineralógico e seus produtos naturais* (Brasília: Senado Federal, Conselho Editorial, 2008).

65. Interrogatory of Custódio Cabinda, Mar. 22, 1864, ANRJ, SJ, IJ1-684.

66. Interrogatory of Teresa Cabinda, Mar. 23, 1864, ANRJ, SJ, IJ1-684.

67. Report of events sent by Bartolomé Bossi to Alexandre Miguel Albino de Carvalho, Mar. 17, 1864, ANRJ, SJ, IJ1-684.

68. "Decreto 3310—Emancipação dos Africanos Livres," Sept. 24, 1864, *Coleção das Leis do Império do Brasil (1808–1889)*, Portal da Câmara dos Deputados, http://www2.camara.leg.br /atividadelegislativa/legislacao/publicacoes/doimperio (accessed Sept. 7, 2021).

69. On this episode and the history of the Mining Society of Mato Grosso, see Zilda Alves de Moura, "Dos sertões da África para os do Brasil: Os africanos livres da Sociedade de Mineração de Mato Grosso (Alto Paraguai-Diamantino, 1851–1865)" (PhD diss., Universidade Federal de Santa Catarina, 2014).

70. Mariana P. Candido and Adam Jones, eds., *African Women in the Atlantic World: Property, Vulnerability, and Mobility, 1660-1880* (Rochester, NY: James Currey, 2019); "Mothering Slaves: Motherhood, Childlessness and the Care of Children in Atlantic Slave Societies," special issue, ed. Camillia Cowling, Maria Helena Pereira Toledo Machado, Diana Paton, and Emily West, *Women's History Review* 38, no. 2 (2017); Cowling, *Conceiving Freedom*; Martha Santos, "'Slave Mothers,' *Partus Sequitur Ventrem*, and the Naturalization of Slave Reproduction in Nineteenth Century Brazil," *Tempo* 22, no. 41 (2016): 467–87; Jennifer L. Morgan, *Reckoning with Slavery: Gender, Kinship, and Capitalism in the Early Black Atlantic* (Durham, NC: Duke University Press, 2021).

71. Francisco da Rosa Quintanilha to Antônio Roiz da Cunha, July 22, 1857; see also Maria Rebola, petição de emancipação, June 17, 1857, ANRJ, GIFI 6D-136.

72. On the violent experiences of liberated Africans throughout the Atlantic, see Maeve Ryan, "'A Moral Millstone'? British Humanitarian Governance and the Policy of Liberated African Apprenticeship, 1808–1848," *Slavery and Abolition* 37, no. 2 (2016): 399–422; Samuël Coghe, "Apprenticeship and the Negotiation of Freedom: The Liberated Africans of the Anglo-Portuguese Mixed Commission in Luanda (1844–1870)," *Africana Studia* 14 (2010): 255–73.

73. Belizário José da Silva Conrado to Diogo Velho Cavalcante de Albuquerque, Mar. 21, 1860, ANRJ, SJ, IJ1-713.

74. Victorina Angola, petição de emancipação, July 4, 1860, ANRJ, SJ, IJ1-713.

75. On the practice of manumission by substitution, in which a slave bought his/her freedom giving another slave in return, see João José Reis, "'Por sua liberdade me oferece uma escrava': Alforrias por substituição na Bahia, 1800–1850," *Afro-Ásia*, no. 63 (2021): 232–90.

76. Belizário José da Silva Conrado to Diogo Velho Cavalcante de Albuquerque, Apr. 2, 1860, ANRJ, SJ, IJ1-713.

77. Conrado to Albuquerque.

78. Victorina Angola, petição de emancipação.

79. Victorina Angola, petição de emancipação.

80. Victorina Angola, petição de emancipação.

81. For more on illiterate litigants as skilled legal practitioners, see Premo, *Enlightenment on Trial*; Kathryn Burns, *Into the Archive: Writing and Power in Colonial Peru* (Durham, NC: Duke University Press, 2010). On literacy and slavery in Latin America, see Graubart, "*Pesa más la libertad*"; Maria Cristina Wissenbach, "Teodora Dias da Cunha: Construindo um lugar para si no mundo da escrita e da escravidão," in *Mulheres negras no Brasil escravista e do pós-emancipação*, ed. Giovana Xavier, Juliana Barreto Farias, and Flávio dos Santos Gomes (São Paulo, SP: Selo Negro Edições, 2012), 228–43; Jouve-Martín, *Esclavos dela ciudad letrada*.

82. On women pursuing their children's emancipation, see also Marília B. A. Ariza, "Mães libertas, filhos escravos: Desafios femininos nas últimas décadas da escravidão em São Paulo," *Revista Brasileira de História* 38, no. 79 (2018): 151–71 and *Mães infames, filhos venturosos: Trabalho, pobreza, escravidão e emancipação no cotidiano de São Paulo (século XIX)* (São Paulo, SP: Alameda, 2020); Isabel Cristina F. dos Reis, "'Uma negra que fugio, e consta que já tem dous filhos': Fuga e família entre escravos na Bahia," *Afro-Ásia*, no. 23 (1999): 27–46.

83. Henry Howard to Brazilian minister of foreign affairs, Antônio Paulino Limpo de Abreu, May 10, 1854, ANRJ, SJ, IJ1-999.

84. Manuela Carneiro da Cunha, *Negros, estrangeiros: Os escravos libertos e sua volta 'a África*, 2nd ed. (São Paulo: Companhia das Letras, 2012); Keila Grinberg, *A Black Jurist in a Slave Society: Antonio Pereira Rebouças and the Trials of Brazilian Citizenship*, trans. Kristin M. McGuire (Chapel Hill: University of North Carolina Press, 2019).

85. Leocádia d'Almeida Soares to Joaquim Luís Soares, n.d. (1854), ANRJ, SJ, IJ1-999.

86. Leocádia d'Almeida Soares to Joaquim Luís Soares.

87. *Annais do Senado do Império de Brasil*, vol. 3, session of July 5, 1871; Maysa Espíndola Souza, "Africanos livres em Desterro: Tutela, trabalho e liberdade" (Bachelor's thesis, Universidade Federal de Santa Catarina, 2012), 30–31.

88. Leocádia d'Almeida Soares to Senator José da Silva Mafra, n.d, 1854, ANRJ, SJ, IJ1-999.

89. Leocádia d'Almeida Soares to Senator José da Silva Mafra.

90. Antônio da Cunha to José Mattoso de Andrade Câmara, May 19, 1854, ANRJ, SJ, IJ1-999. Little is known about José Manoel, except that he married Marcelina in the days before they left for Bahia. He was violently arrested on charges of theft during Leocádia's case, probably due to the active role he played in denouncing the girl's illegal enslavement by Joaquim Luís Soares. Soon after his release from prison, José Manoel was accused by local authorities of being abusive toward Leocádia as he was clearly competing with Soares for authority over her.

91. Henry Howard to Antônio Paulino Limpo de Abreu, May 10, 1854, ANRJ, SJ, IJ1-999.

92. The affidavit carried the signatures of Manoel Paranhos da Silva Vellozo, a judge in the Relação da Corte, the engineer Jerônimo Francisco Coelho, and the merchant José de Araújo Coelho, May 22, 1854, ANRJ, SJ, IJ1-999.

93. "Auto de perguntas feito à crioula Leocádia," May 20, 1854, ANRJ, SJ, IJ1-999. In her original testimony in Portuguese, Leocádia said: "Que como tal foi sempre tratada em casa e pelo Senhor Soares, que muitas noites perdeu com ela quando se achava doente, e era pequena, e que lhe mandou ensinar a ler e escrever, trazendo-a sempre bem vestida e calçada, e mandando-a até a Colégio, ou Escola particular quando era mais pequena."

94. Sílvia Hunold Lara, "Blowin' in the wind: E. P. Thompson e a experiência negra no Brasil," *Projeto História* 12 (1995): 43–56; João José Reis and Eduardo Silva, *Negociação e conflito: A resistência negra no Brasil escravista* (São Paulo: Companhia das Letras, 1989); E. P. Thompson, *The Making of the English Working Class* (New York: Vintage Books, 1966).

95. Cyro's case has been studied by the historian Beatriz Mamigonian in "'Do que 'o preto mina' é capaz': Etnia e resistência entre africanos livres," *Afro-Ásia*, no. 24 (2000): 89–91; and *Africanos livres*, 348–53.

96. Petição de emancipação de Cyro Mina, Mar. 22, 1855, ANRJ, Diversos SDH, cx. 782, pc. 2–3.

97. Mamigonian, *Africanos livres*, 350.

98. Mamigonian, *Africanos livres*, 352.

99. Phillip Troutman, "Correspondences in Black and White: Sentiment and the Slave Market Revolution," in *New Studies in the History of American Slavery*, ed. Edward E. Baptist and Stephanie M. H. Camp (Athens: University of Georgia Press, 2006), 211–42.

100. On slaves and writing in Brazil, see Robert Krueger, "Brazilian Slaves Represented in Their Own Words," *Slavery and Abolition* 23, no. 2 (2002): 169–86; Wissenbach, "Cartas, procurações"; Graham, "Writing from the Margins."

101. Brasil, *Relatório do Ministério da Justiça do Anno 1868 Apresentado à Assembléa Geral Legislativa na 1a Sessão da 14a Legislatura pelo Respectivo Ministro e Secretário de Estado José Martiniano de Alencar* (Rio de Janeiro: Typ. Progresso, 1869).

Chapter 2

1. Marxist historians were among the first to investigate connections between enslaved people's perspectives and international contexts. The work of Eugene Genovese was especially impactful among Brazilian historians. Eugene Genovese, *From Rebellion to Revolution: Afro-American Slave Revolts in the Making of the Modern World* (New York: Vintage Books, 1981). See also C. L. R James, *The Black Jacobins* (London: Secker and Warburg, 1938).

2. Historians have written about the role of the 1848 rebellions in bringing about the end of the slave trade in 1850. See, for example, Sidney Chalhoub, *Visões da liberdade: As últimas décadas da escravidão na Corte* (São Paulo: Companhia das Letras, 1990), 186–212; Robert Slenes, "L'arbre nsanda replanté: Cultes d'affliction kongo et identité des esclaves de plantation dans le Brésil du sud-est (1810–1888)," *Cahiers du Brésil Contemporain*, no. 67/68 (2007): 217–313; Dale Graden, *Disease, Resistance, and Lies: The Demise of the Transatlantic Slave Trade to Brazil and Cuba* (Baton Rouge: Louisiana State University Press, 2014), chapter 5; Mamigonian, *Africanos livres*, chapter 6.

3. From 1831 to 1850, as coffee exports rose from 33,000 tons to 118,000 tons a year, more than 570,000 enslaved Africans arrived at the ports servicing the Paraíba River valley. Parron, *A política da escravidão*. On "second slavery" in Brazil, see Rafael Marquese e Ricardo Salles, eds., *Escravidão e capitalismo histórico no século XIX: Cuba, Brasil e Estados Unidos* (Rio de Janeiro: Civilização Brasileira, 2016); Rafael Marquese and Ricardo Salles, "Slavery in Nineteenth-Century Brazil: History and Historiography," in *Slavery and Historical Capitalism During the Nineteenth Century*, ed. Dale W. Tomich (Lanham, MD: Lexington Books, 2017), 123–69.

4. Tático's interrogatory, Aug. 30, 1848, Arquivo Público do Estado de São Paulo (hereafter APESP), Secretaria de Polícia da Província (SPP), CO 2452.

5. Cross-examination between Tático and Diogo, Sept. 4, 1848, APESP, SPP, CO 2452.

6. Emilia Viotti da Costa, *Crowns of Glory, Tears of Blood: The Demerara Slave Rebellion of 1823* (Oxford: Oxford University Press, 1994); Finch, *Rethinking Slave Rebellion in Cuba*, 137; J. W. C. Pennington, ed., *A Narrative of Events of the Life of J. H. Banks, an Escaped Slave, from the Cotton State, Alabama, in America* (Liverpool: M. Rourke, 1861). On black activism and British antislavery in the Caribbean, see Gelien Matthews, *Caribbean Slave Revolts and the British Abolitionist Movement* (Baton Rouge: Louisiana University Press, 2006); Hilary Beckles, "The Wilberforce Song: How Enslaved Caribbean Blacks Heard British Abolitionists," *Parliamentary History* 26, supplement (2007): 113–26.

7. On enslaved people's notions of diasporic warfare, see especially Reis, *Rebelião escrava no Brasil*; Brown, *Tacky's Revolt*.

8. Katia M. de Queirós Mattoso, *A presença francesa no movimento democrático baiano de 1798* (Salvador: Itapoã, 1969); Ístvan Jancsó, *Na Bahia contra o império: História do ensaio de sedição de 1798* (São Paulo: Hucitec; Salvador: EDUFBA, 1996).

9. Morel, *A Revolução do Haiti*; Laurent Vidal and Tania Regina de Luca, eds., *Franceses no Brasil: Séculos XIX–XX* (São Paulo: Editora UNESP, 2009).

10. Marcus J. M. de. Carvalho, "'Fácil é serem sujeitos de quem já foram senhores': O ABC do Divino Mestre," *Afro-Ásia* 31, no. 1 (2004), 333.

11. Scott, *Common Wind*; Byrd, *The Black Republic*; Alexander, *Fear of a Black Republic*.

12. "Hail the Englishmen" and "Hail freedom." Vicente Ferreira da Silva Bueno to Vicente Pires da Matta, Feb. 23, 1863, ANRJ, SJ, IJ1-518.

13. On rumors, see Machado, *O plano e o pânico*; Azevedo, *Onda negra, medo branco*; Anajn Ghosh, "The Role of Rumor in History Writing," *History Compass* 6, no. 5 (2008): 1235–43; Ranajit Guha, *Elementary Aspects of Peasant Insurgency in Colonial India* (Durham, NC: Duke University Press, 1999); Steven Hahn, "Extravagant Expectations of Freedom: Rumour, Political Struggle, and the Christmas Insurrection Scare of 1865 in the American South," *Past and Present* 157, no. 1 (1997): 122–58; Winthrop D. Jordan, *Tumult and Silence at Second Creek: An Inquiry into a Civil War Slave Conspiracy* (Baton Rouge: Louisiana State University Press, 1995); John D. Garrigus, *A Secret Among the Blacks: Slave Resistance before the Haitian Revolution* (Cambridge, MA: Harvard University Press, 2023).

14. Marcos Couto Gonçalves, "Papéis avulsos: A insurreição dos escravos no Vale do Paraíba," *Revista Acervo Histórico*, no. 3 (2005): 68.

15. In the Lorena court records, his name appears as Jacques Frosser. Arquivo Histórico e Biblioteca Municipal de Lorena, processo-crime no 0155, Feb. 22, 1848, caixa 07, tombo 3637; Luís Fernando Prestes Camargo, "O papel da insurgência escrava na abolição do tráfico africano" (master's thesis, Universidade de Campinas, 2013), 68.

16. Gonçalves, "Papéis avulsos," 70.

17. Gonçalves, "Papéis avulsos," 65.

18. Gonçalves, "Papéis avulsos," 68.

19. Gonçalves, "Papéis avulsos," 67.

20. Morel, *A Revolução do Haiti*, 143, and part 3.

21. Leonídio Adalmir, "Utopias sociais e cientificistas no Brasil, no final do século XIX," *História, Ciências, Saúde-Manguinhos* 14, no. 3 (2007): 921–46.

22. Morel, *A Revolução do Haiti*, 22–24; João José Reis and Flávio dos Santos Gomes, "Repercussions of the Haitian Revolution in Brazil, 1791–1850," in *The World of the Haitian Revolution*, eds. David Patrick Geggus and Norman Fiering (Bloomington: University of Indiana Press, 2009), 284–313; Carlos Eugênio Soares e Flávio Gomes, "Sedições, haitianismo e conexões no Brasil escravista," *Novos Estudos CEBRAP*, no. 63 (2002): 131–44; Luiz Mott, "A revolução dos negros do Haiti e o Brasil," *História: Questões e Debates* 3, no. 4 (1982): 55–62.

23. Morel, *A Revolução do Haiti*, 27.

24. Gonçalves, "Papéis avulsos," 68.

25. Regina Célia Lima Xavier, *Religiosidade e escravidão no século XIX: Mestre Tito* (Porto Alegre: UFRGS Editora, 2008), 87.

26. Lord John Howden compared the movement to the 1835 Malê rebellion in Bahia. Howden to Lord Palmerston, Mar. 20, 1848, FO 84/725.

27. Insurgents in Pelotas shaved the hair on the back of their heads in a straight line from ear to ear as a sign of mutual recognition on the day of the uprising. On the connection with the rebel Nagôs (Yorubas) who participated in the 1835 Muslim slave uprising in Bahia, see *Gazeta Official do Império do Brasil*, Feb. 22, 1848, p. 2.

28. John Morgan to Lord Palmerston, Feb. 15, 1848, and Morgan to Lord Howden, Feb. 9, 1848, FO 84/727.

29. Grinberg, "The Two Enslavements of Rufina"; Secreto and Gomes, *Territórios ao Sul*.

30. Reis and Gomes, "Repercussions of the Haitian Revolution in Brazil." French consuls immediately circulated the April decree, which prohibited the sale of enslaved persons two months after its promulgation. French expatriates then rushed to manage their ties to slavery. *Correio da Tarde*, Dec. 29, 1848, p. 1.

31. Richard Ryan to Lord Palmerston, Dec. 14, 1848, FO 84/727.

32. In July 1831, for instance, enslaved rebels in Carrancas, Minas Gerais, expected that Emperor Pedro I would support their emancipation. Marcos F. de Andrade, "'Nós somos os caramurus e vamos arrasar tudo': A história da revolta dos escravos de Carrancas, Minas Gerais (1833)," in Reis and Gomes, *Revoltas escravas no Brasil*, 262–324. For other examples of royal sponsorship of abolition, see Marcela Echeverri, *Indian and Slave Royalists in the Age of Revolution: Reform, Revolution, and Royalism in the Northern Andes, 1780–1825* (Cambridge: Cambridge University Press, 2016); Elizabeth W. Kiddy, "Who Is the King of Congo? A New Look at African and Afro-Brazilian Kings in Brazil," in *Central Africans and Cultural Transformations in the American Diaspora*, ed. Linda M. Heywood (Cambridge: Cambridge University Press, 2002), 153–82.

33. Tático's interrogatory, Aug. 30, 1848.

34. This was a colloquial expression used by Brazilians to refer to liberated Africans, which embodied the paradox of their liminal status: neither slave nor free, their apprenticeships resembled life in bondage. Cross-examination of Tático and Joaquim, Sept. 4, 1848, APESP, SPP, CO 2452; Enidelce Bertin, *Os meias caras: Africanos livres em São Paulo no século XIX* (Salto, SP: Schoba, 2013).

35. Reginaldo and Ferreira, *África, margens e oceanos*; Luis Nicolau Parés, *The Formation of Candomblé: Vodun History and Ritual in Brazil* (Chapel Hill: University of North Carolina Press, 2013); Ferreira, *Cross-Cultural Exchanges*.

36. Cross-examination of Tático and Joaquim, Sept. 4, 1848. It is possible that Joaquim referred to the 1840 British blockade of the Mozambique harbor, which offered a preamble to the Anglo-Portuguese Slave Trade Treaty of 1842. He probably worked in Indaiatuba alongside "Moçambiques," "Quelimanes," or "Inhambanes," as Bantu speakers from varied East African origins were known in Brazil. It is believed that 18 percent of the enslaved people disembarked in Rio de Janeiro from 1830 to 1852 were from East Africa. Edward A. Alpers, "'Mozambiques' in Brazil: Another Dimension of the African Diaspora in the Atlantic World," in *Africa and the Americas: Interconnections During the Slave Trade*, ed. José C. Curto and Reneé Soulodre-La France (Trenton, NJ, and Asmara: Africa World Press, 2005), 43–68; José Capela, *O tráfico de escravos nos portos de Moçambique, 1717–1904* (Porto: Afrontamento, 2016).

37. Cross-examination of Tático and Diogo, Sept. 4, 1848, APESP, SPP, CO 2452.

38. Cross-examination of Pedro, Rafael, and Luísa, Aug. 30, 1848, APESP, SPP, CO 2452. In 1854, another conspiracy took place in the towns of Taubaté and Pindamonhangaba, led

by enslaved men who claimed to be emissaries of São Benedito. Antônio José da Veiga Cabral to Jovino do Nascimento Silva, May 20, 1854, ANRJ, SJ, IJ1-511; Rafael José Barbi, "Festejos, liberdade e fé: A irmandade de São Benedito de Itu no século XIX (1861–1888)" (master's thesis, Universidade de São Paulo, 2016); Albuquerque, *O jogo da dissimulação*, 134–39; Lucilene Reginaldo, "Rosários dos pretos, São Benedito de Quissamã: Irmandades e devoções negras no mundo atlântico (Portugal e Angola, século XVIII)," *Studia Historica, Historia Moderna* 38, no. 1 (2016): 123–51.

39. Dispatch of José Mendes Ferraz, Sept. 4, 1848, APESP, SPP, CO 2452.

40. Guha, "The Prose of Counter-Insurgency."

41. For reflections about temporal regimes and historical change, see Dan Edelstein, Stefanos Geroulanos, and Natasha Wheatley, eds., *Power and Time: Temporalities in Conflict and the Making of History* (Chicago: University of Chicago Press, 2020); Massimiliano Tomba, *Insurgent Universality: An Alternative Legacy of Modernity* (New York: Oxford University Press, 2019).

42. Hartman, "Venus in Two Acts," 12.

43. Reis, *Rebelião escrava no Brasil*.

44. Slenes, "L'arbre nsanda replanté." The expression *tatés* is probably an iteration of the Bantu word *tatá*, "father," or *tateto*, "our father."

45. Slenes, "L'arbre nsanda replanté."

46. Slenes, "L'arbre nsanda replanté."

47. Drescher, *Abolition*, 291.

48. Martha Abreu, "O caso do Bracuhy," in *Resgate: Uma janela para os oitocentos*, ed. Hebe Mattos and Eduardo Schnoor (Rio de Janeiro: TopBooks, 1995), 165–95; Thiago Campos Pessoa, *O império da escravidão: O complexo Breves no vale do café (Rio de Janeiro, c. 1850–c. 1888)* (Rio de Janeiro: Arquivo Nacional, 2018).

49. *Regeneracão* (Minas Gerais), June 18, 1853, p. 2.

50. *Diário do Rio de Janeiro*, Feb. 18, 1853, p. 3.

51. *Correio Mercantil* (Rio de Janeiro), Feb. 12, 1853, p. 2.

52. *Correio Mercantil* (Rio de Janeiro), Feb. 12, 1853, p. 2.

53. *O Philantropo* (Rio de Janeiro), June 22, 1849, p. 1. The newspaper was published in Rio de Janeiro between 1849 and 1852 by the Sociedade Contra o Tráfico de Africanos e Promotora da Colonização e Civilização dos Indígenas, one of the few antislavery associations in Brazil at the time. The Sociedade was composed of professionals and members of the military and was partially funded by the British embassy in Rio. Despite its name, it advocated emancipation only in the future, when the country would have a large enough number of free workers and settlers (*colonos*). Kaori Kodama, "O debate pelo fim do tráfico no periódico O Philantropo (1849–1852) e a formação do povo: Doenças, raça e escravidão," *Revista Brasileira de História* 28 no. 6 (2008): 407–30.

54. On the relationship between European immigration and the labor question, see Emília Viotti da Costa, *Da senzala à colônia* (São Paulo: Difusão Européia do Livro, 1966); Warren Dean, *Rio Claro: A Brazilian Plantation System, 1820–1920* (Stanford, CA: Stanford University Press, 1976); Giralda Seyferth, "Imigração, colonização e a questão racial no Brasil," *Revista USP*, no. 53 (2002): 117–49.

55. Some European immigrants became slave owners in Southern Brazil. Eugene S. Cassidy, "The Ambivalence of Slavery, the Certainty of Germanness: Representations of Slaveholding and Its Impact Among German Settlers in Brazil, 1820–1889," *German History* 33, no. 3 (2015): 367–84; Paulo Roberto Staudt Moreira and Miquéias H. Mügge, *Histórias de escravos*

e senhores em uma região de imigração europeia (São Leopoldo, RS: Oikos, 2014). On the relationship between capitalism and slavery in Brazil, see Marquese and Salles, *Escravidão e capitalismo histórico no século XIX* and "Slavery in Nineteenth-Century Brazil."

56. Viotti da Costa, *Da senzala à colônia*.

57. Foreign settlers who integrated the various immigration programs of the imperial government during the nineteenth century were known as "colonos" and were usually described as agriculturalists. Antônio de Moraes Silva, *Diccionario da lingua portugueza recopilado de todos os impressos até o presente* (Lisboa: Typographia de M.P. de Lacerda, 1823), 432. Djalma Forjaz, *O Senador Vergueiro: Sua vida e sua época (1778–1859)* (São Paulo: Officinas do Diário Official, 1924); José Eduardo Heflinger Jr., *O sistema de parceria e a imigração européia* (Limeira: Unigráfica, 2014); José Sebastião Witter, *Ibicaba, uma experiência pioneira* (São Paulo: Edições Arquivo do Estado, 1982).

58. André Pinto Rebouças, *Agricultura nacional: Estudos econômicos: propaganda abolicionista e democrática, setembro de 1874 a setembro de 1883* (Rio de Janeiro: A. J. Lamoureux, 1883), 115.

59. From the 1840s to the 1870s, it is estimated that between five thousand and eight thousand immigrants arrived at the province of São Paulo to work as sharecroppers. Sérgio Buarque de Holanda, "Prefácio do tradutor," in Thomas Davatz, *Memórias de um colono no Brasil* (São Paulo: Livraria Martins, 1941), 28–29.

60. Luiz Felipe de Alencastro, "Escravos e proletários," *Novos Estudos CEBRAP*, no. 21 (1988): 37.

61. Hamilton Hamilton to Ernesto Ferreira França, Dec. 17, 1844, José Eduardo Heflinger Jr., *Ibicaba: o berço da imigração européia de cunho particular* (Limeira, SP: Editora Unigráfica, 2007), 31. The Trans-Atlantic Slave Trade Database lists the ships *Maria Segunda*, *Paquete*, *Tejo Aventureiro*, and *Virgínia* as belonging to Vergueiro between 1842 and 1844. In total, these ships disembarked in Rio de Janeiro and Santos around 2,291 Africans coming from the Bight of Benin, Congo, Angola, and Mozambique.

62. Daniel P. Kidder and James C. Fletcher, *O Brasil e os brasileiros* (São Paulo: Companhia Editora Nacional, 1941), vol. 2, 125.

63. Carlos Perret-Gentil, *A colônia Senador Vergueiro: Considerações de Carlos Perret-Gentil, cônsul geral da Suíssa no Rio de Janeiro* (Santos: Typographia Imparcial de F. M. R. D'Almeida, 1851), 37.

64. In his 1858 report, the president of São Paulo listed the ethnic origins of the colonos of Ibicaba: 227 Germans, 267 Swiss-Germans, 41 Swiss-French, 258 Portuguese, and 23 Belgians. Twenty-five coffee plantations employed sharecroppers in the province. Brasil, *Relatório de Abertura da Assembléia Legislativa Provincial*, São Paulo, Feb. 2, 1858.

65. Cassidy, "The Ambivalence of Slavery"; Débora Bendocchi Alves, "Cartas de imigrantes como fonte para o historiador: Rio de Janeiro–Turíngia (1852–1853)," *Revista Brasileira de História*, 23, no. 45 (2003): 155–84. References to "white slavery" were common among workers laboring under contract in slave societies over the nineteenth century. See, for example, Rebecca Scott, *Slave Emancipation in Cuba: The Transition to Free Labor, 1860–1899* (Pittsburgh: University of Pittsburgh Press, 1985).

66. On the 1856 revolt, see Johann Jakob von Tschudi, *Viagem às províncias do Rio de Janeiro e São Paulo* (Belo Horizonte: Itatiaia; São Paulo: EDUSP, 1980); Dean, *Rio Claro*, chapter 4; José Sebastião Witter, *A revolta dos parceiros* (São Paulo: Editora Brasiliense, 1986); José Sebastião Witter, "Ibicaba revisitada," in *História econômica da Independência e do Império*, ed.

Tamás Szmrecsányi and José Roberto do Amaral (São Paulo: ABPHE, 1996), 131–44; Ângela de Castro Gomes, ed., *História de imigrantes e de imigração no Rio de Janeiro* (Rio de Janeiro: 7Letras, 2000).

67. Davatz, *Memórias de um colono*, 123.

68. Holanda, "Prefácio do tradutor," 28–29.

69. José Vergueiro to Francisco Lourenço de Freitas, Sept. 7, 1848, APESP, SPP, CO 2452.

70. Davatz, *Memórias de um colono*, 239, 234.

71. Davatz, *Memórias de um colono*, 61.

72. *Annais do Parlamento Brasileiro, Câmara dos Deputados* (Rio de Janeiro: Typographia Imperial e Constitucional de J. Villeneuve e Comp., 1857), tomo 4, Apêndice, 165.

73. Nicolau Vergueiro to Francisco Diogo Pereira de Vasconcelos, Dec. 31, 1856, ANRJ, SJ, IJ1-512.

74. José Tomás Nabuco de Araújo to the vice president of São Paulo, Feb. 24, 1857, ANRJ, SJ, IJ1-512.

75. Memorandum from the Ministry of Justice for the period Feb. 24 to Mar. 14, 1857, ANRJ, SJ, IJ1-512.

76. Vamireh Chacon, *História das idéias socialistas no Brasil* (Rio de Janeiro: Civilização Brasileira, 1965); Ivone Gallo, "O Brasil e o socialismo do século XIX: Fourieristas no Saí," in Vidal and de Luca, *Franceses no Brasil*, 147–60.

77. H. Ullmann to Nicolau Vergueiro, Feb. 23, 1857, ANRJ, SJ, IJ1-512.

78. Flávio dos Santos Gomes, "Peasants, Maroons, and the Frontiers of Liberation in Maranhão," *Review (Fernand Braudel Center)* 31, no. 3 (2008): 373–99; Case Watkins, *Palm Oil Diaspora: Afro-Brazilian Landscapes and Economies on Bahia's Dendê Coast* (Cambridge: Cambridge University Press, 2021); Judith A. Carney and Richard N. Rosomoff, "Covert Cultivars and Clandestine Communities: Rice and the Making of an Afrodescendant Peasantry in Maranhão, Brazil," *Journal of Peasant Studies*, Jan. 2, 2024, https://doi.org/10.1080/03066150.2023.2296481.

79. *Diário de São Paulo*, Jan. 16, 1868, p. 1; *Correio Paulistano*, July 14, 1877, p. 2.

80. *Correio Paulistano* (São Paulo), June 13, 1877, p. 2.

81. *Diário do Rio de Janeiro*, Jan. 5, 1863, p. 1. On Jan. 5, 1863, Rio de Janeiro newspapers reported the capture of the ships *Áurea, Voadora, Trinta e Um de Outubro*, two unnamed sailing vessels, and the *Paraíba*.

82. Brazil, *Further Correspondence Respecting the Plunder of the Wreck of the British Barque "Prince of Wales" on the Coast of Brazil, in June 1861; and Respecting the Ill-Treatment of Three Officers of Her Majesty's Ship "Forte" by the Brazilian Police, in June 1862* (Cambridge, UK: Proquest LLC, 2006).

83. According to Christie, Rio inhabitants reacted with indignation, reminding him of the days following the passage of the Aberdeen Act in 1845. See Graham, "Os fundamentos da ruptura," 328.

84. The government of Bahia, for example, carried out a detailed assessment of the state of its maritime fortresses and invested in their renovation, allocating several africanos livres for public works. Arquivo Público do Estado da Bahia (APEB), Seção Provincial, 1863, maço 2865.

85. André Pinto Rebouças, Anna Flora Verissimo, and Inacio José Verissimo, *Diário e notas autobiográficas: Texto escolhido e anotações* (Rio de Janeiro: J. Olympio, 1938), 17–18.

86. *Correio Paulistano* (São Paulo), Jan. 18, 1863, p. 3; *Diário do Rio de Janeiro*, Jan. 6, 1863, p. 1.

87. Close to eight hundred people were said to have also marched to the imperial palace of São Cristóvão to demand that Christie surrender his passport to Emperor Pedro II. *Diário do Rio de Janeiro*, Jan. 5, 1863, p. 1.

88. Victor Meirelles was one of the most important visual artists of the Brazilian Empire. Trained at the Imperial Academy of Arts in Rio de Janeiro, he became known for his depictions of historical scenes representing the process of national formation in Brazil. In 1864 he completed the "Study for the Christie Affair," a painting apparently commissioned by the Marquis of Abrantes in the early 1860s. Beatriz Mamigonian, "Building the Nation, Selecting Memories: Vitor Meireles, the Christie Affair and Brazilian Slavery in the 1860s," in *Distant Ripples of the British Abolitionist Wave: Africa, Asia, and the Americas*, ed. Myriam Cottias and Marie-Jeanne Rossignol (Trenton, NJ: Africa World Press, 2017), 235–64.

89. Marcus Rediker, *Between the Devil and the Deep Blue Sea: Merchants, Seamen, Pirates, and the Anglo-American Maritime World, 1700–1750* (New York: Cambridge University Press, 1987); Beatriz G. Mamigonian, "José Monjolo e Francisco Moçambique, marinheiros das rotas atlânticas: Notas sobre a reconstituição de trajetórias da era da abolição," *Topoi* 11 (2010): 75–91; Walter Hawthorne, "Gorge: An African Seaman and His Flights from 'Freedom' Back to 'Slavery' in the Early Nineteenth Century," *Slavery and Abolition* 31, no. 3 (2010): 411–28.

90. On British economic and cultural presence in nineteenth-century Brazil, see Gilberto Freyre and Donald Warren, *Ingleses no Brasil: Aspectos da influência britânica sobre a vida, a paisagem e a cultura do Brasil* (Rio de Janeiro: José Olympio, 1948); Richard Graham, *Britain and the Onset of Modernization in Brazil, 1850–1914* (Cambridge: Cambridge University Press, 1968); Douglas Cole Libby, *Trabalho escravo e capital estrangeiro no Brasil: O caso de Morro Velho* (Belo Horizonte: Itatiaia, 1984); Marshall C. Eakin, *British Enterprise in Brazil: The St. John d'el Rey Mining Company and the Morro Velho Gold Mine, 1830–1960* (Durham, NC: Duke University Press, 1989).

91. Viscount Palmerston to Consul Palmer in Bahia, Feb. 9, 1850, *British and Foreign State Papers*, vol. 38 (1849/1850), 474.

92. See examples of sales of enslaved people by British subjects in Brazil in *British Parliament Papers, House of Commons and Command*, vol. 61 (1861), 33–34. It was also not uncommon for families of diplomats to own slaves. In 1864 thirteen enslaved people belonging to Ms. Benjamin Aveline, widow of the late British consul in Porto Alegre, were liberated at the behest of the acting consul Alex Gollan. Great Britain, Parliament, House of Lords, Accounts and Papers, Slave Trade Correspondence (Class B), *Correspondence with British Ministers and Agents in Foreign Countries and With Foreign Ministers in England Relating to the Slave Trade, from January 1 to December 31, 1864* (London: Harrison and Sons, 1865), 83–84.

93. *Accounts and Papers of the House of Commons*, vol. 56, 30. See also Antônio Penalves Rocha, *Abolicionistas brasileiros e ingleses: A coligação entre Joaquim Nabuco e a British and Foreign Anti-Slavery Society (1880–1902)* (São Paulo: Editora UNESP, 2008).

94. Article from the Liga Constitucional published in the *Revista Commercial*, Feb. 7, 1863, p. 2.

95. In 1852 the government of Campinas listed Antônio Januário Pinto Ferraz among the largest coffee growers in the county, who produced over a thousand arrobas of coffee per year. *Boletim do Arquivo do Estado de São Paulo*, 12 (1952): 120. About the Atibaia plantation, see also Maria Verónica Secreto, "Fronteiras em movimento: O Oeste Paulista e o Sudeste Bonaerense na segunda metade do século XIX: História Comparada" (PhD diss., Universidade de Campinas, 2001), 253.

96. Vicente Ferreira da Silva Bueno to Vicente Pires da Mata, Feb. 23, 1863, ANRJ, SJ, IJ1-518.

97. Bueno to Mata, Feb. 23, 1863.

98. Ferraz witnessed the interrogation of Américo, crioulo; Felizardo, crioulo; Joaquim, Congo nation; Malaquias, Congo; and Tristão, Cabinda, all enslaved by Anna de Campos Paes and involved in the 1832 rebellion. Suely Robles de Queiroz, *Escravidão negra em São Paulo: Um estudo das tensões provocadas pelo escravismo no século XIX* (Rio de Janeiro: Livraria José Olympio Editora, 1977), 214, 220; Ricardo Pirola Figueiredo, *Senzala insurgente: malungos, parentes e rebeldes nas fazendas de Campinas (1832)* (Campinas: Editora da Unicamp, 2011); Maria Thereza Schorer Petrone, *A lavoura canavieira em São Paulo: Expansão e declínio (1765–1851)* (São Paulo: Difel, 1968).

99. Bueno to Mata, Feb. 23, 1863.

100. Queiroz, *Escravidão negra em São Paulo*, 182.

101. Queiroz, *Escravidão negra em São Paulo*, 180.

102. Silva Bueno to Vicente Pires da Mata, Feb. 23, 1863.

103. Damuel Pfromm Netto, *Dicionário de piracicabanos* (São Paulo: IHGP, 2013); Azevedo, *Orfeu de carapinha*, 111. Luiz Gama mentioned Silva Bueno in a letter from 1880, in which he explained his dismissal from the Police Department for being "turbulent and seditious." According to Gama, "the dismissal order was drawn up by Dr. Antônio Manuel dos Reis, a particular friend of mine, who was then police secretary, and signed by the Hon. Dr. Vicente Ferreira da Silva Bueno, who, by this and other similar acts, was appointed judge of the Relação da Corte." Ferreira, *Com a palavra, Luiz Gama*, 199–203.

104. On the importance of "legal localism," see Laura F. Edwards, *The People and Their Peace: Legal Culture and the Transformation of Inequality in the Post-revolutionary South* (Chapel Hill: University of North Carolina Press, 2009).

105. *Correio Mercantil* (Rio de Janeiro), Mar. 7, 1863, p. 2; *Correio Paulistano* (São Paulo), Apr. 29, 1863, p. 3; Xavier, *Religiosidade e escravidão*, 86.

106. Silva Bueno to Vicente Pires da Mata, Feb. 23, 1863.

107. "Insurrection" was the term lawmakers used to define slave rebellion in Brazil. It referred to "the crime of slaves having their freedom by force," for which leaders could be sentenced to death. If considered leaders of an insurrection, free people were subject to the same punishment as the enslaved. Others involved in a supportive capacity could receive life sentences of forced labor (galés perpétuas) in government institutions, shorter terms of forced labor, or flogging. *Código Criminal do Império do Brasil* (Recife: Typographia Universal, 1858).

108. Luis José de Sampaio to Vicente Pires da Matta, Mar. 17, 1863, APESP, SPP, cx. 2.500.

109. José Vergueiro to Pires da Matta, Jan. 19, 1863, APESP, Correspondência de consulados (1825–1903), cx. CO6122.

110. Interrogatory of Benedito, slave of Joaquim Policarpo Aranha, Mar. 15, 1863, APESP, SPP, cx. 2500.

111. Bueno to Mata, Feb. 23, 1863.

112. Xavier, *Religiosidade e escravidão*, 85.

113. Bueno to Mata, Feb. 23, 1863.

114. *Constitucional* (Rio de Janeiro), Mar. 18, 1863, p. 2.

115. Luís José de Sampaio to Vicente Pires da Motta, Mar. 6, 1863, ANRJ, IJ1-518.

116. In the original: "A decantada insurreição de escravos e a questão Anglo-Brasileira." *Correio Paulistano* (São Paulo), Mar. 12, 1863, p. 2.

117. *Correio Paulistano* (São Paulo), Mar. 12, 1863, p. 2.

118. *Diário do Rio de Janeiro*, Mar. 17, 1863, p. 2.

119. Case cited by Mamigonian, "Building the Nation," 235–64.

120. Luiz Francisco da Câmara Leal to Francisco Liberato da Mata, Jan. 23, 1859, ANRJ, SJ, IJ1-541.

121. Policarpo Lopes de Leão to João Luís Vieira Cansansão de Sinimbu, Mar. 18, 1863, ANRJ, SJ, IJ1-465.

122. On the history of British mining investments in Brazil, see João Pandiá Calógeras, *As minas do Brasil e sua legislação* (Rio de Janeiro: Imprensa Nacional, 1904–5); Aires da Mata Machado Filho, *O negro e o garimpo em Minas Gerais* (Belo Horizonte: Itatiaia; São Paulo: EDUSP, 1985); Richard Francis Burton, *Explorations of the Highlands of the Brazil: With a Full Account of the Gold and Diamond Mines; Also, Canoeing Down 1500 Miles of the Great River São Francisco, from Sabará to the Sea* (London: Tinsley Brothers, 1869); Richard Francis Burton, *Viagem do Rio de Janeiro a Morro Velho* (Brasília: Senado Federal, 2001); Courtney J. Campbell, "Making Abolition Brazilian: British Law and Brazilian Abolitionists in Nineteenth-Century Minas Gerais and Pernambuco," *Slavery and Abolition* 36, no. 3 (2015): 521–43.

123. Antônio Manoel Campos de Mello to João Lins Vieira Cansansão de Sinimbu, May 11, 1863, ANRJ, SJ, IJ1-230; Francisco Primo de Souza Aguiar to Francisco de Paula de Negreiros Sayão Lobato, Sept. 23, 1861, ANRJ, SJ, IJ1-228.

124. Antônio Salles do Rego to Antônio Manoel Campos de Mello, May 9, 1863, ANRJ, SJ, IJ1-754.

125. Joaquim Simpliciano Nunes Lisboa to Sebastião José da Silva Braga, Sept. 24, 1864, ANRJ, SJ, IJ1-755.

126. Luis da Anunciação to Antônio Manoel Campos de Mello, Sept. 2, 1864, ANRJ, SJ, IJ1-755.

127. Dispatch of the Ministry of Justice regarding "the proceedings of the English company in Montes Áureos," Nov. 16, 1864, ANRJ, SJ, IJ1-755.

Chapter 3

1. São Luís was founded by the French in 1612, conquered for Portugal in 1615, taken by the Dutch in 1641, and then reconquered by the Portuguese four years later. The province of Maranhão had 359,040 inhabitants in 1872, of whom 284,101 were free and 74,939 enslaved. Pardo (mixed-race) and black people were the majority, adding up to 244,494 people. Within the capital, São Luís, 28 percent of a population estimated at 31,604 residents remained enslaved in 1872. Brasil, Diretoria Geral de Estatística, *Recenseamento da População do Império do Brasil em 1872* (Rio de Janeiro: Leuzinger e Filhos, 1872), 24–26.

2. *Jornal do Commercio* (Rio de Janeiro), Sept. 4, 1861. Brazilian newspapers began tracking the *Sumter*'s movements in April 1861, widely reporting on its voyages across Cuba, where the vessel was said to have captured eight federal ships full of sugar.

3. Howard Jones, *Blue and Gray Diplomacy: A History of Union and Confederate Foreign Relations* (Chapel Hill: University of North Carolina Press, 2009); Howard Jones, *Union in Peril: The Crisis over British Intervention in the Civil War* (Chapel Hill: University of North Carolina Press, 1992).

4. Benevenuto de Magalhães Taques to Brazilian provincial presidents, Aug. 1, 1861, ANRJ, SJ, IJ1-754. Other South American countries, such as Argentina and Colombia, remained more firmly within the Union's sphere of influence but also refrained from recognizing Confederate

ships as "pirates." Though publicly defending Brazil's privileges as a neutral nation, Secretary of State William Seward never ceased to urge the country to take a firmer stand against the Confederacy.

5. David Nixon Porter, *The Naval History of the Civil War* (Mineola, NY: Dover Publications, 1998), 616.

6. *New York Herald*, Nov. 10, 1861.

7. Francisco Primo de Souza Aguiar to Francisco de Paula Sayão Lobato, Oct. 17, 1861, ANRJ, SJ, IJ1-754.

8. Aguiar to Lobato, Oct. 17, 1861.

9. When the *Sumter* arrived in São Luís, the Port Admiral sent a representative on board to inquire about the ship's flag, since he did not recognize the Confederacy emblem. Porter, *Naval History*, 615.

10. On Atlantic approaches to US Civil War history, see Edward B. Rugemer, *The Problem of Emancipation: The Caribbean Roots of the American Civil War* (Baton Rouge: Louisiana State University Press, 2008); W. Caleb McDaniel and Bethany L. Johnson, "New Approaches to Internationalizing the History of the Civil War Era: An Introduction," *Journal of the Civil War Era* 2, no. 2 (2012): 145–50; Rafael Marquese, "The Civil War in the United States and the Crisis of Slavery in Brazil," in *American Civil Wars: The United States, Latin America, Europe, and the Crisis of the 1860s*, ed. Don H. Doyle (Chapel Hill: University of North Carolina Press, 2017), 222–46; Gregory P. Downs, *The Second American Revolution: The Civil War-Era Struggle over Cuba and the Rebirth of the American Republic* (Chapel Hill: University of North Carolina Press, 2019); Gerald Horne, *The Deepest South: The United States, Brazil, and the African Slave Trade* (New York: New York University Press, 2007); Don H. Doyle, ed., *American Civil Wars: The United States, Latin America, Europe, and the Crisis of the 1860s* (Chapel Hill: University of North Carolina Press, 2017); Don H. Doyle, *The Cause of All Nations: An International History of the American Civil War* (New York: Basic Books, 2015); Steve Hahn, *A Nation Without Borders: The United States and Its World in an Age of Civil Wars, 1830–1910* (New York: Viking, 2016).

11. Luiz A. Moniz Bandeira was probably the first Brazilian historian to establish a link between the US Civil War and the 1871 Free Womb Law. Luiz A. Moniz Bandeira, *Presença dos Estados Unidos no Brasil* (Rio de Janeiro: Civilização Brasileira, 1978), 155–61. For a selection of recent studies of the war's impact on Brazil, see Luciana da Cruz Brito, *O avesso da raça: Escravidão, abolicionismo e racismo entre os Estados Unidos e o Brasil* (Rio de Janeiro: Bazar do Tempo, 2023); Maria Clara Sales Carneiro Sampaio, "Não diga que não somos brancos: Os projetos de colonização para afro-americanos do governo Lincoln na perspectiva do Caribe, América Latina e Brasil dos 1860" (PhD diss., Universidade de São Paulo, 2013); Clícea Maria Miranda, "Repercussões da Guerra Civil Americana no destino da escravidão no Brasil, 1861–1888" (PhD diss., Universidade de São Paulo, 2017).

12. Parron, *A política da escravidão*; Marquese, "Civil War"; Jeffrey D. Needell, *The Party of Order: The Conservatives, the State, and Slavery in the Brazilian Monarchy, 1831–1871* (Stanford, Calif.: Stanford University Press, 2006). For Marquese, the Civil War was instrumental in turning the crisis of Brazilian slavery into a systemic issue, even before the conflict with Paraguay in the late 1860s dealt slavery another blow by challenging slaveholders to muster a national army.

13. On the Pan-American imaginary of Southern slave masters, see Matthew Pratt Guterl, *American Mediterranean: Southern Slaveholders in the Age of Emancipation* (Cambridge, MA: Harvard University Press, 2008); Matthew Karp, *This Vast Southern Empire: Slaveholders at the*

Helm of American Foreign Policy (Cambridge, Massachusetts: Harvard University Press, 2016); Horne, *Deepest South*.

14. Raphael Semmes, *The Cruise of the Alabama and the Sumter* (New York: Carleton, 1864), 36.

15. "Opinion of Sérgio Teixeira de Macedo, Advisor to the Ministry of Foreign Affairs," Oct. 25, 1861, in José Antônio Pimenta Bueno, José Maria da Silva Paranhos Rio Branco, and Sérgio Teixeira de Macedo, *Pareceres dos consultores do Ministério dos Negócios Estrangeiros* (Rio de Janeiro: Centro de História e Documentação Diplomática, 2006), 233.

16. David Dixon Porter, *Incidents and Anecdotes of the Civil War* (New York, NY: D. Appleton, 1885), 37; Porter, *Naval History*, 602.

17. Semmes rented out slaves to cut lumber and owned three domestic servants at his home in Mobile. Joseph McKenna, *British Ships in the Confederate Navy* (Jefferson, NC: McFarland and Co., 2010), 19; Stephen Fox, *Wolf of the Deep: Raphael Semmes and the Notorious Confederate Raider CSS Alabama* (New York: Alfred A. Knopf, 2007); Hill, *Diplomatic Relations*.

18. "On the morning of her proposed departure the captain's negro servant went on shore as usual for the day's marketing, when he was waylaid by the worthy Yankee and persuaded indefinitely to postpone his return. Poor fellow!" Semmes, *Cruise of the Alabama and the Sumter*, 55.

19. Raphael Semmes, *Memoirs of Service Afloat: During the War Between the States* (Baltimore: Kelly, Piet, 1869), 210. On Semmes's passage through Brazil, see Peter M. Beattie, *Punishment in Paradise: Race, Slavery, Human Rights, and a Nineteenth-Century Brazilian Penal Colony* (Durham, NC: Duke University Press, 2015). For a discussion of Semmes's proslavery view as he descended into the Caribbean, see Moon-Ho Jung, *Coolies and Cane: Race, Labor, and Sugar in the Age of Emancipation* (Baltimore: Johns Hopkins University Press, 2006), 74.

20. *Jornal do Amazonas*, Sept. 16, 1861, p. 2.

21. Semmes, *Cruise of the Alabama and the Sumter*, 88.

22. Porter, *Naval History*, 616.

23. *O Publicador Maranhense*, Oct. 21, 1861, p. 1.

24. Porter, *Naval History*, 616.

25. With the disruption of southern cotton production between 1861 and 1865, Brazil became one of the largest exporters to the British market, sending its white gold overseas directly from the slaveholding northeast. In 1860 and 1861, only 43,000 bales of Brazilian cotton arrived in Britain each year. In 1863 that number jumped to 56,000 and then skyrocketed to 95,000 bales in 1864 and 138,000 in 1865. Douglas Egerton, "Rethinking Atlantic Historiography in a Post-colonial Era: The Civil War in a Global Perspective," *Journal of the Civil War Era* 1, no. 1 (2011): 83; Sven Beckert, "Emancipation and Empire: Reconstructing the Worldwide Web of Cotton Production in the Age of the American Civil War," *American Historical Review* 105, no. 5 (2004): 1406.

26. *Almanak Administrativo, Mercantil e Industrial do Maranhão para o Anno de 1862* (São Luís: Typ. do Progresso), 33.

27. Reis, *Ganhadores*.

28. The discussions about the *Sumter* held in the Provincial Assembly of Maranhão found their way into the newspapers in November. See, for example, *Publicador Maranhense*, Nov. 4, 1861.

29. The full ad reads: "In around 1855, a slave named Raimundo, known as Surrão ran away, an old mulatto, regular height, kinky hair already going gray, bald, with beard, one eye

askew, works as a tailor, wishes to pass as white saying that he has patent because he knows how to read and write, presents himself as a lawyer, likes spirituous beverages, is very talkative, modest arm, has scars of a beating." *A Coalição*, Aug. 7, 1862.

30. *Publicador Maranhense*, June 13, 1865; Dec. 26, 1866; May 7, 1867.

31. José Cândido Nunes to Júlio César Berenguer de Bittancourt, Nov. 4, 1861, ANRJ, SJ, IJ1-754.

32. Nunes to Bittancourt, Nov. 4, 1861.

33. Nunes to Bittancourt, Nov. 4, 1861.

34. David Clearly, *Anatomy of the Amazonian Gold Rush* (Iowa: University of Iowa Press, 1990); Gomes, *A hidra e os pântanos*; Mundinha Araújo, *Insurreição de escravos em Viana, 1867* (São Luís: Edição AVL, 2006).

35. Reis and Gomes, *Liberdade por um fio*.

36. Report sent by Lieutenant Máximo Fernandes Monteiro to Raimundo Benedito Muniz, Feb. 22, 1862, ANRJ, SJ, IJ1-754.

37. Report of Lieutenant Monteiro, Feb. 22, 1862.

38. Carney and Rosomoff, "Covert Cultivars and Clandestine Communities"; Matthias Röhrig Assunção, "Quilombos maranhenses," in Reis and Gomes, *Liberdade por um fio*, 433–66.

39. Francisco Carlos de Araújo Brusques to Francisco de Paula de Negreiros Sayão Lobato, Feb. 28, 1862, ANRJ, SJ, IJ1-792.

40. Antônio Manoel de Campos Mello to Francisco de Paula Sayão Lobato, Mar. 12, 1862, ANRJ, SJ, IJ1-754.

41. A journalist, poet, teacher, and magistrate from the district of Guimarães, Gentil Homem de Almeida Braga (1835–76) was first elected to the Provincial Assembly of Maranhão in 1857, where he served two subsequent terms before being elected to the Brazilian General Assembly for the 1864–66 term. He considered himself a Liberal, but never openly connected "the *Sumter*'s question" to the problem of slavery in Brazil. His complaints about the privateer's presence in São Luís belonged to the realm of oppositional politics, not abolitionism. Sílvio Romero, *Introdução à história da litteratura brazileira* (Rio de Janeiro: Typographia Nacional, 1880), 1119–33.

42. *Publicador Maranhense*, Oct. 10, 1861.

43. Draft of a letter from Webb to the Ministry of Foreign Affairs, Magalhães Taques (mostly illegible), Oct. 1861, Yale University Manuscripts and Archives, James Watson Webb Papers, box 7.

44. Copy of a "private and strictly confidential" note from Webb to Minister Taques referring to the "Maranhão Affair," Rio de Janeiro, Jan. 28, 1862, James Watson Webb Papers, box 7.

45. Arthur F. Corwin, *Spain and the Abolition of Slavery in Cuba, 1817–1886* (Austin: University of Texas Press, 1967); Seymour Drescher, "Brazilian Abolition in Comparative Perspective," *Hispanic American Historical Review* 68, no. 3 (1988): 429–60; Christopher Schmidt-Nowara, *Empire and Antislavery: Spain, Cuba, and Puerto Rico, 1833–1874* (Pittsburgh: University of Pittsburgh Press, 1999).

46. Brasil, *Ministério das Relacões Exteriores; Ministro Benevenuto Augusto de Magalhães Taques; Relatório do Anno de 1861 Apresentado `a Assembléa Geral Legislativa na 2ª Sessão da 11ª Legislatura*, 1862 (Rio de Janeiro: Typ. Progresso, 1863).

47. "Relatório apresentado à Assembléia Geral Legislativa [. . .] pelo Ministro e Secretário de Estado da repartição dos negócios da Marinha," cited in Silvana Cassab Jeha, "'Anphiteatrical Rio!' Marítimos americanos na baía do Rio de Janeiro, século XIX," *Almanack*, no. 6 (2013): 114.

48. Dispatches of US consuls, Brazil, 1860s, Yale University, Sterling Memorial Library, microfilm.

49. Dispatch from US consul William H. Evans to Ambassador James W. Webb, Dec. 14, 1862, James Watson Webb Papers, box 10.

50. William Seward to James Watson Webb, Nov. 13, 1861, AHI, series 280-1-06.

51. Ferris, "Relations of the United States." See also Harry Bernstein, "The Civil War and Latin America," in *Heard Round the World: The Impact Abroad of the Civil War*, ed. Harold Hyman (New York: Knopf, 1969), 299–326. On American filibustering, see Amy S. Greenberg, *Manifest Manhood and the Antebellum American Empire* (Cambridge: Cambridge University Press, 2005); Robert E. May, *Manifest Destiny's Underworld: Filibustering in Antebellum America* (Chapel Hill: University of North Carolina Press, 2002); Thomas R. Hietala, *Manifest Design: Anxious Aggrandizement in Late Jacksonian America* (Ithaca, NY: Cornell University Press, 1985).

52. "Nota da Legação dos Estados Unidos ao governo imperial," Nov. 1, 1861, AHI, series 280-1-06.

53. Rafael Marquese and Dale W. Tomich, "O Vale do Paraíba escravista e a formação do mercado mundial do café no século XIX," in *O Brasil imperial, 1831–1870*, ed. Keila Grinberg and Ricardo Salles (Rio de Janeiro: Civilização Brasileira, 2009), vol. 2, 339–83; Michelle Craig McDonald and Steven Topik, "Americanizing Coffee: The Refashioning of Consumer Culture," in *Food and Globalization: Consumption, Markets and Politics in the Modern World*, ed. Alexander Nützenadel, and Frank Trentmann (Oxford: Berg, 2008), 109–27.

54. Rood, *Reinvention of Atlantic Slavery*; Saba, *American Mirror*.

55. Leonardo Marques, "The Contraband Slave Trade to Brazil and the Dynamics of U.S. Participation, 1831–1856," *Journal of Latin American Studies* 47, no. 4 (2015): 680.

56. Dale T. Graden, "O envolvimento dos Estados Unidos no comércio transatlântico de escravos para o Brasil, 1840–1858," *Afro-Ásia*, no. 35 (2007): 9–35.

57. Horne, *Deepest South*, 8.

58. Diplomats referred especially to the threat of British invasion, echoing their concerns about the United States. The British government was never entirely pro-Union or pro-emancipation, leading to fears of intervention on both sides of the conflict. British antislavery sentiment was tempered by commercial considerations related to free trade and imperial expansionism in the Atlantic world. R. J. M. Blackett, *Divided Hearts: Britain and the American Civil War* (Baton Rouge: Louisiana State University Press, 2001); Huzzey, *Freedom Burning*; William Mulligan and Maurice J. Bric, eds., *A Global History of Anti-Slavery Politics in the Nineteenth Century* (Houndmills, Basingstoke, Hampshire: Palgrave Macmillan, 2013).

59. Translated letter from Benevenuto de Magalhães Taques to US envoy James W. Webb, Rio de Janeiro, Jan. 23, 1862, James Watson Webb Papers, box 7.

60. Miguel Maria Lisboa to Benevenuto Augusto de Magalhães Taques, Mar. 15, 1862, AHI, series 233-3-12.

61. Bueno, Rio Branco, and Macedo, *Pareceres dos consultores*, 232–41.

62. John DeWitt, *Early Globalization and the Economic Development of the United States and Brazil* (Westport, CN: Praeger, 2002), 119.

63. Federal whalers and coal-laden ships were among the captured: *Morning Star*, *Kingfisher*, *Charles Hill*, *Nora*, *Louisa Hatch*, *Kate Cory*, *Lafayette*, *Nye*, *Dorcas Prince*, *Union Jack*, and *Sea Lark*. The *Alabama* is said to have amassed a total of sixty-five prizes in two years at sea. Semmes, *Cruise of the Alabama*.

64. Antônio Coelho de Sá e Albuquerque to the Ministry of Navy, May 24, 1863, ANRJ, Série Marinha, XM-544.

65. *Diário do Recife* (Pernambuco), May 5, 1863.

66. John M. Taylor, *Semmes: Rebel Raider* (Washington, DC: Brassey's, 2004), 73.

67. Hill, *Diplomatic Relations*.

68. Brian Roleau, *With Sails Whitening Every Sea: Mariners and the Making of an American Maritime Empire* (Ithaca, NY: Cornell University Press, 2014).

69. *Diário do Rio de Janeiro*, May 19, 1863.

70. Semmes, *Cruise of the Alabama*, 180. Ambassador Webb also complained that the *Florida* crew was selling clothes, jewelry, and even family heirlooms stolen from Union sailors on the streets of Recife.

71. Emma Martin Maffitt, *The Life and Services of John Newland Maffitt* (New York: Neale Publishing Company, 1906), 293.

72. Maffitt, *Life and Services*, 289.

73. James Watson Webb to William Seward, May 21, 1863, James Watson Webb Papers, box 10.

74. Arthur Sinclair, *Two Years in the Alabama* (Boston: Lee and Shepard, 1896), 123.

75. Sinclair, *Two Years in the Alabama*, 125.

76. When in Brazil, the USS *Mohican* docked first in Santos and then in Santa Catarina, where the president of the province mistook it for the Confederate *Alabama*. O. A. Glisson, captain of the USS *Mohican*, to James W. Webb, Rio de Janeiro, July 23, 1863, James Watson Webb Papers, box 11.

77. Over time, *O Alabama* became notorious for its mapping of and campaigning against the candomblés of Salvador. I have only identified one edition of *O Mohican*, dating from Jan. 21, 1864, as indicated in the *Revista do Instituto Geográfico e Histórico da Bahia*, 19–22 (1911–15): 551.

78. James Monroe to James W. Webb, Rio de Janeiro, July 23, 1863, James Watson Webb Papers, box 11.

79. *O Alabama* (Bahia), Dec. 21, 1863, p. 1.

80. George Townley Fullam, "Diary of George Townley Fullam, May, 1863," in *Our Cruise in the Confederate States' War Steamer Alabama: The Private Journal of an Officer* (London: A. Schulze, 1863), 64. See also William Stanley Hooley, *Four Years in the Confederate Navy: The Career of Captain John Low on the C.S.S. Fingal, Florida, Alabama, Tuscaloosa, and Ajax* (Athens: University of Georgia Press, 1964); Charles M. Robinson, *Shark of the Confederacy: The Story of the CSS Alabama* (Annapolis, MD: Naval Institute Press, 1995).

81. Composed of lifetime members appointed directly by the emperor, the State Council made influential recommendations on public policy. It had no executive power, but in practice it considered petitions on a wide range of subjects and issued opinions with far-reaching implications. Council members were experienced politicians whose stature lent weight to the opinions, which were drafted as guidelines.

82. Brasil, *O Conselho de Estado e a política externa do Império: Consultas da Seção dos Negócios Estrangeiros (1863–1867)* (Rio de Janeiro: CHDD; Brasília: FUNAG, 2007), 18–37.

83. The circular of Aug. 1, 1861, extended hospitality to foreign cruisers with their prizes for a period of twenty-four hours but stated that they could not dispose of them while in Brazil.

84. Brasil, *O Conselho de Estado e a política externa do Império*, 31.

85. On the incident, see AHI, series 233-3-13 and 233-4-01 (1864).

86. McKenna, *British Ships in the Confederate Navy*, chapter 2.

87. *Correio Mercantil* (Rio de Janeiro), Oct. 16–17, 1864. *A Coalição* (Maranhão), October 22, 1864. Among the U.S. citizens confirmed dead aboard the CSS *Florida* were Lieutenant S. G. Stone, Master T. T. Hunter Junior, Surgeon T. J. Charlton, Chief Engineer W. S. Thompson, and Officer G. F. Sinclair.

88. Ignácio de Avelar Barbosa da Silva to William Seward, Dec. 12, 1864, AHI, series 233-3-13.

89. *Correio Mercantil* (Rio de Janeiro), Oct. 15, 1864, reprint of news published in the *Jornal da Bahia*.

90. *O Constitucional* (Maranhão), Nov. 19, 1864, p. 2.

91. William Seward to Ignácio de Avelar Barbosa da Silva, Dec. 26, 1864, AHI, series 233-3-13.

92. *Times* (New York), Nov. 11, 1864.

93. *Courier des États Unis*, Dec. 12, 1864.

94. "Abraham Lincoln, Fourth Annual Message, Dec. 6, 1864," American Presidency Project, https://www.presidency.ucsb.edu/node/202188 (accessed Apr. 6, 2024).

95. Francisco José Furtado to the president of Bahia, Oct. 26, 1864, APEB, Seção Provincial, maço 903.

96. Antônio Joaquim da Silva Gomes to Francisco José Furtado, Oct. 8, 1864, ANRJ, SJ, IJ1-413.

97. Confidential dispatch from US consul Richard C. Parsons to Ambassador Webb, Oct. 8, 1864, James Watson Webb Papers, box 14.

98. *O Alabama* (Bahia), Oct. 15, 1864, p. 2.

99. Merchant ships sometimes had two names and two flags to fend off the British navy or avoid paying taxes. Marcus J. M. de Carvalho, "A rápida viagem dos 'berçários infernais' e os desembarques nos engenhos do litoral de Pernambuco depois de 1831," in *Do tráfico ao pós-abolição: Trabalho compulsório e livre e a luta por direitos sociais no Brasil*, ed. Helen Osório and Regina Xavier (Porto Alegre: Oikos, 2018), 126–64.

100. Ministry of Justice to the Brazilian legation in Washington, June 6, 1865, AHI, series 233-4-01.

101. Circular from José Antônio Saraiva to the presidents of Brazilian provinces, June 6, 1865, ANRJ, SJ, IJ1-1002.

102. "Mappa aproximado da População da Província de Santa Catharina," "Relatório do Presidente da Província João José Coutinho à Assembleia Legislativa Provincial no ato da abertura de sua sessão ordinária," Mar. 1, 1855, http://brazil.crl.edu/bsd/bsd/942/000037.gif (accessed Dec. 7, 2023).

103. Wellington Castellucci Junior, "Histórias conectadas por mares revoltos: Uma história da caça de baleias nos Estados Unidos e no Brasil (1750–1850)," *Revista de História Comparada* 9, no. 1 (2015): 112. In 1855, Santa Catarina had a population of 19,908 residents, 3,692 of whom were enslaved. João José Coutinho, *Relatório do presidente da província*, Mar. 1, 1855 (Santa Catarina: Presidente da Província, n.d.), 36.

104. Beatriz Mamigonian, "Africanos em Santa Catarina: Escravidão e identidade étnica (1750–1850)," in *Nas rotas do império: Eixos mercantis, tráfico e relações sociais no mundo português*, ed. João Luis Ribeiro Fragoso et al (Vitória: EDUFES, 2014), 563–94; Fabiane Popinigis, "Aos pés dos pretos e pretas quitandeiras: Experiências de trabalho e estratégias de vida em torno do primeiro mercado público de Desterro (1840–1890)," *Afro-Ásia*, no. 46 (2012): 193–226.

105. On the history of whaling in Brazil, see Wellington Castellucci Junior, *Caçadores de baleia: Armações, arpoadores, atravessadores e outros sujeitos envolvidos nos negócios do cetáceo no Brasil* (São Paulo: Annablume, 2009).

106. Maria Cristina Scomazzon and Jeff Franco, *A caminho do ouro: Norte-americanos na Ilha de Santa Catarina* (Florianópolis: Insular, 2016).

107. On maritime marronage, see "Forum: Maritime Marronage: Archaeological, Anthropological, and Historical Approaches," ed., Theresa A. Singleton and Jane Landers in *Slavery and Abolition* 42, no. 2 (2021); Julius S. Scott, "Crisscrossing Empire: Ships, Sailors, and Resistance in the Lesser Antilles in the Eighteenth Century," in *The Lesser Antilles in the Age of European Expansion*, ed. Stanley L. Engerman and Robert L. Paquette (Gainesville: University of Florida Press, 1996), 128–43; Marcus Rediker, "Escapando da escravidão pelo mar na véspera da Guerra Civil Americana: Uma história do trabalho," *Mundos do Trabalho* 14 (2022): 1–18.

108. For more examples, see Álvaro Pereira do Nascimento, "Do cativeiro ao mar: Escravos na Marinha de Guerra," *Estudos Afro-Asiáticos* 38 (2000): 85–112. In Pará, local authorities demanded that the police search ships bound for Peru for escaped slaves. In 1865 two enslaved men escaped on the Peruvian ship *Monna* as it passed through Belém. The captain reported that one of them had written a letter to his mistress asking her not to consider him a fugitive "because he had been contracted by the Peruvian government for certain jobs," after which he would return to Belém. José de Araújo Damim to José Vieira Couto de Magalhães, Jan. 3, 1865, ANRJ, SJ, IJ1-208.

109. William Stafford Jerningham to the Brazilian minister of foreign affairs, José Maria da Silva Paranhos, Jan. 19, 1856, ANRJ, SJ, IJ1-1000.

110. In September, two more enslaved men boarded the *Agatha* in Rio and were found only at sea before arriving at the Cape Colony in Africa. Petition to the chief of police of Rio de Janeiro, João Luis Vieira Cansasão de Sinimbu, with two pages of signatures from owners of enslaved men who either lived nearby or were employed at the city's port, Mar. 4, 1856, ANRJ, SJ, IJ1-1000.

111. Alexandre H. Clemente to the president of the province of Pernambuco, Jan. 23, 1857, ANRJ, SJ, IJ1-328.

112. The historian Myriam Ellis offers an example from Santa Catarina in 1819. Representatives of the São Miguel parish denounced the "theft of slaves" by US ships: "We can further attest that these are not even the greatest damages that foreign fishing ships inflict on this island . . . besides these evils they have resorted to stealing our slaves, as it happened on February 2 of this year, when they took two slaves from Maria Antonia, widow of Antônio Henrique, who left on a ship from the States of America [*sic*] and in March they took another one from an Assistant of the Ratones Fortress on another American Vessel." Ellys, *A baleia no Brasil Colonial* (São Paulo: Melhoramentos, 1969), 178, 179. On US-Brazil relations and whaling, see Wellington Castellucci Junior, "Baleias e Império: Os Estados Unidos e a expansão baleeira nos mares do Atlântico Sul (1761–1844)" *Revista de História*, no. 180 (2021): 1–39.

113. Margaret S. Creighton, *Rites and Passages: The Experience of American Whaling, 1830–1870* (Cambridge: Cambridge University Press, 1995). Castellucci Junior, "Histórias conectadas," 112.

114. *O Despertador* (Santa Catarina), June 27, 1865. About slave flight to US ships in Santa Catarina, see Martha Rebelatto, "Uma saída pelo mar: Rotas marítimas de fuga escrava em Santa Catarina no século XIX," *Revista de Ciências Humanas*, no. 40 (2006): 423–42; Walter Piazza, *A escravidão negra numa província periférica* (Florianópolis: Garapuvu, 1999).

115. Adolfo de B. Cavalcanti de A. Lacerda to José Antônio Saraiva, June 21, 1866, ANRJ, SJ, IJ1-1003.

116. Adolfo de B. Cavalcanti de A. Lacerda to Benjamin Lindsey, June 13, 1866, ANRJ, SJ, IJ1-1003.

117. Interrogatory of Celestino José Machado, May 21, 1866, ANRJ, SJ, IJ1-1003.

118. Interrogatory of Ignácio, May 16, 1866, ANRJ, SJ, IJ1-1003.

119. Interrogatory of the pardo José, May 19, 1866, ANRJ, SJ, IJ1-1003.

120. Interrogatory of Ignácio, May 16, 1866, ANRJ, SJ, IJ1-1003.

121. See Rebelatto, "Uma saída pelo mar," 437.

122. See examples in *O Mercantil* (Desterro), May 3 and 7, 1868.

123. *O Mercantil*, (Desterro), May 17 to 24, 1868.

124. *Anti-Slavery Reporter* (London) 20, no. 2, Apr. 1, 1876, 25.

125. Brasil, *O Conselho de Estado e a política externa*, 181–82.

126. Sue Peabody and Keila Grinberg, eds., *Free Soil in the Atlantic World* (New York: Routledge, 2014), 2–3.

127. Katherine McKittrick and Clyde Woods, eds., *Black Geographies and the Politics of Place* (Cambridge, MA: South End Press, 2007).

Chapter 4

1. Diamond production in the province of Minas Gerais increased by 334 percent between 1819 and 1854. Brazil exported the gems to Europe via the port of Rio de Janeiro to lapidaries in Amsterdam. Slenes, "Múltiplos de porcos e diamantes," 47, 67.

2. Diamantina was the largest urban center in the Comarca do Serro. In 1856, it had a total population of 17,000, while Serro had only 10,584 inhabitants. In the early 1860s, Africans still made up about 23 percent of Diamantina's enslaved population. "Mapa das Freguesias, Distritos, Fogos, Populações parciais e geral do Município do Serro elaborado pelo delegado de polícia Bento Carneiro," Serro, 1856, Arquivo Público Mineiro, Belo Horizonte, Brazil (hereafter cited as APM), Seção Provincial, Presidência da Província, cx. 50, doc. 24; *Anuário estatístico do Estado de Minas Gerais, 1921* (Belo Horizonte: Oficinas Gráficas da Estatística, 1921), 16, 25.

3. João Luís Fragoso, "Alegrias e artimanhas de uma fonte seriada. Os códices 390, 421, 424 e 425: Despachos de escravos e passaportes da Intendência de Polícia da Corte, 1819–1833," in *História quantitativa e serial no Brasil: Um balanço*, ed. Tarcísio Rodrigues Botelho et ali (Goiânia: ANPUH-MG, 2001), 148, 247.

4. African presence survived, for example, in the work songs of miners, who mixed Portuguese and West Central African languages. The linguist and ethnographer Aires da Mata Machado Filho and the musicologist Luiz Heitor Corrêa de Azevedo transcribed and recorded the so-called *vissungos* of São João da Chapada, Diamantina, as part of a larger effort to document folk culture in the 1930s. Machado Filho, *O negro e o garimpo*; Laura lvarez López, "The Dialect of São João da Chapada: Possible Remains of a Mining Language in Minas Gerais, Brazil," *International Journal of the Sociology of Language*, no. 258 (2019): 143–70; Victoria Rose Broadus, "*Vissungo*: The Afro-Descended Culture of Miners and Maroons in Brazil's Diamond District, 1850s–2020s" (PhD diss., University of Georgetown, 2023).

5. Nuno was enslaved to the major Veríssimo Pereira dos Reis in Serro. Processo crime, insurreição, José Cabrinha (escravo), 1865. ANRJ, Corte de Apelação, cx. 3700, maço 5014, 24.

6. Processo crime, insurreição, José Cabrinha, 66. For an in-depth analysis of the 1864 Serro and Diamantina rebellion, see Isadora Moura Mota, "O 'vulcão' negro Chapada: Rebelião

escrava nos sertões diamantinos (Minas Gerais, 1864)" (master's thesis, Universidade de Campinas, 2005).

7. Processo crime, insurreição, José Cabrinha, 24.

8. Needell, *Sacred Cause*; Alonso, *Last Abolition*; Berbel, Marquese, and Parron, *Slavery and Politics*; Carvalho, *Teatro de sombras*.

9. Adão's third testimony, Nov. 21, 1864, Processo crime, insurreição, José Cabrinha, 75.

10. On the intersections of slavery and print culture in Brazil, see Celso Thomas Castilho, "The Press and Brazilian Narratives of *Uncle Tom's Cabin*: Slavery and the Public Sphere in Rio de Janeiro, ca. 1855," *The Americas* 76, no. 1 (2019): 77–106; Godói, *Um editor no império: Francisco de Paula Brito (1809–1861)*; Marialva Barbosa, *Escravos e o mundo da comunicação: Oralidade, leitura e escrita no século XIX* (Rio de Janeiro: Mauad X, 2016); Marco Morel and Mariana Monteiro de Barros, *Palavra, imagem e poder: O surgimento da imprensa no Brasil do século XIX* (Rio de Janeiro: DP&A, 2003).

11. *O Jequitinhonha* (Diamantina), July 13, 1863.

12. On slave literacy in Brazil, see, for example, Iamara da Silva Viana et al., *Dos letramentos: Escravidão, escolas e professores no Brasil oitocentista* (Rio de Janeiro: Editora Malê: 2022); Flávio dos Santos Gomes, Marcelo Mac Cord, and Carlos Eduardo Moreira de Araujo, eds., *Rascunhos cativos: Educação, escolas e ensino no Brasil escravista* (Rio de Janeiro, Editora 7Letras, 2017); Marcus Vinícius Fonseca, *A educação dos negros: A nova face do processo de abolição da escravidão no Brasil* (Bragança Paulista, SP: EDUSF, 2002); Graham, "Writing from the Margins."

13. *Mineiro* refers to people born in the province and later state of Minas Gerais. "Processo de insurreição: José Cabrinha," 24.

14. The Brotherhood of Our Lady of the Rosary was officially founded in Serro, then Vila do Príncipe do Serro Frio, in 1728, although the devotion had been present since the beginning of the eighteenth century through the coronation of black kings and queens. According to its founding statutes, the brotherhood was to accept people of "any quality," that is, free, freed, or enslaved. Danilo Arnaldo Briskievicz, "Um estudo sobre a devoção à Senhora do Rosário na Vila do Príncipe, Minas Gerais, 1713 a 1821," *Saeculum—Revista de História* 27, no. 47 (2022): 48–65; Julita Scarano, *Devoção e escravidão: A Irmandade de Nossa Senhora do Rosário dos Pretos do Distrito Diamantino no século XVIII* (São Paulo: Companhia Editora Nacional, 1978).

15. Processo crime, insurreição, José Cabrinha, 33.

16. Processo crime, insurreição, José Cabrinha, 32.

17. Processo crime, insurreição, José Cabrinha, 66.

18. Processo crime, insurreição, José Cabrinha, 75.

19. Processo crime, insurreição, José Cabrinha, 18.

20. José Maria Brandão to the chief of police of Minas Gerais, Oct. 10, 1864, APM, Seção Provincial, maço 1047.

21. Antônio de Assis Martins e José Oliveira, *Almanack Administrativo, Civil e Industrial da província de Minas Gerais Para o anno de 1864* (Ouro Preto: Tipografia do Minas Gerais, 1863), 269. Among the founders of São João were Bernardina Abelha and Felipe Mina, two black miners credited with building the first chapel in the settlement. Nelson de Senna, *Anuário estatístico de Minas Gerais*, 1913, cited in Machado Filho, *O negro e o garimpo*, 24, 25.

22. The new regulation was codified into law only on Sept. 24, 1845, and amended on Sept. 6, 1852. Joaquim Felício dos Santos, *Memórias do distrito diamantino* (Petrópolis: Vozes; Brasília: INL, 1978), 391.

23. For the royal monopoly on diamond mining, see Júnia Ferreira Furtado, *O livro da Capa Verde: O regimento diamantino de 1771 e a vida no distrito diamantino no período da Real Extração* (São Paulo: Annablume, 1996); Júnia Ferreira Furtado, *Chica da Silva: A Brazilian Slave of the Eighteenth Century* (Cambridge: Cambridge University Press, 2008).

24. Decree 1.081 of Dec. 11, 1852. *Coleção das Leis do Império do Brasil* (Rio de Janeiro: Typografia Nacional, 1872), vol. 1, pt. 2, 460; *O Jequitinhonha* (Diamantina), Aug. 1862, p. 1.

25. Machado Filho, *O negro e o garimpo*, 28. Inventory of Felisberto de Andrade Brant (1897), Biblioteca Antônio Torres, Diamantina (BAT), cartório do 2° ofício, maço 188, pp. 41–43.

26. The enslaved miners Samuel and Justino escaped from the Barro mine in early 1862. *O Jequitinhonha* (Diamantina), Jan. 25, 1862, p. 4.

27. José Ferreira de Andrade Brant to Pedro de Alcântara Cerqueira Leite, Feb. 21, 1863, APM, Ofícios da Presidência da Província, 3.

28. *O Jequitinhonha*, May 27, 1863, p. 1.

29. João Nepomuceno de Aguilar to the president of Minas Gerais, June 16, 1863, APM, Seção Provincial, Indústrias e Terrenos Diamantinos, cód. 1007 (1863).

30. According to the district judge, João Salomé Queiroga, the task of guaranteeing public order in Serro would take time "because there are two fear-inducing quilombos near the town, one of which invaded a farm a few days ago. It is advisable to maintain a detachment of fifteen soldiers here, at least for six or eight months, until the quilombos are defeated, and public peace returns to its normal state." João Salomé Queiroga to Pedro de Alcântara Cerqueira Leite, Dec. 1, 1864, ANRJ, SJ, IJ1-628.

31. Pedro de Alcântara Cerqueira Leite to Francisco José Furtado, Oct. 20, 1864. ANRJ, SJ, IJ1-628.

32. On white fear of black literacy in Brazil, see, among others, Carvalho, "Fácil é serem sujeitos"; for literacy in Arabic among enslaved Muslims in Bahia, see Reis, *Rebelião escrava no Brasil*.

33. Carolyn Eastman, *Nation of Speechifiers: Making an American Public After the Revolution* (Chicago: University of Chicago Press, 2009).

34. *Diário de Pernambuco*, Apr. 12, 1862, p. 1.

35. Chief of Police José Antônio Vaz de Carvalhaes to José Antônio de Albuquerque, Feb. 20, 1862, ANRJ, SJ, IJ-332.

36. Januário Rebolo's testimony, Feb. 15, 1862, ANRJ, SJ, IJ-332. Andrew Pettegree interestingly notes this kind of phenomenon around the emergency of the newspaper in early modern Europe. "It is significant that in this age to 'publish' meant to voice abroad, verbally; books were merely 'printed.'" Andrew Pettegree, *The Invention of News: How the World Came to Know About Itself* (New Haven, CT: Yale University Press, 2014), 11. On the intersection of written and verbal reporting and its connection to popular rebellions, see also Soriano, *Tides of Revolution*.

37. Joaquim pardo's testimony, Feb. 15, 1862, ANRJ, SJ, IJ-332.

38. Geraldo's testimony (*preto escravo* or black slave), Mar. 4, 1862, ANRJ, SJ, IJ-332.

39. I am mindful here of Cristiana Soriano's observations about the development of an incipient public sphere in late eighteenth-century Venezuela, where semiliterate forms of knowledge allowed for the circulation of revolutionary information before the arrival of the printing press. Citing Pablo Piccato, Soriano studies the public sphere as an unfinished historical process through which socially diverse political communities took shape. Soriano, *Tides of Revolution*; Piccato, "Public Sphere in Latin America: A Map of the Historiography," *Social History* 35, no. 2 (2010): 165–92.

40. "Auto de perguntas feitas ao mulato de nome Leandro, escravo do Capitão Jacinto Gomes Borges Uchoa, pelo delegado Cristóvão dos Santos Cavalcante," Mar. 8, 1866, ANRJ, SJ, IJ1-336.

41. On the role of Afro-descendants in the development of Brazilian Portuguese and literate practices in Brazil, see Laura do Carmo and Ivana Stolze Lima, eds., *História social da língua nacional*, vol. 2, *Diáspora africana* (Rio de Janeiro: Edições Casa de Rui Barbosa, 2014); and Laura do Carmo, *Cores, marcas e falas: Sentidos da mestiçagem no império do Brasil* (Rio de Janeiro: Arquivo Nacional, 2003).

42. Sebastião's testimony, Nov. 23, 1864. Processo crime, insurreição, José Cabrinha, 98.

43. Processo crime, insurreição, José Cabrinha, 33.

44. Processo crime, insurreição, José Cabrinha, 79.

45. Letter from Baependi published on the *Correio da Tarde*, Apr. 22, 1848, p. 4. The pieces of paper distributed by Evaristo may have functioned like the passes issued by masters to allow travel. The *papelinhos* would have allowed insurgents license to move around undetected in 1848.

46. Processo crime, insurreição, José Cabrinha, 66.

47. Petition for imperial clemency filed by Francisca de Araújo Padilha, Aug. 20, 1867. ANRJ, SJ, GIFI, 5H-367.

48. *Diário de Minas*, Apr. 14, 1874, p. 3.

49. Burton, *Explorations of the Highlands of the Brazil*, vol. 1, 413.

50. Newspapers lead us into the associational life of enslaved people. Here I apply to them Natalie Zemon Davis's reflections on the printed book "not merely as a source for ideas and images, but as a carrier of relationships." Harvey J. Graff, ed., *Literacy and Historical Development: A Reader* (Carbondale: Southern Illinois University Press, 2007), 128.

51. On literacy in Minas Gerais, see Ivana Stolze Lima, "A voz e a cruz de Rita: Africanas e comunicação na ordem escravista," *Revista Brasileira de História* 38, no. 79 (2018): 41–63; Flávia Silvestre Oliveira and Maria da Conceição Carvalho, "Práticas leitoras em Minas Gerais, século XIX: Bibliotecas públicas e a leitura de jornais," *Informação & informação* 21, no. 1 (2016): 426–47; Luís Carlos Villalta, *Usos do livro no mundo luso-brasileiro sob as luzes: Reformas, censura e contestações* (Belo Horizonte: Fino Traço, 2015); Christianni Cardoso Morais, "Ler e escrever: Habilidades de escravos e forros? Comarca do Rio das Mortes, Minas Gerais, 1731–1850," *Revista Brasileira de Educação* 12, no. 36 (2007): 493–550.

52. Burton, *Explorations of the Highlands of the Brazil*, vol. 2, 81.

53. Maria Helena P. T. Machado, "Os abolicionistas brasileiros e a Guerra de Secessão," in *Caminhos da liberdade: Histórias da abolição e do pós-abolição no Brasil*, ed. Martha Abreu and Hebe Mattos (Niterói: PPGH; Universidade Federal Fluminense, 2011), 10–28.

54. Azevedo, *Onda negra, medo branco*.

55. First published in installments in *O Jequitinhonha* and then in the *Diário do Rio de Janeiro*, *Memórias do distrito diamantino* was released as a book in 1868. Through the writings of Felício, Chica da Silva, the celebrated freedwoman of color who rose to social and economic prominence in colonial Diamantina, first emerged as a historical figure. Furtado, *Chica da Silva*.

56. Teófilo Ottoni (1807–69) was a native of Serro and one of the most famous leaders of the radical wing of the Liberal Party during the Second Reign. He was a provincial and national deputy for Minas Gerais for most of his life and became a senator in 1864. Ricardo Vespucci, *Rebeldes brasileiros: Homens e mulheres que desafiaram o poder* (São Paulo: Editora Casa Amarela, 2001).

57. *O Jequitinhonha*, June 21, 1861, p. 1.

58. On the 1835 law, see Ricardo Figueiredo Pirola, *Escravos e rebeldes nos tribunais do Império: Uma história social da lei de 10 de junho de 1835* (Rio de Janeiro: Arquivo Nacional, 2015).

59. *O Jequitinhonha*, Nov. 30, 1861, 1.

60. *O Jequitinhonha*, Dec. 19, 1861, 2.

61. *O Jequitinhonha*, Dec. 19, 1861, 2.

62. Mariza Lajolo, "The Role of Orality in the Seduction of the Brazilian Reader: A National Challenge for Brazilian Writers of Fiction," in "Loci of Enunciation and Imaginary Constructions: The Case of (Latin) America, I," ed. Walter Mignolo, special issue, *Poetics Today* 15, no. 4 (1994): 555; Lawrence Hallewell, *O livro no Brasil: Sua história* (São Paulo: Editora da USP, 2005).

63. Lilia Moritz Schwarcz, *Retrato em branco e negro: Jornais, escravos e cidadãos em São Paulo no final do século XIX* (São Paulo: Companhia das Letras, 1987); Gilberto Freyre, *O escravo nos anúncios de jornais brasileiros do século XIX* (Recife: Imprensa Universitária, 1963); Flávio dos Santos Gomes, "Jogando a rede, revendo as malhas: Fugas e fugitivos no Brasil escravista," *Revista Tempo* 1, no. 1 (1996): 67–93. On the extensive historiography on the history of the press (and the book) in Brazil, see, for example, Gladys Sabina Ribeiro and Tânia Maria Tavares Bessone, eds., *Linguagens e práticas da cidadania no século XIX* (São Paulo: Alameda, 2010); Isabel Lustosa, *Insultos impressos: A guerra dos jornalistas na independência, 1821–1823* (São Paulo: Companhia das Letras, 2000).

64. *O Jequitinhonha*, June 21, 1862, p. 3.

65. *O Jequitinhonha*, Aug. 23, 1862, p. 3.

66. *O Jequitinhonha*, Sept. 20, 1862, p. 1.

67. *Actualidade* (Rio de Janeiro), Oct. 14, 1862, p. 1. The case is discussed by Silvana Barbosa, "A imprensa e o ministério: Escravidão e Guerra de Secessão nos jornais do Rio de Janeiro (1862–1863)," in *Perspectivas de cidadania no Brasil Império*, ed. José Murilo de Carvalho and Adriana Pereira Campos (Rio de Janeiro: Civilização Brasileira, 2011), 139–41.

68. *O Jequitinhonha*, Nov. 22, 1862, p. 3.

69. *O Jequitinhonha*, Feb. 1, 1863, p. 1.

70. The publicity for the play described it as a comedy that would show like no other "the sordid character of the English." In Diamantina, the Christie Affair would also be a theme of Carnival celebrations, with a group called Zuavos promising to entertain the crowds with "witty exercises alluding to the events of our question—Anglo-Brazilian—thus showing the patriotism of the Diamantinenses even in amusements." *O Jequitinhonha*, Feb. 7, 1863, p. 3. The full script of the play *John Bull* can be found in the paper's edition of Feb. 14, 1863.

71. *O Jequitinhonha*, June 13, 1863, p. 3.

72. *O Jequitinhonha*, June 13, 1863, p. 3.

73. *O Jequitinhonha*, June 13, 1863, p. 3. Only two more editions of the newspaper were published, on February 12 and 14, 1864. *O Jequitinhonha* would be reissued in 1868 as a voice for the emerging republican movement in Brazil.

74. Some original documents about the 1865 uprising were published by Robert Conrad in *Children of God's Fire: A Documentary History of Black Slavery in Brazil* (University Park, PA: Pennsylvania State University Press, 1994), 192–93. On quilombos in northern Brazil, see Oscar de la Torre, *The People of the River: Nature and Identity in Black Amazonia, 1835–1945* (Chapel Hill: University of North Carolina Press, 2018); Flávio dos Santos Gomes, "A 'Safe Haven': Runaway

Slaves, Mocambos, and Borders in Colonial Amazonia, Brazil," *Hispanic American Historical Review* 82, no. 3 (2002), 469–98; Eurípedes Funes, *Nasci nas matas, nunca tive senhor: história e memória dos mocambos do Baixo Amazonas* (Fortaleza: Plebeu Gabinete de Leitura, 2022).

75. When the Pernambuco plantation was sold at public auction in 1867, it had 128 enslaved workers. *Jornal do Pará,* Apr. 13, 1867, p. 2.

76. Brasil, *Relatório do Ministério da Justiça apresentado à Assembléa Geral Legislativa na 4ª Sessão da 12a Legislatura pelo Respectivo Ministro e Secretário de Estado José Thomás Nabuco de Araújo, 1865* (Rio de Janeiro: Typographia Universal de Laemmert, 1866), 8, 9. Vicente Salles, *O negro no Pará sob o regime da escravidão* (Rio de Janeiro: Fundação Getúlio Vargas, 1971), 267–68.

77. Manoel da Natividade de Azevedo to José Vieira Couto de Magalhães, July 5, 1865, ANRJ, SJ, IJ1-792.

78. Historians believe that about a quarter of Pará's population was killed in armed conflicts between 1835 and 1840. The term *cabanagem* refers to the "activity of the people who live in *cabanas*, the region's poorest housing—palm and wood huts. These inhabitants were called *cabanos*, the designation carrying associations of backwardness, poverty and sedition." Mark Harris, *Rebellion on the Amazon: The Cabanagem, Race, and Popular Culture in the North of Brazil, 1798–1840* (Cambridge: Cambridge University Press, 2010), 5.

79. On the conflicts between Carmelites and the enslaved in Bahia, see Walter Fraga Filho, "Histórias e reminiscências da morte de um senhor de engenho no Recôncavo," *Afro-Ásia,* no. 24 (2000): 165–98.

80. Couto de Magalhães to Nabuco de Araújo, July 8, 1865, ANRJ, SJ, IJ1-792.

81. Magalhães to Araújo, July 8, 1865.

82. Case cited in Sandra Rita Molina, "A morte da tradição: A Ordem do Carmo e os escravos da Santa contra o Império do Brasil (1850–1889)" (PhD diss., Universidade de São Paulo 2006), 184.

83. Report from Lieutenant José Geraldo Barroso da Silva, July 24, 1865, ANRJ, SJ, IJ1-792.

84. José Vieira Couto de Magalhães to Nabuco de Araújo, July 29, 1865, ANRJ, IJ1-792.

85. List of escaped slaves from the Pernambuco plantation captured by Lieutenant José Geraldo Barroso da Silva, July 24, 1865, ANRJ, IJ1-792. The list includes the names of five women and two children who were abandoned by their parents.

86. José Vieira Couto de Magalhães to Nabuco de Araújo, July 27, 1865, ANRJ, SJ, IJ1-792.

87. Dispatches of the Ministry of Justice, Aug. 7 and 25, 1865, ANRJ, IJ1-208.

88. Gomes, *A hidra e os pântanos,* 218.

89. Antônio Macedo da Costa to José Vieira Couto de Magalhães, July 10, 1865, ANRJ, SJ, IJ1-792.

90. José Couto de Magalhães to Antônio Macedo da Costa, July 11, 1865, ANRJ, IJ1 792.

91. Magalhães to Costa, July 11, 1865; emphasis added.

92. Nabuco de Araújo to Francisco de Paula da Silveira Lobo, Feb. 20, 1866, ANRJ, SJ, IJ1-977.

93. José de Araújo Roso Dassim to José Vieira Couto de Magalhães, Aug. 12, 1865, ANRJ, SJ, IJ1-977.

94. State Council dispatch, Jan. 29, 1866, ANRJ, Conselho de Estado – Consultas – Seção Justiça, vol. 34.

95. José Antônio Saraiva to Joaquim Maria Nascentes de Azambuja, Nov. 3, 1865, AHI, 235-2-01.

96. Grey Gundaker, *Signs of Diaspora, Diaspora of Signs: Literacy, Creolization, and Vernacular Practice in African America* (New York: Oxford University Press, 1998). On different forms of communication based on cultural codes different from alphabetic literacy, see also Joanne Rappaport and Tom Cummins, *Beyond the Lettered City: Indigenous Literacies in the Andes* (Durham, NC: Duke University Press, 2012); Gabriela Ramos and Yanna Yannakakis, *Indigenous Intellectuals: Knowledge, Power, and Colonial Culture in Mexico and the Andes* (Durham, NC: Duke University Press, 2014).

97. In this respect, Jack Goody interestingly points out that the notion of verbatim recall is not inevitably valued in oral cultures. Quite the contrary, the practice becomes significant only with schooling and the decontextualization of knowledge. Jack Goody, *The Power of the Written Tradition* (Washington: Smithsonian Institution Press, 2000).

98. Azevedo, *Orfeu de carapinha*; Pinto, *Escritos de liberdade*.

99. Ferreira, *Com a palavra, Luiz Gama*.

100. In the original: "Não possuía pergaminhos, porque a inteligência repele os diplomas, como Deus repele a escravidão." *Correio Paulistano*, Dec. 3, 1869, p. 1. Gama once praised Furtado's willingness to welcome "a soldier of black skin, who anxiously solicited the first flashes of elementary instruction."

101. Luiz Gama, *Primeiras trovas burlescas de Getulino* (São Paulo: Typografia Dous de Dezembro de Antonio Louzada Antunes, 1859).

102. Max Fleiuss, *Páginas de história* (Rio de Janeiro: Imprensa Nacional, 1930), 489–90.

103. Godói, *Francisco de Paula Brito*.

104. Godói, *Francisco de Paula Brito*, 132.

105. *O Bom Senso*, Jan. 25, 1855, p. 4.

106. *O Liberal Pernambucano*, Jan. 16, 1857, p. 4.

107. *Diário do Maranhão*, Jan. 6, 1874, p. 4. For more examples of literate slaves in flight, see Alexandra Lima da Silva, "O saber que se anuncia: O poder da palavra em tempos de escravidão (Rio de Janeiro, 1830 a 1888)," *Revista Brasileira de História da Educação*, no. 18 (2018), n.p.

108. Santos, *A Balaiada*; Assunção, "Quilombos maranhenses."

109. Iamara da Silva Viana and Flávio dos Santos Gomes, "Letramento, escravidão e mocambos: Livros encontrados em um rancho quilombola no Espírito Santo oitocentista," *Resgate: Revista Interdisciplinar de Cultura* 28 (2020): 1–20.

110. Sandra Lauderdale Graham, *Caetana Says No: Women's Stories from a Brazilian Slave Society* (New York: Cambridge University Press, 2002), xxi. On the Iberian juridical culture, see Angel Rama, *The Lettered City*, ed. and trans. John Charles Chasteen (Durham, NC: Duke University Press, 1996); Kathryn Burns, *Into the Archive: Writing and Power in Colonial Peru* (Durham, NC: Duke University Press, 2010).

111. Sandra Gustafson, *Eloquence Is Power: Oratory and Performance in Early America* (Chapel Hill: University of North Carolina Press, 2000).

112. Some historians call the movement the War of the Hornets. Guilhermo Palacios, "Revoltas camponesas no Brasil escravista: A 'Guerra dos Marimbondos' (Pernambuco, 1851–1852)," *Almanack Brasiliense*, no. 3 (2006): 9–39.

113. Chalhoub, *A força da escravidão*, chapter 1.

114. Chalhoub, *A força da escravidão*, 21–22. Chalhoub recounts that, in Paraíba, armed groups asked the local judge of Ingá to handle over "the Book, which they called Captivity," referring to the registry.

Chapter 5

1. Scholarship on Brazilian quilombos first developed in relation to Palmares, the largest and longest-lasting network of maroon communities in Brazil's history. Edison Carneiro, *O quilombo dos Palmares* (São Paulo: Editora Brasiliense, 1947); Clóvis Moura, *Rebeliões da senzala: Quilombos, insurreições, guerrilhas* (São Paulo: Edições Zumbi, 1959); R. K. Kent, "Palmares: An African State in Brazil," *Journal of African History* 6, no. 2 (1965): 161–75; Décio Freitas, *Palmares: A guerra dos escravos* (Porto Alegre: Editora Movimento, 1973); John Thornton, "Les États de l'Angola et la formation de Palmares (Brésil)," *Annales. Histoire, Sciences Sociales* 63, no. 4 (2008): 769–97; Flávio dos Santos Gomes, *Palmares: Escravidão e liberdade no Atlântico* (São Paulo: Contexto, 2005).

2. Since the 1980s, scholars have explored marronage in a broader historical context including, for example, relations with indigenous peoples, environmental history, and the formation of black peasantries in Brazil. For a selected overview of this vast scholarship, see Ciro Flamarion Cardoso, *Escravo ou camponês? O protocampesinato negro nas Américas* (São Paulo: Brasiliense, 1987); Flávio dos Santos Gomes, *Mocambos e quilombos: Uma história do campesinato negro no Brasil* (São Paulo: Claro Enigma, 2015); Miki, *Frontiers of Citizenship*; Funes, *Nasci no mato*; Silvia Hunold Lara, *Palmares e Cacaú: O aprendizado da dominação* (São Paulo: EDUSP, 2021); Oscar de la Torre, "The Well That Wept Blood: Ghostlore, Haunted Waterscapes, and the Politics of Quilombo Blackness in Amazonia (Brazil)," *American Historical Review* 127, no. 4 (2022): 1635–58; Marc A. Hertzman, "The 'Indians of Palmares': Conquest, Insurrection, and Land in Northeast Brazil," *Hispanic American Historical Review* 103, no. 3 (2023): 423–60.

3. Gomes, *Histórias de quilombolas*; Grinberg, *As fronteiras da escravidão*; Jonatas Caratti, *O solo da liberdade: As trajetórias da preta Faustina e do pardo Anacleto pela fronteira rio-grandense no contexto das leis abolicionistas uruguaias (1842–1862)* (São Leopoldo: Oikos; Editora Unisinos, 2013).

4. In the 1860s Paraguay had a population of 450,000 inhabitants, while Brazil has just under 10 million (the 1872 census estimated it at 9,930,478). Argentina had 1.7 million inhabitants, while Uruguay had the smallest population, about 250,000. Hendrik Kraay and Thomas Whigham, eds., *I Die with My Country: Perspectives on the Paraguayan War, 1864–1870* (Lincoln: University of Nebraska Press, 2004), 9.

5. Kraay and Whigham, *I Die with My Country*, 7.

6. According to Alex Borucki, the number of captives imported from Brazil and Africa during this period amounted to about 70,000. Alex Borucki, *From Shipmates to Soldiers: Emerging Black Identities in the Río De La Plata* (Albuquerque: University of New Mexico Press, 2015), 2.

7. Grinberg, "Illegal Enslavement, International Relations"; Gabriel Aladrén, "Experiências de liberdade em tempos de guerra: Escravos e libertos nas Guerras Cisplatinas (1811–1828)," *Estudos Históricos* 22, no. 44 (2009): 439–58.

8. Alex Borucki, Karla Chagas, and Natalia Stalla, *Esclavitud y trabajo: Un estudio sobre los afrodescendientes en la frontera uruguaya (1835–1855)* (Montevideo: Pulmón Ediciones, 2004).

9. Francisco Doratioto, *Maldita guerra: Nova história da Guerra do Paraguai* (São Paulo: Companhia das Letras, 2002); Mário Maestri, "A intervenção do Brasil no Uruguai e a Guerra do Paraguai: A missão Saraiva," *Revista Brasileira de História Militar* 5, no. 13 (2014): 6–27.

10. The imperial government spent an estimated 614 thousand *contos de réis* on the war effort, more than ten times the national state budget for 1864. Military recruitment touched

the lives of all Brazilians, with 1 in every 50 men being drafted to the battlefronts of Paraguay, between 150 and 200 thousand in all. Doratioto, *Maldita guerra*, chapter 5.

11. Caetano de Souza Telles Guimarães to the chief of police of Minas Gerais, Sept. 15, 1865, APM, Seção Provincial, cód. 1095, Caeté.

12. "Interrogatório feito pelo delegado João Raymundo Mourão à Vitória da Costa," Diamantina, Nov. 19, 1864, BAT, Processos Criminais, maço 81, 4.

13. Ricardo Salles, *Guerra do Paraguai: Escravidão e cidadania na formação do exército* (Rio de Janeiro: Paz e Terra, 1990).

14. On quilombos in Minas Gerais, see Luiz Luna, *O negro na luta contra a escravidão* (Rio de Janeiro: Leitura, 1968); Waldemar de Almeida Barbosa, *Negros e quilombos em Minas Gerais* (Belo Horizonte: n.p., 1972); Carlos Magno Guimarães, *A negação da ordem escravista: Quilombos em Minas Gerais no século XVIII* (São Paulo: Ícone, 1988). For Maranhão, see Assunção, "Quilombos maranhenses"; Santos, *A Balaiada*; Gomes, *A hidra e os pântanos*.

15. Gomes, *Histórias de quilombolas*, 385.

16. Flávio dos Santos Gomes has coined the term *campo negro* (black field) to describe the social and economic geography that characterized quilombola life, that is, the networks of relationships that brought together runaways with enslaved and marginalized poor people, as well as merchants and other free persons who provided them with food, ammunition, and information on the movements of repressive forces. Gomes, *Histórias de quilombolas*.

17. For examples, see Vitor Izecksohn, "Recrutamento militar no Rio de Janeiro durante a Guerra do Paraguai," in *Nova história militar brasileira*, ed. Celso Castro, Vitor Izecksohn, and Hendrik Kraay (Rio de Janeiro: Editora FGV, 2004), 179–208; Hendrik Kraay, "'O abrigo da farda': O exército brasileiro e os escravos fugidos, 1800–1888," *Afro-Ásia*, no. 17 (1996): 29–56.

18. On recent analyses of quilombola insurgencies, see Brown, *Tacky's Revolt*; Marjoleine Kars, *Blood on the River: A Chronicle of Mutiny and Freedom on the Wild Coast* (New York: New Press, 2020); Reis and Gomes, *Revoltas escravas no Brasil*.

19. The regency period (1831–40), for example, was a decade of popular uprisings. The liberto Cosme Bento dos Santos, as we have seen, led over three thousand escaped slaves during the Balaiada revolt (1838–41) in Maranhão. Araújo, *Em busca de Dom Cosme*.

20. Article reprinted in the *Jornal do Commercio* (Rio de Janeiro), July 17, 1865, p. 2.

21. Processo crime, homicídio, Jerônimo (escravo), Diamantina, 1867. ANRJ, Corte de Apelação, cx. 3699, ap. 5774.

22. Processo crime Jerônimo (escravo), 1867.

23. "Autos de corpo de delito em Carolina Alves da Calçada," Feb. 1, 1862, and Mar. 3, 1862. ANRJ, Corte de Apelação, processo crime, Pedro (escravo), Diamantina, cx. 3698, ap. 4536, 1863.

24. "Auto de perguntas feito a João Alves Nepomuceno," Feb. 7, 1862. ANRJ, processo crime, Pedro, 25.

25. "Auto de perguntas feito a Carolina Alves da Calçada," May 29,1862. ANRJ, processo crime, Pedro, 79; and *O Jequitinhonha* (Diamantina), Feb. 8, 1862, p. 2.

26. "Auto de perguntas feitos a Ana Joaquina Fernandes e sua vizinha Maria Cândida da Serra," June 11, 1865. ANRJ, processo crime, Jerônimo, 1867.

27. "Auto de perguntas feitos a Lucinda Maria Marques," June 12, 1865. ANRJ, processo crime, Jerônimo, 1867.

28. João Nepomuceno de Aguilar to the chief of police of Minas Gerais, Aug. 19, 1865, ANRJ, SJ, IJ1-630.

29. Stephanie McCurry, *Women's War: Fighting and Surviving the American Civil War* (Cambridge, MA: Belknap Press of Harvard University Press, 2019); Thavolia Glymph, *The Women's Fight: The Civil War's Battles for Home, Freedom, and Nation* (Chapel Hill: University of North Carolina Press, 2020).

30. "1º Interrogatório de Praxedes Padilha de Araújo," Aug. 18, 1865. ANRJ, processo crime, Jerônimo, 1867.

31. Processo crime, Jerônimo, 53.

32. Processo crime, Jerônimo, 53.

33. The quilombolas of Minas left a lingering impression on Burton, who described them as most slaveholders would in 1868: "Nowhere, as far as I know Brazil, are negroes so troublesome as those in and around Diamantina. Many of them take to the bush and become 'Quilombeiros,' black banditti, ready for any atrocity which their cowardice judges safe. Here no one travels even by day without having his weapons handy and without looking round the corners. They are skillful as Canidia or Locusta, and much addicted to the use of Stramonium." Burton noted in passing that "when their stronghold was attacked and taken, whites as well as blacks were found in it." Burton, *Explorations of the Highlands of the Brazil*, vol. 2, 97, 109.

34. "1º Interrogatório de Vitória da Costa Pinheiro," Aug. 19, 1865. ANRJ, processo crime, Jerônimo, 1867.

35. "1º Interrogatório de Rita Pereira dos Santos," Aug. 20, 1865. ANRJ, processo crime, Jerônimo, 1867.

36. On the gendered nature of the archives of slave resistance, see Xavier, Farias, and Gomes, *Mulheres negras*; Morgan, *Reckoning with Slavery*; Aisha Finch, "'What Looks Like a Revolution': Enslaved Women and the Gendered Terrain of Slave Insurgencies in Cuba, 1843–1844," *Journal of Women's History* 26, no. 1 (2014): 112–34; Marjoleine Kars, "Dodging Rebellion: Politics and Gender in the Berbice Slave Uprising of 1763," *American Historical Review* 121, no. 1 (2016): 39–69.

37. "1º Interrogatório de Rita Pereira dos Santos," Aug. 20, 1865. ANRJ, processo crime, Jerônimo, 1867.

38. With a certain tone of disdain, Rita also revealed that that her male companions were close to other women outside the quilombo. They once spent three days "dancing [*pagodeando*] with Joaquina Peixe em Pé and Inocência crioula at their house."

39. "1º Interrogatório de Eva Francisca da Conceição," Aug. 24, 1865, and "Auto de qualificação da mesma," Sept. 4, 1865. ANRJ, processo crime, Jerônimo, 1867.

40. "1º Interrogatório de Eva Francisca da Conceição," Aug. 24, 1865.

41. "1º Interrogatório de Eva Francisca da Conceição," Aug. 24, 1865.

42. "1º Interrogatório de Emília Carlota de Oliveira," Aug. 31, 1865. ANRJ, processo crime, Jerônimo, 1867.

43. "Depoimento de Joana Francisca das Neves," Sep. 4, 1865. "1º Interrogatório de Emília Carlota de Oliveira," Aug. 31, 1865. ANRJ, processo crime, Jerônimo, 1867.

44. Rodrigo de Sousa Reis, Misael Felicíssimo de Aguilar, and Vicente José da Trindade, owners of most of the quilombolas, figured on the list of miners with over twenty enslaved men working in the mining services of Diamantina in 1865. Martins e Oliveira, *Almanack*, 1865, 266–67.

45. "Sentença de Pronúncia," Sept. 9 and 27, 1865. ANRJ, processo crime, Jerônimo, 1867.

46. Commander of the National Guard from Sabará, Curvelo, and Santa Luzia, Barão de Curvelo, to President Pedro de Alcântara Cerqueira Leite, Aug. 24, 1865, APM, Seção Provincial,

maço 1105. The reference to the written correspondence between enslaved people at Morro Velho and Diamantina can be found in Barbosa, *Negros e quilombos em Minas Gerais*, 75, 76.

47. "1º Interrogatório de João Rainha, escravo de Vicente José da Trindade," Apr. 4, 1866. ANRJ, processo crime, Jerônimo, 1867.

48. "2º Interrogatório de Eva Francisca da Conceição," May 16, 1866. ANRJ, processo crime, Jerônimo, 1867.

49. "2º Interrogatório de Rita Pereira dos Santos," May 16, 1866. ANRJ, processo crime, Jerônimo, 1867.

50. "2º Interrogatório de Jerônimo, escravo do Barão de Arassuaí," Aug. 29, 1866. ANRJ, processo crime, Jerônimo, 1867.

51. "2º Interrogatório de Eva Francisca da Conceição," May 16, 1866. ANRJ, processo crime, Jerônimo, 1867.

52. "2º Interrogatório de Rita Pereira dos Santos," May 16, 1866. ANRJ, processo crime, Jerônimo, 1867.

53. Petition from the Baron of Arassuaí to Diamantina's municipal judge, Aug. 8, 1866. ANRJ, processo crime, Jerônimo, 1867.

54. "Auto de qualificação" and "1º interrogatório de Jerônimo, escravo do Barão de Arassuaí," Aug. 27, 1866. ANRJ, processo crime, Jerônimo, 1867.

55. Processo crime, Jerônimo, 1867, 137.

56. "2º Interrogatório de Jerônimo, escravo do Barão de Arassuaí," Aug. 29, 1866. ANRJ, processo crime, Jerônimo, 1867. Besides Frutuoso, he named as quilombolas Marcolina; Mateus Barbosa of Alexandre Gomes da Silva; the deceased Francisco and João Pinheiro, both slaves of Rodrigo de Sousa Reis; Germano; João do Dó; Antônio, "slave of Anarante"; Joaquim, slave "of Dona Maria"; Maurício, slave "of the late Manoel da Silva"; Rita; Vitória; Apolinária; Eva; Praxedes; "Rita of Dona Joana"; Joaquim, slave of Misael Felicíssimo de Aguilar; and João Rainha, with whom he had been for the longest time. João Rainha added to Jerônimo's list the names of Cipriano, slave of "Dona Nazareth"; Apolinário, of Manoel de Paula; Miguel, of Dona Clara; and "Joana do Mendanha."

57. "3º Interrogatório de Jerônimo, escravo do Barão de Arassuaí, Oct. 12, 1866. ANRJ, processo crime, Jerônimo, 1867.

58. "2º Interrogatório de João Rainha," Oct. 10, 1866. ANRJ, processo crime, Jerônimo, 1867.

59. "Sentença," Oct. 12, 1866, and "Acórdão da Relação do Rio de Janeiro," June 25, 1867. ANRJ, processo crime, Jerônimo, 1867.

60. "2º Interrogatório de Joaquim," Oct. 31, 1874. ANRJ, processo crime, Jerônimo, 1867.

61. The Brazilian Army estimated that about 91,000 men were recruited to fight in the Triple Alliance War. Brasil, Ministro da Guerra, Relatório 1872, "Mappa da força com que cada uma das Provincias do Império concorreu para a guerra do Paraguay, segundo os mappas remettidos a esta Secretaria de Estado."

62. In 1865–66, separate black regiments known as *zuavos*, *couraças*, and *sapadores* were formed in Bahia and Pernambuco in the tradition of colonial black militias, but the imperial government disbanded these units at the end of 1866. They enlisted roughly one thousand men. Hendrik Kraay, "Os companheiros de Dom Obá: Os Zuavos baianos e outras companhias negras na Guerra do Paraguai," *Afro-Ásia*, no. 46 (2012): 121–61; Eduardo Silva, *Prince of the People: The Life and Times of a Brazilian Free Man of Colour* (London: Verso, 1993).

63. Like regular soldiers, volunteers were also entitled to pay 600$000 réis to purchase exemption from service. Kraay, "Slavery, Citizenship and Military Service in Brazil's Mobilization for the Paraguayan War," *Slavery and Abolition* 18, no. 3 (1997), 233.

64. Decree no. 3.383, Jan. 21, 1865, *Coleção das Leis do Império do Brasil* (Rio de Janeiro: Typografia Nacional, 1872), vol. 1, part 2, 15.

65. Miqueias H. Mugge, "Senhores da guerra: Elites militares no sul do Império do Brasil" (PhD diss., Universidade Federal do Rio de Janeiro, 2016).

66. *Relatório Provincial de Minas Gerais*, May 11, 1865.

67. *Relatório Provincial de Minas Gerais*, Anexo B: "Aquisição de forças para a guerra," 1867.

68. For a social history of the Brazilian military that considers the intersection of honor and gender, see Peter Beattie, *The Tribute of Blood: Army, Honor, Race, and Nation in Brazil, 1864–1945* (Durham, NC: Duke University Press, 2001).

69. Jorge Luiz Prata de Sousa, *Escravidão ou morte: Os escravos brasileiros na Guerra do Paraguai* (Rio de Janeiro: Mauad; ADESA, 1996), 60.

70. José Joaquim do Carmo to Francisco José Furtado, Feb. 11, 1865, ANRJ, SJ, IJ1-437.

71. Eduardo Pindaíba de Mattos to President José Joaquim do Carmo, Feb. 22, 1865, ANRJ, SJ, IJ1-437.

72. Carlos José de Assis to Antônio Barbosa Gomes Nogueira, Feb. 27, 1865, *Relatório Provincial de Minas Gerais*.

73. José Nepomuceno da Fonseca Marques to Pedro de Alcântara Cerqueira Leite, Mar. 4, 1865, *Relatório Provincial de Minas Gerais*.

74. Letter from the Santo Antônio do Monte police to Pedro de Alcântara Cerqueira Leite, Mar. 5, 1865, *Relatório Provincial de Minas Gerais*.

75. Caetano de Souza Telles Guimarães to Pedro de Alcântara Cerqueira Leite, Feb. 19, 1865. *Relatório Provincial de Minas Gerais*.

76. Justino Ferreira Carneiro to Cerqueira Leite, Jan. 29, 1865, ANRJ, SJ, IJ1-778.

77. Antônio da Silva Pereira to Cerqueira Leite, Mar. 4, 1865, APM, Seção Provincial, maço 1093 (1865, 1° trimestre).

78. Antônio Gonçalves da Silva to Pedro de Alcântara Cerqueira Leite, June 21, 1865; dispatch from Cerqueira Leite, Aug. 9, 1865; Justino Ferreira Carneiro to Cerqueira Leite, Sept. 18, 1865, APM, Seção Provincial, maço 1070 (1864–1865). Joaquim Barbosa Lima to Cerqueira Leite, Sept. 4, 1865; Commander of the National Guard in Barbacena, José Rosa Coelho to Cerqueira Leite, Sept. 22, 1865, APM, Seção Provincial, maço 1095 (Sept.–Dec. 1865), *Relatório Provincial de Minas Gerais*, 1865.

79. Caetano de Souza Telles Guimarães to the chief of police of Minas Gerais, Sep. 15, 1865, APM, Seção Provincial, maço 1095.

80. Mário Maestri, "Insurreições escravas no Rio Grande do Sul (século XIX)," in Reis and Gomes, *Revoltas escravas no Brasil*, 458–521.

81. Judge José Alves de Azevedo Magalhães to João Marcelino de Souza Gonzaga, Nov. 20, 1864, ANRJ, SJ, IJ1-586.

82. For a full analysis of the 1864 conspiracy in Taquari, see Paulo Roberto Staudt Moreira, "Porque os brancos eram uns pelos outros, os negros também deviam fazer o mesmo': Revoltas escravas no Rio Grande do Sul na segunda metade do Oitocentos," in Reis and Gomes, *Revoltas escravas no Brasil*, 413–57.

83. President of Rio Grande do Sul to the Ministry of Justice, Feb. 18, 1865, ANRJ, SJ, IJ1-585.

84. Walter Spaulding, *A invasão paraguaia do Brasil* (Rio de Janeiro: Companhia Editora Nacional, 1940), 51.

85. Mário Maestri, *O escravo no Rio Grande do Sul* (Porto Alegre: EST; Caxias do Sul: EDUCS,1984).

86. Mário Maestri, "Pampa negro: Agitações, insubordinações e conspirações servis no Rio Grande do Sul, 1863–1868," *Saeculum—Revista de História* 25 (2011): 68.

87. Chief of Police Belarmino Peregrino da Gama e Melo to Joaquim Vieira da Cunha, June 27, 1868. ANRJ, SJ, IJ1-591. Rui Vieira da Cunha, "Escravos rebeldes em Porto Alegre," *Mensário do Arquivo Nacional* 9, no. 8 (1978): 11–15.

88. Cunha, "Escravos rebeldes," 13.

89. Cunha, "Escravos rebeldes," 14.

90. The circulation of Paraguayan prisoners throughout Brazil extended the war's reach to the provinces on the Atlantic border. On Oct. 1, 1865, a woman enslaved to the notary Manoel Esteves Alves denounced an uprising being prepared by Cândido and other enslaved urban workers. Cândido had told her that he would kill his master's family, saving only Manoel's eldest and most beautiful daughter. Police found firecrackers on the outskirts of Manoel's rural property in Poço, intended as a warning to insurgents. The authorities also suspected the involvement of two Portuguese men and, above all, of "Chileans" who were in Maceió posing as botanists. "Only now is it suspected that these Chileans were Paraguayans who claimed that Lopez was waging war against Brazil to free the slaves." *O Cearense*, Oct. 7, 1865, p. 2.

91. José Araújo Rozo Danino to José Vieira Couto de Magalhães, Oct. 10, 1865, ANRJ, SJ, IJ1-792.

92. Luiza Rios Ricci Volpato, *Cativos do sertão: Vida cotidiana e escravidão em Cuiabá em 1850–1888* (São Paulo: Marco Zero, 1993), 230.

93. *Diário de Minas*, July 3, 1867, p. 2.

94. On Aug. 8, 1871, eighty regular troops raided the Rio Manso quilombo but returned defeated after three and a half months of chasing its inhabitants. Officers captured only three free women with six children and seven slaves with three children. President Francisco José Cardoso João explained his persistence after the raid: "I am seriously committed to the extinction of the Quilombos because they offer shelter to soldiers who desert, to criminals who are persecuted by the action of justice, and to slaves who flee." Letter to Francisco de Paula de Negreiros Sayão Lobato, Aug. 12, 1871, ANRJ, SJ, IJ1-686.

95. Antônio José Carneiro to Saldanha Marinho, Bagagem, Dec. 18, 1866; Manoel Soares Fortuna to Saldanha Marinho, Feb. 2, 1867, *Relatório Provincial de Minas Gerais*, Anexo B, 1867.

96. Francisco de Paula Carneiro Campos to Saldanha Marinho, Feb. 24, 1867, *Relatório Provincial de Minas Gerais*, Anexo B "Aquisição de Forças para a Guerra," 1867.

97. *Escravos da nação* or "slaves of the nation" were enslaved by the Brazilian state. Under government supervision, they usually worked in public institutions. This type of public servitude dates back to colonial times, when the Portuguese crown acquired the slaves of the Jesuits expelled from Brazil in 1760. In 1866, the city council estimated that there were four hundred escravos da nação. Ilana Pelicari Rocha, *Escravos da nação: O público e o privado na escravidão brasileira, 1760–1876* (São Paulo: EDUSP, 2018).

98. Atas do Conselho de Estado, Nov. 5, 1866, https://www.senado.leg.br/publicacoes /anais/pdf/ACE/ATAS6-Terceiro_Conselho_de_Estado_1865-1867.pdf (accessed Apr. 8, 2024).

99. *Fala do trono*, 1867, Brasil, Senado Federal, *Falas do trono: Desde o ano de 1823 até o ano de 1889* (Brasília: Senado Federal, 2019), 488–89.

100. Kraay, "Slavery, Citizenship and Military Service," 229, 245. On black soldiers' participation in the Triple Alliance War, see Jorge Prata de Souza, *Escravidão ou morte: Os escravos brasileiros na Guerra do Paraguai* (Rio de Janeiro: MAUAD: ADESA, c1996); André Amaral de Toral, "A participação dos negros escravos na Guerra do Paraguai," *Estudos Avançados* 9, no. 24 (1995): 287–96; Júlio José Chiavenatto, *O negro no Brasil: Da senzala à Guerra do Paraguai* (São Paulo: Brasiliense, 1982).

101. On slave flight during the Triple Alliance War, see José Maria Bezerra Neto, "A farsa de Elesbão: Escravos, fugas escravas e Guerra do Paraguai (1864–1870)," in *150 anos depois: Reflexões sobre a Guerra do Paraguai, La Guerra Grande, La Guerra de la Triple Alianza*, ed. Johny Santana de Araújo, Eva Paulino Bueno, and Rodrigo Caetano da Silva (Teresina: EDUFPI; Cancioneiro, 2020), 17–40.

102. Malachias and Salomé were enslaved by José Luís de Souza e Oliveira. *Correio Mercantil* (Rio de Janeiro), May 7, 1867, p. 4.

103. *O Liberal de Minas*, June 17, 1868, p. 4.

104. *Correio Mercantil* (Rio de Janeiro), Jan. 31, 1868, p. 4; *Noticiador de Minas*, Nov. 26, 1868, p. 4.

105. *O Jequitinhonha* (Diamantina), Oct. 19, 1869, p. 4.

106. Between 1791 and 1830, Brazil imported an average of forty thousand enslaved Africans per year. See Aline Helg, *Slaves No More: Self-Liberation Before Abolitionism in the Americas* (Chapel Hill: University of North Carolina Press, 2019), 227. On the plural composition of quilombos, see Jan Hoffman French, *Legalizing Identities: Becoming Black or Indian in Brazil's Northeast* (Chapel Hill: University of North Carolina Press, 2009).

107. José Caetano Vaz Júnior to José Thomás Nabuco de Araújo, Sep. 13, 1865, ANRJ, SJ, IJ1-230.

108. Antônio Leitão da Cunha to Francisco José Furtado, Mar. 31, 1865, ANRJ, SJ, IJ1-230.

109. Lafayete Pereira to José Thomás Nabuco de Araújo, Sep. 13, 1865, ANRJ, SJ, IJ1-230.

110. *Publicador Maranhense*, Oct. 26, 1865, p. 1; Gomes, *A hidra e os pântanos*, 219.

111. Deputy Filipe Sá spoke to the assembly during the session of June 13, 1865. *Publicador Maranhense*, July 9, 1867, p. 1.

112. Mundinha Araújo's book, widely cited here, is the seminal account of the 1867 quilombola uprising in Maranhão. In *Insurreição de escravos em Viana*, Araújo published a significant portion of the testimonies collected at the time. The purpose of this section is not to detail the events of 1867 but rather to draw attention to the role of literacy in black struggles for freedom during the Triple Alliance War. See also Reis, "Nos achamos em campo a tratar da liberdade"; Iamara da Silva Viana, Alexandre Ribeiro Neto e Flávio dos Santos Gomes, "Escritos insubordinados entre escravizados e libertos no Brasil," *Estudos Avançados* 33, no. 96 (2019), 155–77.

113. According to the provincial *Almanak*, more than three thousand men had already been recruited for the war effort in 1866 and an imperial decree from March 13, 1867 required Maranhão to send another five hundred guardsmen south. *Almanak administrativo, mercantil e industrial do Maranhão* (São Luís: Ed. B. de Mattos, 1866), 79.

114. *Amocambado* means "from the *mocambo*," another common term to denominate quilombo settlers in Brazil. Viana authorities to President Franklin Américo de Menezes Doria, July 9, 1867, ANRJ, SJ, IJ1-233.

115. Viana authorities to President Franklin Américo de Menezes Doria, July 9, 1867. ANRJ, SJ, IJ1-233.

116. "Auto de perguntas do preto Vicente, escravo de Dona Anna Padilha," Viana, July 18, 1867. Published in Araújo, *Insurreição de escravos em Viana*, 157. Raimundo Antônio da Costa Ferreira, São Vicente Ferrer, to Franklin Américo de Menezes Dória, July 10, 1867, ANRJ, SJ, IJ1-233.

117. At the start of the war in 1865, Joaquim Calisto's father reached out to him in the hopes that his son would take advantage of the general pardon issued by the imperial government and enlist in the army, but Calisto chose to remain on the run with the quilombolas. Cited in Araújo, *Insurreição de escravos em Viana*, 172.

118. Testimony of Plácido Mello dos Santos, July 14, 1867, ANRJ, SJ, IJ1-233.

119. Testimony of Plácido Mello dos Santos, July 14, 1867.

120. Mundinha Araújo has transcribed the original letter with all of its misspellings and abbreviations. I based my translation on a comparison of her transcription with the copy produced by the government of Maranhão, in which the notary public edited the text in formal Portuguese. The original in Portuguese reads: "Ilmos Senhores delegado e Comandante do Destacamento de Viana, Santa Bárbara, 10 de julho de 1867: Communico a V. Sa. que nos ac[h]amos em campo atratar da Liberdade dos Cativos, P. amto. que esperamos P. ella, e como o noço desejo é par contodos e não fazer mal aninguem esperamos P. ella em Santo Ignacio e quando não apareça athe o dia 15 do meis vindouro não teremos remedio senão lançar-mos mão nas armas e la irmos, podendo Vas. Sas. contarem que temos 1000 armas de fogo e contamos com todos os arcos dos gentios em noça defesa e da liberdade, e espero que não tomem este noço aviso P. graça é muito seria essa noça deliberação e assim se privinão, e esperamos pela resposta amanhã P. todo dia. Somos de Vas. Sas." Araújo, *Insurreição de escravos em Viana*, 33–34. In the copy, the letter ends as following: "We are, of your Lordships, thoughtful [*atenciosos*] and [*sic*] servants [*criados*]." ANRJ, Seção Justiça, IJ1-233.

121. The indigenous group of the Akroá-Gamella has inhabited the Baixada Maranhense in the north of Maranhão since the colonial period. Historical documents from 1765 and 1784 attest to the presence of Gamella people as well as to their agricultural activities in the area. Originally, the group possessed an area of 14,000 hectares of land, but today 400 families (1,500 people) occupy only 5 percent of the territory spread over the municipalities of Codó, Viana, Matinha, Penalva, and Cajari. The Gamella people continue to fight for the demarcation of the lands that have historically belonged to them. Maristela de Paula Andrade, "Terra de Índio—terras de uso comum e resistência camponesa" (PhD diss., Universidade de São Paulo, 1990); Cristina Santiago, "Terra e identidade: A luta dos Akroá Gamella no Maranhão," Núcleo Piratininga de Comunicação, Apr. 30, 2020, http://nucleopiratininga.org.br/terra-e-identidade-a-luta-dos-akroa-gamella-no-maranhao/ (accessed on Aug. 31, 2023).

122. In July 1867, Daniel and João belonged to Miguel de Araújo's heirs, Virgílio de Araújo, owner of the Santa Maria plantation, and José Antônio Oliveira.

123. Testimony of Plácido Mello dos Santos, July 14, 1867, ANRJ, SJ, IJ1-233.

124. Benedito de Barros e Vasconcellos to Franklin Américo de Menezes Dória, July 14, 1867, ANRJ, SJ, IJ1-233.

125. The Santana plantation had around three hundred enslaved workers in 1789, some of whom were from West Africa. Stuart Schwartz, *Slaves, Peasants, and Rebels: Reconsidering Brazilian Slavery* (Urbana: University of Illinois Press, 1996), 50–55. About a later movement in the

same plantation, see João José Reis, "Resistência escrava em Ilhéus," *Anais do Arquivo Público da Bahia*, 44 (1979): 285–97.

126. The manuscript, housed in the Arquivo Público do Estado da Bahia, is very clean and shows perfect mastery of writing. It was probably an edited copy of the original document produced in 1789.

127. The document was included as an appendix in a letter Chief of Police Claudio José Pereira da Costa sent to the governor of Bahia on Jan. 22, 1806. Schwartz published a version of the "treaty" in *Slaves, Peasants, and Rebels*, 61–63.

128. The fact that the "treaty" (probably dictated to someone by the insurgents) spoke of returning to work did not mean that the insurgents did not also seek emancipation. When Manoel Ferreira pretended to accept its terms, several others refused to return to the Engenho Santana. Moreover, those who remained on the plantation after the rebellion disrupted sugar production lived for years as quilombolas on the estate. Schwartz, *Slaves, Peasants, and Rebels*, 60.

129. Testimony of Benedito, July 17, 1857, cited in Araújo, *Insurreição de escravos em Viana*, 175.

130. Testimony of Vicente, July 18, 1857, cited in Araújo, *Insurreição de escravos em Viana*, 177.

131. Araújo, *Insurreição de escravos em Viana*, 176–78.

132. Report from the Ensign Antônio Caetano Corrêa, cited in Araújo, *Insurreição de escravos em Viana*, 63–65.

133. Araújo, *Insurreição de escravos em Viana*, 70–72.

134. *Publicador Maranhense*, July 29, 1867.

135. Testimony of Feliciano Corta-Mato, July 23, 1867, cited in Araújo, *Insurreição de escravos em Viana*, 161.

136. Cited in Araújo, *Insurreição de escravos em Viana*, 169.

137. Testimony of José de Colônia, Oct. 5, 1867, cited in Araújo, *Insurreição de escravos em Viana*, 178, 173.

138. Cited in Araújo, *Insurreição de escravos em Vianna*, 80.

139. *Dezenove de Dezembro* (Paraná), Nov. 4, 1868, p. 2.

140. *Diário de São Paulo*, Jan. 5, 1869, p. 2.

141. *Diário de São Paulo*, Dec. 18, 1869, p. 1.

142. Miles Ogborn, *The Freedom of Speech: Talk and Slavery in the Anglo-Caribbean World* (Chicago: University of Chicago Press, 2019), 98.

Epilogue

1. *Revista Ilustrada* 467, Oct. 15, 1887, p. 4. Marcelo Balaban, *Poeta do lápis: Sátira e política na trajetória de Angelo Agostini no Brasil Imperial (1864–1888)* (Campinas, SP: Editora Unicamp, 2009); Isabel Lustosa, ed., *Imprensa, humor e caricatura: A questão dos estereótipos* (Belo Horizonte: Editora da UFMG, 2011); Herman Lima, *História da caricatura no Brasil* (Rio de Janeiro: José Olympio, 1963).

2. *Correio Paulistano*, Oct. 4, 1887, p. 2. The abolitionist newspaper *Rio News*, published in English by the US national Andrew Jackson Lamoureux, also covered what happened in Itatiba. "A S. Paulo provincial paper states that a planter visited his slaves who should have been at work but were found surrounding one of their number who was reading aloud a speech of Senator Dantas." *Rio News*, Oct. 15, 1887, p. 3.

3. See, for instance, *Revista Illustrada* 427, Feb. 18, 1886.

4. On the Brazilian abolitionist press, see Castilho, *Slave Emancipation*; Alonso, *The Last Abolition*.

5. Alonso, *The Last Abolition*, 307. In 1883, Nabuco published what would become in time the most important abolitionist tract in Brazil. *O Abolicionismo* presented a systemic analysis of slavery that called for its elimination as a necessary moral and patriotic step to redeem the nation and redirect the monarchy toward the path of progress and civilization. Joaquim Nabuco, *O Abolicionismo* (London: Abraham Kingdom, 1883), 233.

6. *Revista Ilustrada* 467, Oct. 15, 1887, p. 4.

7. Hailing from Pernambuco, Nabuco was elected deputy in 1878. His passionate defense of abolitionism in the chamber earned him the nickname "Lion of the North."

8. Founded in 1884, *O Paiz* was published in Rio de Janeiro until 1930. Up to 1888, it advocated for abolition and a republican government in Brazil. Alonso, *The Last Abolition*, 281; Andréa Santos da Silva Pessanha, "Memória e missão: *O Paiz* e a *Gazeta Nacional*. Imprensa do Rio de Janeiro (1884–1888)," *Tempos Históricos* 14, no. 2 (2010): 207–25.

9. *O Paiz* (Rio de Janeiro), Aug. 30, 1888, p. 1.

10. Joseli Maria Nunes Mendonça, *Entre a mão e os anéis: A Lei Dos Sexagenários e os caminhos da abolição no Brasil* (Campinas, SP: Editora da UNICAMP, 1999).

11. Needell, *Sacred Cause*.

12. Machado, *O plano e o pânico*, especially chapter 3.

13. Queiroz, *Escravidão negra*; Eduardo Silva, *As camélias do Leblon e abolição da escravatura: Uma investigação de história cultural* (São Paulo: Companhia das Letras, 2003); Célia Marinho de Azevedo, "Batismo da Liberdade: Os abolicionistas e o futuro do negro," *História: Questões e Debates* 9, no. 16 (1988): 38–65.

INDEX

Figures and maps are indicated by page numbers followed by *fig.* and *map* respectively.

ACKNOWLEDGMENTS

Growing up in Brazil, I believed from an early age that storytelling could be a liberating practice, for it seemed to give the least powerful a chance to speak for themselves. Although the History I learned in the books did not feature ordinary people as subjects, I was often taught by them and tried to make sense of life through the knowledge they gladly shared with others. Perhaps this explains why I was drawn to the study of slavery, embedded as it was in the seemingly inexplicable details of so many of their stories, usually set against the backdrop of my hometown of Rio de Janeiro, once the capital of the Brazilian empire. Confronted daily with profound social inequalities, I often wondered: If asked, how would enslaved people describe their experiences of dispossession and hope? How would they explain power? And most importantly, what would they say about what it takes to overcome subjection? This book is an attempt to answer these questions after years of sifting through the many narratives of slavery available in Brazilian archives. I hope these pages express the conviction that historical understanding begins with empathy; for the people we study, for readers interested in the stories we tell, and for a country that continues to grapple with the legacies of chattel slavery in the present.

The emotional and intellectual debts I have incurred while writing this book are now almost impossible to trace, but I will at least try. I first dreamed of studying slavery in Brazil when I was a student at the Federal University of Rio de Janeiro, and my wish came true only because Professor Flávio dos Santos Gomes led me down the path of historical research. I would like to think that this book somehow began during my time as his undergraduate research assistant, when I understood the stakes of the history I wanted to study. To Flávio, my co-conspirator in so many historical projects since then, *um abraço quilombola*. At Unicamp, I learned enormously from my advisor, Robert W. Slenes, Silva Lara, and Sidney Chalhoub, whom I had the pleasure of meeting again after I decided to go to the United States to study. This project would have been impossible without the support of staff members, archivists, and librarians who, like me, enjoy spending much of their lives in the archives. As I navigated the collections of the Arquivo Nacional, the Arquivo do Itamaraty, the Arquivo Público Mineiro, the Biblioteca Antônio Torres in Diamantina, and the Fórum of Serro, in particular, they were invaluable. I would like to thank everyone at Brazilian and US institutions for so kindly guiding me toward the materials that brought this book to life.

I started to write *Freedom's Horizon* as a dissertation at Brown University, where I was fortunate to count on the cheerful guidance of my advisor James N. Green, and on the generosity of Roquinaldo Ferreira, whom I thank for encouraging and preparing me to embrace the many challenges that made this work possible. My heartfelt thanks go also to my teachers: Michael Vorenberg, Cynthia Brokaw, Amy G. Remensnyder, Seth Rockman, Tara Nummedal, Naoko Shibusawa, Françoise Hamlin, Douglas Cope, Rebecca A. Nedostup, and Linford Fisher. At Brown, I received funding from the Department of History, the Center for Latin American and Caribbean Studies (CLACS), the Cogut Institute for the Humanities, and the Center for the Study of Slavery and Justice. The Social Sciences Research Council awarded me an International Dissertation Research Fellowship to spend a year lost among nineteenth-century manuscripts, providing invaluable support for research in Brazil.

My professional journey continued at the University of Miami, where I found a wonderful group of colleagues who welcomed a young scholar with open arms. Mary Lindemann, Eduardo Elena, Martin Nesvig, Kate Ramsey, Michael Bernath, Krista A. Goff, and Ashley White commented on my work and offered precious advice as I figured out my way in academia. Tracy Devine Guzmán, Dominique Reill, and Merike Blofield made me feel like part of an extended family, and with them I built my fondest memories of the sweltering Miami Christmas. Scott Heerman read and commented on every chapter of this book, probably five times each, and cheered me on to the finish line. I will be forever grateful for his brilliant insights and friendship over the years. The journey here would not have been fun without you.

At Princeton, I met an incredible group of scholars who have continued to inspire my work. Gyan Prakash, Keith Wailoo, Michael Gordin, Angela Creager, Tera Hunter, Laura Edwards, Vera Candiani, Michael Laffan, and Matt Karp have been especially generous in their comments on early versions of this book. Special thanks also to David Bell and the 2022 Fellows at the Davis Center for Historical Studies for providing me with another intellectual home as we all struggled to overcome the Covid-19 pandemic. At Princeton, I am also grateful for the continued support of Judy Hanson, Judie Miller, Jennifer Loessy, and Millie Ndiritu. He Bian, Divya Cherian, Iryna Vushko, and Rosina Lozano have been wonderful role models as well as friends along the way. I would also like to thank Vincent Brown, Ada Ferrer, and Flávio Gomes for participating in a manuscript workshop held at Princeton in 2021 that widened the scope of this book considerably. I am grateful to my colleagues at the Brazil Lab, especially Miqueias Mugge, João Biehl, Lillia Schwartz, and Pedro Meira Monteiro for the years of collaboration that are also reflected in my thinking about Brazilian history.

I have been supported by a number of grants and benefited from feedback at multiple institutions and workshops. In 2018, I spent a semester at the Gilder Lehrman Center for the Study of Slavery, Resistance, and Abolition, where I exchanged ideas with David W. Blight, Edward Rugemer, Marcela Echeverri, Luis C. de Baca, and Michelle Zacks. I presented different portions of this book at the Atlantic History Workshop at NYU and the New York City Latin American History Workshop, the International History Workshop at Columbia University, the University of Pennsylvania's McNeill Center for Early American Studies, the Latin America History Workshop at the University of Chicago, the Global History Workshop at the University of California, Santa Barbara, the Latin American and the Caribbean Workshop at Princeton, and the seminar "Global Slaveries, Fugitivity, and the Afterlives of Unfreedom" at Indiana University. My sincere thanks to all those who have offered comments to my work.

While working on this book I have benefited from the feedback of several editors and colleagues who have reviewed essays derived from my research on slave activism in Brazil. My second chapter has been substantially strengthened by the publication of "Cruzando caminhos em Ibicaba: escravizados, colonos e abolicionismo durante a *Revolta dos Parceiros* (São Paulo, 1856-7)," in *Afro-Ásia* 62 (2021), 291–326; and "On the Verge of War: Black Insurgency, the 'Christie affair,' and British Antislavery in Brazil," in *Slavery & Abolition* 43, no. 1 (2022), 120–39. Portions of Chapter 3 have appeared in "Other Geographies of Struggle: Afro-Brazilians and the American Civil War," *Hispanic American Historical Review* 100, no. 1 (2020), 35–62. My gratitude also to Rhae Lynn Barnes and Glenda Goodman for their insightful comments on my chapter in *American Contact: Objects of Intercultural Encounters and the Boundaries of Book History*. As I neared completion of the manuscript, João José Reis read my book manuscript carefully, a true labor of love, and offered suggestions beyond anything I could have expected. At the University of Pennsylvania Press, Bob Lockhart was an amazing editor, whose intellectual work is evident throughout this book. Lily Palladino and Sara Lickey have also patiently reviewed my text. Finally, I owe these pages to the trust and support of my students from whom I continue to learn so much.

I am truly indebted to my friends and family, who are sometimes hard to tell apart. At Brown, I was lucky enough to meet Justina Hwang, a sister from Taiwan that I didn't know I had. *Muitíssimo obrigada* for standing by me all these years, for keeping me young at heart, and for never letting me give up. To Margaret Groesbeck, my gratitude for the years of friendship and witty banter since our library days. To my *comadre* Lily, gracias for all the support and encouragement that have made me feel less like a foreigner in a new land. And, most of all, thank you for bringing Tato into my life. To Alan, Josie, Anila, and Sidney, I owe more than I can say in words. Thank you for your enduring friendship and for sharing your passion for social justice. To Kamilla Cardoso, Nina Gordon, Durba Chattaraj, and Sara Kozameh, my sincere thanks for always standing by me. To my parents, Rose and Moacir, my sisters Isis and Isabela, I am grateful for the love that has kept me strong even when I am an ocean away from home. Timothy Van Compernolle has been an attentive reader of this manuscript in its various iterations and, along with Cate, an important source of encouragement.

My daughter Chloe grew up with this book, sometimes literally coloring its printed drafts and giving it a greater sense of purpose. She has been an incredible partner in research trips to Brazil that would not have been possible without her auntie Isis's unwavering and loving support. Once Chloe asked me the very pertinent question: "Mommy, you say you cannot come outside to play with me because you are writing a book, but where is it? I just see a computer." I dedicate this work to her and to my querida Dudi, the mother I lost while writing the dissertation that inspired *Freedom's Horizon*, whose intelligence and laughter continue to guide me. I stand on the shoulders of these two generations of strong women and hope to make them proud. Here is the book, Chloe!